Psychology for Physical Educators

Student in Focus

SECOND EDITION

Jarmo Liukkonen, PhD

Yves Vanden Auweele, PhD
Beatrix Vereijken, PhD
Dorothee Alfermann, PhD
Yannis Theodorakis, PhD

EDITORS

A project of the
European Federation of Sport Psychology

Human Kinetics

Library of Congress Cataloging-in-Publication Data

Psychology for physical educators : student in focus / Jarmo Liukkonen . . . [et al.]. --
2nd ed.

    p. cm.
   "A project of the European Federation of Sport Psychology."
   Includes bibliographical references and index.
   ISBN-13: 978-0-7360-6240-4 (hard cover)
   ISBN-10: 0-7360-6240-8 (hard cover)
  1. Physical education and training--Europe--Psychological aspects. 2. Physical
education and training--Study and teaching--Europe.   I. Liukkonen, Jarmo.   II. European
Sport Psychology Association.
  GV342.22.P79 2007
  796´.01--dc22

                                2006038970

ISBN-10: 0-7360-6240-8
ISBN-13: 978-0-7360-6240-4

The Web addresses cited in this text were current as of February 22, 2007, unless otherwise noted.

Acquisitions Editor: Scott Wikgren; **Developmental Editor:** Jacqueline Eaton Blakley; **Assistant Editors:** Bethany J. Bentley, Jackie Walker; **Copyeditor:** Patsy Fortney; **Proofreader:** Red Inc.; **Indexer:** Craig Brown; **Permission Manager:** Dalene Reeder; **Graphic Designer:** Nancy Rasmus; **Graphic Artist:** Angela K. Snyder; **Photo Manager:** Jason Allen; **Cover Designer:** Robert Reuther; **Art Manager:** Kelly Hendren; **Illustrators:** Keri Evans, Al Wilborn; **Printer:** Sheridan Books

Printed in the United States of America   10 9 8 7 6 5 4 3 2 1

Human Kinetics
Web site: www.HumanKinetics.com

United States: Human Kinetics
P.O. Box 5076
Champaign, IL 61825-5076
800-747-4457
e-mail: humank@hkusa.com

Canada: Human Kinetics
475 Devonshire Road Unit 100
Windsor, ON N8Y 2L5
800-465-7301 (in Canada only)
e-mail: orders@hkcanada.com

Europe: Human Kinetics
107 Bradford Road
Stanningley
Leeds LS28 6AT, United Kingdom
+44 (0) 113 255 5665
e-mail: hk@hkeurope.com

Australia: Human Kinetics
57A Price Avenue
Lower Mitcham, South Australia 5062
08 8372 0999
e-mail: liaw@hkaustralia.com

New Zealand: Human Kinetics
Division of Sports Distributors NZ Ltd.
P.O. Box 300 226 Albany
North Shore City
Auckland
0064 9 448 1207
e-mail: info@humankinetics.co.nz

contents

preface

The many, apparently different physical education curricula in European countries have all developed after the millennium shift in much the same direction. In addition to the traditional focus on motor and physical development, recent curriculum goals include health and fitness and the development of positive self-perceptions and social skills. The rapid increase in adult and child obesity during the last few decades has created a special challenge for school physical educators, who in their work meet the whole adolescent population. Thus, today, even more than at the time the first edition of this book was published, enhancing children's positive emotions related to physical education lessons and creating a motivationally favourable atmosphere are paramount. Although many have endorsed the importance of these goals, few have offered advice and suggestions about how to implement them.

That is the gap that this second edition of this textbook wants to bridge. Its intention is to give physical educators the psychological knowledge and practical guidelines necessary for realising current curriculum goals. Unlike the many general textbooks on educational psychology that are currently available, this book relates directly to the physical education domain, offering physical educators practical tools and thus supporting the valuable work they do.

This book will be useful for physical educators in every aspect of the field—for physical education teachers, students and teachers in physical education teacher education courses; curriculum specialists; university and predoctoral physical education students; health educators; psychologists and counsellors. The book is also useful for trainers and coaches who are involved in youth sports and youth trainer academies. The book's straightforward explanation of theory and guidelines for educators can also help parents, politicians and concerned citizens better understand both the importance of physical education for children's health and well-being and the relevance of psychological factors modulating the way physical education is put into practice.

Why have we taken on the development, writing and editing of this book? The regular contact of like-minded professionals in FEPSAC (the European Federation of Sport Psychology) in the relatively new field of sport and exercise psychology stimulated discussions about common problems and common issues. We wanted to present a work that displays the European traditions and expertise in our field. It became clear that the greatest single need was for a book in which sport and exercise professionals present their knowledge to physical education teachers. This book gave us the opportunity to work together on a text that we each think is necessary to have in our own country.

Each of the five editors of this text might have attempted to write such a book alone. But it would have lacked the breadth and depth that this collaboration offers, both in terms of psychology and in terms of addressing Europe as a whole. After agreeing on a structure, explained in the prologue, authors from across Europe were invited to propose chapters. Although we would have liked to have a better representation of authors from the whole of Europe, we ended up with 29 experts representing seven European countries: Belgium, Finland, Germany, Greece, the Netherlands, Norway and the United Kingdom.

The absence of some important names from Eastern Europe may be due to the continuing difficult working and living conditions there and subsequently to the difficulties in communications and contacts between East and West European colleagues. Overcoming this gap is one of the major challenges for European sport psychology.

Regarding the applicability, readability and flow of the chapters, the authors balance theory, research findings and action ideas. They include relevant examples, summaries, exercises and study questions.

We hope you find this book useful, and we invite your comments and feedback on where we have succeeded and where more work could still be done.

Jarmo Liukkonen, Jyväskylä, Finland
Yves Vanden Auweele, Leuven, Belgium
Beatrix Vereijken, Trondheim, Norway
Dorothee Alfermann, Leipzig, Germany
Yannis Theodorakis, Thessaloniki, Greece

acknowledgments

I am grateful to the numerous experts who have contributed to the development of this book: part editors, chapter authors, reviewers and the editors at Human Kinetics. The department of sport sciences at Jyväskylä University in Finland has supported this project by allowing me to use a remarkable number of academic working days during the long editing process. Special thanks are devoted to the president and the managing council of FEPSAC for initiating and supporting the production of this book, which is partially new and partially an update of the *Psychology for Physical Educators* textbook published in 1998. It has been a great pleasure to work with this team of outstanding experts in pedagogical psychology and physical education. I am convinced that this book, the result of a four-year FEPSAC project, presents the topics of primary importance in European physical education today.

I would like to acknowledge the important contribution of the part editors: Yves Vanden Auweele, Beatrix Vereijken, Dorothee Alfermann and Yannis Theodorakis. They were responsible for ensuring that the chapter manuscripts were comprehensive, included relevant theory and research and provided significant applications to various contexts of physical education. We appreciate the involvement of the following authors and other experts:

- Vassilis Barkoukis, author, Greece
- Øyvind Bjerke, author, Norway
- Philippe Brunel, France
- Stiliani Chroni, author, Greece
- Nikolaos Digelidis, author, Greece
- Veikko Eloranta, author, Finland
- Ingunn Fjørtoft, author, Norway
- Marios Goudas, author, Greece
- Kari Aasen Gundersen, author, Norway
- Antonis Hatzigeorgiadis, author, Greece
- Johan Hovelynck, author, the Netherlands
- Timo Jaakkola, author, Finland
- Urban Johnson, Sweden
- Marja Kokkonen, Finland
- Evdoxia Kosmidou, author, Greece
- Marjo Kuusela, author, Finland
- Pierre-Nicolas Lemyre, author, Norway
- Taru Lintunen, author, Finland
- Dilwyn Marple-Horvat, author, UK
- Dimitris Milosis, author, Greece
- Thanasis Mouratidis, author, Greece
- Yngvar Ommundsen, author, Norway
- Athanasios Papaioannou, author, Greece
- Singa Polvi, author, Finland
- Maria Psychountaki, Greece
- Geert Savelsbergh, author, the Netherlands
- Roland Seiler, Switzerland
- Reinhard Stelter, Denmark
- Jeannine Stiller, author, Germany
- Risto Telama, author, Finland
- Kaivo Thomson, Estonia
- Nikolaos Tsigilis, author, Greece
- John van der Kamp, author, the Netherlands
- Yves Vanden Auweele, author, Belgium
- Martine Verheul, author, UK
- Paul Wylleman, Belgium
- Klaudia Zuskova, Slovakia

Jarmo Liukkonen

message from the president of FEPSAC

The publication of a book is always a big moment of pride and satisfaction. In the case of this book, I am especially proud because it is a milestone in the history of FEPSAC for several reasons. First, the book addresses two of the most important areas in modern Western societies: children, and sport and exercise. Experts generally agree that physical activity and sport are of central importance in children's development, helping them to reach important educational goals such as adopting prosocial behaviour, increasing self-concept and self-esteem and learning basic motor skills. Physical education promotes a positive attitude toward sport and exercise and encourages children to adopt active lifestyles and continue those habits into their adult lives, which is important for the health of our society. However, physical education in schools is under economic pressure and is in danger of being reduced in most Western countries. A high quality of work on the part of physical educators is therefore required. This book is designed to provide the psychological knowledge physical educators need to meet these demands. I hope this book will increase the interest of physical educators in psychology and also encourage sport psychologists to continue to study the field of physical education.

The second reason this book is a milestone in the history of FEPSAC is linked with the aim of FEPSAC to promote cooperation among European sport psychologists. Representing the knowledge and competencies of 29 authors from seven countries and representing 11 institutions, this book is an excellent tool for establishing networks all over the continent and for giving European sport psychology a unified voice.

Third, I am especially proud that in recent years FEPSAC has increased its visibility through publications. After *European Perspective on Exercise and Sport Psychology,* published in 1995 and edited by Stuart Biddle, and *Psychology for Physical Educators,* published in 1999 with Yves Vanden Auweele as senior editor and Frank Bakker, Stuart Biddle, Marc Durand and myself as co-editors, this book is the third edited book published by Human Kinetics. Together with the official FEPSAC journal *Psychology of Sport and Exercise,* these publications ensure that the work of European colleagues is now well retrievable and publicly available.

As president of FEPSAC, I would like to acknowledge the outstanding efforts and energy of the senior editor, Jarmo Liukkonen. FEPSAC owes him, the editors and the authors our thanks. We hope that physical educators will adopt their proposals and recommendations in their professional work—which would be the highest form of recognition for the book.

Roland Seiler, PhD

message from the president of the European Network of Sport Science, Education and Employment (ENSSEE)

It is one of the objectives of the European Network of Sport Science, Education and Employment to work toward the convergence of education for sport-related professions in the European Union and to develop a body of knowledge in this respect for the community of European students and teachers. We therefore are very happy that a number of outstanding colleagues in the field of sport psychology have succeeded in publishing this fine book you are reading. On behalf of the European Network, I congratulate the authors and thank them for bringing their knowledge closer to the students who are preparing themselves for professional work in the field of physical education. We also thank FEPSAC for giving us the opportunity to endorse this initiative. We are prepared to play our role as ambassador for this edition, and we are convinced that many will wish to include this textbook in their libraries.

Walter Tokarski, PhD
President, European Network of Sport Science,
Education and Employment

prologue

Physical education curricula in European countries reflect the educational needs of each society. However, the trend toward globalisation—in Europe, the development of the European Union as a strong contributor—has meant increased cooperation among educational organisations throughout Europe and globally. PE curricula have developed during the past few decades in much the same direction.

This textbook is structured around most common physical education curriculum goals of European school systems. Despite many differences, today's PE curricula throughout Europe have several similarities. In addition to motor skills, fitness and health education, most European curricula have given increased importance to the development of children's life skills, such as self-perceptions and socio-emotional skills. The general focus in PE is twofold: education to and via physical activity. Both of these general goals, to be fulfilled by PE professionals, challenge understanding of the regularities of human behaviour and the mechanisms of behaviour change. Sport and exercise psychology has much to give in this body of knowledge through the massive theoretical and empirical research activities, which are reflected in the increasing number of professionals in the field. New educational programs, such as the European master of sport and exercise psychology program, have been constructed in order to enhance the knowledge of professionals. New journals in sport and exercise psychology have been founded, such as *Psychology of Sport and Exercise*. An increased number and diversity of authors in the journals as well as the tightened criteria for acceptance of articles submitted for publication in the journals reflect the increased interest and knowledge in the field of human behaviour in the various contexts of physical activity, including physical education.

Promoting a physically active lifestyle is the main challenge in the physical education of today's European societies. A large body of evidence points to the health benefits of physical activity. In all European school systems, the major goal of physical education is to enhance physical activity. Numerous interventions have focused on enhancing the health and increasing the physical activity of various target groups. However, empirical studies give only vague support to the effects of these strivings. The problem we face when trying to bring about behaviour change is related to individual psychological mechanisms. What motivates one person may not have any effect on another.

Physical educators work with pupils from preschool through elementary, secondary and gymnasium levels up to later professional education levels. This presents a challenge to understand human behaviour and the mechanisms behind it on a large scale. For young children, physical activity should be an end in itself. Children do not want to continue to participate in activities that are not intrinsically motivating. Youth and adults have more and more external reasons to participate in physical activities as they age. But intrinsic factors remain remarkable determinants of behaviour.

At first glance the PE curricula of the many countries and cultures of Europe may not seem similar. The diversity in school curricula reflects various values and cultural differences between the peoples and areas in Europe. However, today's PE curricula throughout Europe, despite many differences, contain basic similarities related to their roots and their continuing development reflected in the concepts and terminology used in discussions of the topic. In the European Union, the past years have shown an increasing tendency to adopt common goals, curricula and policies in educational systems. International school evaluation programs, such as the Programme for International Student Assessment (PISA, at www.pisa.oecd.org), have revealed effective practices in educational policies in some countries. Modeling these has directed the development of school physical education in other countries, increasing the similarity among physical education curricula throughout Europe.

The ambivalence of some European countries toward the development of the European Union into the United States of Europe reflects the desire to value both the undeniable similarities with fellow Europeans and the differences. The latter is captured in one of the EU mottos (Be European—Be Different), referring to the great richness in the diversity of peoples, cultures and educational systems.

The writing of the second edition of this book has been structured around common curriculum goals found in European Union countries. This is a practical decision that allows the presentation of psychological concepts and examples to the widest range of readers throughout Europe and further abroad.

It may be useful to consider how curricula are generated and what influences the form they take. In each country, policy makers in education try to define their own philosophy of education. This is done through systematic reflection and deliberation about the fundamental assumptions of people in each society. In this process, policy makers rely on the norms and expectations of their countries. Curricula, as such, are written expressions of such concepts of education, whether at the national, local or school level or at the level of the teacher in the classroom. At each level a curriculum directs the planning and implementation of lessons, describing the goals, means and content to be used to produce the desired learning. The closer one gets to the classroom, the more the curriculum is refined and applied. The designed curriculum has implications for the pedagogic interactions that take place between teachers and students. The socio-cultural context in which these interactions take place co-determines how the curriculum is worked out and applied.

The many countries and cultures that make up Europe have different norms and expectations regarding education. The interactions between teachers and students also vary from one country to the next. How can it be, then, that these differ-

ent countries have in common basic curriculum goals for physical education? Most European PE curricula find their roots in German *Turnen,* Swedish *gymnastics* or English *sports.* Although we are aware of the fact that what can be called new in one country is considered traditional in another, we think that in more recent times most European PE curricula have placed increased importance on the development of students' self-perceptions and social skills. Movement and exercise are considered appropriate means for achieving these newer goals.

The two new foci of self-perception and social skills have not supplanted but have instead supplemented the traditional goals of physical and motor development and health and fitness education. Nevertheless, it should not be assumed that the traditional goals have received less attention as a result. Of course, important differences in PE curricula remain among countries. We acknowledge differences in approaches ranging from the philosophical to the descriptive and from the conservative to the critical. Differences in PE history and cultural heritage are prominent both within and between East and West European countries. And there are also differences in terminology, reflecting the philosophical and cultural differences (e.g., *Körperkultur, sport, exercise, Bewegungserziehung, education par le movement, physical education* and *movement education*).

European Physical Activity Goals

Despite the importance of each of the differences, the PE curricula of all European countries have been developed more or less with the same four main points, two directed at the physical aspects and two at the more psychological goals. It may be said that the function of PE in every European country has been generalized to the production of happy, healthy people who are able to use their bodies as tools for self-actualization in various aspects of their lives, including work and leisure. The physical activity goals that are designed to have a direct effect on the body and its functioning are physical and motor development and health and fitness. The curriculum goals for physical activity, which are designed to have an effect on personality and social functioning, are the development of positive self-perceptions and social skills.

Another modern development common to various European countries has been the term *physical education,* which has generally been accepted as the most suitable label for the previously mentioned conceptualization. The term *physical education* includes but goes beyond the more restricted traditional conceptions of body, physical training and movement education to the broader and newer conceptions of personality education through movement and exercise.

The developments in European physical education curricula have not been independent of those of North America and, specifically, the United States. But the relationship has changed over the years. Since before the beginning of the 20th century, the European way of presenting PE dominated how topics were taught and studied in the United States. After the two World Wars, the U.S. system of education and its vision weighed very strongly on the European perspective and its practice. A comparison of a U.S. and a classical European physical education textbook would reveal clear similarities, as would a look at a typical PE lesson in most countries or states in these two continents. In fact, the similarities extend to the basic curriculum goals as well.

One of the major assets of using the four curriculum goals to structure this textbook is their compatibility with the traditional structuring of educational goals. This follows a taxonomy that most physical educators are familiar with: cognitions, behaviours and emotions. Within each of the four sets of goals, three subsets can easily be formulated in terms of knowledge, attitude and skill (see table P.1).

Format of This Book

These similarities across Europe as well as in the United States, Canada and Australia provide us with a structure for this book, which has four parts that come directly from the four major sets of common European curriculum goals. The title of this book, *Psychology for Physical Educators: Student in Focus,* reflects the emphasis on individual learning-oriented approaches.

Part I, Promotion of Lifelong Health and Fitness, is devoted to physical activity and the development of a healthy and safe lifestyle. This part approaches the issue of lifelong health and fitness through the prism of two motivational theories: motivational climate and goal setting. The third approach to physical education is related to emotions, specifically to the individual perception of anxiety. In this book, *fitness* has been defined more broadly than a mere increase in physical activity and more extensively than what can be measured by fitness tests. Fitness involves the integration of a healthy lifestyle into personal life goals, self-perception and identity. Factors that enhance students' motivation toward physical activity play an important role in part I, reflecting

Table P.1   Major Curriculum Goals in European Countries

	Fitness, health and safety	Psycho-motor competence	Positive self-perception	Social development
Knowledge (cognition)	Know the principles that contribute to fitness as part of a healthy lifestyle.	Know the essential elements of efficient performance.	Have a working knowledge of how to improve self-esteem.	Know which behaviour is acceptable in the context of today's norms.
Skill (behaviours)	Demonstrate an acceptable level of endurance and fitness.	Demonstrate a variety of sport-specific skills and expressive movements.	Demonstrate self-esteem and intrinsic motivation in physical activities.	Demonstrate acceptable social and emotional behaviours in physical activities, sports and games.
Attitude (emotions)	Demonstrate an appreciation of the role of fitness as an element of a high quality of life.	Demonstrate an appreciation for efficient and creative movement in sports and games.	Demonstrate an appreciation for physical and emotional abilities and a desire to improve self-esteem.	Demonstrate respect and an appreciation for individual differences.

concepts such as intrinsic motivation, goal orientation and motivational climate.

Part II, Promotion of Social Skills for Life, deals with the development of social skills, which is a basic physical education curriculum goal in its own right because contemporary life places a premium on citizens' abilities to relate to others and to work effectively in groups. This part addresses social development and related issues, such as how students learn to behave as members of a class, what a teacher can expect regarding how a class develops, how a teacher can understand and cope with deviant and aggressive behaviours and how a teacher can learn to communicate effectively with students. The quality of the relationship between the teacher and the students, as well as the quality of the relations among the students, has a critical effect on learning. Teaching students new ways to work effectively in groups and to deal with conflicts and tensions is crucial for their success in physical education as well as their success in future endeavours outside of physical education.

Part III, Promotion of Self-Concept and Cognitive Skills, deals with psychological outcomes of physical education, including the development of positive self-perceptions through physical activity. The goals of part III are to show how PE can influence various aspects of the self and cognitive skills and how teachers can promote self-concept and cognitive skills through physical education.

The level of dynamic physically active interactions between the teacher and the students as well as the interaction among the students will produce several positive psycho-social outcomes. Knowing oneself and what others think, knowing how to function in groups, and knowing how to adapt to various situations are all features of the self that can be influenced by exercise and sports. This goal is associated with the other goals: fitness and motor development. During skill and fitness training in a group, students perceive successes and failures. They try to explain these experiences and search for explanations. They continually evaluate their perceived abilities, capacities and progress. They are also aware of the evaluations and judgments that others make about them.

Part IV, Promotion of Motor Skills for Life, focuses on the area of motor competence and performance, which is defined more broadly than teaching and learning of sport skills, techniques and tactics. It entails reflecting on the quality and quantity of information needed as well as the considerations of task difficulty and learning strategies. It means thinking about movement, exercise and performance in their appropriate contexts as well as complex skill acquisition, coordination and perception of motor competence. Teaching of motor skills remains the central task for physical educators. This involves teaching not only traditional sport skills but also basic motor skills in life, such as general body control and coordination, locomotor and manipulative skills, balance, flexibility and adaptability. Furthermore, teaching of motor skills can stretch across the entire life span, from preschool children to the elderly.

Jarmo Liukkonen and Yves Vanden Auweele

part one

Promotion of Lifelong Health and Fitness

Yannis Theodorakis and Jarmo Liukkonen

Part I of the book approaches the issue of lifelong health and fitness through the prism of two motivational theories: *motivational climate* and *goal setting*. It also addresses the measurement of the perceived motivational climate in physical education as well as the individual perception of anxiety.

In chapter 1, 'Establishing a Positive Motivational Climate in Physical Education', Timo Jaakkola and Nikolaos Digelidis define positive motivational climate, distinguish among several motivational climate dimensions and help physical education teachers apply specific motivational strategies in educational settings by giving examples from school praxis.

A *motivational climate* is a situation-induced environment directing the goals of an action in achievement situations. A person's perception of a motivational climate is *task involving* or *ego involving,* depending on how the person perceives and interprets the structure of the achievement environment. Motivational climate is considered to affect a person's interpretation of the criteria of success and failure in the given context, and the perceived motivational climate and dispositional goal orientation determine whether people become task involved or ego involved in the activity.

In a task-involving motivational climate, children are involved in decision making, and group-ing is not based on ability. In addition, success is defined and evaluated based on individual effort, improvement and learning. A task-involving motivational climate is created when a teacher or coach emphasises self-reference and task involvement as criteria for determining success and failure.

On the other hand, in an ego-involving motivational climate, children typically are rewarded for performing better than others, mistakes are treated negatively, evaluation is based on normative standards, grouping of students is based on ability and learning time is not flexible. An ego-involving motivational climate is created when a teacher or coach emphasises various forms of ego involvement as criteria for determining success and failure.

Chapter 2, 'Goal Setting in Physical Education', describes the benefits of an operative goal-setting system in physical education and presents guidelines for implementing goal-setting strategies. Practical applications and suggestions are provided for the development of a favourable motivational climate and effective goal setting in physical education.

The chapter begins with an introduction of goal-setting theory in sport and exercise. Definitions, principles of goal setting and basic research findings are presented, with references to the beneficial effects of goal setting on performance, confidence, effort, commitment and autonomy.

Subsequently, the role of goal setting in physical education is considered. The importance of applying goal setting in a class environment is discussed with regard to the teacher and also the students. Following, guidelines for developing effective goal-setting plans are presented. This involves preparation, education and acquisition, goal evaluation, implementation and follow-up, and goal reevaluation. Goal setting is also examined as a strategy for enhancing healthy habits and lifestyles.

Within a life-skills context, suggestions and practical guidelines are given for organising physical education and transferring these practices from physical education to other school subjects, such as math and language.

In chapter 3, 'Measuring Perceived Motivational Climate in Physical Education', Papaioannou and colleagues review the existing measures of perceived motivational climate in physical education and provide guidelines to help teachers choose the best measure for their needs. They also describe the different types of validity and reliability when employing climate questionnaires.

In recent years a number of instruments have been developed to assess students' perceptions of class climate. Using these tools, several studies have investigated perceived climate in relation to students' cognitions, emotions and behaviours in physical education. The interest in the subjective climate is hardly surprising given that perceived climate has a stronger impact on people's actions than the objective climate recorded by unbiased observers has.

Chapter 3 also describes the validity and reliability of climate questionnaires. The authors provide examples from their research that illustrate the process of establishing validity and reliability. They also describe the principle of compatibility and how one investigates the validity of motivational climate measures based on this principle.

Anxiety is a largely studied topic in sport psychology. It is considered one of the most important psychological factors affecting physical performance in the context of competitive sport. In exercise settings, research has mostly concentrated on the acute and chronic effects of exercise on feelings of anxiety. In educational psychology, research on anxiety has focused mainly on test anxiety. Physical education has largely been studied from the viewpoints of intrinsic motivation and enjoyment. Although students generally enjoy physical education lessons, feelings of anxiety may be triggered as a result of the comparative, competitive and evaluative nature of many physical education settings. So far, there is only limited research on the experience of anxiety in physical education lessons. Chapter 4, 'Experience of State Anxiety in Physical Education', provides an insight into the experience of state anxiety in physical education. It also suggests practices that may diminish the feelings of state anxiety and reinforce the experience of positive affective states.

chapter one

Establishing a Positive Motivational Climate in Physical Education

Timo Jaakkola
University of Jyväskylä, Finland
Nikolaos Digelidis
University of Thessaly, Greece

After reading this chapter, you will be able to do the following:

- Define positive motivational climate
- Distinguish among several motivational climate dimensions
- Apply specific strategies in school settings to create a task-involving climate

A **motivational climate** is defined as a situation-induced environment directing the goals of an action in achievement situations (Ames, 1992; Ames & Archer, 1988; Dweck & Leggett, 1988; Nicholls, 1984, 1989). Motivational climates can be either **task involving** or **ego involving,** depending on how people perceive and interpret the structure of the achievement environment (Duda, 2001; Duda & Hall, 2001; Treasure, 2001). Motivational climate is considered to affect a person's interpretation of the criteria of success and failure in achievement environments. It is also assumed to affect adaptive and maladaptive achievement behaviour, as well as affective and cognitive responses.

Ames (1992) suggested that motivational climate is a multidimensional structure. The most often applied presentation of task- and ego-involving motivational climate is Epstein's (1989) TARGET model, which is presented in table 1.1. Treasure and Roberts (1995) and Papaioannou and Goudas (1999) have presented examples of applications in school settings of TARGET structures.

In addition, several other definitions of task- and ego-involving climates exist in the literature. According to Newton and Duda (1993), a task-involving climate is characterised by cooperative learning, students' important role, and a focus on individual improvement. Newton and Duda (1999) also suggested that an ego-involving climate is characterised by punishment for mistakes, unequal recognition and intrateam rivalry. Papaioannou (1994) defined a task-involving motivational climate as having a teacher-initiated learning orientation and a student-initiated learning orientation. Students' competitive orientation, students' worries about mistakes and an outcome orientation without effort characterise the ego-involving motivational climate. In addition, Ames and Archer (1988) described motivational climate as constructs of task- and ego-involving structures. These constructs are categorised as follows:

- Definition of success (improvement vs. normative performance)
- Value (on effort and learning vs. normatively high ability)
- Reasons for satisfaction (hard work vs. outperforming others)
- Teacher orientation (learning vs. performing)

- View of errors (part of learning vs. performing normatively well)
- Attention (on learning processes vs. normative performance)
- Reasons for effort (learning new material vs. performing normatively well)
- Evaluation criteria (progress vs. normative)

The teacher has an important role in creating the motivational climate in physical education lessons. A teacher's pedagogical and didactical alternatives (e.g., feedback and discussions with students) affect the motivational climate of a class (Ames, 1992). The members of the class constitute another major factor influencing motivational climate. For example, if the majority of students, or the leading students of the class, are task oriented, the climate will be biased toward task involvement. Conversely, if students are primarily ego oriented, the climate will be biased toward ego involvement.

It is important to note that each student perceives the climate in a personal manner (Roberts, 2001). For example, goal orientation, perceived competence and intrinsic motivation toward activity affect these perceptions. The role of the teacher in regulating the climate is important because the climate generated by the teacher may be different from the climate generated by the students. The teacher may emphasise a more task-involving climate even though students are ego oriented (Duda, 2001; Roberts, 2001).

Correlates of Motivational Climates

A task-involving motivational climate has been found to be associated with adaptive cognitive, affective and behavioural responses. These are **task orientation** (Biddle et al., 1995; Ebbeck & Becker, 1994; Newton & Duda, 1993), perceived competence (Kavussanu & Roberts, 1996), increased **intrinsic motivation** and identified regulation (Brunel, 1999; Goudas, 1998). A task-involving climate has also been linked with enjoyment (Kavussanu & Roberts, 1996; Liukkonen, 1998; Seifriz, Duda & Chi, 1992), satisfaction (Carpenter & Morgan, 1999; Walling, Duda &

Table 1.1 TARGET Principles in Physical Education

TARGET principles	Description of principle	How to support a task-involving climate	What should be avoided
Tasks	Design of learning activities and assignments	• Include variety, challenge and purpose for each activity. • Give students the opportunity to choose from a variety of tasks. • Encourage students to set their own goals.	Basing task goals on who will be first or who will score the most points, and so on
Authority	Students' opportunities to develop a sense of personal control, independence and participation in the instructional process	• Foster active participation and a sense of autonomy. • Use questioning skills. • Give students the opportunity to choose (within the assigned content framework). • Involve students in decision making during teaching (e.g., how to complete tasks, what materials to use, and so on).	• Assuming all the responsibility as the teacher • Giving students orders and no choices
Rewards	Formal and informal use of incentives and praise. Reasons for recognition.	• Focus on individual progress and improvement. • Recognition of students' accomplishments is kept private and rewards are given for improvement.	Recognition of students' accomplishments is public and rewards are given in comparison with others.
Grouping	• Manner and frequency of students working together • Arrangements utilized in classroom to allow students to master course content.	• Use individual and cooperative learning. • Students work on individual tasks, in dyads or in small cooperative groups. • Grouping is flexible and heterogeneous.	Grouping is based in ability.
Evaluation	• Methods used to assess and monitor learning • Standards for performance and feedback	• Evaluation is self-referenced and private. • Give opportunities to improve. • Use diverse methods. • Progress is judged on the basis of individual objectives, participation, effort and improvement. • Students are encouraged to evaluate their own performances.	Evaluation is based in norms and in comparing with others.
Time	Includes workload, pace of instruction and learning	• Allow students to participate in scheduling. • Time limits for task completion are flexible. • Students help schedule timelines for improvement.	Time is not flexible.

Adapted from Epstein 1989; Ames 1992; Treasure and Roberts 1995.

Chi, 1993), intrinsic interest (Cury et al., 1996), the intention to be physically active (Biddle et al., 1995), effort (Kavussanu & Roberts, 1996) and lowered tension (Carpenter & Morgan, 1999; Kavussanu & Roberts, 1996; Ommundsen, Roberts & Kavussanu, 1997). In addition, research has shown that a task-involving motivational climate was related to the use of effective learning strategies, training, a lowered chance of avoiding practice (Ommundsen & Roberts, 1999; Roberts & Ommundsen, 1996), the development of meta-cognition in physical education (Theodosiou & Papaioannou, 2006) and respect for the rules and social conventions of sport (Papaioannou, 1997). Associations between task-involving motivational climate and the belief that effort and hard work lead to success (Seifriz et al., 1992; Treasure & Roberts, 1998; Yoo, 1997) and the belief that the purpose of sport is to develop social and lifetime skills (Ommundsen & Roberts, 1999; Ommundsen et al., 1997) have been found. In addition, Balaquer, Crespo and Duda (1996) reported a link between task-involving motivational climate and the development of leadership. Finally, Digelidis and Papaioannou (2002) supported the notion that a task-involving climate positively affects task orientation and students' enjoyment in physical education lessons, while ego-involving climate positively affects ego orientation.

Studies have shown that an ego-involving motivational climate was associated with **ego orientation** (Newton & Duda, 1993) and **extrinsic motivation** (Brunel, 1999). In addition, an ego-involving motivational climate has been found to be related to worrying (Walling, Duda & Chi,

1993), tension, anxiety and pressure (Ntoumanis & Biddle, 1998; Seifriz et al., 1992; Walling et al., 1993) and decreased interest (Cury et al., 1996; Ommundsen et al., 1997). The belief that superior ability causes success (Papaioannou, 1997; Seifriz et al., 1992), the belief that the purpose of sport is to increase social status (Ommundsen et al., 1997), maladaptive behavioural patterns such as dropping out from sport (LeBars & Gernigon, 1998; Whitehead, Andree & Lee, 1997), lowered effort and adherence (Yoo, 1997), strategies of avoiding practice (Ommundsen & Roberts, 1999) and deception (Papaioannou, 1997) have all been demonstrated to be linked with an ego-involving motivational climate.

Motivational Climate Interventions

Several interventions have been implemented to alter motivational climate. Two of these involve short-term interventions concentrating on one practice session (Vallerand, Gauvin & Halliwell, 1986; Walsh, Crocker & Bouffard, 1992). Findings indicated that a task-involving motivational climate was associated with adaptive cognitive, affective and behavioural responses, whereas an ego-involving climate was linked with maladaptive responses.

In addition, several long-term task-involving interventions have been conducted in this area. Intervention periods ranged from two weeks to one academic year. Papaioannou and Digelidis

DEVELOPMENTAL DIFFERENCES CONCERNING MOTIVATIONAL CLIMATE

Digelidis and Papaioannou (1999) examined age-group differences in self-perceptions, goal orientations, motivational climate, effort and enjoyment in physical education classes. The results showed that senior high school students scored lower than junior high school and elementary school students on the scales assessing intrinsic motivation, perceived learning orientation of the lesson, task orientation and perceived athletic ability. High school students had lower scores than elementary school students on the *Perceived Physical Appearance Scale* (Fox & Corbin, 1989) and higher scores on the measure assessing perceptions of students' worries about mistakes. The results suggested that ego orientation remained rather stable from elementary to high school and that learning orientation should be strengthened. The preceding results were confirmed also by a longitudinal study (Digelidis & Papaioannou, 2004).

(1998) implemented a one-year intervention for 8- to 12-year-old elementary school children in Greece. Results indicated that the intervention increased students' perceptions of a task-involving climate, task orientation, intrinsic interest in the lesson, attitudes toward exercise and attitudes toward helping mates. In addition, as a result of the intervention, ego orientation and ego-involving motivational climate decreased.

Digelidis, Papaioannou, Laparidis and Christodoulidis (2003) and Christodoulidis, Papaioannou and Digelidis (2001) implemented two one-year interventions with junior (12- to 14-year-old) and senior (15- to 17-year-old) high school students. The results showed that the intervention increased students' task orientation, their perceptions of a task-involving motivational climate and their attitudes toward exercise. The intervention decreased students' ego orientation and perceptions of an ego-involving motivational climate.

Jaakkola (2002) conducted a one-academic-year intervention for ninth-grade students in Finland. The intervention positively affected students' self-determined motivation and task orientation during the year.

Weigand and Burton (2002) conducted an intervention with 16-year-old English students. The results revealed that students in the task-involving climate group perceived higher levels of task orientation and perceptions of competence, and were more satisfied and less bored compared with those in the control group. In addition, the task climate group decreased their ego orientation during the intervention.

Morgan and Carpenter (2002) implemented a seven-week intervention with secondary school students. The results showed that students in the task climate group increased their task orientation, preferred more challenging tasks and indicated more satisfaction and positive attitudes during the intervention.

Papaioannou and Kouli (1999) conducted an intervention with junior high school students. The study included task-involving and ego-involving tasks in a physical education lesson. In the lesson comprising task-involving tasks, the students had higher states of self-confidence and lower somatic anxiety and perceived a higher task-involving and a lower ego-involving climate than those in the lesson consisting of the ego-involving tasks. In both lessons, task orientation and the perception

of a task-involving climate were positive predictors of concentration, autotelic experience and loss of self-consciousness. In both lessons, males perceived the climate as more ego involving than females did.

Solmon (1996) implemented an intervention for seventh- and eight-grade students. Solmon found that a manipulated task-involving climate was associated with students' persistence during practice at difficult levels of physical activity. An ego-involving climate was related to the belief that ability leads to success.

Theeboom, De Knop and Weiss (1995) conducted a three-week intervention with participants divided into task- and ego-involving teaching groups. The results revealed that the task group participants reported greater enjoyment and perceived competence compared with the ego group.

Treasure (1993) implemented a 10-week intervention in a middle school in North America. Participants were divided into task and ego climate groups. After the intervention, participants in the task group preferred more challenging tasks, believed that effort and motivation lead to success and experienced higher feelings of interest and satisfaction compared with their counterparts in the ego group.

Lloyd and Fox (1992) conducted a six-week intervention in the United Kingdom. They incorporated both task-involving and ego-involving teaching approaches. The results showed that the task-involving group perceived higher enjoyment and motivation compared with their counterparts in the ego-involving group. In addition, participants in the ego group increased in ego orientation, whereas those in the task group displayed a reduced level of ego orientation.

Marsh and Peart (1988) implemented a 14-session intervention study in Australia. They divided students into task- and ego-involving groups. Participants in the task group reported higher physical ability and perceived physical appearance compared with those in the ego group.

It should be noted that within the set of studies reviewed, interventions have primarily been implemented in sport settings, with only four interventions conducted in school physical education settings. The overall trend of these intervention studies indicated that the teacher can alter motivational climate and that an increase in task involvement is associated with adaptive cognitive, affective and behavioural responses.

In addition, Goudas, Biddle, Fox and Underwood (1995) implemented an intervention for a group of adolescent girls. They used two different teaching styles: direct (in which decisions were made by the teacher) and differentiated (in which the teacher gave the children choices). Results indicated that students in the differentiated group showed higher levels of intrinsic motivation and task involvement than students in the direct-style group. Morgan and Carpenter (2002), Weigand and Burton (2002), Solmon (1996), Theeboom, De Knop and Weiss (1995) and Treasure (1993) implemented their interventions based on the TARGET model of Epstein (1989). In other investigations, the structures of the intervention were adopted indirectly from Epstein's (1989) model.

Limited interventions have been applied in adapted physical education. For example, Valentini and Rudisill (2004) designed a 12-week intervention with developmentally delayed kindergarten children. The results showed that the mastery climate (task-involving) group demonstrated significantly better locomotor performance and higher perceived physical competence after the intervention than did the low-autonomy (ego-involving) group, although both groups improved in locomotor and object-control skill performance. Their second investigation (Valentini & Rudisill, 2004) extended the findings of the first study by determining that the intervention effects were present six months later. In summary, the mastery climate group showed positive changes in skill development and perceived physical competence, and this positive pattern of change was maintained over time.

Practical Ways to Establish a Positive Motivational Climate

This section gives practical guidance for physical education teachers who would like to work on creating a positive motivational climate. All ideas expressed in this section have been assessed using several short-term and long-term interventions in physical education contexts.

One of the ways teachers establish a positive motivational climate is through values. While talking with students, teachers invariably reveal hidden thoughts that reflect their values. Some of these values and ideas may help establish a positive climate, whereas others may not (see table 1.2). The main purpose of schools in our societies is to provide learning. Because one of teachers' primary responsibilities is creating this learning environment, the ideas they emphasise should stem from learning theories.

Increase Autonomy

Autonomy is the cornerstone of human motivation (Deci & Ryan, 1985, 2000). It is also important for promoting self-determination and self-regulation in educational settings (Pelletier, Fortier, Vallerand & Brière, 2001), which is vital for the learning process. Therefore, increasing autonomy plays an important role when creating the task-involving motivational climate. Increasing autonomy means individualising the instructional process by letting students become part of it. It means giving a personal character to teaching while at the same time giving every student who participates in a

Table 1.2 Values to Avoid and Emphasise

Values to Avoid	Values to Emphasise
It's impossible to teach you anything!	Everybody can learn.
Are you stupid?	Everybody can improve.
You are always wrong!	Everyone learns at his or her own pace
You are not talented!	When someone is trying to learn, it is possible that he or she will make mistakes.
You have to do it.	Learning depends on your will and effort.
If you don't, your grades will drop off.	Learning depends on how much time you are going to devote.
You must do it.	Learning depends on how committed you are to learning goals.

physical education lesson a sense of personal meaning. It can be done by giving the students opportunities to select from given alternatives and actions and to develop drills and games by themselves. In addition, teachers can involve students in decision-making processes concerned with various aspects of the physical education class. From the preceding statements, it is obvious that student-centred teaching styles give more autonomy and enhance students' self-determination. At the same time, teachers should emphasise that responsibility comes with the increased autonomy (Hellison, Siedentop & Hellison, 2003). Table 1.3 summarises some of the most critical points of teacher-centred and student-centred teaching styles.

But what kinds of choices can teachers offer to students? The answer to this question depends on some prerequisites. A physical education teacher should consider at least three main issues before organising a class for greater autonomy:

- Is this choice safe for the students?
- Do students have the responsibility to react appropriately?
- How should I organise this kind of choice in my lesson?

One way to increase students' autonomy might be to offer two or more alternative warm-up options (e.g., ropes or running) and let students choose the warm-up they prefer. Or, when preparing to play a game, a teacher can let students make teams, choose roles and choose how they are going to change their roles in the team (e.g., who will be the goalkeeper or how many minutes one will play in defence).

Teachers must apply these changes gradually in order to be effective—perhaps one kind of choice at a time. Otherwise, giving students all these choices simultaneously could lead to a teaching disaster! Teachers should decide which choice to give students, considering that different choices could affect the way they organise their teaching. For example, if teachers want to let students choose which exercise to do first, they have to make sure that all necessary athletic equipment is usable.

Individualise

Students' perceived competence is vital for their intrinsic motivation (Deci & Ryan, 1985, 2000). A student with high perceptions of his athletic competence will likely maintain his effort. On the other hand, a student who thinks that she may be humiliated in front of others may give up trying. Teachers can effectively increase students' perception of their competence by using individualisation. The first prerequisite in applying individualisation is that the student, not the teacher, should be responsible for individualising a task. In this way, the teacher avoids the self-fulfilling prophecy phenomenon (Martinek, 1989; Martinek & Hellison, 1997). The second prerequisite is creating a climate of acceptance for all students.

When circumstances allow, teachers should let students change drill parameters that have to do with task difficulty (e.g., distance, target size, execution technique). Safety issues should dictate whether to allow individualisation (e.g., setting the minimum or the maximum distance that one can kick to goal). Figure 1.1 shows an example of how a teacher might customise a volleyball service lesson.

Table 1.3 Teacher-Centred and Student-Centred Teaching Styles

Teacher-centred styles (low autonomy)	Student-centred styles (high autonomy)
Students follow teacher's orders.	Students have choices.
Students do not participate in the instructional process.	Students have roles and responsibilities in the instructional process.
Games and activities are controlled by the teacher.	Games and activities are controlled by the students.
Students have no option to alter the games' rules or drills' parameters.	Students have the opportunity to modify the games' rules and drills' parameters to meet their own needs and capacities according to their understanding.

TASK CARD CHOICES

Teachers who like using task cards in their lessons could give the following choices to students:

Which exercises do you choose? (You can skip one exercise.)

How many repetitions will you do?

Which exercise will you do first?

Which exercise will you do last?

How much time are you going to devote to an exercise?

Teachers who like working with the practice style of teaching or generally organising stations could give the following choices to students:

Which station will you go to first?

How many times are you going to repeat a station?

You may skip one station. Which will you skip?

How much time are you going to devote to a station?

You have two (or more exercises) to choose from during the transition phase. Which do you choose?

Offer Goal-Setting Programmes

Goal setting is a practical tool when emphasising students' personal development in physical education. Zimmerman and Kitsantas (1996) suggested that in physical activity contexts, goals can be distinguished as either process or product. When students set *process* goals, they try to perform the correct movement pattern of a skill. When they set *product* goals, they try to achieve an outcome that is usually expressed in numbers. Process goals, such as performing a skill correctly, help students to improve themselves and should be considered conducive to a task-involving climate. On the other hand, based on the analysis of Ames (1984), product goals can be classified

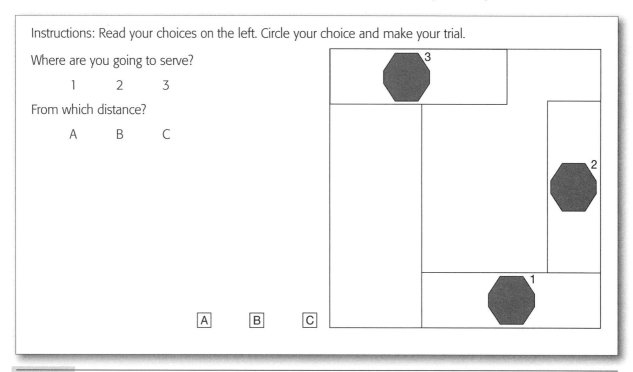

Figure 1.1 A simple example of task individualisation in volleyball service.

as competitive, cooperative or personal development. Trying to overcome others is obviously a competitive goal. A cooperative goal is set when, for example, students try to keep the ball in the air for 10 consecutive overhead sets in volleyball. Finally, students set a personal development goal when they are trying to improve their performance from two out of five free shots in basketball to three out of five.

Teachers setting competitive goals create an ego-involving atmosphere, whereas teachers setting cooperative or personal development goals create a task-involving environment (Papaioannou & Kouli, 1999; see also in the same book, Milosis & Papaioannou, 'Effects of Interdisciplinary Teaching on Multiple Goals, Intrinsic Motivation,

Self-Concept and School Achievement'). Teachers can request that students voluntarily choose two or three special sport skills they want to develop (e.g., volleyball hit and endurance). After students select these skills, the teacher can advise them how to measure these variables three or four times before the end of the season. It is also important that teachers help students develop methods for improving their special skills in school physical education and their leisure time. Teachers can give students free time (e.g., during breaks or following physical education lessons) to practise chosen skills. It is also important that students seek teachers' assistance in establishing purposefully developed skills. One example of goal setting in physical education is presented in figure 1.2.

Name: _____

Set three goals for increasing your fitness during your leisure time this year (for example, 'I will go jogging twice a week').

My goals are:

1._____

2._____

3._____

Set three goals for yourself that you want to achieve during the year in physical education (your teacher will give examples of sport skills you may want to develop).

My goals are:

1._____

2._____

3._____

Write down what you can do to help you achieve your goals in practice (e.g., 'I have to . . . three times a week').

1._____

2._____

3._____

Figure 1.2 Example of a goal-setting model for students.

Use Positive Evaluation Practices

Mastery of goals is most likely to occur when assessment and evaluation are focused on individual progress, improvement and understanding. Evaluation is usually linked with goal-setting programmes. Often this means that the teacher will make the final judgment. Creating a task-involving climate means that teachers use a variety of evaluation methods (e.g., traditional skill tests, written tests, portfolios, homework), and students have the responsibility to evaluate themselves. Teachers should avoid evaluating or grading students based on norms or curves.

Evaluation is different from grading. Grading is a function of evaluation. Assessments should demonstrate what students know or are able to do, but the main issue is how results are communicated to students. Low grades should mean low effort. The following tips may be helpful to physical education teachers who are using assessment techniques in their classrooms:

- Be very clear about what is being assessed. Whatever is being assessed has to be worth learning. Students need to know what information is included in their grades.
- Allow students to get involved in the process (e.g., by using your criteria they can evaluate themselves, a partner or others; you could allow students some choices in the way they want to be assessed).
- Share the information with students.

In almost all European countries, grading is the teacher's responsibility. Because grading can have a great effect on students' goal orientations and motives, physical education teachers should follow these tips when they have to grade their students:

- Grades should be a synthesis of as many students' performance elements as possible.
- Grades should be connected with goal achievement and especially the effort that students expend.
- Grades should provide useful information to students for further personal improvement.

When learning, we inevitably make some mistakes. But as we keep trying, mistakes diminish until finally we master the skill. So what's the use of mistakes? Do they mean that we are stupid or incapable of learning? Of course not! Clearly, everybody needs time to learn. This means that everybody can learn if given time. What, then, is the purpose of evaluation? If it is to assess someone's skill or effort only for the academic season, then it's OK. But if the purpose is to assess someone for the rest of his life, then it is not helpful.

Use Positive Feedback

Feedback is vital for learning motor skills and for establishing a positive learning climate. In general, feedback should have the following characteristics:

- It should be given personally and not publicly (not in front of other people).
- It should be self-referenced and not norm-referenced.
- It should be given using positive phrases (e.g., expressing positive feelings).
- Mistakes should be accepted as part of the learning process.
- Trying should be emphasised.
- It should be immediate.

Maximise Learning Time

Time on task is vital for learning motor skills. In fact, time is vital for teaching and learning in general. It is important to be realistic about the amount of time it takes to learn a simple or complex motor skill or complex subject matter. Furthermore, learning is more effective when students engage in deliberate practice, monitor their progress and set personal goals for improvement.

Maximising students' learning time seems to be one of the crucial issues for establishing a task-involving motivational climate because it's related to learning itself. In a previous study, it has been shown that a task-involving climate was linked with higher academic learning times (Papaioannou, 1993). For example, Papaioannou (1993), by combining measures of perceived motivational climate and the ALT-PE observational system, showed that classes with higher scores in task-involving climate had increased academic learning time and also increased practice time. On the contrary, classes that had lower scores in task-involving climate had more students off task and playing without supervision. Although direct paths between learning and time have not been proved, it is obvious that higher levels of students' activity and participation are related with learning and also with task-involving climate. Teachers who want to maximise students' learning time could organise students in small teams and avoid having students in long queues. See table 1.4 for further suggestions.

Recognise Students Appropriately

In the world of sport, external rewards (e.g., trophies and medals) are used extensively. Such rewards do exist in PE classes in different forms and under different circumstances (e.g., a teacher's smile after a student's successful performance). Early research (e.g., Deci, 1971) suggested that external rewards could undermine intrinsic motivation. After a rather short period of debate and some contradictory findings (e.g., Cameron & Pierce, 1994), it is now widely accepted that external rewards can undermine intrinsic motivation (Ryan & Deci, 2000; Vallerand & Losier, 1999), but perhaps not in all cases (Deci & Ryan, 1985). Therefore, one has to seek information from this area of research because intrinsic motivation is related with task orientation and task-involving climate (Brunel, 1999; Digelidis & Papaioannou, 2002; Goudas, 1998).

Task-involving contexts base recognition and rewards on effort and task mastery (Newton, Duda & Yin, 2000). Investigation has also suggested an additive relationship between the TARGET structures, with recognition and evaluation being the most influential in determining pupils' climate perceptions (Morgan, Sproule, Weigand & Carpenter, 2005). According to the present knowledge base (Deci & Ryan, 1985; Epstein, 1989; Midgley,

Table 1.4   Maximising Learning Time

Ineffective strategies	Effective strategies
Bad use of athletic equipment (e.g., we use only two balls when we could use 20)	Use all the available athletic equipment. Try also using alternative equipment (e.g., you can use volleyballs for soccer).
Bad use of space (e.g., all students are exercising in a narrow area while our school has a big yard)	Use a practice style of teaching (e.g., stations, task cards).
Bad grouping strategies (e.g., big teams)	Group students in small teams, at least most of the time.
Use of unstable signals (e.g., in order to stop an exercise we shout "stop", and the next time we use a whistle)	Use the same signals consistently in order to communicate effectively with the students.
Lack of space or equipment preparation (e.g., we wait for the bell to ring, and then we try to organize our gym or bring in balls)	Prepare for teaching before arriving to class.
Big lines in tasks	Have small teams; use all available athletic equipment and space; organise students in stations.
Lessons with many different forms of organization (e.g., first in pairs, then in threes, then again in pairs, then in teams)	Exercises with the same organisational form may go one after another. Exercises that need the same equipment or space may go one after another.

2002; Ryan & Deci, 2000; Stipek, 2002; Weinberg & Gould, 2003), suggestions for proper use of praise and recognition that enhance task-involving climate should include the following:

- Give recognition privately when possible and not publicly.

- Link rewards to the performance of specific behaviours (e.g., in order to inform students how well they are doing or to give information about their progress).

- Avoid recognising the absence of mistakes (e.g., rewarding only students with fewer than five mistakes on a balance test).

- Recognise students for stretching their own capabilities and for coming up with novel ways to solve a problem.

- Acknowledge the quality of students' work rather than the quantity of work completed (e.g., offering praise for dealing with one challenging situation rather than completing five easy tasks).

Manage the Class

Many teachers, especially in the beginning of their careers, worry about keeping students disciplined. Sometimes discipline is a big headache, and some teachers become obsessed with class management. Unfortunately, this may lead to decreased student autonomy, enjoyment and individualisation.

Students who are basically intrinsically motivated are likely to be well behaved in the physical education lesson for intrinsic reasons (e.g., because they enjoy the lesson, because they care about each other, because they believe that what they are doing is important for them, because they believe they can do it). On the other hand, students who are basically extrinsically motivated are likely to behave for extrinsic reasons (e.g., because the teacher has rules, because they may be afraid of being embarrassed publicly by the teacher, because there are penalties for student misbehaviour) (Papaioannou, 1998). Because of the complexity of this issue, physical education teachers should basically do two things: (1) have rules and protocols, especially for students who are extrinsically motivated, and (2) increase students' intrinsic motivation by creating a task-involving climate.

Summary

A motivational climate is defined as a situation-induced environment directing the goals of an action in achievement situations. Motivational climates are either task involving or ego involving depending on how people perceive and interpret the structure of the achievement environment. Motivational climate is considered to affect a person's interpretation of the criteria of success and failure in achievement environments. It is also assumed to affect adaptive and maladaptive achievement behaviour, as well as affective and cognitive responses.

If children are involved in decision making, and grouping is not based on ability, the environment is task involving. In addition, in the task-involving motivational climate, success is defined and evaluated according to individual effort, improvement and learning. A task-involving motivational climate is created when a teacher emphasises self-reference and task involvement as criteria for success and failure.

The teacher has an important role in creating the motivational climate in physical education lessons. A teacher's pedagogical and didactical alternatives (e.g., feedback and discussions with students) affect the motivational climate of a class. The members of the class constitute another major factor influencing motivational climate. For example, if the majority of students, or the leading students of the class, are task oriented, the climate will be biased toward task involvement. Conversely, if students are ego oriented, the climate will be biased toward ego involvement. Each student perceives the climate in a personal manner. For example, goal orientation, perceived competence and intrinsic motivation toward activity affect these perceptions. The role of the teacher in regulating the climate is important, because the climate generated by the teacher may be different from the climate generated by the students. The teacher may emphasise a more task-involving climate, even though students are ego oriented.

Teachers have many practical tools for increasing the task-involving motivational climate in physical education. Increasing the autonomy of the class is important to encourage students' intrinsic motivation. Through individualisation, the teacher confirms that each student practises at his or her own skill level. This contributes to students' perceived competence. By using an individual goal-setting programme and task-involving evaluation, the teacher is able to increase self-referenced criteria for success. The teacher's feedback and rewarding behaviour also affect how the students perceive the motivational climate. Private feedback and rewards for personal development and effort can have a major influence on students' motivation. Lastly, it is important that the teacher provide enough time for learning.

Clearly, a positive motivational climate is important in physical education. But establishing a task-involving climate is a rather complex and demanding issue. Teachers must apply many strategies simultaneously to achieve consistency. Nevertheless, they don't have to do everything simultaneously from the beginning! They may start by increasing autonomy, for example, which could take one or more weeks. Then they can choose another subcategory of strategies in their daily teaching. Realistically, establishing a positive motivational climate may take more than a month.

Review Questions

1. What is the meaning of a motivational climate?
2. What characteristics does a task-involving motivational climate have?
3. What characteristics does an ego-involving motivational climate have?
4. What cognitive, affective and behavioural responses on the part of students have changed as a result of motivational climate interventions?
5. What kinds of strategies can a teacher use to foster a task-involving motivational climate?

Critical Thinking Questions

1. How can you foster autonomy in a 30-student class in which discipline is lacking?
2. How can you increase the perceptions of competence of most students in an extremely heterogeneous group?
3. Which teaching styles seem proper for enhancing a task-involving climate?
4. How can you maximise academic learning time?
5. If you could choose the content of a physical education lesson whose primary focus was fostering a task-involving motivational climate, what would it look like?
6. In the process of learning, we all make mistakes. How can you offer feedback to correct students' mistakes?
7. What forms of evaluation and what criteria would you use to evaluate and grade students?

Key Terms

ego-involving motivational climate—A motivational climate perspective based on normative evaluation.

ego orientation—A goal orientation perspective based on normative criteria for success.

extrinsic motivation—Motivation based on the potential external rewards that may be received as a result.

intrinsic motivation—Motivation based on one's enjoyment of the behaviour itself rather than on external reinforcement.

motivational climate—A situation-induced environment directing the goals of an action in achievement situations.

task-involving motivational climate—A motivational climate perspective based on self-referenced criteria for success, effort and personal development.

task orientation—A goal orientation perspective based on self-referenced criteria for success.

References

Ames, C. (1984). Competitive, cooperative, and individualistic goal structures: A cognitive-motivational analysis. In R. Ames and C. Ames (Eds.), *Research on motivation in education, Vol. 1. Student motivation* (pp. 177-207). New York: Academic Press.

Ames, C. (1992). Achievement goal, motivational climate, and motivational processes. In G.C. Roberts (Ed.), *Motivation in sport and exercise* (pp. 161-176). Champaign, IL: Human Kinetics.

Ames, C., & Archer J. (1988). Achievement goals in the classroom: Students' learning strategies and motivation processes. *Journal of Educational Psychology, 80,* 260-267.

Balaquer, I., Crespo, M. & Duda, J.L. (1996). The relationship of motivational climate and athletes' goal orientations to perceived/preferred leadership style. *Journal of Sport & Exercise Psychology, 18,* S13.

Biddle, S., Cury, F., Goudas, M., Sarrazin, P., Famose, J.-P. & Durand, M. (1995). Development of scales to measure perceived physical education class climate: A cross-national project. *British Journal of Educational Psychology, 65,* 341-358.

Brunel, P. (1999). Relationship between achievement goal orientations and perceived motivational climate on intrinsic motivation. *Scandinavian Journal of Medicine & Science in Sports, 9,* 365-374.

Cameron, J. & Pierce, W.D. (1994). Reinforcement, reward and intrinsic motivation: A meta-analysis. *Review of Educational Research, 64,* 363-423.

Carpenter, P. & Morgan, K. (1999). Motivational climate, personal goal perspectives, and cognitive and affective responses in physical education classes. *European Journal of Physical Education, 19,* 302-312.

Christodoulidis, T., Papaioannou, A. & Digelidis, N. (2001). Motivational climate and attitudes towards exercise in Greek senior high school: A year-long intervention. *European Journal of Sport Science, 1,* 1-12.

Cury, F., Biddle, S., Famose, J.P., Goudas, M., Sarrazin, P. & Durand, M. (1996). Personal and situational factors influencing intrinsic interest of adolescent girls in school physical education: A structural equation modelling analysis. *Educational Psychology, 16,* 305-315.

Deci, E.L. (1971). Effects of externally mediated rewards on intrinsic motivation. *Journal of Personality and Social Psychology, 18,* 105-115.

Deci, E.L. & Ryan, R.M. (1985). *Intrinsic motivation and self-determination in human behaviour.* New York: Plenum Press.

Deci, E.L. & Ryan, R.M. (2000). The "what" and "why" of goal pursuits: Human needs and the self-determination of behaviour. *Psychological Inquiry, 11,* 227-268.

Digelidis, N. & Papaioannou, A. (1999). Age-group differences in intrinsic motivation, goal orientations and perceptions of athletic competence, physical appearance and motivational climate in Greek physical education. *Scandinavian Journal of Medicine & Science in Sports, 9,* 375-380.

Digelidis, N. & Papaioannou, A. (2002). Interactions between effort, enjoyment, perceived motivational climate and task and ego orientations in physical education classes during a school year. *Athlitiki Psychologia, 13,* 35-55.

Digelidis, N. & Papaioannou, A. (2004). Developmental differences concerning effort, enjoyment, goal orientations, perceived motivational climate and self-perceptions in physical education classes: A longitudinal study. *Athlitiki Psychologia, 15,* 3-16.

Digelidis, N., Papaioannou, A., Laparidis, K. & Christodoulidis, T. (2003). A one-year intervention in 7th grade physical education classes aiming to change motivational climate and attitudes towards exercise. *Psychology of Sport and Exercise, 4,* 195-211.

Duda, J.L. (2001). Goal perspective research in sport: Pushing the boundaries and clarifying some misunderstandings. In G.C. Roberts (Ed.), *Advances in motivation in sport and exercise* (pp. 129-182). Champaign, IL: Human Kinetics.

Duda, J.L. & Hall H.K. (2001). Achievement goal theory in sport: Recent extensions and future directions. In R.N. Singer, H.A. Hausenblas & C.M. Janelle (Eds.), *Handbook of research in sport psychology* (2nd ed., pp. 417-443). New York: Wiley.

Dweck, C.S. & Leggett, E.L. (1988). A social-cognitive approach to motivation and personality. *Psychological Review, 95,* 256-273.

Ebbeck, V. & Becker, S.L. (1994). Psychosocial predictors of goal orientations in youth soccer. *Research Quarterly for Exercise and Sport, 65,* 355-362.

Epstein, J.L. (1989). Family structures and student motivation: A developmental perspective. In C. Ames & R. Ames (Eds.), *Research on motivation in education,* Vol. 13 (pp. 259-295). San Diego, CA: Academic Press.

Fox, K.R. & Corbin, C.B. (1989). The physical self-perception profile: Development and preliminary validation. *Journal of Sport and Exercise Psychology, 11,* 408-430.

Goudas, M. (1998). Motivational climate and intrinsic motivation of young basketball players. *Perceptual and Motor Skills, 86,* 323-327.

Goudas, M., Biddle, S., Fox, K. & Underwood, M. (1995). It ain't what you do, it's the way that you do it! Teaching style affects children's motivation in track and field lessons. *The Sport Psychologist, 9,* 254-264.

Hellison, D.R., Siedentop, D. & Hellison, D. (2003). *Teaching responsibility through physical activity.* Champaign, IL: Human Kinetics.

Jaakkola, T. (2002). Changes in students' exercise motivation, goal orientation, and sport competence as a result modifications in school physical education teaching practices. *Research Reports on Sport and Health no. 131.* University of Jyväskylä, Finland: LIKES-Research Center for Sport and Health Sciences.

Jaakkola, T., Pakkala, P., Piirainen, U., Liukkonen, J., Kokkonen, J. & Telama R. (1999). The reliability and validity of the observation scale of the motivational climate in physical education lessons. In V. Hosek, P. Tilinger & L. Bilek (Eds.), *Psychology of sport and exercise: Enhancing the quality of life* (pp. 271-273). Proceedings of the 10th European Congress of Sport Psychology: European Federation of Sport Psychology.

Kavussanu, M. & Roberts, G.C. (1996). Motivation in physical activity contexts: The relationship of perceived motivational climate to intrinsic motivation and self-efficacy. *Journal of Sport and Exercise Psychology, 18,* 264-280.

LeBars, H. & Gernigon, C. (1998). Perceived motivational climate, dispositional goals, and participation withdrawal in judo. *Journal of Sport and Exercise Psychology, 20,* S58.

Liukkonen, J. (1998). Enjoyment in youth sports: A goal perspectives approach. *Research Reports on Sport and Health no. 114.* University of Jyväskylä, Finland: LIKES-Research Center for Sport and Health Sciences.

Lloyd, J. & Fox, K. (1992). Achievement goals and motivation to exercise in adolescent girls: A preliminary intervention study. *British Journal of Physical Education Research Supplement, 11,* 12-16.

Marsh, H.W. & Peart, N.D. (1988). Competitive and cooperative physical fitness training programs for girls: Effects on physical fitness and multidimensional self-concepts. *Journal of Sport & Exercise Psychology, 10,* 390-407.

Martinek, T.J. (1989). Children's perceptions of teaching behaviors: An attributional model for explaining teacher expectancy effects. *Journal of Teaching in Physical Education, 8,* 318-328.

Martinek, T.J. & Hellison, D. (1997). Fostering resiliency in underserved youth through physical activity. *Quest, 49,* 34-49.

Midgley, C. (2002). *Goals, goal structures, and patterns of adaptive learning.* Mahwah, NJ: Erlbaum.

Morgan, K. & Carpenter, P. (2002). Effects of manipulating the motivational climate in physical education lessons. *European Physical Education Review, 8,* 207-229.

Morgan K., Sproule, J., Weigand, D. & Carpenter, P. (2005). A computer-based observational assessment of the teaching behaviours that influence motivational climate in physical education. *Physical Education and Sport Pedagogy, 10,* 83-105.

Newton, M. & Duda, J.L. (1993). Elite adolescent athletes' achievement goals and beliefs concerning success in tennis. *Journal of Sport & Exercise Psychology, 15,* 437-448.

Newton, M., Duda, J.L. & Yin, Z. (2000). Examination of the psychometric properties of the *Perceived Motivational Climate in Sport Questionnaire—2* in a sample of female athletes. *Journal of Sports Sciences, 18,* 275-290.

Newton, M.L. & Duda, J.L. (1999). The interaction of motivational climate, dispositional goal orientation and perceived ability in predicting indices of motivation. *International Journal of Sport Psychology, 30,* 63-82.

Nicholls, J.G. (1984). Conceptions of ability and achievement motivation. In R. Ames & C. Ames (Eds.), *Research on motivation in education: Student motivation, Vol. 1* (pp. 39-73). New York: Academic Press.

Nicholls J.G. (1989). *The competitive ethos and democratic education.* Cambridge, MA: Harvard University Press.

Ntoumanis, N. & Biddle, S. (1998). The relationship between competitive anxiety, achievement goals, and motivational climates. *Research Quarterly for Exercise and Sport, 69,* 176-187.

Ommundsen, Y. & Roberts, G.C. (1999). Effect of motivational climate profiles on motivational indices in team sport. *Scandinavian Journal of Medicine & Science in Sports, 9,* 389-397.

Ommundsen, Y., Roberts, G.C. & Kavussanu, M. (1997). Perceived motivational climate and cognitive and affective correlates among Norwegian athletes. In R. Lidor & M. Bar-Eli (Eds.), *Innovations in sport psychology: Linking theory into practice* (pp. 522-524). Proceedings of the 9th World Congress of Sport Psychology: International Society of Sport Psychology.

Papaioannou, A. (1993). *Characteristics of physical education classes differing in achievement orientations.* In S. Serpa, J. Alves, V. Ferreira & A. Paula-Brito (Eds.), *Proceedings of the 8th World Congress of Sport Psychology* (pp. 799-803). Lisbon: International Society of Sport Psychology.

Papaioannou, A. (1994). Development of a questionnaire to measure achievement orientations in physical education. *Research Quarterly for Exercise and Sport, 65,* 11-20.

Papaioannou, A. (1997). Perceptions of motivational climate, perceived competence, and motivation of students of varying ages and sport experience. *Perceptual and Motor Skills, 85,* 419-430.

Papaioannou, A. (1998). Goal perspectives, reasons for behaving appropriately, and self-reported discipline in physical education lessons. *Journal of Teaching in Physical Education, 17*(4), 421-441.

Papaioannou, A. & Goudas, M. (1999). Motivational climate in physical education. In Y. Vanden Auweele, F. Bakker, S. Biddle, M. Durand & R. Seiler (Eds.), *Textbook: Psychology for physical educators* (pp. 51-68). Champaign, IL: Human Kinetics.

Papaioannou, A. & Kouli O. (1999). The effect of task structure, perceived motivational climate and goal orientations on students' intrinsic motivation and anxiety. *Journal of Applied Sport Psychology, 11,* 51-71.

Pelletier, L., Fortier, M., Vallerand, R. & Brière, N. (2001). Associations among perceived autonomy support, forms of self-regulation, and persistence: A prospective study. *Motivation and Emotion, 25,* 279-306.

Roberts, G.C. (2001). Understanding the dynamics of motivation in physical activity: The influence of achievement goals, personal agency beliefs, and the motivational climate. In G.C. Roberts (Ed.), *Advances in motivation in sport and exercise* (pp. 1-50). Champaign, IL: Human Kinetics.

Roberts, G.C. & Ommundsen, Y. (1996). Effect of goal orientation on achievement beliefs, cognition and strategies in team sport. *Scandinavian Journal of Medicine & Science in Sports, 6,* 46-56.

Ryan, R.M., & Deci, E.L. (2000). Self-determination theory and the facilitation of intrinsic motivation, social development and well-being. *American Psychologist, 55,* 68-78.

Seifriz, J.J., Duda, J.L. & Chi, L. (1992). The relationship of perceived motivational climate to intrinsic motivation and beliefs about success in basketball. *Journal of Sport & Exercise Psychology, 14,* 375-391.

Solmon, M.A. (1996). Impact of motivational climate on students' behaviours and perceptions in physical education setting. *Journal of Educational Psychology, 88,* 731-738.

Stipek, D. (2002). *Motivation to learn: Integrating theory and practice.* Boston: Allyn & Bacon/ Longman.

Theeboom, M., De Knop, P. & Weiss, M.R. (1995). Motivational climate, psychological responses, and motor skill development in children's sport: A field-based intervention study. *Journal of Sport & Exercise Psychology, 17,* 294-311.

Theodosiou, A. & Papaioannou, A. (2006). Motivational climate, achievement goals and metacognitive activity in physical education and exercise involvement in out-of-school settings. *Psychology of Sport and Exercise, 7,* 361-379.

Treasure, D.C. (1993). *A social cognitive approach to understand children's achievement behaviour, cognitions and affect in competitive sport.* Unpublished doctoral dissertation, University of Illinois at Urbana-Champaign.

Treasure, D.C. (2001). Enhancing young people's motivation in youth sport: An achievement goal approach. In G.C. Roberts (Ed.), *Advances in motivation in sport and exercise* (pp. 79-100). Champaign, IL: Human Kinetics.

Treasure, D.C. & Roberts, G.C. (1995). Applications of achievement goal theory to physical education: Implications for enhancing motivation. *Quest, 47,* 475-489.

Treasure, D.C. & Roberts, G.C. (1998). Relationship between female adolescents' achievement goal orientations, perception of motivational climate, beliefs about success and sources of satisfaction in basketball. *International Journal of Sport Psychology, 29,* 211-230.

Valentini, N.C. & Rudisill, M.E. (2004). An inclusive mastery climate intervention and the motor skill development of children with and without disabilities. *Adapted Physical Activity Quarterly, 21,* 330-347.

Vallerand, R.J., & Losier, G. (1999). An integrative analysis of intrinsic and extrinsic motivation in sport. *Journal of Applied Sport Psychology, 11,* 142-169.

Vallerand, R.J., Gauvin, L.I. & Halliwell, W.R. (1986). Negative effects of competition on children's intrinsic motivation. *The Journal of Social Psychology, 126,* 649-657.

Walling, M.D., Duda, J.L. & Chi, L. (1993). The perceived motivational climate in sport questionnaire: Construct and predictive validity. *Journal of Sport & Exercise Psychology, 19,* 98-109.

Walsh, J., Crocker, P.R.E. & Bouffard, M. (1992). The effects of perceived competence and goal orientation on affect and task persistence in a physical activity skill. *The Australian Journal of Science and Medicine in Sport, 24,* 86-90.

Weigand, D.A. & Burton, S. (2002). When anxiety is not always a handicap in physical education and sport: Some implications of the defensive pessimism strategy. *European Journal of Sport Science, 2,* 1-14.

Weinberg, R.S., & Gould, D. (2003). *Foundations of Sport and Exercise Psychology.* Champaign, IL: Human Kinetics.

Whitehead, J.R., Andree, K.V. & Lee, M.J. (1997). Longitudinal interactions between dispositional and situational goals, perceived ability, and intrinsic motivation. In R. Lidor & M. Bar-Eli (Eds.), *Innovations in sport psychology: Linking theory into practice* (pp. 750-752). Proceedings of the 9th World Congress in Sport Psychology: International Society of Sport Psychology.

Yoo, J. (1997). Motivational and behavioural concomitants of goal orientation and motivational climate in the physical education context. In R. Lidor & M. Bar-Eli (Eds.), *Innovations in sport psychology: Linking theory into practice* (pp. 773-775). Proceedings of the 9th World Congress in Sport Psychology: International Society of Sport Psychology.

Zimmerman, B.J. & Kitsantas, A. (1996). Self-regulated learning of a motor skill: The role of goal setting and self-monitoring. *Journal of Applied Sport Psychology, 8,* 60-75.

chapter two

Goal Setting in Physical Education

Yannis Theodorakis
Antonis Hatzigeorgiadis
Stiliani Chroni
Marios Goudas
University of Thessaly, Greece

After reading this chapter, you will be able to do the following:

- Identify the value of goal setting in physical education
- Comprehend the basic principles of effective goal setting
- Develop, implement and evaluate goal-setting plans
- Build your physical education lesson on the grounds of goal setting
- Educate students on the application of goal setting in physical education
- Endorse a holistic approach to physical education through the use of goal setting

Despite what many people believe, **goal setting,** like sport psychology, is not just for elite athletes. Teachers and students at the elementary, secondary and higher education levels can benefit from setting goals. Physical education teachers who have used a goal-setting approach have found that it sustains their own motivation to teach while bringing students new knowledge and enhancing their self-confidence and commitment to do the work.

Both students and teachers often pursue results and forget all about the process, the means that take them to the next level. A simple definition of a **goal** is something of value to a person. Achieving a goal involves a process of recognising where one wants to go and deciding how to get there. The level of self-awareness that is attained through this process is an added bonus on the journey to success. Self-awareness will help young students grow into self-possessed people and will help PE teachers become effective educators.

Goal-Setting Theory

The theory supporting goal setting was developed in industrial or organisational settings, but research has proven the effectiveness of this technique in other fields as well (Burton, Naylor & Holliday, 2001). Goal-setting theory assumes that human action is directed in general by conscious goals and intentions. The goals people have for a task influence what they will do and how well they perform.

Assigned goals facilitate performance because they influence both self-efficacy and personal goals (Locke, 1996; Locke & Latham, 1990). According to the theory, goals direct attention to important elements of the skill being performed, mobilise effort, encourage persistence and foster the development of new learning strategies. Goals influence behaviour by causing changes in important psychological factors such as self-confidence, anxiety, commitment and satisfaction (Weinberg & Gould, 2003).

For goal setting to be effective, a number of **goal-setting principles** should be considered (Weinberg & Gould, 2003). Goals should be *specific* rather than vague, *challenging* rather than easy, and *controllable* by the individual rather than dependent on others. Because **goal attainment** should be evaluated frequently, goals should

also be *measurable.* People should set *short-term* and *long-term* goals, in relation to **performance goals** (what they want to achieve) and **process goals** (how they are going to achieve it). Goals should be *self-determined* rather than imposed, or at least *endorsed* by the person. Finally, goals should be set down *in writing* and *announced to significant others* to increase commitment. **Goal evaluation** with regard to these principles helps identify whether the goals are appropriate.

Many studies have examined various elements of goal setting in relation to sport and exercise (e.g., Boyce, 1994; Smith & Lee, 1992; Weinberg, Burton, Yukelson & Weigand, 1993; Weinberg, Stitcher & Richardson, 1994). Burton and colleagues (2001) provided a comprehensive review of goal-setting research in sport. These studies have focused primarily on the areas of goal specificity, goal difficulty and goal proximity. Other studies (Lerner & Locke, 1995; Theodorakis, 1995, 1996) showed that commitment to goals related positively to self-efficacy and performance. In general, the more confident, the more satisfied and the more committed athletes are, the higher their personal goals and performance attainment appear to be. In the physical activity and exercise domains, numerous studies have supported the effectiveness of goal setting in various fitness and skill tests, including sit-ups, running, swimming, basketball free throws and dribbling, tennis skills, and golf putting (for a review, see Weinberg & Butt, 2005). Kyllo and Landers' (1995) meta-analysis indicated that, overall, setting goals improves performance in sport. Moderate, absolute and combined short- and long-term goals were associated with the greatest benefits.

Designing a Goal-Setting Process in the Physical Education Environment

Researchers have described extensively the process of setting goals, offering the necessary information for implementing the technique correctly. Weinberg and Gould (2003) emphasised that 'goal setting is an extremely powerful technique for enhancing performance, but it must be implemented correctly' (p. 333) and described a three-phase goal-setting system:

1. Planning and preparation
2. Education and acquisition
3. Implementation and follow-up

In the following sections we discuss these three phases in greater detail.

Planning and Preparation

Theoretically, PE teachers should spend at least an hour per day preparing for their classes. In reality, though, daily preparation does not happen. A critical question is whether daily planning and preparation are essential. At the onset of their teaching careers, most teachers devote enough time daily to prepare and organise their classes for the next day. This preparation time shrinks as experience grows. Nonetheless, preparing and planning one's work is always vital for a number of reasons:

- Limited hours for physical education in the school setting and the limited time actually spent working with students
- Large numbers of students in each class
- Lack of facilities and equipment
- Dependence on weather conditions
- Teachers' lack of knowledge about various sport skills and techniques
- Variability in students' fitness levels or sport knowledge

Spending a significant amount of time preparing a goal-setting system for their classes will save

In reality, daily preparation does not always happen.
© Bob Vincke.

PE teachers hours of work and help them avoid frustrations during class. Furthermore, such a system makes teaching easier and more efficient, and its value is recognised by students and the school as a whole.

All physical educators can plan and organise their classes based on their personal philosophies while following this book's and their state's or school board's guidelines. Designing an ideal PE class by following this book's guidelines may seem easy. Having that class run smoothly in a real-world setting, however, may be more difficult. A successful PE class meets the needs and preferences of the students using the existing facilities and equipment. Because every school and every PE teacher's knowledge are different, the most pragmatic starting point for devising a successful PE class is the teacher's personal philosophy.

The planning and preparation phase of a goal-setting system in a physical education class should include the following steps:

1. Assess students' needs and abilities.
2. Set goals in different areas.
3. Identify influencing factors.
4. Plan goal-attainment strategies.

The first step in the planning and preparation phase is *assessing students' needs and abilities* based on their skill and fitness levels to identify areas that need improvement. Goals that are imposed by teachers are not always recognised and adopted by students. Weinberg and Gould (2003) suggested that PE teachers present students with a list of necessary skills or behaviours and ask the students to rate themselves.

Because students are attracted to and motivated by different kinds of physical activity, the second step in planning and preparation is *setting goals in different areas* (e.g., individual and team sport skills, fitness, fun, playing time, healthy habits and behaviours). Some PE teachers focus primarily on their students' fitness levels, whereas others place more emphasis on improving motor skills, teaching new sport skills or teaching their students to cooperate. All of these objectives are important for students' growth and development as long as they are presented in well-planned and well-organised classes. When physical educators plan to teach motor skills and activities, planning is relatively easy. However, when they want to emphasise the learning process, planning becomes more complicated. When planning their classes, PE teachers should start by clarifying their teaching objectives.

The third step in the preparation and planning phase is *identifying influencing factors* on the goal-setting system. Influencing factors will either help or hinder goal attainment. For example, students' commitment and opportunities for practice must be considered. If students will be asked to practise outside of PE class time, their personal and family habits ought to be considered too.

Finally, PE teachers should *plan goal-attainment strategies* to provide students with task-specific ways of approaching the next level that is within their capabilities. The strategies should be simple and clear and should include a detailed timetable. Goals do not attain themselves. Goal-attainment strategies offer step-by-step guidelines for daily improvement or learning that will lead to goal achievement.

For example, when working on free-throw shooting in basketball, the goal-attainment strategy for improvement may include the following:

- At the end of each class (10 minutes), students attempt 20 free throws, aiming to succeed at a specific number of throws (depending on their individual abilities).
- At the beginning and end of each free-throw shooting session, students mentally rehearse a successful free-throw shot.

Education and Acquisition

During the education and acquisition phase, PE teachers spend ample time with their students educating them about goals and goal setting. Examples and informative discussions can help students improve their skills without having to struggle with unreasonable comparisons with their peers or out-of-reach standards.

Physical educators can begin their classes with a 10- or 15-minute meeting during which they provide information on goal-setting principles and challenge their students to think about objectives they would like to achieve in physical education. Students may not be able to list their goals right away. As these meetings continue, some of the students' goals and goal-attainment strategies should be discussed with 'respect to their importance, specificity and realistic nature' (Gould, 2001, p. 199).

Launching the school year with common goals for all students in a class is a good way to start. Subsequently, as students get acquainted with the goal-setting system, teachers can use short meetings (two to three minutes) with individual students during the class hour to set personalised goals. When educating students on goal setting, teachers should take their age into consideration. Elementary school students need more teacher guidance when setting goals. As they grow older, more experienced and more confident, they will need less direction from their teachers.

Implementation and Follow-Up

The worst thing a PE teacher can do is to set goals at the beginning of the year and then forget all about them! The most common excuse for putting goal setting aside is a lack of time and busy work schedules. Some students, though, may work systematically on their goals and expect some type of evaluation and feedback from their teachers. The absence of follow-up for the goals they set and tackled results in disappointment and feelings of distrust for the teacher: 'He doesn't do what he says he will!'

Therefore, teachers should, first and foremost, plan how they are going to assess improvement and when and how they will give feedback to their students. Some teachers use evaluation form copies; one evaluation form goes to the student and the other is kept by the teacher. Table 2.1 presents a sample short-term goal-setting follow-up sheet for two fitness tests.

Many physical activity skills and techniques cannot be measured with precision. In this case goals are hard to set and then evaluate. Goals may be evaluated using performance measures or tests, meters, time or repetitions. To avoid subjective evaluations and build trust with their students, PE teachers should set goals with their students and help them see daily improvement through their work. Task-specific performance tests that are valid and reliable should be used for evaluating students' technique and performance. A plethora of tests can be found in physical measurement textbooks (Barrow, McGee, & Tritschler, 1989; Dunham, 1994) and national fitness tool kits (from the American Alliance for Health, Physical Education, Recreation and Dance in the United States or from the British Association of Sport and Exercise Science in the United Kingdom), which provide specifics for different age groups, motor skills, sports and fitness levels.

Table 2.2 offers useful ideas and guidelines to help physical educators develop and evaluate their goal-setting plans and to make their classes more interesting, challenging and valuable for students.

Physical educators should plan their classes based on the goal-setting principles described in the previous section. The goal-setting process aids both teachers and students to succeed at what they choose to accomplish. Properly set goals add quality to students' workouts, clarify and specify students' expectations, keep students engaged by offering challenging tasks and enhance their satisfaction and confidence. These benefits help students enjoy their participation in physical education or health education classes.

Table 2.1 Sample Goal-Setting Follow-Up Sheet for Two Fitness Tests for 12-Year-Old Students

Fitness tests	Pre-goal-setting evaluation	My performance goal	My process goal (strategy)	4-week evaluation	6-week evaluation	8-week evaluation
1,600 m (1 mi) test	10:00 minutes	9:00 minutes	1 km (0.62 mi) jogging 3 times per week	9:30 minutes	9:15 minutes	9:00 minutes
1-minute sit-up test	30 sit-ups	50 sit-ups	20 sit-ups 5 times a week	38 sit-ups	45 sit-ups	50 sit-ups

Table 2.2   Goal Setting for Physical Education Teachers

Goal	Skills for goal attainment	Evaluation
To give all students the opportunity to participate regardless of their fitness and skill levels	1. Use my imagination. 2. Learn about students' participation motives. 3. Ask students what they prefer to do and to learn. 4. Select and write down activities.	• Number of participating students • Time spent on each activity
To prepare six lectures for rainy or winter days	1. Identify six topics (e.g., aggression and violence in sports, ways to work out and feel good, ways to work out during the summer, healthy eating, sport rules). 2. Find relevant literature. 3. Find or develop activities for better understanding. 4. Prepare presentations.	• Three lectures ready by August 1 • Six lectures ready by September 1
To plan and prepare my classes for the next month	1. Read the literature on goal setting. 2. Select and write down activities appropriate for my students.	• Class material ready by last week of the month
To provide the opportunity to my students to develop responsibility and confidence	1. Read the literature on relevant topics. 2. Identify sources of responsibility and confidence. 3. Choose activities that will enhance these sources.	• Observe how students move and behave during class. • Ask them how they feel. • Ask them what they learned and how they can apply it to daily life.

As mentioned before, students can become frustrated if goals are not set properly, if the goal-attainment strategies are not appropriate for them, if they have too many goals or if they are not involved in choosing their goals. Consider the following discussion between a physical education teacher and a 17-year-old overweight student during lunch break at school:

Teacher: You eat very little. Are you trying to lose weight?

Student: That's one of my goals for this year, Mr. X.

Teacher: What are your goals for this year?

Student: To get straight *As*, to lose weight and to become a strong tennis player.

Teacher: What are your goals for this week? How will you get stronger at playing tennis?

Student: I will practise three times this week.

Teacher: How do you plan to get straight *As*?

Student: Since the beginning of this year, I have been studying four hours every day.

Teacher: What about losing weight? What's the plan?

Student: The plan is to lose 10 kilos (22 pounds). I am trying to cut down on how much I eat.

Teacher: Do you set specific goals every week to work on your three year-long goals?

Student: No, those are my only goals for the year.

Teacher: Have you gotten closer to achieving your goals?

Student: I don't know yet. I will know at the end of this year. The problem is that when I don't do well at a school test, I go home and gobble down all kinds of junk food, and of course those days I hate going to tennis practice. I stay home and watch TV. I don't even feel like studying.

Teacher: How does that make you feel?

Student: Angry! It has been very tough to work on my goals. I have been setting the same goals for the past three years. My weight goes up instead of down. My tennis skills have not improved a bit, and my grades are not the best.

My best friend still gets better grades, and he studies only two hours every day. That's not fair! My mom says I am not as smart as he is.

Teacher: Why do you want to be a strong tennis player?

Student: So I can be selected for the school team and become popular at school. Girls will pay attention to me then.

Teacher: What about losing weight? Why do you want to lose weight?

Student: The tennis coach at school told me that I need to lose at least 10 kilos (22 pounds) to play for him. And of course girls will like me more then!

Teacher: So what happens then? How do you get back to your goals after having a few bad days?

Student: After I've had a few bad days of eating and not practicing, my mother gets frustrated. I receive the good-old sermon, and then she locks the TV. All I can do is study or go to tennis practice. When I play tennis for a couple of days, then I feel good about myself, and I start cutting down on food intake once again! I hate this goal-setting thing; it's been like a roller-coaster ride!

In this case the student had been setting the same goals for three years without having a clear and precise plan for achieving them. The goals appeared to be interrelated, and a poor performance on one goal triggered worse behaviours toward all goals. Adolescents often waste their time and energy on idealistic expectations and unrealistic desires. It is of vital importance to educate our youth how to approach their wants and desires, how to turn them into goals and dreams and, most important, how to tackle these goals and live their dreams!

Examples of Goal Setting in Physical Education Classes

Physical education has always been considered the most appropriate setting for the development of fitness and sport skills. Nevertheless, contemporary approaches emphasise that PE should do more than simply develop the physical self; it should also play an important role in the development of social and life skills. Health education is one of the domains that can be fostered through PE, especially in schools in which health education classes are not taught. Health education aims to educate students about healthy habits and attempts to instill in students at least a few of those habits. Moral development is another area in which PE can play an important role. Games are an excellent socialising agent, providing valuable opportunities for the development of moral values. Furthermore, within the PE context, useful psychological life skills, such as positive thinking, can be developed. Bearing in mind the previously mentioned objectives of the contemporary PE class, the section that follows presents detailed examples of three-phase goal-setting plans designed to enhance students' holistic development.

Example 1: Fitness Tests

This example focuses on the development of fitness level, using fitness tests for initial evaluation and goal setting. The example addresses initial testing, goal setting, student commitment and goal attainment evaluation.

Session 1: Testing and Goal Setting

Describe and demonstrate the execution of the fitness tests; then group the students in pairs and distribute copies of the goal-setting card (figure 2.1) and the commitment card (figure 2.2). One student executes while the other checks for correct

Name: _____		Date: _____	
Task	Today's score	Goal for next month	Retest score
Sit-ups			
Push-ups			

Figure 2.1 Goal-setting card: fitness tests.

To achieve my goals, I will do the following:

I will participate in all classes until the next test.	___ No	___ Yes
I will execute all the requested repetitions.	___ No	___ Yes
I will concentrate on the teacher's instructions.	___ No	___ Yes
I will have extra practice at home 10 minutes per day.	___ No	___ Yes

Figure 2.2 Commitment card.

execution and keeps the score. Inform students that after some sessions there will be a reevaluation using these tests and ask them to specify a goal for this testing. Emphasise personal improvement. Ask students to complete the 'Today's score' and 'Goal for next month' columns in figure 2.1. Ask students to keep the goal-setting card for the next test and keep a copy for themselves.

Session 2: Commitment

In the next session take a few minutes to explain to the students the importance of committing to their goals. Then ask them to complete the commitment card (figure 2.2), and remind them of the retest date.

Session 3: Goal Attainment Evaluation

At the time specified in figure 2.1, a retest should take place to assess whether the students have achieved their goals. Remind the students of their goals, and repeat the procedure of the initial evaluation. At the end of the session, ask them to set new goals for the next month or to select new fitness tasks.

Example 2: Individual Skill— Basketball Free Throw

This example describes a goal-setting strategy for the basketball free-throw shot. The example addresses initial testing, goal setting, the evaluation of goals based on the goal-setting principles and a goal attainment evaluation.

Session 1: Testing and Goal Setting

Adjust the distance of the free throw so that students can achieve a score that will not disappoint them, but that allows space for improvement (e.g., an average success rate of 4 out of 10). Arrange students in pairs. One student executes the test, and the other gives the ball back and keeps score. Each student performs two trials of 10 repetitions. After concluding the test, they complete the 'Today's score' and 'Goal for next two weeks' columns in the goal-setting card shown in figure 2.3. Ask students to keep the goal-setting card for the next test.

Session 2: Goal Evaluation

In the next session take a few minutes to discuss with students the characteristics of effective goals. Then ask them to complete the goal evaluation form shown in figure 2.4 and to adjust their goals in figure 2.3, if necessary.

Today's score	Goal for next two weeks	Retest score
Trial 1:		Trial 1:
Trial 2:		Trial 2:
Total :	Total :	Total :

Figure 2.3 Goal-setting card: free throw.

My goal is	Not at all				Very much
Realistic	1	2	3	4	5
Challenging	1	2	3	4	5
Controllable	1	2	3	4	5
Specific	1	2	3	4	5
Measurable	1	2	3	4	5

Figure 2.4 Goal evaluation form.

Adapted from D. Gould and R. Weinberg, 1996, Instruction guide for foundations of sport and exercise psychology (Champaign, IL: Human Kinetics), 38.

Session 3: Goal Attainment Evaluation

Have students repeat the test, complete the retest scores on the goal-setting card and set their next goal.

Example 3: Team Skill— Volleyball Reception

This example refers to team goals using a volleyball task that involves serve reception. The key here is to develop communication codes, team encouragement and team compliments. The example addresses initial skills testing, goal setting for communication and performance and goal attainment evaluation.

Session 1: Skills Testing and Goal Setting

Create two teams of six players. One team is serving and one is receiving. Each set should consist of six repetitions, so that all players on the serving team execute one serve (false serves could be repeated). On the receiving team, five players are receiving and one waits close to the net for the reception (the 'setter': the player to whom the ball should be directed from the receivers). Each of the five players in the reception has an area of responsibility. Players rotate positions after each execution, until all players have been to all positions. After concluding the set, the teams swap roles. The teacher should check for the correct execution of ball reception and team talk and keep score for successful receptions and not for points won. The teacher and students can set goals for the number of successful receptions using the goal-setting card (e.g., three out of six). Accordingly, goals can be set for the players of the serving team.

Session 2: Communication Goal Setting

In the next session take a few minutes to explain the importance of team talk, and develop team codes.

- *Team encouragement.* Before each execution the target player in the receiving team gives an encouragement cue (e.g., 'Let's go').

- *Team communication.* On execution, the player who is responsible for the area toward which the ball is directed should shout that he or she is going to receive the ball (e.g., 'Me').
- *Team compliments.* After the reception, all players on the receiving team compliment the player who received the ball (e.g., 'Well done').

Select the team codes that the students prefer and assess whether and how frequently they use the codes during execution. Students should aim to use the team codes in every execution. After the set, the players complete the team talk evaluation cards (figure 2.5).

Session 3: Goal Attainment Evaluation

In the retest the teacher can assess the frequency and quality of team talk. Team performance in reception can be also assessed with the use of a goal-setting card, as in examples 1 and 2.

Example 4: Healthy Habits

This example refers to the use of goal setting to improve health. The example includes the evaluation of current habits, goal setting for healthy habits, goal attainment evaluation and problem solving (missed goals analysis and reassessment).

Session 1: Evaluation

Figure 2.6 presents a number of healthy and unhealthy habits. Have students fill out the form, stating whether they have these habits. If they answer yes, they should specify how often or how much per week they engage in these behaviours (e.g., run 20 minutes three times per week, drink one Coke per day).

Session 2: Goal Setting

Based on the list in figure 2.6, students should make specific goals on selected behaviours (figure 2.7, columns 1-3).

- In column 1, students write down which of the healthy habits they don't have, but will follow as of today, and which of the

Frequency	Never				All the time
How often did the team use team encourage-ment?	1	2	3	4	5
How often did the team use team communica-tion?	1	2	3	4	5
How often did the team use team compliments?	1	2	3	4	5

Quality	Not at all				Very much
How vigor-ous was the encourage-ment?	1	2	3	4	5
How clear was the com-munication?	1	2	3	4	5
How enthusi-astic was the compliment?	1	2	3	4	5

Figure 2.5 Team talk evaluation card.

unhealthy habits they have and will reduce or stop.

- In columns 2 and 3, students write down how frequently and for how long they will be doing the selected behaviours for the next week (e.g., bike for 20 minutes every day, eat fruits daily, go shopping on a bike).

			How often/much per day/week
1. During school breaks I play games.	No	Yes	
2. I participate on school teams.	No	Yes	
3. I use the stairs rather than the elevator.	No	Yes	
4. In my spare time, I play outdoor games.	No	Yes	
5. I go biking to stay fit.	No	Yes	
6. I run.	No	Yes	
7. I go walking.	No	Yes	
8. I use a bike for short trips (school, shopping, etc.).	No	Yes	
9. I eat fruits.	No	Yes	
10. I eat vegetables.	No	Yes	
11. I drink fresh juices.	No	Yes	
12. I play video games.	No	Yes	
13. I watch TV.	No	Yes	
14. I eat junk food (chips, sweets, etc.).	No	Yes	
15. I have soft drinks (Coke, Pepsi, etc.).	No	Yes	
16. I drink alcohol.	No	Yes	
17. I smoke.	No	Yes	

Figure 2.6 Healthy habits evaluation card.

What exactly I'm going to do	Sessions per week	Time per week	Goal met?	Why or why not?	Plan for meeting unmet goals

Figure 2.7 Healthy goals card.

Session 3: Goal Attainment Evaluation

Once per week ask students to evaluate their progress toward their goals (figure 2.7, columns 4-6).

- In column 4, students record whether they have achieved their goal after a week.

- In column 5, students write down the reasons they achieved or failed to achieve their goals.

- In column 6, students describe how they are going to meet unmet goals.

Example 5: Moral Development

This example describes ways to promote fair play in team games. The selected actions aim to develop behaviours that reflect respect for opponents and referees. The example addresses the identification of fair and unfair play, the application for fair play and goal setting for fair play.

Session 1: Identifying Desirable and Undesirable Behaviours

Discuss with students the importance of fair play and make a list of actions that promote respect for opponents and referees. Also make a list of unfair actions. (Following are examples of such lists.)

Fair Play

Before the start of the game, I shake hands with the opponents.

I congratulate opponents for a good play.

I stop the game when an opponent is injured.

I admit having fouled an opponent.

I shake hands with opponents after the game, regardless of the result.

Unfair Play

I object to the referee's decisions.

I fake being fouled to win a referee's decision.

I hit an opponent when he hits me first.

I play hard to win.

I fake injury to have an opponent penalised.

I try to upset opponents.

Session 2: Application

Before the start of a team game, each student has 10 small pieces of paper in his or her left-hand pocket. For each of the identified fair-play actions, students move one piece of paper to the right-hand pocket. In contrast, for each of the unfair-play actions, students move one piece from the right-hand pocket back to the left. At the end of the game, the team with the most pieces in their right-hand pockets receives the 'special fair-play award of the day'. Each player writes down the number of pieces found in his or her right-hand pocket at the end of the game on a goal card. At the end of the month, students with the highest scores receive the 'fair-play award of the month'.

Session 3: Goal Setting

Before the start of the game, each player sets a goal for the number of pieces of paper to collect in his or her right-hand pocket, on the fair-play goal card (figure 2.8). After the game each player counts the collected pieces and sets a goal for the next game.

Example 6: Positive Thinking

This example is about reducing negative thoughts during task performance and developing positive thinking. The example addresses testing and goal setting, positive thinking practice and goal attainment evaluation.

Name: _____		Date: _____
	Today's goal	Today's score	Goal for next game
Number of pieces of paper in right-hand pocket			

Figure 2.8 Fair-play goal card.

Session 1: Testing and Goal Setting

The first step in this process is to identify how often students have negative thoughts. To do that, administer the negative thoughts form in figure 2.9 immediately after an exam or test situation. Students should then set a goal for the retest and complete the negative thoughts goal card (figure 2.10).

During the test I had thoughts	Never				Very often
1. that I was not doing well	1	2	3	4	5
2. that I should be more careful	1	2	3	4	5
3. that others are better than me	1	2	3	4	5
4. about how difficult the test was	1	2	3	4	5
5. that I felt confused	1	2	3	4	5
TOTAL SCORE:					

Figure 2.9 Negative thoughts form.

Name: _____	Date: _____
Today's score	**Goal for next exam**
Negative thoughts	

Figure 2.10 Negative thoughts goal card.

Session 2: Changing Negative Thoughts

In the next session explain to the students that negative thoughts are counterproductive, and show them how they can transform negative thoughts into positive ones. For example, 'I can't' can become 'I can, if I . . .' or 'It is difficult' can become 'It is a challenge', and 'I feel confused' can become 'I will be OK, if . . .'.

Then, ask students to identify specific negative thoughts they experience. To do that, students should complete the negative thoughts column in the changing negative thoughts card (figure 2.11). Subsequently, ask them to change each negative thought to a positive one and complete the positive thoughts column. Set goals for daily or weekly practice (e.g., 10 minutes exercise per day).

Session 3: Evaluation of Goal Attainment

Two weeks after the initial test, give students another test and reassess the frequency of their negative thoughts with the negative thoughts form (figure 2.10).

Summary

Goal setting is for the everyday use of teachers and students at the elementary, secondary and higher education levels. PE teachers set goals that help them plan and organise their classes. Plan-

	Negative thoughts	Positive thoughts
1.	→	
2.	→	
3.	→	
4.	→	
5.	→	

Figure 2.11 Changing negative thoughts card.

ning ahead is critical for running fluid classes and avoiding last-minute calls and decisions and the mistakes that follow them. Moreover, goal setting helps PE teachers improve professionally because it brings new knowledge, sustains their motivation by increasing their effectiveness and enhances their self-confidence and commitment to their jobs.

Review Questions

1. Why is goal setting effective?
2. What are the characteristics of effective goals?
3. What are the phases of effective goal setting, and what does each phase include?
4. What are the domains to which goal setting can be applied?

Critical Thinking Questions

1. Design a complete goal-setting plan with regard to a personal goal of yours in relation to your PE class.
2. Design a detailed year-long goal-setting form for your students in relation to an individual skill and a team skill.
3. How can you motivate your students to use goal setting in all their achievement situations?
4. Think of a student in your PE class who will benefit if he or she used some goals to improve skills. How would you apply the three phases of goal setting to the student's specific needs?

Key Terms

goal attainment—The process of achieving goals that were set.

goal evaluation—An evaluation of the degree to which goals that have been set are in line with the goal-setting principles.

goals—Objectives or results that people consciously plan to achieve.

goal setting—An organised, ongoing process that includes assessment, planning, monitoring and evaluating and that helps people attain their goals.

goal-setting principles—Guidelines regarding how goals should be set; they facilitate the goal-setting process and improve goal effectiveness.

performance goals—Goals that focus on the quality of a person's performance, as opposed to an outcome.

process goals—Goals that focus on the strategies that should be followed to achieve a performance goal.

References

Barrow, H., McGee, R. & Tritschler, K. (1989). *Practical measurement in physical education and sport*. Philadelphia: Lea & Febiger.

Boyce, B.A. (1994). The effects of goal setting on performance and spontaneous goal-setting behavior of experienced pistol shoots. *The Sport Psychologist, 8,* 87-93.

Burton, D., Naylor, S. & Holliday, B. (2001). Goal setting in sport: Investigating the goal effectiveness paradox. In R.N. Singer, H.A. Hausenblas & C.M. Janelle (Eds.), *Handbook of sport psychology* (pp. 497-528). New York: Wiley.

Dunham, P. (1994). *Evaluation for physical education.* Englewood, CO: Morton.

Gould, D. (2001). Goal setting for peak performance. In J.M. Williams (Ed.), *Applied sport psychology: Personal growth to peak experience* (4th ed., pp. 190-205). Mountain View, CA: Mayfield.

Kyllo, B. & Landers, D. (1995). Goal setting in sport and exercise: A research synthesis to resolve the controversy. *Journal of Sport and Exercise Psychology, 17,* 117-137.

Lerner, B. & Locke, E. (1995). The effects of goal setting, self-efficacy, competition, and personal traits on the performance of an endurance task. *Journal of Sport and Exercise Psychology, 17,* 138-152.

Locke, E. (1996). Motivation through conscious goal setting. *Applied and Preventive Psychology, 5,* 117-124.

Locke, E. & Latham, C. (1990). *A theory of goal setting and task performance.* Englewood Cliffs, NJ: Prentice Hall.

Smith, M. & Lee, C. (1992). Goal setting and performance in a novel coordination task: Mediating mechanisms. *Journal of Sport & Exercise Psychology, 14,* 169-176.

Theodorakis, Y. (1995). Effects of self-efficacy, satisfaction and personal goals on swimming performance. *The Sport Psychologist, 9,* 245-253.

Theodorakis, Y. (1996). The influence of goals, commitment, self-efficacy and self-satisfaction on motor performance. *Journal of Applied Sport Psychology, 8,* 171-182.

Weinberg, R.S., Burton, D., Yukelson, D. & Weigand, D. (1993). Goal setting in competitive sport: An exploratory investigation of practices of collegiate athletes. *The Sport Psychologist, 7,* 275-289.

Weinberg, R.S. & Butt, J. (2005). Goal setting in sport and exercise domains: The theory and practice of effective goal setting. In D. Hackfort, J. Duda & R. Lidor (Eds.), *Handbook of research in applied sport psychology: International perspectives.* Morgantown, WV: Fitness Information Technology.

Weinberg, R.S. & Gould, D. (2003). *Foundations of sport and exercise psychology* (3rd ed.). Champaign, IL: Human Kinetics.

Weinberg, R.S., Stitcher, T. & Richardson, P. (1994). Effects of a seasoned goal-setting program on lacrosse performance. *The Sport Psychologist, 8,* 166-175.

chapter three

Measuring Perceived Motivational Climate in Physical Education

Athanasios G. Papaioannou*
Evdoxia Kosmidou
Nikolaos Tsigilis
University of Thessaly, Greece
Dimitris Milosis
Democritus University of Thrace, Greece

After reading this chapter, you will be able to do the following:

- Describe the differences between perceived motivational climate scales and other perceived climate scales in physical education

- Explain the reasons to choose each of the existing perceived motivational climate measures

- Explain the principle of compatibility in perceived motivational climate measures and exemplify it in physical education

- Describe the different types of validity in perceived motivational climate measures

- Explain intraclass correlation and why it is important in perceived climate measurement

- Explain how we examine the reliability of perceived climate measures

*The studies presented here were conducted while the first author was at the Democritus University of Thrace.

Choosing Among the Existing Measures

Over the past years a number of instruments have been developed to assess students' perceptions of class climate. Using these tools, researchers have conducted several studies investigating perceived climate in relation to students' cognitions, emotions and behaviours in physical education (e.g., Ntoumanis & Biddle, 1999). The interest in the perceived, or subjective, climate is hardly surprising because it has a stronger impact on people's actions than the objective climate recorded by unbiased observers (Fraser, 1986). Taking into consideration the different climate measures, one meaningful question is, Which instrument should I use? The answer to this question is, It depends on your purpose.

If you are interested in students' effort, their preferences for particular tasks or teaching styles, their persistence in accomplishing a task, the effect of teaching on physical activity outside of school and the cognitions and emotions that are linked with all these student behaviours, you are obviously interested in students' motivation. In that case you should select one of the motivational climate measures.

If your primary interest is in social issues such as cliques, democracy, equality or aspects of class organisation that are not directly relevant to students' motivation (e.g., rule clarity, class organisation), you should select a climate measure developed particularly for physical education that fits your purpose. If no instrument appropriate for physical education captures what you want, but you are aware of an instrument in the general educational domain (e.g., Fraser, 1986; Weinstein, 1989), you may be able to adapt it for physical education (e.g., Papaioannou, 1995).

This chapter is devoted to motivational climate. If you are interested in motivational climate, you can select a measure among several existing tools.

School Teams or Physical Education Classes

Newton, Duda and Yin (2000) developed a measure that is appropriate for school teams and competitive sport. The *Perceived Motivational Climate in Sport Questionnaire—2 (PMCSQ-2)* is composed of six factors: cooperative learning, a perceived important role for each team member and emphasis on effort and improvement, which are features of a task-involving climate; and punishment for mistakes, unequal recognition and intrateam member rivalry, which characterise ego-involving climates.

A detailed description of task-involving and ego-involving climates is presented in other chapters of this book. Here, we will briefly note that these concepts stem from the research of Nicholls (1989) and Ames (1992), who suggested that in achievement contexts such as sport and physical education, two major goals prevail: When a *task-involving goal* prevails, self-referenced criteria of ability and task difficulty are used, success is defined as personal progress and students focus on task mastery and skill development. When an *ego-involving goal* is emphasised, success is normatively defined; that is, ability and task difficulty are judged in relation to the ability and performance of others, and students focus on overcoming others to prove that they are more competent than most of their schoolmates. Hence, a class climate is either task involving or ego involving, depending on which goals are emphasised by teachers and students (Nicholls, 1989). Others have used the terms *learning oriented* (Dweck, 1999) or *mastery oriented* (Ames, 1992), for a concept similar to task involving, and the term *performance oriented* for a concept similar to ego involving (Ames, 1992).

The *PMCSQ-2* was designed for competitive sport and not for regular physical education classes. As most teachers and coaches know, the two contexts differ markedly in climate dimensions. Intrateam rivalry is meaningless in typical physical education settings. Moreover, several climate structures in physical education are not observed in sport—for example, many types of grouping, grades and so on. So at present, someone wanting to evaluate motivational climate in a regular physical education class would be safe to choose among the measures described in the following sections.

Motivational Climate and Students' Goals

At times it is useful to assess both the motivational climate and its effects on students' goals. The early motivational climate questionnaires were developed to capture several dimensions of the motivational climate. Because these self-reports assessed too many dimensions, they did not explicitly assess whether students perceived that the class climate is intended to affect their achievement goals.

Three measures belong to this category of motivational climate. Papaioannou (1992, 1994) developed the *Learning and Performance Oriented Physical Education Classes Questionnaire (LAPOPECQ)* to assess two dimensions of the task-involving climate (*teacher-initiated learning orientation* and *students' learning orientation*) and three dimensions of the ego-involving climate (*students' competitive orientation, students' worries about mistakes* and *outcome without effort*). Later, Goudas and Biddle (1994) presented the *Physical Education Class Climate Scale (PECCS)*. This instrument was based on *LAPOPECQ*, but it did not include the *outcome without effort* subscale. Moreover, the authors added two new subscales to assess task-involving climate: *teachers' support* and *students' perceptions of choice*.

Mitchell (1996) presented a third measure to assess perceptions of *threat, competition* and *challenge* in physical education. The author did not link this instrument with achievement goals theory. Another limitation of this tool is the large number of items starting with the word *I*, something that is also found in some items of the *students' learning orientation* subscale of *LAPOPECQ*. When this happens, the measure captures what students perceive to be the goal

Students with ego-involving goals focus on proving themselves more competent than their classmates.
© Bob Vincke.

structure operating in their classes as well as their personal goal orientations rather than just the goal structure of the class (Duda & Whitehead, 1998). To circumvent this problem, in subsequent research Papaioannou (1998) used a two-factor instrument assessing perceptions of *teacher-initiation of mastery* and *performance orientation,* respectively (see also Papaioannou, Marsh & Theodorakis, 2004).

Mitchell's (1996) instrument was not designed to assess whether students perceive that the structure of their class climate is intended to affect their achievement goals. The same also applies to the *teacher support* and *perceptions of choice* subscales of the *PECCS*. For example, the item 'the teacher is more a friend than a figure or authority' of the *teacher support* subscale (Biddle et al., 1995) primarily assesses teacher caring and not teacher emphasis on task involvement. Likewise, a student who agrees with the item 'pupils have a choice of what activities they take part in' does not necessarily denote that students try to develop their competence. Of course, students who are allowed to choose an activity are often more intrinsically motivated and therefore more likely to pursue competence, but this is not always the case. They can select it just for the sake of play or even to compete with others! Lack of explicit focus on achievement goals also characterizes the *important role for each team member, punishment for mistakes* and *unequal recognition* subscales of the *PMCSQ-2*.

Finally, because the *LAPOPECQ* and the *PECCS* were developed some time ago, they were not tested with regard to a new development in achievement goals theory. Elliot and his colleagues split the ego/performance goal into two dimensions: **performance-approach goals** and **performance-avoidance goals** (Elliot & Harackiewicz, 1996; Elliot & Church, 1997). When performance-approach goals are adopted, students seek positive evaluations of their competence from others; but when performance-avoidance goals are adopted, students focus on avoiding negative evaluations from others. Hence, although the items of the *students' worries about mistakes* subscale in *LAPOPECQ* and *PECCS* capture an important dimension of ego-involving climate in physical education, this climate emphasises performance-avoidance goals (Elliot & Harackiewicz, 1996). On the other hand, the other ego-involving climate dimensions of *LAPOPECQ* and *PECCS* emphasise performance-approach goals.

To summarise, if you want to examine perceived motivational climate in relation to students' goals, you should select a measure that really captures students' perceptions of the emphasis placed on these goals in their classes. To make things easier, the measures should be based on the *principle of compatibility* introduced next. The remainder of this chapter focuses on these instruments. On the other hand, if you want to examine a wide variety of motivational climate dimensions that are generally and indirectly related to the adopted goals, then the assessment of climate dimensions such as *teacher support* and *perceptions of choice* could be useful. You should be aware, however, that students' achievement goals may have a weaker relationship with these climate dimensions than with climate dimensions directly emphasising achievement goals, such as the *teacher initiation of mastery* and *performance orientation* subscales developed by Papaioannou (1998).

Principle of Compatibility

When we want to investigate students' perceptions of the achievement goals emphasised in their classes, the perception items should be based on what we call the **compatibility principle.** According to this principle, the perception and goal measures should be compatible with each other to the extent that their *target, action domain, life context* and *time* elements are assessed at identical **levels of generality** or specificity. This approach and terminology were borrowed from Ajzen and Fishbein (1977), who formulated the principle of compatibility in their theory focusing on attitude–behaviour relations.

The principle of compatibility was formatted based on the common grounds of classic social-psychology theories explaining the links between perceptions, goals and other cognitive-affective mental representations (expectations, emotions, beliefs, strategies) and the ensuing dynamics in self-regulation process (Bandura, 1986; Carver & Scheier, 1998; Mischel & Shoda, 1998). All these theories assume that the activation of goals is always the outcome of an encoding process, which can be either a perception of an external feature of a situation or self-generating stimuli (such as thinking, fantasy and daydreaming).

To explain this principle in the context of physical education, when we assess perceptions of a particular situation, we should capture whether this situation is intended to affect students' goals. Many items and scales today do not meet the requirements of the principle of compatibility, such as the *teacher support* and *students' perception of choice* subscales of the *PMCSQ-2*. Moreover, items in classroom environment instruments that are labeled 'task orientation' do not meet this requirement either. For example, one item of the *task orientation* subscale of the *Classroom Environment Scale* (Moos & Trickett, 1987) reads, 'Getting a certain amount of classwork done is very important in this class'. A student who agrees with this item does not necessarily indicate that this class facilitates high task involvement and personal improvement for all students because the 'certain amount of work' may be an easy task for some students and a hard task for others. The items should also capture whether the structure of this situation is intended to affect students' task orientation too, as in the item 'our teacher makes sure that I understand how to perform a skill before we move on to another' (Papaioannou, 1998).

Components of Motivational Climate Questionnaires

Central to the principle of compatibility are the four components that should be at identical levels of specificity for perception and goal scales: target, action domain, life context and time. We will explain these components by presenting the stages that we followed to develop two instruments.

Common to the instruments presented here is the *life context,* which is physical education. However, we have developed similar instruments for other life contexts, such as language classes and peer contexts (Papaioannou, 2006; see also chapter 10 in this book). Hence, both the perception and goals scales presented here are compatible with each other in terms of life context, which is physical education.

Within each life context we can observe countless *actions*. Usually we classify them in higher-order conceptual categories, such as achieving, social, moral behaviours and so forth. These higher-order categories are what we mean by the term *action domain*. The two instruments presented here focus on the achievement domain. Hence, in the two following instruments, goals and perceptions are identical in terms of the action domain, which is achievement.

Actions have countless *targets* too. Each action at a particular moment has a specific target, which is usually different from the target of an action following a few moments later. We will treat the target concept as equivalent to a goal. As explained, in the achievement domain the goals of behaviours have been classified in three classes: *task/mastery, performance approach* and *performance avoidance.* More recently a fourth achievement goal was introduced: *mastery avoidance* (Conroy, Elliot & Hofer, 2003; Elliot & McGregor, 2001). Because research based on this goal is still in its infancy, we have not attempted to assess mastery goals in the studies presented here. Hence, the present instruments are based on the trichotomous model of achievement goals (Elliot & Church, 1997).

Apart from these three goals, a fourth goal was also assessed: *social approval.* Some theorists consider this a social goal (Wentzel, 1999), but in the first version of achievement goals literature it was considered an achievement goal (Maehr & Nicholls, 1980). Indeed, in collectivistic cultures, social approval goals lead to important motivational outcomes in physical activity contexts (Hayashi, 1996; Schilling & Hayashi, 2001). Moreover, cross-cultural research supports the importance of social approval goals in the achievement domain in collectivistic societies (McIrney, Hinkley, Dowson & Van Etten, 1998; Niles, 1998) and among minority students of collectivistic cultures living in Western societies (Verkuyten, Thijs & Canatan, 2001). It seems, then, that in collectivistic cultures, social approval goals are not clearly discernible from achievement goals, such as **mastery** and performance.

To summarise, the instruments presented here focus on the measurement of four goals: mastery, performance approach, performance avoidance and social approval. According to the principle of compatibility, both the perception and goal scales should capture these four goals.

In all aforementioned climate measures the *time* element, although not clearly specified, is regarded as the academic year because the students and the teacher of a class remain constant during that time. Students are asked 'In this physical education class . . .', and then they respond to items concerning the climate of the class at that time. Sometimes, however, we need to assess the motivational climate at a particular moment or on a particular day (e.g., Papaioannou & Kouli, 1999).

Later in this chapter we will present an instrument assessing climate on a particular day. We will refer to this measure using the term **situational level of generality** (Vallerand, 2001). When we discuss perceptions and goals in physical education in general, we will speak of perceptions and goals at the **contextual level of generality** (Vallerand, 2001).

This differentiation of the time element has important implications. When teachers want to evaluate the temporary effects of teaching on motivational climate, they should capture perceptions at the situational level of generality. For example, the use of a teaching task or type of grouping on one particular day has temporary effects on motivational climate. On the other hand, the instrument at the contextual level of generality is recommended for the assessment of relatively sustainable effects of teaching, such as the motivational effects from the yearlong adoption of a particular curriculum.

Recommended Motivational Climate Scales

In this section we present two measures that were used in Greece to capture motivational climate at the contextual and situational levels of generality. The development of both was based on the principle of compatibility. These instruments can be used by teachers and researchers in other countries, but be aware that the present wording is a direct translation of the Greek items. Hence, if teachers use them in another language, they should first examine the validity and reliability of these measures. Later we describe how to examine validity and reliability, and then we explain how we established the validity and reliability of the present measures.

Principle of Validity

When we examine the **validity** of a test, we investigate whether it measures what it is supposed to measure. Does it measure perceived climate or not? Are the captured goals what achievement goals theory suggests or not? And so on. We respond to some of these questions later, using two of our recent climate measures as examples.

We classify the many types of validity into two general categories: **content validity** and **construct validity.**

Content Validity

Content validity is important in the first stage of development of any test. It involves the judgment of experts in the field with regard to whether the items measure what they are presumed to measure. In addition, we can also acquire the judgment of a sample of the population under investigation. In that case we usually ask some students whether they understand all the items. We also explain the purpose of our items to the teachers and ask them whether they are comprehensible to their students.

Construct Validity

When we investigate the construct validity of a measure, we can adopt within-network and between-network investigations, which are also called tests of internal and external construct validity, respectively.

Internal Construct Validity

Within-network investigations focus on the internal structure of the measure (Marsh, 1998). Accordingly, we will call them tests of **internal construct validity.** Two types of analyses are usually adopted to examine the internal construct validity of a measure. Using a statistical analysis called **factor analysis,** we can examine the structure of the measure to provide evidence of structural or factorial validity. For example, when we test the motivational climate measures, we want to prove that they have at least two distinct multidimensional components: mastery and performance-oriented climate. Another technique in within-network studies involves the correlations among the factors or dimensions of the measure.

Confirmatory factor analysis (CFA) is an important statistical analysis used to establish construct validity. With CFA we can specify that the items that were designed to assess a particular factor are associated with this factor only and no other factors. The association of the items with the factor is given by a statistic called **loading.** With CFA we can find the magnitude of the loading and learn whether it is statistically significant. Hence, this analysis is theory driven because we test a model that was developed based on some theory. In addition, CFA has the advantage of taking into account the error and unexplained variance inherent in all statistics in behavioural science. Moreover, with CFA we can compare alternative models and establish which is best.

CFA can be conducted using statistical packages such as *LISREL* (Joreskog & Sorbom, 1993), *EQS* (Bentler, 1995) and *AMOS* (Arbuckle & Wothke, 1999). Following the specification of the model, we examine how well it fits the data. This is achieved with the help of goodness-of-fit indexes, such as the chi square. When the model fits the data perfectly, the chi square is not statistically significant ($p > .05$). However, because chi square values depend on sample size, with large sample sizes producing significant chi squares, additional fit indexes have been developed to examine the model fit. Initially, the ratio of the chi square to the degrees of freedom was considered, which should be less than 2. Nevertheless, studies revealed that this ratio is also affected by sample size (Fan, Thompson & Wang, 1999; Marsh, Balla & MacDonald, 1988). These authors suggested that the least unaffected goodness-of-fit indexes by sample sizes are the Tucker-Lewis index (TLI; Tucker & Lewis, 1973), also called the nonnormed fit index (NNFI); the comparative fit index (CFI; Bentler, 1990) and the root mean square error of approximation (RMSEA; Browne & Cudeck, 1993). According to Hu and Bentler (1999), RMSEA should be .06 or lower, and CFI and NNFI should be close to .95 or higher.

External Construct Validity

With between-network investigations, we attempt to establish a logical, theoretically consistent pattern of relations between our measure and other constructs (Marsh, 1998). We will call these investigations tests of **external construct validity.** The techniques can be classified into two general categories. The first includes correlational studies in which we usually try to establish *convergent validity, discriminant validity* and *predictive validity.* **Convergent validity** (convergence) means that evidence from different sources collected in different ways indicates similar meaning of the construct. Usually we correlate the new measure with another similar construct and look for substantial relationships. **Discriminant validity** (discriminality) means that the new measure can differentiate the construct from other constructs that may be similar, and it is unrelated to a construct with which it has nothing in common. Hence, here we try to establish low correlations with measures of a different construct or no correlations at all. Usually discriminant validity follows evidence of convergent validity. **Predictive validity** is established when our measure predicts another construct that is measured some time in the future. When external variables are discrete, such as gender, age group, religion, athlete or nonathlete, one can prove construct validity by revealing differences between the groups.

The second technique for testing external construct validity includes experimental studies. For example, after an intervention aiming to emphasise mastery goals, do we find an increased mastery-oriented climate? Concurrently, we can try to ascertain that the intervention had no influence on constructs that it is not meant to influence (e.g., effects on performance approach goals). This approach is very useful because it establishes construct validity for the measure and concurrently identifies the causal processes underlying the intervention and its effects on the measures. An example follows later.

The Individual and Class as Units of Measurement

An important issue in the establishment of validity is the unit of measurement. Students are individuals, but they also participate in groups such as classes or schools. When we test the validity of climate measures, we should use two units of measurement and maybe their interaction—that is, the individual, the group or class, and the interaction between the individual and the class. Usually we find statistics in which the unit of analysis is the individual. Within a class differences in climate perceptions are meaningful and important. As Ames (1992) and Maehr (1984) observed, within the same class, students give different meanings to similar things. They interpret a great deal of the situation based on their own goals.

Nevertheless, apart from individual perceptions there are also collective perceptions of class climate—that is, the aggregate perception of all students in the class. In that case the unit of measurement is the class. We should expect that a valid climate measure should discriminate between classes or teachers emphasising different goals. Finally—because motivational outcomes

depend on the individual, the teaching process and the interaction between the person and the environment—when we examine predictive validity, we receive additional information when we add the interaction effects into the analysis. Multilevel modeling is an advanced statistical analysis that focuses on both the individual and the group. Papaioannou and colleagues (2004) provided a relevant application in physical education. At the very least, we should test the validity of climate measures by investigating the proportion of variance of perceived climate that is due to class or teacher differences. This is called **intraclass correlation** (Kenny & Lavoie, 1985).

The percent of variance due to between-class differences (that is, differences in the collective perceptions of class climate) depends on the particular climate dimension that is captured. For example, classmates are more likely to agree how orderly their class is than whether their teacher emphasises ego-oriented goals. Students bring their own goals to school, which are formed at home and in sport and peer contexts. Students' goals are more likely to affect their perceptions of teachers' emphasis on goals than their perceptions of climate dimensions that are irrelevant to their goals. A high ego-oriented student is much more likely to interpret ambiguous teacher feedback as evaluative than is a low ego-oriented student (Ames, 1992; Maehr, 1984). But much of a teacher's feedback is relatively ambiguous with regard to the goals it promotes. For example, when teachers just say 'good' to their students, high task-oriented students might interpret it as

Students have individual perceptions, as well as collective perceptions.
© Bob Vincke.

'good motion', which facilitates task involvement, but high ego-oriented students might construe it as 'you are good at this', which promotes ego involvement. Hence, important within-class disagreement exists with regard to what goals the teacher promotes.

In addition, despite differences in teachers' preferences for particular goals, many times teachers are obliged to promote similar goals—that is, goals that are set by the curriculum or the educational policy (e.g., adopting common grading practices). This reduces even further the possibility of capturing large between-teacher variations in the promotion of achievement goals.

To summarise, finding a low proportion of variance attributable to teacher or class differences in motivational climate instruments is common, particularly when measures are based on the principle of compatibility. On the other hand, if we randomly select an adequate number of teachers or classes (e.g., 20 to 30 classes), this proportion of variance should be statistically significant. Teachers often make the goals they want to promote quite clear, and we should expect between-teacher differences in the goals they emphasise. Hence, a minimum degree of within-class agreement should also be expected with regard to class motivational climate.

Principle of Reliability

Questions such as, Are people's responses to this scale consistent over time? refer to the **reliability** of the scale. When we investigate the reliability of a scale, we examine two general issues: the internal consistency of the scale and the stability of the scale over time.

Scales are usually composed of multiple items. **Internal consistency** provides information about the degree to which all items measure the same construct. For example, if a student tends to respond at one end of the scale for most items while another student responds at the other end of the scale for most items, then this scale is internally consistent. Cronbach (1951) developed a statistic called **alpha reliability** that ranges from 0 to 1. A scale with an alpha reliability higher than .70 has an acceptable level of internal consistency (Nunnally & Bernstein, 1994).

A high internal consistency does not provide information about **temporal stability.** We need responses to the scale from the same participants at least two different times to investigate temporal

stability. In that case the easiest way to examine **test-retest reliability** is to investigate the magnitude of the relationship between the two sets of scores.

One should be cautious, though: a low test-retest relationship does not necessarily imply that the measure is unreliable because the construct itself (true score) may have changed. For example, early perceptions are likely to change a few weeks later when students become more familiar with their class environment. Hence, it is important to differentiate temporal stability from reliability. A more sophisticated approach to investigating stability is structural equation modeling (SEM), which gathers responses from the same people at least three times. This is quite a sophisticated statistical technique. Schutz (1998) provided a good presentation of this approach in how to examine temporal stability.

Investigating Validity and Reliability for Two Motivational Climate Measures

We conducted two studies to investigate validity and reliability for two instruments assessing perceived motivational climate in physical education at the contextual and situational level of generality.

Study 1: Participants and Procedures

Fifteen Greek physical education teachers randomly selected and unknown to the researchers were told that the scope of the study was to examine the validity of instruments assessing students' perceptions and motivation in physical education. In total, 25 coeducational classes participated in the study. All students ($n = 297$ male; $n = 283$ female) were in the first year of junior high school (aged 12.5 ± 0.5). The study took place seven months after the beginning of the academic year. At first, the students responded on two scales: the perceived motivational climate at the contextual level of generality questionnaire and a scale of motivation in physical education (intrinsic motivation and amotivation) (Pelletier et al., 1995). One week later they participated in the following experiment.

Five teachers were instructed to follow a physical education lesson comprising drills aiming to promote mastery goals, five teachers were asked to organise a lesson consisting of drills aiming to promote performance-approach goals and the remaining five teachers were told to teach as usual. The collected student reports from these three groups were 185, 174 and 221, respectively. Following the 35-minute class, the students completed instruments assessing their perceptions of teachers' emphasis on goal orientation, intrinsic-extrinsic motivation, amotivation and satisfaction at the situational level of specificity.

The subject of all classes was volleyball. Students had already learned this subject and were familiar with the drills. The first five minutes were devoted to warming up. In the mastery and performance groups, three drills followed, each of them lasting about 10 minutes. The three drills aiming to promote mastery were as follows:

1. Two by two, the students performed volley overhead sets; the goal was to keep the ball in the air for 20 consecutive passes.

2. Two by two, one student threw the ball and the other responded with a volley overhead set; the goal was to set passes using the proper technique; every 10 sets the students changed roles.

3. Two by two, one student threw the ball and the other responded with volley forearm passes; the goal was to bump the ball using the proper technique; every 10 passes the students changed roles.

In all cases the students adjusted the distance between each other by themselves.

In the group consisting of drills aiming to promote performance-approach goals, the activities were as follows:

1. Two by two, each student set overhead passes to himself or herself; the goal was to outperform one's partner.

2. Each student served three consecutive times; the goal was to perform more successful serves than the others.

3. Each student served three consecutive times while two students played defence; the goal was to score the most points from serves or defences.

The selected schools had more than two volleyball courts; hence students did not wait long to participate in the activities.

Past research has shown that the preceding drills and manipulations resulted in high mastery and performance-oriented climates, respectively (Papaioannou & Kouli, 1999).

Study 2: Participants and Procedures

Three weeks after the beginning of the academic year, two physical education teachers carried out an intervention in seven classes of four junior high schools for a period of three weeks (nine consecutive lessons). Seven classes from three physical education teachers who followed the typical curriculum served as the control groups. The intervention groups consisted of 170 students, and the control groups consisted of 181 students. All classes were coeducational.

One week earlier, at the end of one physical education lesson, students had completed questionnaires assessing their perceptions of teachers' emphasis on goals, intrinsic-extrinsic regulation and satisfaction at the situational level of generality. Two weeks before the intervention, they responded to questionnaires assessing the same constructs at the contextual level of generality.

The students were in their first year of junior high school, so they were new to this environment. Following the completion of the questionnaires the week prior to the intervention, the physical education teachers told the students that the aim of the lesson for the next month was to teach them how to set challenging personal goals, how to pursue them and how to evaluate their improvement.

Three simple tasks that students could perform during their free time were chosen that would allow students to have immediate feedback on their performance. Students tested themselves in sit-ups, balance and endurance in jumping (continuous side jumping). They kept their scores and set weekly goals. Every third day of the week, the students assessed themselves, set their new personal goals and participated in the remaining activities of the lesson. At the end of the lesson, they completed the instruments at the situational level of generality. The two teachers in the intervention study were asked to plan their lessons according to existing instructions for the creation of a task-involving climate in physical education (e.g., Papaioannou & Goudas, 1999; Treasure & Roberts, 1995; see also chapter 1 of this book). One week after the intervention, students completed the measures at the contextual level of generality.

To use the class as the unit of analysis, we computed the class means for all climate variables (both before and after the intervention) separately for boys and girls. Then we created a new data file composed of 28 records representing the collective perceptions of the boys and girls in 14 classes.

Results Supporting the Validity of the Measures

As was mentioned, to investigate the validity of a measure, various statistical analyses should be used. Some of them follow.

Motivational Climate at the Contextual Level of Generality

Initially content validity was examined, followed by analyses focusing on the construct validity of this measure.

Content Validity and Preliminary Analyses

One of the authors selected a pool of items from existing goal orientation and motivational climate measures. Then these items were adapted to the purposes of the study—that is, to fit the context of physical education, the goals (four goals and four corresponding perceptions), the action domain (achievement) and the time (we used the stem 'in this physical education class'). Next, three researchers familiar with the tenets of goal perspectives theory judged the appropriateness of each item and reduced the number of items to 32 (8 for each subscale). A 5-point Likert-type scale was selected for students' responses to these items (5 = *strongly agree,* 1 = *strongly disagree*). After the completion of items by the students participating in a pilot study ($n = 96$), the data were analysed via exploratory factor and scale reliability analyses. Items with low loadings on the expected factors were excluded by subsequent analyses and were replaced by new ones. The new version was given to a second sample of students ($n = 105$), and the data were analysed again using exploratory factor and reliability analyses. Following this procedure, we arrived at the items appearing in table 3.1.

Confirmatory Factor Analysis (CFA)

After the second pilot study, we administered the measures to the 580 students in study 1 and to the

351 students in study 2. The responses of these 931 students were analysed via CFA. Based on theory, we expected to capture four perceptions assessing teachers' emphasis on mastery, performance approach, performance avoidance and social approval, respectively. As is shown in table 3.1, the loadings were either moderate (i.e., higher than .40) or high (i.e., higher than .70), and all of them were statistically significant. Moreover, this four-factor model fit the data quite well because the goodness-of-fit indexes approached the criteria suggesting a robust factor structure (chi square = 612, df = 224, CFI = 930, TLI = .921, RMSEA = .048).

Factor Correlations: Internal Convergent and Discriminant Validity

The factor correlations shown in table 3.2 provide important insights into the internal validity of the measure. The strong positive relationship that emerged between the two performance factors is an index of convergent validity. Teachers focusing on who is the best student promote performance-approach goals and create a highly evaluative climate in their classes. In this environment many students are afraid of the evaluation and pursue performance-avoidance goals by trying to avoid being evaluated. Hence, when teachers encourage performance-approach goals, many students perceive that performance-avoidance goals are promoted at the same time in their classes.

On the other hand, both performance factors had no positive relationship with the mastery factor, which is an index of discriminant validity. Teachers promoting mastery goals adopt subjective criteria of evaluation and not normative, which is the case in high performance-oriented classes. Hence, the promotion of mastery goals is unrelated to the promotion of performance goals.

The positive association of social approval factors with both mastery and performance-approach factors is expected and provides further support to the convergent validity of this measure. As Maehr and Nicholls (1980) noted, socially approved behaviours are those indicating high levels of effort and commitment. Hence, in a climate nurturing social approval goals, students are likely to perceive that high effort and mastery goals are also encouraged. Thus, the positive relationship between mastery and social approval factors is an index of internal convergent validity. On the other hand, when social approval goals are encouraged, the criteria of evaluation are not subjective

Table 3.1 Perceptions of Teacher Emphasis on Goals Questionnaire at the Contextual Level of Generality

	My physical education teacher . . .	Factor loadings***			
		1	2	3	4
1	. . . often makes me worried if he says that I'm not capable in physical education.	.650			
2	. . . wants me to learn skills and games for which my schoolmates will love* me.		.621		
3	. . . encourages students to play better than the others.			.505	
4	. . . makes me afraid of the evaluation in physical education.	.657			
5	. . . is happy when what I learn in physical education makes other people love me.		.704		
6	. . . is absolutely satisfied only with students whom everyone recognises as more capable in physical education.			.548	
7	. . . often makes me worry about how others view my athletic abilities.	.687			
8	. . . is very satisfied when I try to learn a skill that will make other people love me.		.715		
9	. . . insists that we fight to prove that we are more capable in skills and games than others.			.537	
10	. . . makes me want to avoid questions in the lesson that could make others laugh at me.	.543			
11	. . . believes it's important to do well at a skill or game so other people will love me.		.716		
12	. . . is very happy when I learn new skills and games.				.647
13	. . . often makes me worry about others calling me incapable in drills or games.	.705			
14	. . . pays particular attention to whether my skills are improving.				.575
15**	. . . praises only students who are more capable than others in physical education.				
16	. . . likes me to learn new skills and games and to earn others' love.		.729		
17	. . . is absolutely satisfied when he sees that I am improving all my physical abilities.				.706
18	. . . believes that students should prove that they are more capable than others in all skills and games.			.797	
19	. . . feels great when I learn a new skill and my classmates love me.		.755		
20	. . . helps me learn how to improve my abilities in games and exercises.				.649
21	. . . wants us to appear more capable than others in all exercises.			.663	
22	. . . makes me want to avoid exercises or games that could cause others to comment negatively on my abilities.	.590			
23	. . . insists that errors in skills and games help me to find my weaknesses and improve my abilities.				.634
24	. . . makes sure that I understand how to perform a new skill before the class moves on to learning other skills.				.588

*The word love is a culture-specific term indicating social approval in Greek groups. In other cultures other terms can be used, such as accept or approve.

**Item 15 was excluded from the confirmatory factor analysis.

***Loadings indicate standardised beta weights.

anymore and a given performance is judged as successful by the teacher or the peers but not by the student herself. Hence, when social approval goals are promoted, students expect others to evaluate their performances, as it happens in performance-oriented environments. Therefore, the positive association that emerges between performance and social approval factors supports the convergent validity of the scale.

Class Influences

Next we computed the intraclass correlations for the four climate subscales at the contextual level of generality. In other words, we investigated the proportion of variance of perceived climate that was attributable to class differences. Using the data from study 1, we computed the class means for the four climate scores. Then we computed four regression analyses. In each analysis one of the climate scores was the dependent variable and its corresponding class mean was the independent variable. Class differences explained a significant amount of the variance of perceptions of teachers' emphasis on (1) mastery goals (18%, $p < .001$), (2)

performance-approach goals (17%, $p < .001$), (3) performance-avoidance goals (19%, $p < .001$) and (4) social approval goals (16%, $p < .001$). These findings imply that the four climate subscales capture a significant proportion of variance that is attributable to class differences.

External Convergent and Discriminant Validity

Vallerand (2001) asserted that the *Sport Motivation Scale* (*SMS;* Pelletier et al., 1995) is a measure of intrinsic-extrinsic motivation at the contextual level of generality. In study 1 we used the *SMS* to investigate intrinsic motivation and amotivation in physical education and their correspondence to perceived motivational climate at the contextual level of generality. Theory and research evidence suggest that perceptions of mastery climate facilitate high self-determination and intrinsic motivation, but perception of performance climate is linked with low self-determination and amotivation (e.g., Duda, Chi, Newton, Walling & Catley, 1995; Papaioannou, 1994). Indeed, the correlations in table 3.3 indicate that intrinsic

Table 3.2 Factor Correlation Matrix and Alpha Reliabilities in the Diagonal for the Motivational Climate Scale at the Contextual Level

Factor	Factor			
	1	2	3	4
1. Mastery	*.80*			
2. Performance approach	−.05	*.73*		
3. Performance avoidance	−.22	.58	*.80*	
4. Social approval	.55	.44	.20	*.86*

Table 3.3 Pearson's Correlation Coefficients Among Perceptions of Teacher's Emphasis on Goals and Intrinsic Motivation and Amotivation at the Contextual Level of Generality

	Intrinsic motivation	Amotivation
Perceptions of teacher's emphasis on		
Mastery	.36*	−.14*
Performance approach	.12	.24*
Performance avoidance	−.08	.32*
Social approval	.29*	.06

*$p < .001$

motivation was positively related to mastery climate, and amotivation was positively associated with performance factors.

On the other hand, the lack of a positive association between mastery climate and amotivation and between performance-oriented climate and intrinsic motivation supports the external discriminant validity of the climate measure.

Experimental Evidence

We used the data from study 2 to investigate the differences between intervention and control groups in the perceived motivational climate at the contextual level of generality. We expected that after the intervention, students in experimental classes should perceive stronger teacher emphasis on mastery goals than students in control classes. The results shown in table 3.4 supported these expectations. Controlling for possible differences in the perception of motivational climate prior to the intervention, the results suggested that after the intervention students in experimental classes perceived a stronger mastery-oriented climate than students in control classes did. On the other hand, there were no differences in students' perceptions of performance-oriented climate because the intervention did not attempt to alter performance orientation in the experimental classes.

Motivational Climate at the Situational Level of Generality

Evidence for content and construct validity of the motivational climate instrument at the situational level of generality is described in the following discussion.

Content Validity

To determine the content validity at the situational level of generality, we followed the same procedure that we used to determine content validity at the contextual level of generality. The items are shown in table 3.5.

Confirmatory Factor Analysis (CFA)

The results from the CFA suggested that the four-factor model fit the data well because the goodness-of-fit indexes approached the criteria indicating a robust factor structure (chi square = 701, df = 318, CFI = 950, TLI = .940, RMSEA = .036). Moreover, the loadings in table 3.5 were either modest or high, and all of them were statistically significant. These findings support the factorial validity of the motivational climate questionnaire at the situational level of generality.

Factor Correlations: Internal Convergent and Discriminant Validity

The correlations shown in table 3.6 establish the internal convergent validity of the measure. The reasoning is the same as that for the measure at the contextual level. The positive association pattern between the two performance factors and the social approval factor is in line with hypotheses. On the other hand, the lack of positive relationship between mastery and performance factors establishes the discriminant validity of the questionnaire.

Table 3.4 Differences in the Final Measurement Controlling for Initial Differences Prior to the Intervention

	Experimental group	Control group		
	M_{adj}	M_{adj}	F	p
Contextual level of generality				
Perception of teacher emphasis on				
Mastery	4.35	4.03	14.2	.000
Performance approach	2.81	2.83	.02	.882
Performance avoidance	2.91	2.79	.85	.358
Social approval	4.07	3.87	3.8	.053

M_{adj} = adjusted means, controlling for differences in the measurement prior to the intervention.

Table 3.5 Perceptions of Teacher Emphasis on Goals Questionnaire at the Situational Level of Generality

	My physical education teacher . . .	Factor loadings*			
		1	2	3	4
1.	. . . made me worry by saying I am not capable.			.633	
2.	. . . was pleased with students who were more capable than others.		.639		
3.	. . . was happy when others admired us for what we achieved in the gym.				.677
4.	. . . looked satisfied with students whom everyone recognised as most capable.		.728		
5.	. . . often made me think about how the others see my abilities.			.551	
6.	. . . was very pleased when I was trying to learn a skill that made others love** me.				.731
7.	. . . was very satisfied when someone was showing improvement after hard effort.	.629			
8.	. . . made me want to avoid questions that would possibly result in others making fun of me.			.631	
9.	. . . seemed to believe that it's important to do well in a drill or game so others will love me.				.701
10.	. . . was mostly pleased when I was improving my abilities in a drill or game in which I was not so good.	.592			
11.	. . . was absolutely satisfied with students whom performed better than others.		.675		
12.	. . . often made me worry that others would call me incapable in the lesson.			.702	
13.	. . . was happy when I was loved by my classmates for what I accomplished.				.699
14.	. . . was absolutely satisfied when I was improving in skills and games after hard effort.	.718			
15.	. . . praised the students who were more capable than others.		.601		
16.	. . . often made me think about how to protect myself from negative evaluation of my abilities.			.584	
17.	. . . liked me to learn new skills and games and gain the love of others.				.740
18.	. . . was absolutely satisfied with every student who improved his or her abilities.	.608			
19.	. . . believes we should prove that we are more capable than others in skills and games.		.567		
20.	. . . felt wonderful when others loved me for what I learned in the lesson.				.740
21.	. . . particularly cared whether I was improving my skills.	.586			
22.	. . . paid attention to me only when I was performing better than others.		.636		
23.	. . . made me avoid skills and games in which my abilities could be negatively criticised.			.624	
24.	. . . was really happy when I performed well and gained the love of others.				.701
25.	. . . insisted that mistakes in games and drills help us to find our weaknesses and improve our abilities.	.574			
26.	. . . was enthusiastic about students who appeared more capable than others.		.578		
27.	. . . made sure that students showed improvement in a skill before continuing to another.	.539			

* Loadings indicate standardised beta weights.

**The word *love* is a culture-specific term indicating social approval in Greek groups. In other cultures other terms can be used, such as *accept* or *approve*.

Table 3.6 Factor Correlation Matrix and Alpha Reliabilities in the Diagonal for the Measure at the Situational Level

Factor	Factor			
	1	2	3	4
1. Mastery	.81			
2. Performance approach	.11	.81		
3. Performance avoidance	−.01	.66	.78	
4. Social approval	.57	.44	.36	.88

Table 3.7 Pearson's Correlation Coefficients Among Perceptions of Teacher Emphasis on Goals and Intrinsic Motivation and Amotivation at the Situational Level of Generality

	Intrinsic motivation	Amotivation
Perceptions of teacher emphasis on		
Mastery	.48*	−.20*
Performance approach	.06	.36*
Performance avoidance	.01	.54*
Social approval	.35*	.12

*$p < .001$

Evidence of External Construct Validity

Intrinsic-extrinsic motivation in the present was assessed with the *Situational Motivational Scale* (Guay, Vallerand & Blanchard, 2000). The relationship between the *SMS* and the motivational climate measure at the situational level of generality appears in table 3.7. The expected relationships and the reasoning are the same as those that were described for the measures at the contextual level of generality. In line with hypotheses, mastery climate was positively associated with intrinsic motivation, and performance-oriented factors were positively linked with amotivation. These findings support the external convergent validity of the scale. On the other hand, mastery orientation was not related positively with amotivation, and performance orientation factors were not associated with intrinsic motivation. These results support the discriminant validity of this measure.

Construct Validity Based on Experimental Techniques

We conducted two sets of analyses to determine construct validity at the situational level of gener-

ality. First, based on students' responses in study 1, we examined differences in perceived motivational climate at the situational level between the three groups of this study: (1) the group in which mastery goals were emphasised, (2) the group in which performance approach goals were emphasised and (3) the control group.

The results shown in table 3.8 suggest that students in the mastery-oriented group reckoned that their teachers placed higher emphasis on mastery goals and lower emphasis on performance-approach and performance-avoidance goals than did the control group. On the other hand, in the group that performed drills aiming to promote performance goals, students reckoned that their teachers placed higher emphasis on performance-approach and performance-avoidance goals than did students in the group that performed mastery-oriented drills. The relatively high scores on performance subscales that appeared in the control group are expected given the competitive nature of the sport-oriented Greek physical education curriculum. These findings support the external construct validity of the measure at the situational level of generality.

The second set of analyses was based on students' responses in study 2. We expected that in the nine physical education lessons that took place during the intervention, students in experimental classes should have perceived the climate as more mastery oriented than students in control classes. We investigated this assumption with a repeated measures design, using perceptions of teachers' emphasis on mastery goals in times 2, 3 and 4 as the repeated measures factor, controlling for initial differences in the aforementioned perceptions. The results shown in figure 3.1 imply that students in the intervention group perceived their classes as more mastery oriented than students in the control groups did. These findings provide further evidence of construct validity for the climate measure at the situational level of generality.

Results Supporting the Reliability of the Measures

Finally, the reliability of the two measures was examined. Tests of internal consistency preceded analyses focusing on the temporal stability of the scales.

Table 3.8 Means (*M*), Standard Deviations (*SD*) and Significant Differences (*F*) of Perceptions in Experimental Conditions

| | Type of drills or lessons | | | | | | |
| | Task involving | | Ego involving | | Typical (control) | | |
	M	*SD*	*M*	*SD*	*M*	*SD*	*F*
Perception of a teacher promoting							
Mastery	4.20$_a$	.78	4.08$_{ab}$	.66	3.93$_b$	.83	4.80**
Performance approach	2.71$_a$	.98	3.15$_b$	1.10	3.05$_b$	1.00	6.67***
Performance avoidance	2.48$_a$	.80	2.77$_b$	.88	2.75$_b$	.85	5.98**
Social approval	3.23$_a$	.98	3.69$_b$	.92	3.40$_a$	.99	6.59**

Note: Means sharing the same subscript are not statistically significant ($p > .05$).

* $p < .05$, ** $p < .01$, *** $p < .001$.

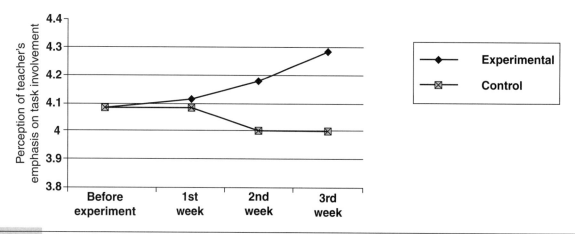

Figure 3.1 Perception of teacher's emphasis on mastery goals at the situational level of generality in three weeks on the intervention.

Internal Consistency of the Scales

As shown in the diagonals of tables 3.2 and 3.6, all scales had acceptable internal consistencies; that is, the alpha reliabilities were higher than .70.

Temporal Stability

The following analyses concern the motivational climate measure at the contextual level of generality. Using the data from study 2, we computed the test-rest correlation coefficients for the six-week period between the two time points of students' responses—that is, before and after the intervention. All were significant ($p < .001$), and their magnitude was moderate: for perceived teacher emphasis on mastery, $r = .46$; for perceived teacher emphasis on performance-approach goals, $r = .59$; for perceived teacher emphasis on performance-avoidance goals, $r = .45$; and for perceived teacher emphasis on social approval, $r = .51$.

Summary

In this chapter we presented the existing motivational climate measures and explained in which circumstances they can be used in applied research and assessment in physical education settings. The development of instruments is an ongoing process. As theories are refined, new measures appear. Accordingly, two new motivational climate scales were presented that we believe have some advantages over older measures. These scales can be used to assess the type of goals that are promoted by teachers in physical education classes. The scale at the contextual level of generality can be used to examine the relatively permanent effects of teaching on goal adoption. The scale at the situational level can be used to assess the type of goals that are encouraged in one particular teaching episode.

Because the present items are a direct translation from Greek, physical educators who use these tools in other languages should examine the validity and reliability of these scales. We explained the major psychological properties that can be examined, and we provided examples based on our research in Greece. We hope that these measures will be helpful to physical educators who want to assess whether their teaching really promotes an adaptive motivational climate in their classes.

Review Questions

1. How do perceived motivational climate scales differ from other perceived climate scales in physical education?
2. What are some reasons for choosing each of the existing climate measures?
3. What is the principle of compatibility in perceived motivational climate measures, and how is it exemplified in physical education?
4. Which are the different types of validity, and how are they defined?
5. What is intraclass correlation, and why is it important in perceived climate measurement?
6. How would you examine the reliability of perceived climate measures?
7. What are the limitations of test-retest correlations?

Critical Thinking Questions

1. If you wanted to adapt one of the motivational climate measures presented here in a language other than Greek, what steps should you follow to establish content and construct validity?
2. Select two previous motivational climate instruments. How can you examine their convergent and discriminant validity adopting a within-network studies approach? What are the expected interfactor correlations?

Key Terms

alpha reliability—Coefficient indicating the degree of internal consistency of a scale; it ranges from 0 to 1 with high values indicating acceptable level of internal consistency.

compatibility principle—Consistency between perception and goals, to the extent that their target, action domain, life context and time elements are assessed at identical levels of generality or specificity.

confirmatory factor analysis—A statistical technique applied to a set of variables in order to confirm that some variables in the set which have been chosen a priori based on theoretical grounds form coherent subsets that are relatively independent of one another.

construct validity—Research evidence confirming the conceptualization of the construct.

content validity—Definitional evidence of validity of written tests.

contextual level of generality—Category in the hierarchy of goals' level of abstraction, specifying that goals and their antecedents and consequences should refer to the same life context and action domain.

convergent validity—Evidence from different sources collected in different ways indicating similar meaning of the construct.

discriminant validity—Evidence that the test can differentiate the construct from other constructs that may be similar. It is unrelated to constructs that have nothing in common.

external construct validity—Research evidence establishing a logical, theoretically consistent pattern of relations between the measure of the construct and other constructs.

factor analysis—A statistical technique applied to a set of variables in order to discover which variables in the set form coherent subsets that are relatively independent of one another.

internal consistency—Evidence that each item of an instrument measures the same general construct.

internal construct validity—Research evidence confirming the conceptualization of the internal structure of a construct.

intraclass correlation—The proportion of variance attributed to group effects.

levels of generality—A hierarchy of categories describing different degrees of goal abstraction, ranging from a global level that incorporates very abstract goals generally in life to a situational level that refers to specific goals in a particular situation at a particular moment.

loading—The relationship between each observed variable and the subsets of variables (factors) resulting from factor analysis.

mastery goal—A goal to improve competence.

performance-approach goal—A goal to indicate high normative ability.

performance-avoidance goal—A goal to avoid negative evaluation of their competence from others.

predictive validity—Evidence that the measure of a construct predicts another construct which is measured some time in the future.

reliability—Evidence of consistency of measurement.

situational level of generality—Category in the hierarchy of goals' level of abstraction, specifying that goals and their antecedents and consequences should refer to the same situation, action and time.

social approval goal—A goal to exhibit high effort in order to gain social approval.

temporal stability—Consistency of measurement across some time period.

test-retest reliability—The correlation between scores on the same construct assessed at two time periods.

validity—The extent to which a test measures what it purports to measure.

References

Ajzen, I. & Fishbein, M. (1977). Attitude-behavior relations: A theoretical analysis and review of empirical research. *Psychological Bulletin, 84*(5), 888-918.

Ames, C. (1992). Achievement goal, motivational climate, and motivational processes. In G.C. Roberts (Ed.), *Motivation in sport and exercise* (pp. 161-176). Champaign, IL: Human Kinetics.

Arbuckle, J.L. & Wothke, W. (1999). *Amo's 4 user's guide.* Chicago, IL: Smallwaters Corporation.

Bandura, A. (Ed.). (1986). *Social foundations of thought and action: A social-cognitive theory.* Englewood Cliffs, NJ: Prentice Hall.

Bentler, P.M. (1995). *EQS: Structural equations program manual.* Encino, CA: Multivariate Software, Inc.

Bentler, P.M. (1990). Comparative fit indices in structural models. *Psychological Bulletin, 107,* 238-246.

Biddle, S., Cury, F., Goudas, M., Sarrazin, P., Famose, J.P. & Durand, M. (1995). Development of scales to measure perceived physical education class climate: A cross-national project. *British Journal of Educational Psychology, 65,* 341-358.

Browne, M.W. & Cudeck, R. (1993). Alternative ways of assessing model fit. In K.A. Bolen & J.S. Long (Eds.), *Testing structural equation models* (pp. 136-162). Newbury Park, CA: Sage.

Carver, C.S. & Scheier, M.F. (1998). *On the self-regulation of behavior.* New York: Cambridge University Press.

Conroy, D.E., Elliot, A.J. & Hofer, S.M. (2003). A 2 × 2 achievement goals questionnaire for sport: Evidence for factorial invariance, temporal stability and external validity. *Journal of Sport and Exercise Psychology, 25*(4), 456-476.

Cronbach, L. (1951). Coefficient alpha and the internal structure of test. *Psychometrika, 16*(3), 297-334.

Duda, J.L., Chi, L., Newton, M.L., Walling, M.D. & Catley, D. (1995). Task and ego orientation and intrinsic motivation in sport. *International Journal of Sport Psychology, 26,* 40-63.

Duda, J.L. & Whitehead, J. (1998). Measurement of goal perspectives in the physical domain. In J. Duda (Ed.), *Advances in sport and exercise psychology measurement* (pp. 21-48). Morgantown, WV: Fitness Information Technology.

Dweck, C.S. (Ed.). (1999). *Self-theories and goals: Their role in motivation, personality, and development.* Philadelphia: Taylor & Francis.

Elliot, A. & Church, J. (1997). A hierarchical model of approach and avoidance achievement motivation. *Journal of Personality and Social Psychology, 72*(3), 218-232.

Elliot, A. & Harackiewicz, J. (1996). Approach and avoidance achievement goals and intrinsic motivation: A mediational analysis. *Journal of Personality and Social Psychology, 70*(3), 461-475.

Elliot, A. & McGregor, H. (2001). A 2 × 2 achievement goal framework. *Journal of Personality and Social Psychology, 80,* 501-519.

Fan, X., Thompson, B., & Wang, L. (1999). Effects of sample size, estimation methods, and model specification on structural equation modeling fix indexes. *Structural Equation Modeling, 6,* 56-83.

Fraser, B.J. (Ed.). (1986). *Classroom environment.* London: Croom Helm.

Goudas, M. & Biddle, S. (1994). Perceived motivational climate and intrinsic motivation in school physical education classes. *European Journal of Psychology of Education, IX*(3), 241-250.

Guay, F., Vallerand, R.J. & Blanchard, C.M. (2000). On the assessment of situational intrinsic and extrinsic motivation: The Situational Motivation Scale (SIMS). *Motivation and Emotion, 24*(3), 175-213.

Hayashi, C. (1996). Achievement motivation among Anglo-American and Hawaiian male physical activity participants: Individual differences and social contextual factors. *Journal of Sport & Exercise Psychology, 18,* 194-215.

Hu, L. & Bentler, P.M. (1999). Cutoff criteria for fit indexes in covariance structure analysis: Conventional criteria versus new alternatives. *Structural Equation Modeling, 6,* 1-55.

Joreskog, K.G. & Sorbom, D. (1993). *LISREL 8: Structural equation modeling with the SIMPLIS command language.* Chicago, IL: Scientific Software International.

Kenny, D.A. & Lavoie, L. (1985). Separating individual and group effects. *Journal of Personality and Social Psychology, 48,* 339-348.

Maehr, M. (1984). Meaning and motivation: Toward a theory of personal investment. In R. Ames & C. Ames (Eds.), *Research on motivation in education: Student motivation in education* (Vol. 1; pp. 115-207). Orlando, FL: Academic Press.

Maehr, M.L. & Nicholls, J.G. (1980). Culture and achievement motivation: A second look. In N. Warren (Ed.), *Studies in cross-cultural psychology* (Vol. 3; pp. 221-267). New York: Academic Press.

Marsh, H.W. (1998). Foreword. In J.L. Duda (Ed.), *Advances in sport and exercise psychology measurement* (pp. xv-xix). Morgantown, WV: Fitness Information Technology.

Marsh, H.W., Balla, J.R. & McDonald, R.P. (1988). Goodness-of-fit indices in confirmatory factor analysis: The effect of sample size. *Psychological Bulletin, 102,* 391-410.

McIrney, D., Hinkley, J., Dowson, M. & Van Etten, S. (1998). Aboriginal, Anglo and immigrant Australian students' motivational beliefs about personal academic success: Are there cultural differences? *Journal of Educational Psychology, 90,* 621-629.

Mischel, W. & Shoda, Y. (1998). Reconciling processing dynamics and personality dispositions. *Annual Review of Psychology, 49,* 229-258.

Mitchell, S. (1996). Relationships between perceived learning environment and intrinsic motivation in middle school physical education. *Journal of Teaching in Physical Education, 15,* 369-383.

Moos, R.H. & Trickett, E.J. (Eds.). (1987). *Classroom environment scale manual* (2nd ed.). Palo Alto, CA: Consulting Psychologists Press.

Newton, M., Duda, J. & Yin, Z. (2000). Examination of the psychometric properties of the *Perceived Motivational Climate in Sport Questionnaire—2* in a sample of female athletes. *Journal of Sports Sciences, 18*(4), 275-290.

Nicholls, J. (1989). *The competitive ethos and democratic education.* Cambridge, MA: Harvard University Press.

Niles, S.G. (1998). Achievement goals and means: A cultural comparison. *Journal of Cross-Cultural Psychology, 29,* 656-667.

Ntoumanis, N. & Biddle, S.J.H. (1999). A review of motivational climate in physical activity. *Journal of Sports Sciences, 17*(8), 643- 665.

Nunnally, J.C. & Bernstein, I.H. (Eds.). (1994). *Psychometric theory.* New York: McGraw-Hill.

Papaioannou, A. (1992). *Students' motivation in physical education classes, perceived to have different goal perspectives.* Unpublished doctoral dissertation, Manchester University, UK.

Papaioannou, A. (1994). Development of a questionnaire to measure achievement orientations in physical education. *Research Quarterly for Exercise and Sport, 65,* 11-20.

Papaioannou, A. (1995). Differential perceptual and motivational patterns when different goals are adopted. *Journal of Sport & Exercise Psychology, 17,* 18-34.

Papaioannou, A. (1998). Students' perceptions of the physical education class environment for boys and girls and the perceived motivational climate. *Research Quarterly for Exercise and Sport, 69,* 267-275.

Papaioannou, A. (2006). Muslim and Christian students' goal orientations in school, sport and life. *International Journal of Sport & Exercise Psychology, 4,* 250-282.

Papaioannou, A. & Goudas, M. (1999). Motivational climate in physical education. In Y. Vanden Auweele, F. Bakker, S. Biddle, M. Durand & R. Seiler (Eds.), *Psychology for physical educators* (pp. 51-69). Champaign, IL: Human Kinetics.

Papaioannou, A. & Kouli, O. (1999). The effect of task structure, perceived motivational climate and goal orientations on students' task involvement and anxiety. *Journal of Applied Sport Psychology, 11,* 51-71.

Papaioannou, A., Marsh, H.W. & Theodorakis, Y. (2004). A multilevel approach to motivational climate in physical education and sport settings: An individual or a group level construct. *Journal of Sport and Exercise Psychology, 26*(1), 90-118.

Pelletier, L.G., Fortier, M.S., Vallerand, R.J., Tuson, K.M., Brière, N.M. & Blais, M.R. (1995). Toward a new measure of intrinsic motivation, extrinsic motivation, and amotivation in sports: The Sport Motivation Scale (SMS). *Journal of Sport and Exercise Psychology, 17,* 35-53.

Schilling, T.A. & Hayashi, C.T. (2001). Achievement motivation among high school basketball and cross-country athletes: A personal investment perspective. *Journal of Applied Sport Psychology, 31*(1), 103-128.

Schutz, A. (1998). Assessing the stability of psychological traits. In J.L. Duda (Ed.), *Advances in sport and exercise psychology measurement* (pp. 393-408). Morgantown, WV: Fitness Information Technology.

Treasure, D. & Roberts, G.C. (1995). Applications of achievement goal theory to physical education: Implications for enhancing motivation. *Quest, 47*(4), 475-489.

Tucker L.R. & Lewis, C. (1973). A reliability coefficient for maximum likelihood factor analysis. *Psychometrica, 38,* 1-10.

Vallerand, R.J. (2001). A hierarchical model of intrinsic and extrinsic motivation in sport and exercise. In G.C. Roberts (Ed.), *Advances in motivation in sport and exercise* (pp. 263-320). Champaign, IL: Human Kinetics.

Verkuyten, M., Thijs, J. & Canatan, K. (2001). Achievement motivation and academic performance among Turkish early and young adolescents in the Netherlands. *Genetic, Social, and General Psychology Monographs, 127*(4), 378-408.

Weinstein, R.S. (1989). Perceptions of classroom processes and student motivation: Children's views of self-fulfilling prophecies. In R. Ames & C. Ames (Eds.), *Research on motivation in education, Volume 3: Goals and cognitions* (pp. 187-221). New York, NY: Academic Press.

Wentzel, K.R. (1999). Social-motivational processes and interpersonal relationships: Implications for understanding motivation at school. *Journal of Educational Psychology, 91,* 76-97.

chapter four

Experience of State Anxiety in Physical Education

Vassilis Barkoukis

Aristotle University of Thessaloniki, Greece

After reading this chapter, you will be able to do the following:

- Understand the nature of anxiety

- Identify feelings of anxiety in your students

- Obtain a measure to estimate the levels of your students' state anxiety

- Have a good understanding of the association between state anxiety and other psychological constructs in physical education

- Increase your awareness of possible strategies to reduce the experience of state anxiety

Anxiety is one of the most extensively studied topics in sport psychology. It is considered one of the most important psychological factors affecting physical performance. A plethora of theories have been developed to describe and explain the relationship between state anxiety and physical performance in the context of competitive sport. Most of these theories have focused on the anxiety–performance relationship. In exercise settings, research has mostly concentrated on the acute and chronic effects of exercise on feelings of anxiety. In educational psychology, research on anxiety has been focused mainly on the anxiety–performance relationship during testing in different disciplines, such as mathematics, science, learning a foreign language, computers and so on.

Physical education is a somewhat unique situation because it combines both physical activity and educational elements. Regarding educational elements, the physical education class differs in context and teaching methods from other educational disciplines. Additionally, unlike sport, school physical education should give all students fundamental movement experiences and positive cognitive and affective experiences that will eventually lead to active lifestyles. However, although physical education lessons are usually seen as fun and enjoyable, they may trigger feelings of anxiety because of their comparative, competitive and evaluative nature (Tremayne, 1995).

So far, there is only limited research on the experience of anxiety in physical education. Furthermore, physical education teachers have rarely focused on the possibility of triggering negative feelings in their students. The purpose of this chapter is to provide an insight into the experience of state anxiety in physical education and to suggest practices that may diminish the feelings of state anxiety and reinforce the experience of positive affective states.

Understanding Anxiety

The term *anxiety* is often used interchangeably with the terms **arousal** and **stress.** Psychologists, though, argue that these constructs represent different psychological states, and, as such, they should be distinguished. The term *arousal* has typically referred to the activation of the autonomic nervous system as a response to a stimulus. Furthermore, many researchers have argued that

arousal also incorporates the cognitive activation of the organism. Arousal can be defined as a physiological and psychological activation that varies on a continuum from deep sleep to intense excitement (Gould, Greenleaf & Krane, 2002; Hardy, Jones & Gould, 1996; Weinberg & Gould, 2003).

Stress is defined as the biological reactions (physical, mental and emotional) to an unfavourable and unfamiliar environmental stimulus that disturbs a person's homeostasis. Based on McGrath's (1970) stress process model, stress is currently viewed as a process that has specific effects on the person rather than simply as a reaction (emotional or physical) to a stimulus. The stress process involves four stages. At stage 1 a physical or psychological demand is imposed on the person. An example can be a student who has to perform a difficult skill for the first time or after repeated failures in front of the class.

At the second stage the student interprets the demand and decides how to respond to the stressor. Some students may interpret being asked to perform a new task in front of the class as a challenge and a sign of the teacher's trust in their abilities; others may view it as a threatening situation in which they may demonstrate low ability and feel embarrassment and disgrace. Similarly, a physical education teacher might choose to work with a less skilled student separately on a difficult and novel task; in this case some students may see it as a sign of interest in their personal improvement, whereas others might see it as an index of low ability.

The response of the student to the demand is organised at stage 3. This response is heavily dependent on the perception of the demand the student held in the previous stage. If the student experiences an imbalance between the demands of the environment and her capabilities (i.e., she interprets the demand as threatening and perceives that she cannot adequately cope with it), she will respond with elevated levels of state anxiety.

Stage 4 involves the consequences of the response made at stage 3. The feelings of state anxiety usually have negative consequences such as low performance, perceptions of low capability and negative self-evaluation. In the previous cases the stress process starts from the beginning: a similar demand will be interpreted as threatening, the student will respond with elevated levels of state anxiety and then the performance is more likely to be low and negative self-evaluation will be formed (Gould et al., 2002; Weinberg & Gould, 2003). If this cycle is repeated, the student is very likely to develop a low physical self-concept and learned helplessness. As a result he might drop out of compulsory physical education. To manifest the function of stress as a succession of events and not just as a stimulus, Martens (1977) defined it as 'the process that involves the perception of substantial imbalance between environmental demand and response capability, under conditions where failure to meet the demand is perceived as having important consequences and is responded to with increased levels of A-state' (p. 9).

Anxiety, on the other hand, has been defined as an unpleasant emotional state elicited by a nonspecific and nonconscious danger (May, 1977) or as the emotional reaction evoked by a stimulus that is perceived as threatening (irrespectively of its objective nature) (Spielberger, 1972). The experience of anxiety is characterised by arousal of the autonomic nervous system, accompanied by feelings of tension and apprehension and unpleasant and negative thoughts (Martens, Vealey & Burton, 1990; Spielberger, 1972). The stress process operates as an objective demand that produces the arousal response; the person interprets the situation as threatening and responds with elevated levels of arousal and negative thoughts, the basic elements of anxiety.

The definition and characteristics of anxiety presented earlier involve a transient emotional state, namely **state anxiety.** However, anxiety can also be a relatively stable personality trait (i.e., **trait anxiety**). Trait anxiety refers to 'differences in the disposition to perceive a wide range of stimulus situations as dangerous or threatening, and in the tendency to respond to such threats with A-state reactions' (Spielberger, 1972, p. 39). Trait anxiety reflects individual differences in the frequency and intensity of the experience of state anxiety. According to state-trait theory, high trait anxious people will perceive more situations as threatening and react with higher levels of state anxiety than people with low levels of trait anxiety.

Anxiety was initially viewed as a unidimensional construct. Further research, however, indicated that there are at least two distinct dimensions of anxiety. In the sport literature, Martens, Vealey and Burton (1990) formulated these conceptions and developed the multidimensional

anxiety theory. According to this theory, there are two basic dimensions of anxiety: **cognitive anxiety** and **somatic anxiety.** Cognitive anxiety in sport is defined as negative expectations about performance, cognitive concerns about oneself (and thus negative self-evaluation) and cognitive concerns about the situation at hand and the consequences of a potential failure. Somatic anxiety refers to the physiological and affective elements of anxiety; it is characterised by bodily symptoms such as rapid heart rate, shortness of breath, clammy hands and tension in the stomach and muscles. Cognitive anxiety and somatic anxiety are generated by different sources and affect behaviour differently. With respect to performance, cognitive anxiety was found to have a negative linear association with performance. An increase in cognitive anxiety will result in a decrease of performance. Somatic anxiety showed a curvilinear relationship with performance. An increase in somatic anxiety will lead to gradual improvement in performance up to an optimum level; a further increase in somatic anxiety will gradually decrease performance levels (see figure 4.1). Research on cognitive and somatic anxiety revealed that they are interrelated, albeit independent, constructs (Martens et al., 1990). Researchers have adopted the view that anxiety is a multidimensional emotional state, and the concept now dominates this sport and exercise literature.

State Anxiety in Physical Education

An important aspect of the anxiety definition is the role of a person's perceptions. Anxiety can be evoked by a stimulus that is nonspecific and nonconscious and objectively may not be dangerous at all. Hence, state anxiety could be experienced in any context and situation in which a person perceives an imbalance between environmental demands and personal capabilities, even if this context or situation is enjoyable for others. This is the case in physical education. For many students, physical education is a fun and enjoyable course, with playful drills and a structure that is less strict than that of other classes. But for others, it may be a context eliciting negative feelings. The sources of state anxiety and its manifestation in physical education lessons will be discussed in the following section.

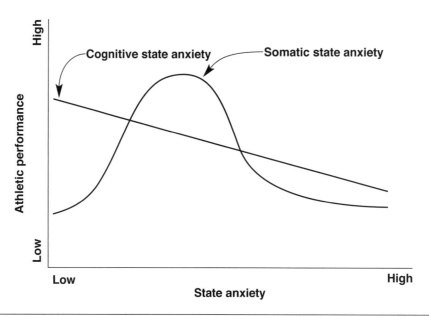

Figure 4.1 Relationship between anxiety dimensions and sport performance.

Reprinted from R. Cox, 1994, *Sport psychology: Concepts and applications,* 3rd ed. (New York: McGraw-Hill Companies), 109. Reproduced with permission of The McGraw-Hill Companies.

State anxiety can be detrimental to performance in achievement contexts.

© Lambros Lazuras

Sources of State Anxiety in Physical Education

Research in sport has shown that there are different sources of anxiety in different sports. Research into anxiety in the context of physical education, however, is limited. Tremayne (1995) listed a number of physical factors (e.g., low fitness levels, temporary sickness, inadequate body build), psychological factors (e.g., low interest, fear, shame, dislike of the subject or teacher) and environmental factors (e.g., poor facilities and equipment, bad weather) resulting in feelings of alienation and threat during involvement in sporting activities at school. These and other factors that seem to be more anxiety evoking will be discussed.

Trait Anxiety

The levels of a person's disposition to perceive environmental stimuli as threatening has long been associated with elevated levels of state anxiety in the context of sport and physical activity. High trait anxious children are more prone to respond with state anxiety in objectively less threatening situations, and they are expected to respond with higher levels of state anxiety in the presence of an appropriate stimulus (Spielberger, 1972).

Perceptions of Low Competence

Every child has an innate desire for competence. When this desire is threatened, state anxiety is likely to occur. For example, obese and less coordinated children face more threats to their competence perceptions when participating in physical education lessons. Thus, they prefer less active roles during the lesson, such as being the goalkeeper in soccer and handball. Their poor competence is apparent to themselves and their peers, and unless the structure of the lesson helps them, they may experience anxiety and helplessness.

The maturity level of the students is another important issue related to perceptions of competence. During adolescence, major bodily and emotional changes take place. These changes affect motor coordination and physical performance. Precocious children are more competent at physical education drills than are children who mature more slowly. On the other hand, children with delayed maturation can feel awkward when interacting with and competing against precocious children during physical education. The situation can be further complicated when children with delayed maturation catch up to the precocious children; the former watch their skills improve disproportionately to those of their skilled peers, while the latter begin to question their motor excellence. These continuing changes and the subsequent changes in bodily and emotional reactions are apparent in the physical education lesson and can cause students stress that may lead to an elevation of state anxiety.

Another feature of physical education that is associated with perceptions of competence is the organisation of the learning process. Teaching tasks that are not based on previous experience will result in decreased self-efficacy and increased state anxiety. For example, a physical education teacher who plans to teach the triple jump to students without prior experience with the long jump technique may elevate the students' uncertainty about their capabilities, and subsequently her actions may lower their sense of self-efficacy and increase the probability for feelings of state anxiety. Practising the long jump first will give

Perceptions of competence can affect the experience of state anxiety in physical education.

© Lambros Lazuras

students the opportunity to experience the approach run, the takeoff and the landing phases. Preliminary experiences can lessen the uncertainty of the novel task, promote self-efficacy and diminish state anxiety. In the same vein, the use of difficult and complex drills without previous practice will have similar results on self-efficacy and state anxiety (Bandura, 1997).

Peer Comparison

Achievement goal theory has provided substantial evidence that performance-oriented students (i.e., students with the tendency to define success relative to others by seeking either to outperform them or to avoid failure) experience more often negative affect than mastery-oriented students (Ntoumanis & Biddle, 1999; Rawsthorne & Elliot, 1999). Performance-oriented students focus on winning or avoiding losing and not on the process of the activity or personal improvement. When the outcome of the activity is ambiguous, performance-oriented students are more likely than mastery-oriented students to experience state anxiety.

Besides the students' general tendencies, the teacher-initiated motivational climate can also influence students' affective states. A performance-oriented climate focuses on performance goals, extrinsic motivation and, subsequently, negative affect. On the contrary, a mastery-oriented climate fosters personal improvement and is more likely to avoid stressful situations for students (Roberts, 2001; Treasure, 2001).

Social Evaluation

Recent research has shown that social goals, such as social affiliation and acceptance, are very important in sport contexts. Children value themselves through peer recognition and want to hang out with the most popular of their peers (Allen, 2003). However, research evidence suggests that less competent and less skilled students have fewer playmates and are asked to play with other children less often. Additionally, they report less enjoyment and more anxiety during participation in their usual activities (Skinner & Piek, 2001). Hence, evaluation by peers can be a powerful stressor. A student who faces the possibility of negative evaluation by her peers, and possibly social rejection, is likely to respond with elevated levels of state anxiety.

The physical educator may also constitute a strong source of evaluative anxiety. School teachers, along with parents, relatives and peers, are included in children's 'significant others'. Children value their opinions and seek their positive feedback and affection. This is more evident with physical education teachers because of the unique nature of the physical education class, in which the teacher and students interact in a rather

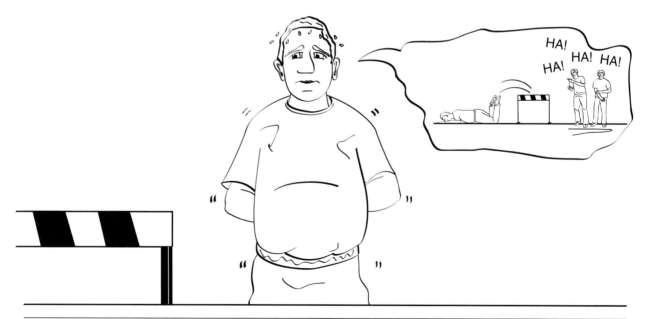

Peer evaluation can be a powerful source of state anxiety in physical education.

© Lambros Lazuras

informal way. Therefore, students who believe they cannot adequately perform a task and will therefore disappoint the teacher and evoke negative evaluations from peers are likely to experience feelings of state anxiety.

Grading

The evaluation of students in the physical education class may also be anxiety provoking. An evaluation based on normative criteria will reinforce a performance orientation that is associated with feelings of anxiety. Additionally, in such a normative environment, the examination procedures themselves may be state-anxiety-evoking situations (Ames, 1992).

Manifestation of State Anxiety in Physical Education

State anxiety in physical education can manifest in several ways. A close examination of students' behaviour during physical education lessons revealed cognitive-emotional, physiological, behavioural and information-processing symptoms of anxiety (Lox, Martin & Petruzzello, 2003; Weinberg & Gould, 2003). Although many of these symptoms can be caused by other factors, the presence of two or three of these symptoms in a child with certain personality characteristics can alert a physical educator to the presence of state anxiety.

Cognitive Symptoms

Low performance expectations are a very common symptom of state anxiety. For example, the teacher sets a feasible goal such as succeeding at 5 out of 10 free-throw basketball shots (with a previous performance goal of 4 out of 10), and the student refuses to participate. In this case, the student may have low performance expectations as a result of inadequate preparation to move on, or he may be anxious about failing and the subsequent negative evaluation. Low expectations can also be expressed as worries about failure. If a highly skilled student expresses worries about demonstrating a new but attainable skill, this might be because she believes that the demands of the task exceed her capabilities. In both cases, low performance expectations and worries about failure suggest the experience of state anxiety.

To avoid the negative outcomes of a possible failure, students often use excuses, such as 'I am not feeling very well', 'I was ill yesterday' or 'I twisted my ankle during training'. The use of such self-handicapping statements has also been associated with state anxiety. If these behaviours become chronic, then students develop an obsession with poor performance. They feel incapable of performing most of the physical education tasks. When they perform a task, they don't expect a successful outcome: 'I knew I couldn't do it right'. This obsession leads to learned helplessness and amotivation (i.e., 'No matter what I do, I can't perform the tasks correctly, so why waste my time in physical education?'). Amotivation is strongly associated with negative affect in physical activity contexts (Ntoumanis & Biddle, 1999).

Emotional Symptoms

Anxiety is, by definition, an unpleasant emotional state. Unpleasant feelings such as discomfort, embarrassment, shame and feeling overwhelmed are closely associated with state anxiety. When a student feels uncomfortable about performing a task, this is due to negative thoughts about performance and evaluation—that is, the experience of state anxiety. Furthermore, a student who feels ashamed about his physical skills is possibly experiencing state anxiety as a result of his fear of failure or of his peers' and teacher's negative evaluations. Another common situation in physical education is for a student to feel embarrassed about a previous poor performance. This embarrassment will generate feelings of state anxiety when the student is faced with another task.

EXERCISE 1

Write down as many situations as you can from everyday life at school that might have caused state anxiety in your students. Ask your students how they feel about these situations. Make a list of the stressful situations in your class.

Anxious students show lower levels of fun and enjoyment during physical education and report less satisfaction. They try to avoid the lesson with several excuses, and they question its utility. Additionally, uncertainty about the demands of a new task is thought to elicit feelings of apprehension. Anxious students seem preoccupied, and they don't demonstrate enthusiasm about learning new tasks. They claim that they don't like the new task, although they haven't tried it before. A careful observation of students' body language can provide valuable information about their thoughts and feelings.

Physiological Symptoms

Physiological arousal is an important indicator of state anxiety. However, in physical education it can be difficult to distinguish between positive activation derived from playful activities and negative activation associated with state anxiety. Thus, observations of muscle tension and autonomic hyperactivity alone cannot provide solid information concerning the levels of state anxiety. Physical educators should evaluate these symptoms jointly with other anxiety symptoms to ensure that what they are witnessing is state anxiety.

Behavioural Symptoms

Behavioural symptoms are more obvious to observe and interpret than are physiological symptoms in the physical education environment. The most common behavioural symptom of state anxiety is the avoidance of a situation. A high anxious student will refuse to demonstrate or perform a difficult and demanding task. In milder situations she will express her doubts about her abilities to perform the task at hand, her worries about failure, her concerns about negative evaluations and, in some cases, her embarrassment about performing. The experience of state anxiety can also lead to unusually poor performances and poor class attendance.

Disturbance of Cognitive Processes

Physical education, as an educational discipline, involves the teaching of many new motor skills. However, the time available for training these skills is less than that available in competitive sport. Hence, the lesson may elicit a great amount of stress on cognitive processes, such as attention, memory and problem solving. In sport psychology research, substantial evidence suggests that increased state anxiety deteriorates the efficacy of several cognitive processes (Hardy et al., 1996). Although there is no such research in physical education, a similar pattern is likely to exist. Anxious students are likely to show attentional narrowing, paying attention to a limited number of cues regarding the task at hand. For example, they may focus on the ball's course and forget to move according to the team's tactics, or they fail to see free players in a ball game. Furthermore, anxious students are more easily distracted. High anxious children divide their attention between self-relevant and task-relevant matters, whereas low anxious students focus more on the task at hand. Additionally, state anxiety is expected to result in an impaired working memory. For example, an anxious student will ask the physical educator to describe the elements of a new task many times, or he will continuously forget the instructions on how to improve a movement. Furthermore, anxiety may result in long-term memory impairment (i.e., anxious students will not be able to use the elements of tasks taught in the past to perform a new task).

Measurement of State Anxiety in Physical Education

State anxiety in sport and exercise has been assessed through overt behaviour, physiological indexes and self-report measures, with the self-report measures being the most commonly used method. Researchers in general and sport psychology developed different instruments to estimate

EXERCISE 2

Identify a high anxious student. Write down the symptoms through which this student expresses state anxiety. Repeat this procedure with another high anxious student. Make a list of the symptoms of state anxiety in your class.

state and trait anxiety. Furthermore, researchers developed multidimensional measures of trait and state anxiety. Spielberger (1972), Nitsch (1975) and Martens (1977) proliferated long ago the use of sport-specific rather than general anxiety scales for the estimation of anxiety in sporting situations. In this vein, Hackfort and Schwenkmezger (1993) argued that a simple transfer of anxiety measures from general to sport psychology is not very promising and supported the distinction among different sport-related situations with respect to the task at hand (i.e., the type of sport). This need for diverse anxiety measures is more evident across different sporting contexts such as competitive sport, physical education and recreation, where the focus of involvement may differ. With regard to state anxiety in sport, the most widely used instrument in sport research is the *Competitive State Anxiety Inventory—2* (*CSAI-2;* Martens et al., 1990). *CSAI-2* was developed to measure cognitive and somatic anxiety and self-confidence in competitive situations. This instrument has been mainly employed in research on anxiety in physical education (Cecchini et al., 2001; Papaioannou & Kouli, 1999; Stadulis, MacCraken, Eidson & Severance, 2002).

Nevertheless, several practical and theoretical issues have caused some researchers to question the use of *CSAI-2* in the context of school physical education. Notwithstanding the wide acceptance of *CSAI-2* in the scientific community, recent studies questioned its factorial validity in sport (Cox, Martens & Russell, 2003; Lane, Sewell, Terry, Bartram & Nesti, 1999). Stadulis and colleagues (2002), who attempted to adapt the scale to school-age children and in the context of physical education, did not confirm the original factor structure and presented an alternative structure of 15 items. Furthermore, the *CSAI-2* assesses the dimensions of state anxiety experienced prior to a competitive situation, not during the learning process. Because of the highly stressful nature of competition, it could also be argued that the anxiety symptoms measured with *CSAI-2* are rather intense and not likely to manifest in school physical education environments. Moreover, physical education, as an educational discipline, places more emphasis on learning new tasks than sport does. Both anecdotal evidence and research, as mentioned earlier, revealed that students are likely to experience state anxiety during the learning process and not

only in the face of competition. Based on these considerations, Barkoukis (2001) developed an instrument to measure state anxiety in the specific context of physical education: the *Physical Education State Anxiety Scale (PESAS).*

Physical Education State Anxiety Scale

The development of *PESAS* was based on the distinction in multidimensional anxiety theory between cognitive and somatic anxiety. Both dimensions were included in the scale accompanied by a third subscale, *cognitive processes.* Therefore, *PESAS* consists of *somatic anxiety, worry** and *cognitive processes* subscales. The *somatic anxiety* subscale—similar to that of *CSAI-2*—assesses bodily symptoms. *CSAI-2* uses items to assess more intense symptoms of body tension such as 'My body feels tense', 'I feel jittery', 'My body feels tight', 'My heart is racing' and 'I feel my stomach sinking'. On the other hand, *PESAS* incorporated milder symptoms of body tension such as 'I feel as though I am short of breath', 'I sense a feeling of pressure on my chest' and 'I feel as if something is choking me'. The use of such statements was preferred because a physical education lesson is not as competitive as sport is.

The *worry* subscale, similar to *CSAI-2*'s *cognitive anxiety* subscale, assesses negative expectations about performance and the consequences of potential failure. *CSAI-2*'s items are mostly focused on competition ('I am concerned about this competition', 'I am concerned about losing', 'I am concerned about performing poorly', 'I am concerned that I may not do as well in this competition as I could') and less on process and evaluative issues ('I am concerned that others will be disappointed with my performance', 'I am concerned I won't be able to concentrate', 'I am concerned about reaching my goal'). On the other hand, *PESAS* gives equal emphasis to the learning process ('I am concerned about making errors during task execution', 'When performing the task, I feel uneasy about potential mistakes'), the evaluation ('I am concerned about the results of failure when performing the task', 'I think about the consequences of possible mistakes in the task') and performance ('I worry that I will perform badly', 'I worry a lot about the physical test'). These statements were found, through

* The term *worry* was selected over the term *cognitive anxiety* to avoid confusion with the *cognitive processes* subscale.

pilot studies, to be more appropriate in physical education lessons involving the learning process and the evaluation of learning.

A *cognitive processes* subscale was introduced to estimate symptoms related to information processing during physical education lessons. As mentioned earlier, the experience of state anxiety can create cognitive interference during learning and performing physical skills. Smith, Smoll and Schutz (1990) included such a subscale (namely, *concentration disruption*) in their *Sport Anxiety Scale.* Stadulis and colleagues (2002) attempted to adapt this subscale with elementary school children and include it in the revised-for-children version of *CSAI-2,* without success. Barkoukis (2001) expanded this subscale to include more cognitive processes, such as memory, attention, thinking and problem solving. In the initial pool of items, these processes were entered as separate factors, but statistical analyses suggested one global factor, which integrated all these processes. The items of this subscale measure aspects of attention ('I find it difficult to focus on the PE tasks presented'), working memory ('I find it difficult to retain information in my memory regarding the tasks presented'), long-term memory recall ('I find it difficult to remember PE tasks I already know'), thinking ('Irrelevant thoughts disturb my thinking') and problem solving ('I have difficulty understanding the pattern of such complex tasks').

Development of *PESAS* followed a systematic procedure (Barkoukis, 2001). An initial pool of 75 items assessing cognitive anxiety, somatic anxiety, self-confidence and the cognitive processes was developed. The items were derived from general and sport psychology anxiety scales and adapted for the physical education context or were developed for this purpose. Sport psychology experts tested the face validity of the items. Exploratory factor analyses suggested a four-factor structure: *worry, somatic anxiety, cognitive processes* and *self-confidence.* A subsequent pilot study resulted in the rejection of the *self-confidence* subscale because there was no clear theoretical framework

integrating it as an anxiety dimension. Thus, the final form of the scale consisted of three subscales: *worry, somatic anxiety* and *cognitive processes.*

A preliminary test of the scale's psychometric properties confirmed the proposed factor structure (CFI = .92; RMSEA = .06), supported the internal consistency of the subscales (alphas ranged from .79 to .83) and provided some evidence of the predictive validity of the scale; the *anxiety* subscales were negative predictors of shot put performance (Barkoukis, Tsorbatzoudis, Grouios & Rodafinos, 2005). Barkoukis (2003) administered jointly the *PESAS* and the Greek version of *CSAI-2* (Tsorbatzoudis, Barkoukis, Sideridis & Grouios, 2002) in physical education classes. The multitrait-multimethod approach used with the data supported the construct validity of the scale. The examination of both scales' factor structure confirmed the structure of *PESAS* (CFI = .93), whereas the fit indices were not acceptable for *CSAI-2* (CFI = .84).

Data from Barkoukis (2003) indicated also that the subscales of *PESAS* were significant predictors of several cognitive, affective and behavioural elements of the physical education lesson. Worry was found to be a negative predictor of performance in a basketball drill, of self-efficacy to perform this drill and of the effort applied. Cognitive processes were negative predictors of effort and intrinsic interest, and positive predictors of self-handicapping and obligatory participation in the task. These findings provide evidence of the predictive validity of the scale. More importantly, they denote the existence of state anxiety in physical education lessons and its association with a maladaptive response pattern. Finally, the findings underscore the significance of measuring the information-processing symptoms of state anxiety in school physical education because they seem to have contributed substantially to the understanding of cognition, affect and behaviour in physical education lessons. To sum up, the *PESAS* (see figure 4.2) has been found to have satisfactory levels of factorial, construct and predictive

EXERCISE 3

Administer **PESAS** to your class to measure the state anxiety in your students. Identify the students experiencing state anxiety. Discuss with them the situations in the class that trigger the anxiety response.

Directions: Below you will find some statements about how boys and girls feel when they perform tasks in physical education lessons. Please read each statement; then circle the appropriate number to the right of the statement to indicate *how you feel right now* prior to the execution of physical education tasks. There are no right or wrong answers. Do not spend too much time on each statement, but choose the answer that best describes your feelings *right now.*

	Not at all	Some- what	Moder- ately so	Fairly	Very much
1. I find it difficult to remember information about the tasks presented.	1	2	3	4	5
2. I feel as though I am short of breath.	1	2	3	4	5
3. I am concerned about making errors during task execution.	1	2	3	4	5
4. I find it difficult to focus on the PE task presented.	1	2	3	4	5
5. I feel discomfort when I breathe.	1	2	3	4	5
6. When performing the tasks, I feel uneasy about potential mistakes.	1	2	3	4	5
7. I find it difficult to memorise information regarding the tasks presented.	1	2	3	4	5
8. I feel dizzy.	1	2	3	4	5
9. I worry a lot about the physical tests.	1	2	3	4	5
10. I find it difficult to remember PE tasks I already know.	1	2	3	4	5
11. I sense a feeling of pressure on my chest.	1	2	3	4	5
12. I am concerned about failing when per- forming the tasks.	1	2	3	4	5
13. Irrelevant thoughts disturb my thinking.	1	2	3	4	5
14. My body is aching.	1	2	3	4	5
15. I think about the consequences of pos- sible mistakes in the test.	1	2	3	4	5
16. I have difficulty understanding the pattern of such complex tasks.	1	2	3	4	5
17. I feel as if something is choking me.	1	2	3	4	5
18. I worry that I will perform badly.	1	2	3	4	5

Note: Items 1, 4, 7, 10, 13 and 16 represent cognitive processes; items 2, 5, 8, 11, 14 and 17 represent somatic anxiety; items 3, 6, 9, 12, 15 and 18 represent worry.

Figure 4.2 The Physical Education State Anxiety Scale (PESAS).

validity, and reliability. Thus, it is considered a valid and reliable tool to measure state anxiety in physical education.

Research on State Anxiety in Physical Education

Although some research on negative affect in physical education exists (Ntoumanis & Biddle, 1999), state anxiety in physical education has drawn little attention in the literature so far. Papaioannou and Kouli (1999) examined the effect of class structure on state anxiety. Students in task-involving environments reported lower somatic anxiety. Moreover, students who perceived their teachers as mastery oriented were less anxious than those who perceived their teachers as performance oriented. Barkoukis (2001), who also examined the influence of motivation climate on feelings of state anxiety, found similar results. Ten weeks after the application of an intervention programme fostering a task-involving motivational climate, labeled TARGET, students in the experimental group reported lower levels of somatic anxiety than those of the control group. By manipulating class climate, Cury and his associates (Cury, Da Fonséca, Rufo, Peres & Sarrazin, 2003; Cury, Elliot, Sarrazin, Da Fonséca & Rufo, 2002) created a mastery condition, a performance-approach condition and a performance-avoidance condition. In both studies, the performance-avoidance condition elicited higher levels of state anxiety, whereas the performance-approach condition generated higher anxiety levels than did the mastery condition. Furthermore, state anxiety was negatively associated with intrinsic motivation and investment in learning. In contrast to these, Cecchini and colleagues (2001) showed that a mastery motivational climate—apart from enjoyment, perceived ability and commitment—was also associated with somatic anxiety after four weeks of TARGET application.

With regard to the dispositional achievement goals, data from Barkoukis (2003) indicated that performance-avoidance goals were positive predictors of all the state anxiety dimensions measured with PESAS (worry, somatic anxiety and cognitive processes). Furthermore, performance-approach goals positively predicted PESAS' cognitive processes, whereas mastery goals were negative predictors of PESAS' cognitive processes. Ommundsen (2001) had similar findings with

respect to trait anxiety; ego-oriented students experienced higher levels of trait anxiety in physical education lessons than task-oriented students did. In general, these findings support the achievement goal theory, which states that (1) the adoption of performance goals is associated with a maladaptive pattern of affective responses in physical activity contexts, and (2) the adoption of a mastery-oriented motivational climate will have a positive influence on students' affective experiences.

Practical Recommendations

Research has shown that a mastery-oriented motivational climate is associated with the promotion of positive experiences and a decrease in state anxiety and other negative affective states. Therefore, physical education teachers should adopt such a motivational climate. The TARGET is an intervention protocol that provides a framework for strategies enhancing a mastery-oriented motivational climate. Ames (1992) and Treasure (2001) described the TARGET dimensions in detail. Following are some strategies most likely to reduce state anxiety in physical education lessons:

1. Use playful drills and allow children to learn through play. Children are more likely to 'forget' their concerns and negative thoughts in a playful, fun and enjoyable environment.

2. Organise the lesson according to students' needs and abilities. Select drills that the majority of students can perform, and increase difficulty gradually. Let the students' pace guide the learning process. Do not use very complex drills unless the students are ready to perform them.

3. When introducing a difficult or novel task, form groups of similar capability. For example, in the introductory unit of the floater serve, you can form a group of students who can pass the ball over the net and a group of student who cannot. In this case, the less skilled students compare themselves with students of similar ability. In subsequent units or during play, mixed ability groups are considered more effective.

4. Provide alternative drills at which less skilled and less competent children can

succeed. When some student can't perform a drill, offer them an easier drill that practices the same task. When they succeed, move them to a more difficult drill. Likewise, if they are not good in a sport, introduce them to a different sport and let them spend more time on it.

5. Help students establish a positive ratio between effort and achievement. Make clear to students that effort will lead to adequate performance. Use activities at which students can succeed with some effort.

6. Provide opportunities for all students to achieve. It is important for all students to feel able. This will foster intrinsic interest and enjoyment. For example, change the characteristic of a drill (intensity, distance, etc.) to allow less competent students to perform the drill adequately.

7. Use the goal-setting cycle: Help students set personal goals; give them time to work on their goals; help them evaluate the attainment of their goals; and then help them set new, more challenging goals. Personal and challenging goals keep students focused on the task at hand and on personal improvement regardless of the normative level of their abilities.

8. Provide feedback on personal improvement. Make clear to students that personal improvement is what you care about. Praise and reinforce effort, personal improvement

and attainment of personal goals, but do not emphasise winning. Provide feedback to all students, not just the skilled ones.

9. Explain the evaluation procedures to students. During lessons, use drills similar to those you will use in testing. Adopt effort and personal improvement, not normative standards, as grading criteria. Provide students with opportunities to evaluate themselves.

Summary

Anxiety is an unpleasant emotional state experienced in achievement settings such as school physical education. After reading this chapter, you should understand the nature of anxiety and distinguish it from other relevant terms such as *arousal* and *stress*. You should also understand the main sources of state anxiety in physical education (i.e., trait anxiety, perceptions of low competence, peer comparison, social evaluation and grading) and be able to identify the major cognitive, emotional, physiological, behavioural and information-processing symptoms of state anxiety. The measure used to estimate the levels of your students' state anxiety described in this chapter should help you identify the occurrence and the levels of state anxiety in your students. Current research in physical education illustrates the association between state anxiety and other psychological constructs in physical education. This

---

EXERCISE 4

- Go back to the list of stressful situations you created in exercise 1. Find the most appropriate strategy to overcome each one.

- Reorganise the daily plan for your next lesson to include anxiety-reducing strategies, such as alternative drills for less competent students, opportunities for achievement for all students and an emphasis on personal improvement.

- Select one or two drills for each sport that you believe to be crucial for adequate performance and employ the goal-setting cycle.

- Videotape a teaching unit. Write down how many times you provided feedback on personal improvement, if you provided alternative drills to less competent students and if you provided opportunities for achievement. Write down how exercise groups were formed and how students interacted. Evaluate yourself on the effective application of anxiety-reducing strategies.

chapter included recommendations to reduce the experience of state anxiety in your students. The application of these recommendations to physical education classes will promote a task-involving motivational climate, reduce state anxiety and foster positive cognitive and emotional experiences in physical education.

Review Questions

1. What is anxiety, and how does it differ from stress and arousal?
2. What is the difference between state anxiety and trait anxiety?
3. What is the difference between cognitive anxiety and somatic anxiety?
4. What are the major sources of anxiety in physical education?
5. How is anxiety manifested in physical education lessons?
6. Why should cognitive processes be measured in a scale assessing state anxiety in physical education?
7. How are achievement goals and motivational climate associated with anxiety in physical education?
8. What strategies could physical educators employ to diminish the experience of state anxiety in their students?

Critical Thinking Questions

1. Observe and compare students' behaviour in several sport activities during recesses and physical education lessons. Are there any differences in the performance and affective state of the students?
2. Integrate the recommendations of this chapter with those reported in other chapters regarding motivational climate to develop a task-oriented environment in your physical education classes.
3. Identify self-handicappers and students who are ashamed to perform in front of others. Do they perform worse than the other students or report less satisfaction and enjoyment from the lesson? What can you do (and why) to change these behaviours?
4. You are a teacher at the beginning of a school year of a class in which many students try to avoid new and challenging tasks. What kind of strategies can you employ to reverse this situation?

Key Terms

anxiety—An unpleasant emotional state elicited by a nonspecific and nonconscious danger.

arousal—Activation of the autonomic nervous system; it varies from deep sleep to intense excitement.

cognitive anxiety—Negative expectations about performance and cognitive concerns about oneself and the task at hand.

somatic anxiety—The bodily symptoms of the anxiety experience.

state anxiety—A transitory emotional state characterised by feelings of tension and apprehension.

stress—The reactions to a threatening stimulus that disturb a person's homeostasis.

trait anxiety—A tendency to perceive environmental stimuli as threatening and to respond with state anxiety.

References

Allen, J.B. (2003). Social motivation in youth sport. *Journal of Sport and Exercise Psychology, 25,* 551-567.

Ames, C. (1992). Classrooms: Goals, structures, and student motivation. *Journal of Educational Psychology, 84,* 261-271.

Bandura, A. (1997). *Self-efficacy: The exercise of control.* New York: W.H. Freeman.

Barkoukis, V. (2001). *The effect of motivational climate on motivation, anxiety and learning of track and field tasks.* Unpublished doctoral dissertation: Aristotle University of Thessaloniki, Greece.

Barkoukis, V. (2003). *Extending research on the achievement goal approaches with the study of multiple goals and their effect on cognitive and emotional variables during physical education lessons.* Unpublished postdoctoral dissertation: National Scholarship Foundation, Athens, Greece.

Barkoukis, V., Tsorbatzoudis, H., Grouios, G. & Rodafinos, A. (2005). The development of a physical education state anxiety scale: A preliminary study. *Perceptual and Motor Skills, 100,* 118-128.

Cecchini, J.A., González, C., Carmona, A.M., Arruza, J., Escartí, A. & Balagué, G. (2001). The influence of the physical education teacher on intrinsic motivation, self-confidence, anxiety, and pre- and post-competition mood states. *European Journal of Sport Science, 1,* 1-12.

Cox, R., Martens, M. & Russell, W. (2003). Measuring anxiety in athletics: The revised Competitive State Anxiety Inventory—2. *Journal of Sport and Exercise Psychology, 25,* 519-533.

Cury, F., Da Fonséca, D., Rufo, M., Peres, C. & Sarrazin, P. (2003). The trichotomous model and investment in learning to prepare for a sport test: A mediational analysis. *British Journal of Educational Psychology, 73,* 529–543.

Cury, F., Elliot, A., Sarrazin, P., Da Fonséca, D. & Rufo, M. (2002). The trichotomous achievement goal model and intrinsic motivation: A sequential mediational analysis. *Journal of Experimental Social Psychology, 38,* 473–481.

Gould, D., Greenleaf, C. & Krane, V. (2002). Arousal-anxiety and sport behavior. In T. Horn (Ed.), *Advances in sport psychology* (2nd ed., pp. 207-241). Champaign, IL: Human Kinetics.

Hackfort, D. & Schwenkmezger, P. (1993). Anxiety. In R. Singer, M. Murphy & L. Tennant (Eds.), *Handbook of research on sport psychology* (pp. 328-364). New York: Macmillan.

Hardy, L., Jones, G. & Gould, D. (1996). *Understanding psychological preparation in sport: Theory and practice of elite performers.* Chichester, UK: Wiley.

Lane, A.M., Sewell, D.F., Terry, P.C., Bartram, D. & Nesti, M.S. (1999). Confirmatory factor analysis of the Competitive State Anxiety Inventory—2. *Journal of Sport Sciences, 17,* 502-512.

Lox, C.L., Martin, K.A. & Petruzzello, S.J. (2003). *The psychology of exercise: Integrating theory and practice.* Scottsdale, AR: Holcomb Hathaway.

Martens, R. (1977). *Sport competition anxiety test.* Champaign, IL: Human Kinetics.

Martens, R., Vealey, R. & Burton, D. (1990). *Competitive anxiety in sport.* Champaign, IL: Human Kinetics.

May, R. (1977). *The meaning of anxiety.* New York: Norton.

McGrath, J.E. (1970). Major methodological issues. In J.E. McGrath (Ed.), *Social and psychological factors in stress* (pp.19-49). New York: Holt, Rinehart, & Winston.

Nitsch, J. (1975). Sportliches Handeln als handlungsmodell [Action in sport as action model]. *Sportwissenschaft [Sport Science], 5,* 39-55.

Ntoumanis, N. & Biddle, S.J.H. (1999). Affect and achievement goals in physical activity: A meta-analysis. *Scandinavian Journal of Medicine and Science in Sport (Special issue: European perspectives in Sport Motivation Research), 9,* 315-332.

Ommundsen, Y. (2001). Pupils' affective responses in physical education classes: The association of implicit theories of the nature of ability and achievement goals. *European Physical Education Review, 7,* 219-242.

Papaioannou, A. & Kouli, O. (1999). The effects of task structure, perceived motivational climate and goal orientations on students' task involvement and anxiety. *Journal of Applied Sport Psychology, 11,* 51-71.

Rawsthorne, L.J. & Elliot, A.J. (1999). Achievement goals and intrinsic motivation: A meta-analytic review. *Personality and Social Psychology Review, 3,* 326-344.

Roberts, G. (2001). Understanding the dynamics of motivation in physical activity: The influence of achievement goals on motivational processes. In G. Roberts (Ed.), *Advances in motivation in sport and exercise* (pp. 1-50). Champaign, IL: Human Kinetics.

Skinner, R.A. & Piek, J.A. (2001). Psychological implications of poor motor coordination in children and adolescents. *Human Movement Science, 20,* 73-94.

Smith, R., Smoll, F. & Schutz, R. (1990). Measurement and correlates of sport-specific cognitive and somatic trait anxiety: The Sport Anxiety Scale. *Anxiety Research, 2,* 263-280.

Spielberger, C. (1972). Anxiety as an emotional state. In C. Spielberger (Ed.), *Anxiety: Current trends in theory and research* (pp. 23-49). New York: Academic Press.

Stadulis, R.E., MacCracken, M.J., Eidson, T.A. & Severance, C. (2002). A children's form of the Competitive State Anxiety Inventory: The CSAI-2C. *Measurement in Physical Education and Exercise Science, 6*(3), 147-165.

Treasure, D. (2001). Enhancing young people's motivation in youth sport: An achievement goal approach. In G. Roberts (Ed.), *Advances in motivation in sport and exercise* (pp. 263-320). Champaign, IL: Human Kinetics.

Tremayne, P. (1995). Children and sport psychology. In T. Morris & J. Sunders (Eds.), *Sport psychology: Theory, applications and issues* (pp. 516-537). Chichester, UK: Wiley.

Tsorbatzoudis, H., Barkoukis, V., Sideridis, G. & Grouios, G. (2002). Confirmatory factor analysis of the Greek version of the Competitive State Anxiety Inventory—2 (CSAI-2). *International Journal of Sport Psychology, 33,* 182-194.

Weinberg, R. & Gould, D. (2003). *Foundations of sport and exercise psychology.* Champaign, IL: Human Kinetics.

part two

Promotion of Social Skills for Life

Yves Vanden Auweele

Social skills development is a basic physical education curriculum goal in its own right because contemporary life places a premium on citizens' ability to relate well to others, to work effectively in groups and to deal with interpersonal conflicts and tensions. Schools have an increased responsibility for helping pupils learn the skills needed to cope with these life challenges. A class that develops mutual support and trust contains opportunities for constructive peer feedback and feelings of acceptance (Gallagher, 1994; Weinstein, 1991). Positive school relationships play an important role in developing social resilience in adult life, whereas poor school relationships can lead to social vulnerability (Vettenburg, 1988).

A second justification for having social skills development as a curriculum goal is the important part social processes play in the creation of a supportive emotional and motivational climate. Such a climate can facilitate the implementation of the other major curriculum goals: 'development of a mature self concept, the acquisition of motor skills, and the development of the right attitude in children to enable them to develop and maintain an active and healthy lifestyle'. The physical education task will benefit from relational issues being settled to some degree; it is very difficult to focus on learning when one feels rejected by peers (Schmuck & Schmuck, 1992; Tuckman, 1992).

Part II includes three chapters, drawing on expertise from Finland, Belgium and Greece. In chapter 5, 'Social and Emotional Learning in Physical Education', Taru Lintunen and Marjo Kuusela describe the teaching and use of social and emotional skills in the physical education context. The emphasis of the chapter is on the description of the basic social and emotional skills, and not so much on the research behind these skills. Supportive emotional climate, positive experiences and enjoyment are important goals—and means—in physical education classes. They provide the participants with a good foundation for the practice of lifelong exercise activity. The teaching and use of social and emotional skills are ways of achieving a supportive learning atmosphere.

Chapter 5 defines the concept of social and emotional skills. The skills taught to the students are the basic counselling skills used in many forms of psychotherapy, such as active listening; clear expression of feelings, beliefs and thoughts and problem-solving skills. Because they are skills, like motor skills, practice is an important part of learning. Student-centred, action-oriented teaching and learning methods are essential. Narratives are presented as examples of the use of social and emotional skills in the physical education context.

In chapter 6, 'Facilitating Prosocial Behaviour in Physical Education', Risto Telama and Singa Polvi discuss prosocial behaviour, which they define as positive social behaviour, including consideration of others, a willingness to cooperate genuinely with others, altruistic feelings and especially helping behaviour. It is also defined as the lack of negative social behaviour, such as violence and bullying. In modern educational programmes, cultivating altruism and prosocial behaviour may be considered one of the most important attitudinal goals. It is desirable for adults in our society to be concerned not only for their own well-being but also for the well-being of others. Altruistic and prosocial behaviours must be acquired.

Physical education in schools has for a long time regarded the promotion of prosocial behaviour as one of its main goals. However, the implementation of this goal has not been consistent and deliberate because of the belief that physical activity, in and of itself, develops prosocial behaviour. Even though we must give up the old belief that physical activity naturally develops people ethically and socially, it remains a fact that physical activity and physical education share features that lend themselves to such development. In physical activity it is easy to create genuine interactive relations that encourage people to observe, give feedback to, support and help others. Physical activity also offers opportunities for solving conflicts between individuals through dialogue and discussion.

Prosocial skills are learned just as any other skills are. Chapter 6 provides a teaching methodology that focuses on real social interaction and genuine cooperation among students.

Chapter 7, 'Group Development in the Physical Education Class', by Johan Hovelynck, Yves Vanden Auweele and Thanasis Mouratidis, considers the physical education class as a task group that is more than a collection of individuals. It is a social system in which evolving goals, roles, procedures and interpersonal relationships are important issues to be understood in order to make the class more manageable and a good medium for social skill development.

The rationale for chapter 7 is based on the following key propositions. First, a physical education class group, like any other class or group of people, is more than a mere collection of students. As individuals do, the class as a whole develops during an academic year. Second, the group processes within a class can enhance the social development of individual students. Third, the social experiences that students acquire as their class develops are also learning experiences. Moreover, a well-developed classroom, in which students feel competent in dealing with their academic tasks and their interpersonal relations, constitutes an appropriate learning environment.

At the core of group development theory lies the assumption that the interactions that take place among group members are the driving force of class development. At each stage of development, students have certain needs that should be met to enable them to mature both as individuals and as a class. However, because neither individual students nor the class as a whole develops automatically toward a more mature stage, teachers must create strategies to influence class development. The authors of chapter 7 describe and exemplify several class management approaches to facilitate group development at each of the developmental stages.

References

Gallagher, J. (1994). Teaching and learning: new models. *Annual Review of Psychology, 45,* 171-195.

Schmuck, R., & Schmuck, P. (1992). *Group processes in the classroom.* Dubuque, IA: Brown.

Tuckman, B. (1992). *Educational psychology: From theory to application.* Fort Worth, TX: Harcourt.

Vettenburg, M. (1988). *Schoolervaringen, delinkwentie en maatschappelijke kwetsbaarheid [School experiences, delinquency and social vulnerability].* Leuven: Report of the K.U.L. research group on youth criminology.

Weinstein, C. (1991). The classroom as a social context for learning. *Annual Review of Psychology, 42,* 493-526.

chapter five

Social and Emotional Learning in Physical Education

Taru Lintunen
Marjo Kuusela
University of Jyväskylä, Finland

After reading this chapter, you will be able to do the following:

- Explain the relevance of social and emotional learning in physical education

- Consider the physical education experience as an opportunity to use and teach social and emotional skills

- Define active listening, clear expression of emotions, problem-solving skills, team-building skills and the ecosystemic approach

- Start practising basic social and emotional skills in your personal and professional life

The purpose of this chapter is to describe the teaching and use of social and emotional skills in the physical education context. Socioemotional skills have a particular importance for both the teachers and students of physical education. Socially and emotionally competent behaviour helps to create a supportive learning atmosphere, positive experiences and enjoyment, which are important goals—and means—in physical education classes. Students who have received positive experiences and enjoyment from physical education have a good foundation for the practice of lifelong exercise activity. In addition, because PE classes are action oriented, they provide a lot of interaction and real-life situations that teachers can use to advantage.

PE lessons are public in the sense that everybody present can see how each student performs. As a result, embarrassment may stop a student from participating. It is no wonder that the PE classroom has been seen as a laboratory of emotional and social skills. These skills are also tools for teachers to use to cope with the stress caused by the demands at work. Moreover, there is increasing recognition of the need to incorporate social and emotional learning into the regular instructional programme.

The importance of social and emotional learning for youth has been well documented in the literature. Such learning has a critical role in improving children's academic performance and lifelong learning (Zins, Weissberg, Wang & Walberg, 2004). Social and emotional skills are becoming increasingly important as young people face difficult challenges at school and in their personal lives. Research indicates that psychologically competent young people are likely to avoid high-risk activities that can have dangerous consequences for their health and well-being (Ross, Powell & Elias, 2002).

Social and Emotional Skills, Competencies and Learning

Social and emotional skills must be taught to students and athletes. Even though physical education and sports often have goals related to social and emotional skills, such as fair play and character education, we seldom seek to improve these skills by applying a specific method. However,

numerous programmes have been constructed for advancing socioemotional skills. Illustrative of this diversity is the fact that many terms have been used to describe the construct we call social and emotional skills, including *life skills, emotional intelligence, emotional literacy, emotional skills, social skills* and *social and emotional learning.*

Social and emotional competence can be defined as the ability to understand, manage and express the social and emotional aspects of one's life in ways that enable the successful management of life tasks such as learning, forming relationships, solving everyday problems and adapting to the complex demands of growth and development (Elias et al., 1997, p. 2; Saarni, 2000). Social and emotional learning refers to how these competencies are learned through the curriculum and the whole school experience (Elias, 2006; Weare, 2004, p. 7). Social and emotional competence is often seen to consist of individual characteristics, such as skills, attitudes and behaviours. In addition, social and emotional learning is also a social process and systemic phenomenon (Zins, Bloodworth, Weissberg & Walberg, 2004). It can be seen, for example, in the atmosphere of the class, and in participants' boldness and willingness to express their thoughts, emotions and needs openly; to make suggestions to the teacher; and to give feedback to other members of the class (Kuusela, 2005). Even though social and emotional competence is an individual characteristic, it becomes apparent in the interaction with the person and the environment. It is a question of communal-level learning. The aim is not only to teach teachers and the students individually but also to help the whole school community develop good practices.

We follow the school of thought that social and emotional skills are—at least partly—learned. Emotional skills have their conceptual origin in emotional intelligence research. Emotional intelligence encompasses four interrelated abilities involved in the processing of emotional information: perceiving emotions, using emotions to facilitate thinking, understanding emotions and regulating one's own emotions and the emotions of others (Mayer & Salovey, 1997). These abilities are thought to be important for social interaction because emotions serve communicative and social functions. Out of these four abilities, emotion regulation is probably the most important for social interaction because it influences emotional expression and behaviour directly. One inappropriate outburst of anger can destroy a relationship forever. Emotion regulation can operate through cognitive, expressive, behavioural and physiological processes. It is a domain in which, as with sport skills, practising is essential for expert performance (Lopes, Salovey, Côté & Beers, 2005).

The concept of emotional intelligence is useful in describing emotional aspects. However, a great deal of the content of the programme we have developed and use with teachers and students comes from the practical experience of social and clinical psychology and psychotherapy. The skills include the basic counselling skills used in many forms of psychotherapy, such as **active listening**; the clear expression of feelings, beliefs and thoughts; and problem-solving skills (see Geldard, 1989; Gordon, 2003; Greenberg & Paivio, 1997;

Hill, 2004; Ivey & Bradford Ivey, 2003). The skills of taking responsibility, collaborating and team-building skills are derived from the social psychological research on group dynamics (Carron & Hausenblas, 1998; Rovio, Lintunen, Eskola, 2007). In addition, the **ecosystemic approach** (Molnar & Lindquist, 1989) is also useful for teachers, especially in problem situations. According to research findings and practical experience, these tools are useful for improving social and emotional learning at school.

Reading books is not the most effective way to learn social and emotional skills. Like motor skills, they must be practised. Learner-centred, dialogical and action-oriented teaching and learning methods are essential (McCombs, 2004). Skills, attitudes and values are all important. Genuineness, empathy and unconditional acceptance of students are all preconditions of effective learning.

Genuineness, empathy and unconditional acceptance of students are all preconditions of effective teaching.

Guidelines for Practice

The narratives, or stories, in this section illustrate how a change of perspective or choice of words can have a great impact on the learning atmosphere.

Active Listening

Active listening is a basic skill in communication and an essential aspect of every orientation course in counselling. It is a method of listening in which the listener reflects back to the speaker his or her understanding of what the person has said. This is meant to confirm that the listener has understood the message and to give the speaker a chance to correct the listener if necessary. More important, however, is that active listening communicates the listener's acceptance of the speaker's thoughts and emotions (Gordon, 2003, pp. 91-124; Hill, 2004, pp. 99-160; Ivey & Bradford Ivey, 2003, pp. 125-147; Weare, 2004, pp. 116-119).

Active listening does not involve dispensing advice or making suggestions, and it is nonjudgmental. It requires that the listener make the speaker believe that he is really listening to her and valuing her and wants to understand what she has to say. Unfortunately, teachers seldom use active listening, and it is not always included in teacher training programmes, even though it might be of value in many of the social interaction occasions that arise in school. Consequently, hardly any research exists on the use of active listening in the school context. Our study (Kuusela, 2005; Lintunen, Kuusela & Millner, 2007) seeks to redress this situation by examining the effects of the use of active listening by the physical education teacher. Examples follow.

Teacher Assumes a Positive Role

At the beginning of a physical education lesson, students often explain why they are unable to participate. Students believe that they need to convince the teacher that they really have, for example, a malady that prevents them from participating in the lesson. Such a situation may, despite the teacher's intention, lead to a negative and teacher-controlled atmosphere. In these cases the teacher can use active listening. The following example illustrates how one such discussion went at the beginning of a PE lesson:

Student: Teacher, I can't do PE today, but my mother didn't remember to write you a note about it.

Teacher: What's the matter with you?

Student: Well, I fainted yesterday, and I thought that it might not be wise to do PE.

Teacher: You're afraid that you'll faint again in the middle of the class?

Student: Yes.

Teacher: It makes sense to be careful.

When the class began, this student was sitting and watching on the sidelines. However, after a while the teacher realised that the student was exercising with the others. In the middle of the class the teacher even had to remind the girl to take it easy because she was carrying her friend on her back. In spite of the fact that students ask to be exempted from lessons, they often choose to participate, at least to the extent that their physical problems allow.

In our study, the atmosphere improved as a result of the teacher's use of active listening at the onset of the physical education lessons (Kuusela, 2005; Lintunen et al., 2007). The students were more open and willing to talk about their feelings and perceptions as compared to earlier. The role of the teacher changed from one of controlling dishonesty to one of ensuring that the students do not overstrain themselves—a much more positive role.

Participants Get More Energy

Students are usually encouraged to achieve, try harder and endure more. Students may find the situation difficult when they run out of strength or reach the limit of their skills. By recognising that they do not need to encourage students constantly or push them to succeed, teachers may help in these situations. Just listening to students' feelings and accepting them seems to give students more energy and motivation.

Student: Running is so heavy on this mat.

Teacher: You are tired of running on this kind of soft surface.

After this discussion, the student continued running.

New Solutions Are Found

At times students cannot participate in physical education because they have other tasks to do. They might have a rehearsal for a play or choir practice, or perhaps need to see the school nurse. In such cases the student asks the teacher for permission to be absent from the lesson. Normally, the teacher will decide whether to excuse the student. The situation is rarely solved constructively, or the student's point of view or position is rarely heard. By means of active listening, teachers can help students make their own decisions, which often results in constructive and well-thought-out solutions. Sometimes students come up with alternatives that even the teacher has not considered. Students seem to have a strong sense of responsibility when they are allowed and encouraged to resolve their problems by themselves. The solution is their own, not one handed down by an authority, as in the following example:

Student: I have to miss class because I have choir practice.

Teacher: You would like to go to choir practice?

Student: Yeah. Well, I'm not sure. I would also really like to play basketball.

Teacher: And now you don't know what to do.

Student: No, not really.

After a little while, the student found a solution.

Student: What if I played basketball for 15 minutes and went to choir practice for the other 15 minutes?

Teacher: That sounds like a good decision.

This solution, to divide the available time into parts and enjoy the result, might not have entered the mind of the teacher.

Clear Expression of Thoughts, Emotions and Needs

When problem situations arise, students are often unable to express their thoughts and emotions clearly. Consequently, they do not take responsibility for themselves. Some students easily stop work and withdraw from the group when everything does not go their way. Sometimes in these situations the student gives up and goes to the locker room muttering something inappropriate. When students are taught to express their feelings and thoughts clearly, this kind of 'speaking in the language of action', or acting-out behaviour, decreases (Kuusela, 2005). Students who can express their needs become more capable of taking responsibility for themselves.

For example, at the end of a planning session for a gladiator competition, one girl raised her hand and said, looking worried, that she did not have the courage to run another time because she was afraid that the balls thrown by the gladiators would hurt her. At the end of a joint discussion, the group changed the rules so that every student could choose a role she felt was best for her. Changing the rules didn't have any influence on the task itself, but it gave the class more responsibility. As a result, the student was able to concentrate on the game without pressure or fear. Instead of trying to opt out of the activity, the student spoke on her own behalf and was able to engage in the task.

When a student causes the teacher or another student a problem, confrontative or problem-solving **I-messages** can be used. With an I-message teachers can explain to the student that his behaviour is causing the teacher a problem, but in a nonblameful manner that reduces the student's resistance to the message. The idea here is to influence the student to want to change his behaviour in consideration of the teacher's needs (and those of other students). A well constructed I-message encourages students to cooperate, and it leaves their self-esteem intact. But more than that, it teaches them a valuable lesson in self-discipline: Students change their behaviour not because they fear the teacher (or because they'll get some sort of reward), but out of consideration for the needs of the teacher and of the class—because they see value in the request. This is how students learn empathy (Gordon, 2003, pp. 142-155).

A problem-solving I-message contains three parts:

1. A description of the unacceptable behaviour: 'You are speaking too loud'.

2. A description of the effect the behaviour has on me: 'It is difficult to teach'.

3. My own feeling: 'And I feel frustrated'.

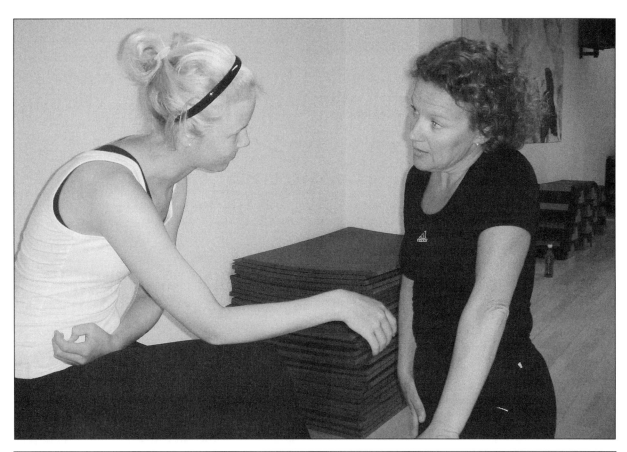

An I-message is an effective way to influence students to want to change their behaviour in consideration of others' needs.

Ecosystemic Methods

In ecosystemic methods, misbehaviour is not looked at as a problem, with a cause and a cure, but as an ecosystem. The ecosystem in which a misbehaviour occurs contains many environmental factors, all of which could have an impact on the behaviour. Changing any one of the factors in an ecosystem could result in the behaviour disappearing. The emphasis in ecosystemic methods is on involvement in the system rather than on observation of the system. The change of perspective enables people to think and behave differently in relation to their experiences.

Ecosystemic techniques (Molnar & Lindquist, 1989) are a form of positive discipline. The method can be individually tailored for specific situations. Instead of trying to control a situation, we should try to change the dynamics that make the situation happen. Instead of assuming that a student is bad, we should try to see things from his or her point of view. We can change a situation without being authoritarian.

For example, consider a scenario in which a student did not want to stop listening to her mp3 player during physical education class. The teacher had already asked her to stop, but talking did not seem to work. Finally, the teacher decided to use the ecosystemic symptom-commanding technique (Molnar & Lindquist, 1989) to solve the problem. Once again the student came to class without the proper attire for physical education and listening to music. Unsuccessfully the teacher asked the student to stop the player and leave it in the locker room.

Teacher: The music you are listening to must be good if you cannot stop it.

Student: Umm . . . .

Teacher: Would it be possible for all of us to listen to it at some point during the lesson?

Student: Yes?

The student plugged her mp3 player in and got changed. The entire class was now able to listen to her music during the lesson, and it brightened the atmosphere. At the end of the lesson everybody was asked to say what had delighted and what had annoyed them during this lesson. Most of the students said that they had been delighted by the music. After this lesson the student with the mp3 player became the class music representative. Every now and then she brought music for the class to listen to. There were no more problems with the issue.

Summary

Students develop emotional skills when teachers plan to include them and model behaviour for the students. Although questions remain regarding the efficacy of social and emotional skills interventions, our position is that effective social and emotional skills interventions are possible and that good treatment effects can be achieved by designing interventions that (1) target specific skills rather than general problems; (2) are comprehensive, intensive, culturally appropriate and long term: and (3) promote the use of skills beyond the training setting (Elksnin & Elksnin, 2003; McCombs, 2004).

Reading books is not the most effective way to learn social and emotional skills. Like motor skills, they must be practised. Learner-centred, action-oriented teaching and learning methods are essential.

By using active listening, encouraging clear self-expression and using ecosystemic methods, teacher can feel competent in dealing with problem situations. Many conflict situations can be resolved without the use of power or displeasure; instead the responsibility for solving problems and changing behaviour can be transferred to students. This confirms their autonomy and gives them a positive self-image. It also gives students more motivation and energy for performance. Thanks to these tools, the teacher can experience problem situations as interesting challenges that become natural situations in which to model emotional skills.

Students are usually motivated to learn social and emotional skills. The students' skill development is made manifest in an improved social atmosphere and in positive behaviour and attitudes toward the other students, the teacher and the lessons in general. The students express their opinions more, and more often share ideas about how the PE lessons should be conducted. This helps to make the lessons more pleasurable for everyone. The overall result is an improvement in the student-teacher relationship and an increase in democracy. Everybody gains something by developing and using emotional skills. Encouraging all teachers and students to acquire emotional skills would do a great deal to empower everyone in the school community.

Review Questions

1. What is the importance of social and emotional skills?
2. In what way is social and emotional learning both an individual characteristic and a social phenomenon?
3. What is active listening?
4. What are three consequences of active listening in PE class?
5. When should I-messages be used?
6. How is misbehaviour looked at according to ecosystemic methods?

Critical Thinking Questions

1. As a PE teacher, you see that a student throws bats away and looks upset. How would you act in this situation? Why do you think your student is doing this?

2. Create positive I-messages and send them to at least three people. Be sure to include the three parts of an I-message. Describe the process of creating these messages and the possible consequences of them.

Key Terms

active listening—A method of listening in which the listener reflects back to the speaker his or her understanding of what the person has said. This is meant to confirm that the listener has understood the message and to give the speaker a chance to correct the listener if necessary.

ecosystemic approach—An approach in which misbehaviour is not looked at as a problem, with a cause and a cure, but as an ecosystem. The ecosystem in which a misbehaviour occurs contains many environmental factors, all of which could have an impact on the behaviour. Changing any one of the factors in an ecosystem could result in the behaviour disappearing.

I-message—A message that includes a description of the behaviour, the effect the behaviour has on the person and the person's feeling.

social and emotional competence—The ability to understand, manage and express the social and emotional aspects of one's life in ways that enable the successful management of life tasks such as learning, forming relationships, solving everyday problems and adapting to the complex demands of growth and development (Elias et al., 1997, p. 2; Saarni, 2000).

References

Carron, A.V. & Hausenblas, H. (1998). *Group dynamics in sport* (2nd ed.). Morgantown, WV: Fitness Information Technology.

Elias, M., Zins, J., Weissberg, R., Frey, K., Greenberg, M., Haynes, N., Kessler, R., Schwabstone, M. & Shriver, T. (1997). *Promoting social and emotional learning.* Alexandria, VA: Association for Supervision and Curriculum Development.

Elias, M.J. (2006). The connection between academic and social-emotional learning. In M. J. Elias & H. Arnold (Eds.), *The educator's guide to emotional intelligence and academic achievement: Social-emotional learning in the classroom* (pp. 4-14). Thousand Oaks, CA: Corwin Press.

Elksnin, L.K. & Elksnin, N. (2003). Fostering social-emotional learning in the classroom. *Education, 124*(1), 63-75.

Geldard, D. 1989. *Basic personal counseling: A training manual for counselors.* Sydney, Australia: Prentice Hall.

Gordon, T. (2003). *Teacher effectiveness training: The program proven to help teachers bring out the best in students of all ages.* New York: Three Rivers Press.

Greenberg, L. & Paivio, S. (1997). *Working with emotions in psychotherapy.* New York: Guilford.

Hill, C.E. (2004). *Helping skills: Facilitating exploration, insight, and action.* Washington, DC: American Psychological Association.

Ivey, A.E. & Bradford Ivey, M.B. (2003). *Intentional interviewing and counselling: Facilitating client development in a multicultural society.* Pacific Grove, CA: Brooks/Cole-Thomson.

Kuusela, M. (2005). *Sosioemotionaalisten taitojen harjaannuttaminen, oppiminen ja käyttäminen perusopetuksen kahdeksannen luokan tyttöjen liikuntatunneilla [Teaching and learning socio-emotional skills in girls' physical education].* A doctoral dissertation. *Liikunnan ja kansanterveyden julkaisuja [LIKES-Research Reports on Sport and Health], 165.* Jyväskylä, Finland: LIKES.

Lintunen, T., Kuusela, M. & Millner, V. (2006). *Teaching and using social and emotional skills in physical education: A qualitative case study.* Manuscript submitted for publication.

Lopes, P.N., Salovey, P., Côté, S. & Beers, M. (2005). Emotion regulation abilities and the quality of social interaction. *Emotion, 5,* 113-118.

Mayer, J.D. & Salovey, P. (1997). What is emotional intelligence? In P. Salovey & D.J. Sluyter (Eds.), *Emotional development and emotional intelligence: Implications for educators* (pp. 3-31). New York: Basic Books.

McCombs, B.L. (2004). The learner-centered psychological principles: A framework for balancing academic achievement and social-emotional learning outcomes. In J. Zins, R., Weissberg, M., Wang & H. J. Walberg (Eds.), *Building academic success on social and emotional learning: What does the research say?* (pp. 23-39). New York: Teachers College Press.

Molnar, A. & Lindquist, B. (1989). *Changing problem behavior in schools.* San Francisco: Jossey-Bass.

Ross, M.R., Powell, S.R. & Elias, M.J. (2002). New roles for school psychologists: Addressing the social and emotional learning needs of students. *School Psychology Review, 31,* 43-52.

Rovio, E., Lintunen, T. & Eskola, J. (2007). Team building method in sport. A review. Paper submitted for publication.

Saarni, C. (2000). Emotional competence: A developmental perspective. In R. Bar-On & J. Parker (Eds.), *Handbook of emotional intelligence* (pp. 68-91). San Francisco: Jossey-Bass.

Weare, K. (2004). *Developing the emotionally literate school.* London: Paul Chapman.

Zins, J.E., Bloodworth, M.R., Weissberg, R.P. & Walberg, H.J. (2004). The scientific base linking social and emotional learning to school success. In J. Zins, R. Weissberg, M. Wang & H. J. Walberg (Eds.), *Building academic success on social and emotional learning: What does the research say?* (pp. 3-22). New York: Teachers College Press.

Zins, J.E., Weissberg, R.P., Wang, M.C. & Walberg, H.J. (Eds.). (2004). *Building academic success on social and emotional learning: What does the research say?* New York: Teachers College Press.

chapter six

Facilitating Prosocial Behaviour in Physical Education

Risto Telama
Singa Polvi
University of Jyväskylä, Finland

After reading this chapter, you will be able to do the following:

- Understand the importance of facilitating prosocial behaviour
- Know the main elements of prosocial behaviour
- Know the psychological correlates and moral basis of prosocial behaviour
- Explain how physical education can promote prosocial behaviour
- Teach prosocial behaviour in the context of physical education

During a physical education class in which soccer is being played, one student plays very effectively and scores often but tackles very aggressively, causing pain and injuries to other players. In a volleyball lesson, the game is going well, but one newer student passed the ball and seems bored. In an ice hockey game, players are skating skilfully, but they mock a clumsy goalkeeper who is unable to catch the puck. As a teacher, what do you see in these situations, and how do you evaluate them? Are you satisfied because the game is run well, or do you pay attention to the negative social issues? If you disregard the aggressive tackling and the mocking of the clumsy goalkeeper, then you are teaching your students that aggression and mockery are acceptable. In physical education you can concentrate on physical skills such as motor skills and fitness. However, you also implement social education, either consciously or unconsciously, and the results may be positive or negative. In this chapter we will show you how to implement *positive* social education *consciously* in physical education.

Why Facilitate Prosocial Behaviour?

Surveys on values held by young people and adults have revealed that individualistic values (such as egoism) have increased during past decades, which means that people are more inclined to focus on what benefits them and less inclined to care about others. In many societies there is an increased need for solidarity, tolerance and willingness to help because of growing numbers of people at risk of alienation, such as immigrants. Although information technology has provided many people the opportunity to work alone in many occupations, cooperation with other people is necessary. While the number of employees in many sectors is decreasing as a result of automation, the number of people working in various service trades and providing human relations services is increasing.

Inclusion is a term that reflects recent developments in education that focus on giving everybody an equal opportunity for learning. In pedagogical discussions, inclusion has often been connected with teacher behaviour, but we should remember that inclusion cannot exist without good cooperation and a prosocial atmosphere among pupils.

For a long time physical education in schools has regarded as one of its main goals the promotion of **prosocial behaviour.** However, the implementation of this goal has not been consistent and deliberate. An extensive observation study has shown that in the majority of physical education lessons, very little real cooperative work (e.g., helping each other) among pupils was found (Varstala, Paukku & Telama, 1983). In youth sports the situation was the same (Liukkonen, Telama & Laakso, 1996). There are many reasons for this. One is the old belief that physical activity and sports, as such, promote prosocial behaviour, and therefore it is not necessary to pay attention to social issues in teaching. Another reason may be that physical education has been seen as addressing primarily the 'physical' because it is the only school subject in which the body and its functions are the target of teaching. As such, the social and psychological aspects of physical activity have been ignored. One reason for the poor implementation of prosocial goals may be the lack of an appropriate definition of prosocial goals in the context of the physical activity curriculum, which in turn may lead teachers to believe that prosocial skills are difficult to teach. In the next section we define prosocial behaviour in more detail.

Elements of Prosocial Behaviour

Prosocial behaviour—or positive social behaviour—is defined as voluntary actions that are intended to aid or benefit another person. **Altruism** and **empathy,** which are closely related to prosocial behaviour, involve concrete psychological help and maintaining friendship. Altruism is a form of prosocial behaviour that people engage in for its own sake with no intention of getting any outward reward. Empathy is defined as being able to match one's own feelings with those of another person or to understand another person's position.

Helping behaviour involves concrete helping as well as psychological helping. Concrete helping means assisting to perform motor skills. **Psychological helping** involves such actions as caring, supporting verbally, encouraging and comforting.

Prosocial behaviour often results in promoting the development of positive relationships with other people. Although often explained in terms of sympathy and empathy, prosocial behaviour also addresses skills such as the **ability to help** and moral reasoning. Because morals are associated with interpersonal relationships, morality is related to prosocial behaviour. People who look to help others when faced with a moral conflict are exhibiting prosocial behaviour.

Children's social interactions and cooperating behaviour increase with age. As their feelings of competence increase, so does the frequency of prosocial behaviour. Therefore, to promote prosocial behaviour in the classroom, teachers must develop and enhance children's **self-esteem** while encouraging productive interpersonal relations. Studies have shown that children from cooperative classrooms are more helpful than children from competitive classrooms. Concrete interactive relations are essential preconditions for learning prosocial skills such as giving psychological support, caring about other people, taking others into consideration, sharing and giving concrete assistance such as verbal and physical help, advice and correction. By interacting with each other, pupils in the class learn to understand and to internalise the social skills needed for working with others. People choose certain friends because they see them as generous, cooperative and skilled helpers.

The term *social qualification* refers to the skill of interacting effectively with the environment, both physically and socially. Social interaction is based on the relationships between people, which, in the form of overt behaviour, can be either positive or negative. Positive social behaviour, or prosocial behaviour, involves being interested in and concerned about others, resolving conflicts constructively and offering concrete assistance. Those with prosocial skills are able to work cooperatively with others.

Prosocial behaviour is associated with a high level of social acceptance. Popular children and adolescents behave more sociably and less aggressively than do those who are less popular or rejected.

Prosocial Behaviour and Moral Behaviour

The motives for helping behaviour or other forms of prosocial behaviour may be multifarious. A person may help just for selfish reasons—for example, expecting a reward or a service in return. On the other hand, the motive may be purely altruistic, based on the concept that one has a responsibility to help others. The prosocial behaviour that is the aim of education should be based on morality (**moral behaviour**), or a concept of right and wrong. In society, decisions about right and wrong most often concern other people. Selfish reasons may change from one situation to another, but people who help based on altruistic values are likely to help regardless of the situation or possible rewards.

The research literature on moral development emphasises peer interaction. Through their social exchanges with peers and adults, children construct two different understandings of their social world and two sets of rules to guide behaviour. Through interactions with those in power who are familiar with a system the child has yet to learn, the child learns conformity, or how to act in accordance with others' social expectations. However, with peers, children discover a social system that they create with others, one that is open to modification and offers a sense of mutual understanding. In peer interaction, because there is initially no set structure, no one is initially superior or inferior; the system is open to redefinition through democratic processes (Youniss, 1980). By interacting with peers, children learn about affection and attitudes. Positive feelings of affection and attitudes increase the readiness for prosocial behaviour, such as a willingness to help.

Psychological Correlates of Prosocial Behaviour

An important psychological structure behind prosocial behaviour is self-esteem. Studies have shown that children with a positive self-concept are more likely to demonstrate helping, sharing and cooperating behaviours than children with a less positive self-concept. The child with a positive self-concept is also more likely to be concerned about other children's needs and is more capable of feeling empathy. Studies have also shown that positive responses to children's prosocial behaviour, especially by peers, strongly reinforce that behaviour.

Self-esteem is based on self-perceptions concerning one's competence in different life activities, such as academic, social and physical activities. Regarding physical education, particularly important is a child's perceived competence in motor skills, fitness and sports. Therefore, teachers of physical education can promote prosocial behaviour by supporting perceived physical competence and, through it, self-esteem.

Promotion of Prosocial Behaviour in Physical Education

Although it is time to give up the old belief that physical activity in and of itself develops people ethically and socially, we must keep in mind that physical activity and physical education share features that lend themselves to such development. Social skills, such as collaboration, showing consideration to others and helping others, are learned as other skills are: by doing. Physical education can offer opportunities for social interaction in more varied environments and activities than those encountered in any other school subject. In physical education it is easy to create genuine interactive activities in which students can observe, give feedback to, support and help others. Physical activity also contains genuine conflict situations that offer opportunities for solving conflicts with dialogue and discussion. Showing consideration toward peers in a peaceful classroom is relatively easy, but in tension-packed situations, such as games in physical education, much more self-control is needed to behave in a socially acceptable way. Because children exhibit more of their social skills in physical education than they do in the lessons of other school subjects, physical education is a good environment for organising cooperative activities and enhancing prosocial behaviour.

Physical educators can either encourage or inhibit the development of prosocial behaviour in their students.
© Bob Vincke.

Class Social Structure

Social behaviour can vary from prosocial behaviour to negative social behaviour. One of the most harmful negative social behaviours is **bullying.** Bullying is always an intentional, repeated action and is usually directed toward the same people. In most classes there is at least one pupil who is bullied. Bullying can last for years. Typical bullying actions include calling pupils names, making fun of pupils, rejecting pupils and making pupils look ridiculous. Girls typically bully indirectly, whereas boys bully directly. Bullying victims often have character traits such as being sensitive, shy, uncertain, aggressive or different. The pupil being bullied often has poor self-esteem, and the bully often has a need to dominate and is often unable to tolerate even small criticisms.

In a bullying situation the pupils of the class take one of five roles: teaser, teaser's helper, supporting role, defender, or outsider. The roles are permanent unless an intervention is undertaken.

To decrease bullying, teachers should pay attention to the whole class. The most common practice for decreasing bullying is to hold discussions between the teaser and the victim in the presence of their parents or the whole class. One way to decrease bullying is called the reciprocal method: Every pupil is systematically everybody's partner while practising physical tasks. To be successful, students must learn to help, support, encourage, give feedback and take the partner into consideration. In this method students see many different models of behaviour and get feedback from their peers.

If a less skilled and perhaps rejected pupil can help and advise a more skilled pupil—perhaps a teaser—successfully, this can give an invaluable boost to that pupil's sense of self-esteem and self-worth and may stop the bullying. Because pupils rarely report bullying, the teacher must determine the social structure of the class, either through *sociometry* or by observing how the pupils work together.

Following are some important questions teachers should answer concerning the social structure of the class:

- How many pupils are rejected or even mocked in the class, and how badly?

- How well are pupils accepted in the class?

- How are different pupils accepted as working partners in their own class?

- What is the atmosphere of the class?

- Is there democracy in the class?

- Are there 'cliques' in the class?

To answer these questions, teachers need information about the social structure of their class. One of the best means to acquire that information is the **sociometric test,** which shows how many pupils are rejected or accepted in the class. This helps the teacher identify starting points for planning programmes for developing social behaviour. A sociometric test requires the teacher to ask pupils, for example, who they want to work with and who they don't want to work with. The same questions can be asked concerning other situations such as breaks or leisure time. A **sociogram** of the answers to a sociometric test can result in a map of the class climate and the relations among the children.

Following are examples of sociometric questions:

1. Which two pupils do you prefer to work with in lessons?

2. Which pupils do you *not* want to work with in lessons, in any situation?

3. Which two pupils do you prefer to spend your recess at school with?

4. Which pupils do you *not* want to spend your recess at school with, in any situation?

Table 6.1 shows results for questions 1 and 2, and figure 6.1 shows a graph of those results.

Preparing a sociogram may seem troublesome and difficult, but it is not difficult if the circle is big enough. Minimally, the teacher should find out the pupils who are accepted by nobody or rejected by several pupils. Of course, it is useful for the teacher to know the most popular students and the possible friendship cliques.

The acceptances in the sociogram in figure 6.1 show us that three of the girls, Ann, Mary and Kate, chose each other, indicating that they are friends with each other and possibly a clique. Meanwhile, Donna and Liz are not accepted by anyone. Kate is very popular, and so is Mary, even if Donna rejected her. Nobody in the group has rejected Kate. Three girls have rejected Sara

Table 6.1 Acceptances and Rejections Concerning Work During Lessons

Pupils (girls): Ann, Mary, Kate, Donna, Liz, Sara

	Acceptances	Rejections
Ann	Mary	Sara
	Kate	Liz
Mary	Ann	Sara
	Kate	Liz
Kate	Ann	Sara
	Mary	Liz
Donna	Kate	Mary
	Sara	
Liz	Mary	Ann
	Kate	
Sara	Kate	Liz
	Mary	

Acceptances

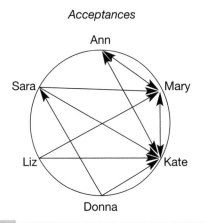

Rejections

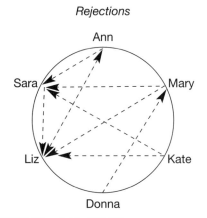

Figure 6.1   Sample sociogram.

and four girls have rejected Liz, so they are the most discriminated girls in the group. Ann and Liz rejected each other. Donna is a girl to whom nobody gives any notice; she is neither accepted nor rejected. So, if everyone in the group has to choose a working partner, what is going to happen to Donna, or to the two rejected girls, Sara and Liz? These girls are called surplus pupils. In such a situation, the teacher can solve the problem by using a teaching method that promotes prosocial behaviour among pupils.

In a study (Kahila, 1993) of four groups of 11-year-old pupils (grade level 5), one group worked cooperatively in physical education for one school year; their activity was based on helping and advising pupils of different abilities. In the group in which children changed partners, the results of the sociometric measurement at the end of the year showed that positive choices had increased and negative choices (i.e., rejections) had decreased significantly and more than in the group where the partners were not changed and in the group working individually. Also, positive choices concerning interactions during breaks increased. Interestingly, in the academic year following the study, when the same pupils were allowed to choose their own partners, they often chose based on others' willingness to cooperate, help and advise rather than on their physical skills or friendship.

There are a lot of discussions on the assets and liabilities of negative choices or rejections in sociometry. Our recommendation is that negative choices should not be used in the lowest grades of elementary school or in a new class until the teacher has come to know the pupils. Although only the teacher knows the results of the sociom-

etry, young children will talk about most of their rejections, and it can be very anxious for some of the pupils. On the other hand, we recommend that teachers use negative choices (rejections) among the older pupils because the most serious social problems in the class concern alienated, rejected and bullied pupils, and it is very difficult to get information about those pupils without sociometry and the negative choices in particular.

In addition to sociometric tests, teachers can acquire information about the social relationships in their classes through **observation.** While observing the performances of pupils, physical educators can also pay attention to social issues. For example, if some pupils always want to be together, they may form a clique and perhaps reject others. Teachers should also be attentive to pupils who seem always to be left alone and probably are rejected or even mocked. Sometimes it may be useful to discuss social issues with the class.

Teaching Prosocial Behaviour

Prosocial behaviour can be learned and taught in the same way as other objectives of physical education. Studies have shown that sharing, helping and cooperative behaviours are affected by reinforcement, modelling and doing things together. But before starting any learning process, teachers should specify the goals of a programme for enhancing prosocial behaviour (i.e., what kinds of behaviour they want to improve). They can then choose the methods that will help them achieve their goals. The reciprocal (cooperative) method, for example, is designed to encourage helping behaviour, responsibility, reliability, politeness, a social atmosphere, and the giving and receiving of feedback.

General Principles

Researchers disagree about the socialising effect of physical education. The old myth that taking part in sport, particularly in team sport, brings pedagogical benefits because it automatically leads to positive social and moral results is questioned nowadays. Instead of saying that physical activity and sport have intrinsic value, many believe that they have a potential instrumental value in teaching and promoting social and moral behaviour. However, physical education can sometimes enhance selfish and egocentric behaviour, especially when the teaching method focuses on competition between pupils. Physical education's ability to enhance prosocial behaviour, ability and willingness to help depends very much on how it is socially organised and what kinds of teaching methods the instructor uses.

A key point of this chapter is the value of learning by doing and the need for working cooperatively. Social skills, such as collaborating, showing consideration toward others and helping others, can be learned by doing. Learning by doing here means that pupils work in cooperative peer interactions. When pupils are playing volleyball or soccer, it may look as though they are cooperating. A closer look, however, will reveal that they are playing egocentrically, in a competitive way that emphasises their own abilities as players. They pass only because they have to, and some pupils are never passed the ball. Real cooperative work means that all participants are needed to reach a mutual goal.

The dominant teacher styles used in physical education have been the command style and the individual practice style. These methods are teacher centred. Even if the pupils have some possibility for self-regulation, they seldom have any chance to communicate or cooperate with each other. Doing a task individually often also results in competition among learners. By using only competition as a teaching method, teachers risk inciting situations in which pupils become either aggressive or submissive. Another way to teach physical education is to use the learning process

as an instrument to promote prosocial behaviour. This means that pupils practise together in a cooperative way.

Prosocial behaviour is also learned through observation. Social learning theory posits that behaviour such as helping and complimenting can be learned by observing. A person who observes another person acting prosocially is more inclined to demonstrate similar prosocial behaviour. However, observing alone is not enough. The key word is *cooperation.* Concrete interactive relations are essential preconditions for learning social skills, such as giving psychological support; caring about other people; taking others into consideration; and giving concrete assistance such as verbal and physical help, advice and corrections. By interacting with each other, pupils learn to understand and to internalise the social skills needed for working with many different people.

To learn prosocial behaviour, people must interact and work with many individuals. In so doing, they learn their own and others' weaknesses and strengths and learn to see situations from others' points of view.

Often teachers say that they have no time to teach prosocial skills, or they worry about the implementation of 'more important' objectives, such as motor skills and fitness. Studies have shown that pupils' achievements in physical fitness and motor skills were at least as good in classes using the reciprocal (cooperative) method as in classes using so-called traditional methods. This indicates that facilitating prosocial behaviour in physical education does not prevent the implementation of other objectives. And promoting prosocial behaviour does not require any extra time.

The primary ways of facilitating prosocial behaviour are using the reciprocal (cooperative) teaching style, creating a task-oriented motivational climate and allowing rule changes and adaptations of team games.

Reciprocal Teaching Style (Cooperative Method)

The **reciprocal teaching style** (Mosston & Ashworth 2002), or cooperative method, is based on pair work in which one pupil is the doer while the other monitors the performance of the task, gives advice and demonstrates how to do it properly, corrects errors, offers psychological support, gives feedback and, if needed, asks the teacher for further advice. The teacher is a facilitator in the background, helping if needed and providing feedback about social cooperation and social skills. The teacher has to demonstrate and give very clear information about both roles, that of the performer and the observer, at the beginning of the task. The main point of this method is that the pupils don't choose their pairs themselves. At some point in the class, every pupil is paired with every other pupil. This is organised by changing pairs systematically after some weeks, such as every three or four weeks.

The reciprocal model can be used in many activities—skating, volleyball, gymnastics, apparatus gymnastics and so on. Teachers must give clear information, show how to help, explain roles and responsibilities and perhaps provide different levels of difficulty depending on the students' abilities. With this method, young people learn to work together and take responsibility. Pupils may not like having to work with every other pupil in the class in the beginning, but they will get used to it. As they get to know more pupils and learn to get along with them, it will affect the whole atmosphere in the physical education lessons.

Teacher's Role

The teacher's own values and beliefs, which are expressed in goals and teaching methods, build the foundation for the teaching process. The focus is in the questions, What is worth teaching? and Why and how should I teach it?

The teacher has to give clear instructions for practice and performance, demonstrate the task, give criteria, show how to help and explain how to use supporting equipment. With new tasks, teachers should guide pupils through the task. During the practice the teacher's role is to be a facilitator in the background, helping if needed and providing feedback about social cooperation. As pupils become accustomed to cooperating with each other, their dependence on the teacher will decrease and their number of friends and working partners will increase. Teachers who use the reciprocal style must learn to trust their pupils and allow them to teach each other. This develops responsibility among pupils.

The teacher should prepare a task sheet and post it at the place of practice. The task sheet can be in the form of written instructions or figures. It should include (1) the main points of the task performance, (2) phases of the task, (3) practice models and (4) how to help (see figure 6.2 for a

1. Main point of the task performance	Keep the body straight and the legs up at the moment the weight is on the hands.
2. Phases of the task	Step 1. Take a step forward with the left leg, lifting up the right leg. Step 2. Shift the weight to the left hand. Step 3. When the weight is going to the right hand, legs are straight up. Step 4. Use the hands to push up to the standing position as the weight moves to the right leg.
3. Practice models	Step 1. Before practicing the cartwheel, one must be able to do a controlled handstand. Step 2. After performing a good handstand position, move the left leg to the left side and bend the body from the hip joints, coming down to the left leg. Step 3. Push up with the hands to the standing position.
4. How to help	A partner can stand behind the doer and put his hands on the doer's hips to assist with the movement. A partner can observe the line of the cartwheel and the position of the body during the performance (rolling X).

Figure 6.2 Sample task sheet for execution of a cartwheel.

sample sheet). The task sheet will help the pair determine the best way to practise the task.

Because of the preparation the teacher must do at home, the reciprocal teaching style may require more work at the outset. Once pupils have learned to really work together, helping, advising and giving feedback, this method makes the teaching process much easier than traditional methods.

Feedback

Apart from advising and helping, a partner has a very important role in giving feedback, especially in the practice of physical skills. Feedback is also important in maintaining the level of motivation in practising all kind of sports. In the reciprocal teaching style, most of the responsibility of doing the task and giving the feedback is given to the pupils.

In the reciprocal teaching style, because many pairs of pupils are practising at the same time, the teacher will not be able to advise and support everyone. Instead, the teacher can discuss with the class as a whole how to give advice and feedback to each other. This is appropriate, given that an important goal of the lesson is to learn and practise prosocial behaviour.

Teaching Young Children to Cooperate

Children must have a certain level of moral development (an understanding of right and wrong) before they can be expected to undertake prosocial actions. The earlier they begin to rehearse social skills in the school, the better they learn to cooperate and the better the results. Tasks for children in the first grades of elementary school should be very easy. Teachers of very young children should understand that, even though they have been taught social skills and cooperation, younger children may tend to work individually more than older children will.

Methods of Choosing Pairs

Students often want to exercise and play in physical education lessons with their friends. As a result, teachers often allow pupils to choose their own partners. This method has its weaknesses. First of all, because the children may have socialised extensively in their spare time with their friends, mutual enjoyment may be a lot more important than actual goal-oriented activity in physical education. Second, some pupils may not have a friend to pair with, causing them to withdraw from social contact in physical education. A comparison of the advantages and disadvantages of self-selecting pairs is shown in table 6.2.

Success in working cooperatively requires both partners to respect each other, to accept each other as a working partner and to accept each other's levels of performance and opinion. Cooperation also requires giving and receiving help, advice and feedback. To be successful in cooperating and interacting, caring for others, feeling responsible and sharing aspirations with others, one must practise working with different kinds of people. Acquiring a new partner on a regular basis facilitates the learning of prosocial behaviour.

To set up pairs systematically, teachers can make a list of the pupils and then circulate the pupils to work with each other. They can also pick names of pupils randomly and then make

Table 6.2 Self-Selected Pairs: Advantages and Disadvantages

Advantages	Disadvantages
Pupils like to work with their best friends.	Not every pupil will have a best friend to choose.
Friends know each other's skills.	Motivation can be very low.
Pupils feel safe with friends.	Pupils may focus on enjoyment instead of working.
	Pupils will have limited social contacts.
	Friendship pairings can be unbalanced (physically or psychologically).
	Friends may approve of each other's performances too readily (and not correct errors).

a list of pairs. Using sociometry, teachers can be more conscious about their choices—for example, making sure that pupils who dislike each other are not paired at the beginning. Whatever method the teacher uses, it is important to explain the system, show the list of pairs and clarify the goals, including the social goals, of physical education. By taking the time to prepare groupings ahead of time, the teacher can ensure that the lesson starts without any problem concerning pairs or groups. The teacher is then free to focus on demonstrating and giving advice, and the pupils can focus on practising. The earlier pupils are used to systematically changing pairs, the easier it will be. Beginning a new method with teenagers can be problematic. In this case it may be best to begin by choosing pairs of pupils who like each other and moving to other pairings gradually. If a critical situation arises, the teacher should take the pupil aside, discuss the problem and then try to solve the problem with the help of the pupil(s) involved. Advantages and disadvantages of systematically choosing pairs are shown in table 6.3.

Mastery-Oriented Motivational Climate

In addition to teaching methods, the socioemotional climate or atmosphere prevailing in gyms affects the development of prosocial behaviour. Research studies have shown that different sport teams have different moral atmospheres and that players' and coaches' attitudes toward fair play and rule violation vary according to the atmosphere of the team. An important development in the research on classroom climate concerns findings on motivational climate and, in particular, its division into ego-oriented and mastery-oriented (or task-oriented) climates.

Ego-oriented and mastery-oriented climates in physical education differ in the ways they address competition and cooperation. In general, in a mastery-oriented climate, pupils can concentrate on their own learning and develop according to their own skill level without any need to be better than others. Such a climate also offers pupils more

Table 6.3 Systematically Changing Pairs: Advantages and Disadvantages

Advantages	Disadvantages
There are no surplus pupils.	In the beginning pupils don't know each other's skills.
Many social contacts occur.	Pupils may have difficulty working with someone new at first.
Every new pupil brings a new challenge.	
Every pupil has an opportunity to work with every other pupil.	
An opportunity to make new friends is created.	
The climate of the class may improve.	

ABILITY TO HELP

The **ability to help** and to advise is not as dependent on physical abilities and skills as is generally thought. When a pupil who is less skilled physically is able to help and advise successfully a more skilled pupil, the experience can be an invaluable boost to that pupil's sense of self-worth. It may also change the pupil's attitude toward physical education and sport in a positive way.

opportunities to help others, something that is almost impossible in competitive situations. The teacher creates the motivational climate through verbal behaviour, grouping of pupils, selecting task levels and so on.

Other Means of Promoting Prosocial Behaviour in Physical Education

Any activity that increases participation and involvement in physical education is favourable for developing prosocial behaviour. Team games, which many believe promote social interaction and prosocial behaviour, may actually isolate many pupils when the best players are passing to each other and scoring. Therefore, teachers should pay attention to the social behaviour of pupils during team games, observing and intervening when appropriate. A simple method is to stop the game and demonstrate the situation. For example, a teacher can ask the good players if they have noticed that some players have not touched the ball at all. She might ask how they would feel if they were an outsider in the game all the time. The teacher also can encourage shy pupils to participate and try harder.

A more effective way to intervene in games in which some are not playing is to change the rules of the game to increase participation. For example, in soccer the rule could be that the ball must be passed to all players before kicking to the goal. If there are more than five players on the team, the rule could be that at least five players must touch the ball before scoring. In volleyball, when playing four on four (which in school is more appropriate than six on six), more than three touches of the ball can be accepted, but at least three players must touch the ball before hitting it to the opponents. This enhances not only social behaviour but also playing skills.

Positive feedback is important when teaching prosocial behaviour. In team games the teacher should give feedback when pupils exhibit prosocial behaviour, such as when a good player offers other players the possibility for scoring instead of trying it by himself. Positive feedback can also be made systematic by changing the scoring. An example is so-called 'fair play games', in which

scores can be given for behaviours such as fair play and sportsmanship in addition to goals.

In team games an important educational objective may be to learn to understand and follow the rules. Children should learn that rules help make the game fun while also guaranteeing the same opportunities for all. When children are playing by themselves, they usually understand that without rules and without respecting rules, the game does not go on. But if winning is emphasised and a referee is observing the rules, children easily learn to delegate the responsibility of enforcing the rules to the referee. They learn that everything that the referee does not see or that the referee does not deny is accepted. This is not a good situation from the point of view of social education. Therefore, in school physical education, pupils should learn to play games without referees. Because school rules can and should be different from the rules in competitive sport, teachers should make sure that the accepted rules are clear to everybody. They should also emphasise that the rules are a common agreement that increases their enjoyment.

An important aspect of prosocial behaviour is feeling responsible for others. Don Hellison's (2003) method of enhancing feelings of responsibility is one of the best known. According to Hellison's philosophy, before someone can feel responsible for another person, he must feel responsible for himself. There are five levels in Hellison's method of promoting responsibility (see figure 6.3). At level zero a person shows irresponsible behaviours, usually in the form of blaming others. At level I a person shows some kind of self-control and respects the rights and feelings of others, although she is not yet ready to participate in anything. At level II a person is ready to participate and to show some effort, tries new things and may have a personal definition of success. At level III a person shows self-direction, is on task independently and may have a personal plan. At level IV a person cares about and helps others and shows compassion. Hellison developed his method when working with alienated and at-risk youth. Pedagogically, an important feature of his method is the emphasis given to self-esteem and the need to take responsibility for oneself first before focusing on helping others. A programme to encourage students to take more responsibility for themselves may be beyond the duties of a physical

Level IV, Caring

Students at Level IV, in addition to respecting others, participating and being self-directed, are motivated to extend their sense of responsibility beyond themselves by cooperating, giving support, showing concern and helping.

Level III, Self-direction

Students at Level III not only show respect and participation but also are able to work without direct supervision. They can identify their own needs and begin to plan and carry out their physical education programs.

Level II, Participation

Students at Level II not only show at least minimal respect for others but also willingly play, accept challenges, practice motor skills and train for fitness under the teacher's supervision.

Level I, Respect

Students at Level I may not participate in daily activities or show much mastery or improvement, but they are able to control their behavior enough that they don't interfere with the other students' right to learn or the teacher's right to teach. They do this without much prompting by the teacher and without constant supervision.

Level Zero, Irresponsibility

Students who operate at Level Zero make excuses, blame others for their behavior and deny personal responsibility for what they do or fail to do.

Figure 6.3 Hellison's levels of responsibility.

Reprinted, by permission, from D Hellison, 2003, *Goals and Strategies for Teaching Physical Education,* 2nd ed. (Champaign, IL: Human Kinetics), 28.

educator, but teachers could use Hellison's levels as a scale to evaluate the level of their students' social behaviour.

Applications to Youth Sport

Everything that has been said so far in this chapter can also be applied to competitive youth sport. You may wonder why cooperative work is important in youth sport when the purpose of sports is to prepare young people for competitions. Competition teaches young people to compete, win and lose. The research literature shows that too much emphasis on competition and winning in youth sport results in rule violating, unfair play, low levels of moral reasoning and other behaviours that are not acceptable from the point of view of education. Team sports often place too heavy an emphasis on winning and may also cause intrateam rivalry, which is not in line with the goals of team sport itself. Therefore, it is important

to facilitate cooperative interaction and prosocial behaviour in youth sports.

Youth sport coaches can encourage prosocial behaviour by organising skill-learning drills cooperatively as pair work or group work. Commonly in youth sport, positive feedback is given for motor performances and negative feedback is given for behavioural issues. In general, of course, positive feedback is more effective than negative feedback. Therefore, good behaviour and fair play should be rewarded with positive feedback. One effective way to do this is to have referees use green cards to reinforce fair play in team games.

If winning and competing are overemphasised in youth sports, the players of the opposing team are often seen as enemies. To keep competition at a moderate level, youth sports should be organised at low and local levels only.

In a study by Polvi (1998), young people who took part in organised sport showed more willingness to help than did young people who participated in nonorganised sport or did not take part in sport. This may be due to selection, but it also may be connected with the fact that when engaging in sport activities, people must combine their psychic and physical egos. In other words, people take part in sport not only as physical beings but also as psychological beings with feelings, values and attitudes. Clearly, youth sport has the potential of being an environment for social education.

Recommendations for Teachers and Coaches

The following recommendations point out important issues that may help you to implement social education in practice.

■ *Reflect on your teaching.* Are you ready to promote your students' prosocial behaviour? Is social education important to you? Do you think that it is part of your job to facilitate students' prosocial behaviour, and not simply to enhance fitness and motor development? How do you understand prosocial behaviour and social education? Discuss these issues with your colleagues. For instance, is it important that students learn to work together and help each other, and can students teach each other? Think about your role and students' role in physical education lessons. How many peer interactions occur during your lessons? Have you given responsibility to your students? How often do your verbal interventions deal with prosocial issues?

■ *Use methods that encourage collaborative interaction.* When arranging work in groups or pairs, take care that students learn to work with all other students, not only with their best friends. Pay attention to social skills. For instance, demonstrate how to help another student and how to give feedback to other students.

■ *Think about your verbal behaviour.* Through your verbal behaviour you can influence the socioemotional atmosphere of your lessons. Remember to give feedback on social behaviour, not only on motor performance and learning. For instance, you can say, 'Sara, your encouragement of Larry was great' or 'Thanks, Ron, for stopping the game when Donna fell down'.

■ *Promote empathy by encouraging students to consider the feelings and points of view of other students.* For instance, after an aggressive reaction in a game, you can ask, 'How do you think Mary feels?' If some students have not been involved in the game, you can ask good players, 'Do you think it's fun to play the game without touching the ball at all?'

■ *Use all kinds of physical activities for social education.* The impact of physical education on prosocial behaviour depends more on the social structure of the situation than on the activity itself. When teaching games, discuss with students how the games and rules could be modified to increase all participants' involvement. Encourage students to plan and make these modifications.

As a physical education teacher, you are a very important person in students' social development at school. Moreover, by increasing social interaction and fairness in your lessons, you can make physical education more enjoyable for your students. This is very important, too.

Summary

After reading this chapter, you should have a better understanding of how prosocial behaviour can be facilitated in physical education by increasing interaction and cooperation among students and focusing on the social and moral aims of education. Prosocial behaviour can be learned and taught in the same way as other objectives of physical education: by doing. To facilitate prosocial behaviour, you should be aware of the social and moral characteristics of physical activities in PE class. Another prerequisite for teaching prosocial behaviour is a good knowledge of the social structure of your class; sociometric methods may help you here. Because prosocial behaviour is learned in cooperative interaction with others, the main teaching method should be one that offers opportunities for interaction. The reciprocal teaching method—in which students work in pairs or in small groups and teach each other, give feedback and help—is the most effective method for facilitating prosocial behaviour. Physical education offers excellent opportunities for teaching prosocial behaviour but only if it is done consciously and deliberately.

Review Questions

1. Why is it important to facilitate prosocial behaviour in physical education?
2. What are the primary elements of prosocial behaviour?
3. What is the relationship between prosocial behaviour and moral behaviour?
4. How can sociometric inquiry be used to promote prosocial behaviour?
5. Compare and contrast physical education and other school subjects as environments of social education.
6. What are the principles and primary elements of the reciprocal teaching style?
7. Discuss the methods of choosing pairs in a cooperative learning situation.

Critical Thinking Questions

1. Think about what was said about promoting self-esteem in other chapters of this book and try to relate it to facilitating prosocial behaviour.
2. You are starting a new school year with a class you do not know. What would you do to get to know your students and the social relationships among them?
3. Recall your memories from the past school year and describe three situations in which the promotion of prosocial behaviour was clearly the focus of your teaching. Describe one situation in which, in your opinion, you would have done better to take prosocial behaviour into account.

Key Terms

ability to help—A capacity and willingness to give support and feedback, monitor others' performances and offer psychological help.

altruism—A form of prosocial behaviour that people engage in for its own sake with no intention of getting any outward reward.

bullying—Annoying or teasing another person deliberately. Typical bullying actions in school are calling pupils names, making fun of pupils, rejecting pupils and making pupils look ridiculous.

empathy—The quality of being able to match one's own feelings with those of another person or to understand another person's position.

moral behaviour—Behaviour based on a concept of right and wrong. In society, decisions about right and wrong most often concern other people.

observation—The acquisition of information about student behaviours in classes by watching and listening. In practical class situations, observation is informal, such as eyeballing or filling out checklists. In research situations, observation is usually systematic.

prosocial behaviour—Voluntary actions intended to aid or benefit another person; a positive form of social behaviour.

psychological helping—Helping in the form of caring, supporting verbally, encouraging and comforting.

reciprocal teaching style (cooperative method)—A method of teaching in which one pupil is the doer while the other monitors the performance of the task, gives advice and demonstrates how to do it properly, corrects errors, offers psychological support, gives feedback and, if needed, asks the teacher for further advice.

self–esteem—Self-perceptions concerning one's competence to act in different life activities, such as academic, social and physical activities.

sociogram—A graph that illustrates social relationships studied by sociometric tests.

sociometric test (or sociometric inquiry)—A method of studying social relationships in a certain group; for instance, in a class of schoolchildren.

References

Hellison, D. (2003). *Teaching responsibility through physical activity* (2nd ed.). Champaign, IL: Human Kinetics.

Kahila, S. (1993). The role of teaching method in pro-social learning: Developing helping behaviour by means of the co-operative teaching method in physical education. Jyväskylä, University of Jyväskylä, *Studies in Sport, Physical Education and Health, 29.*

Liukkonen, J., Telama, R. & Laakso, L. (1996). Youth sport coach as an agent of socialization: An analysis of observed coaching behaviours. *International Journal of Sport Psychology, 3.*

Mosston, M. & Ashworth, S. (2002). *Teaching physical education* (5th ed.). New York: Benjamin Cummings.

Polvi, S. (1998). *Am I doing right?* Jyväskylä, Finland: LIKES-Foundation for Sport and Health Sciences. (In Finnish with English abstract)

Varstala, V., Paukku, P. & Telama, R. (1993). Teacher and pupil behaviour in P.E. classes. In R. Telama et al. (Eds.), *Research in school physical education* (pp. 47-57). Jyväskylä, Finland: Reports of Physical Culture and Health 38.

Youniss, J. (1980). *Parents and peers in social development: A Sullivan-Piaget perspective.* Chicago: University of Chicago Press.

chapter seven

Group Development in the Physical Education Class

Johan Hovelynck
Yves Vanden Auweele
Thanasis Mouratidis
Katholieke Universiteit Leuven (K.U. Leuven), Belgium

After reading this chapter, you will be able to do the following:

- Explain the relevance of group dynamics to physical education
- Describe the difference between the issue and the topic of an interaction
- Discuss how a collection of people becomes a group or a team
- Understand relational messages and describe the interactions in a class group in terms of a few basic dimensions, using the sociogram technique
- Describe the development of a class group as a sequence of stages in terms of the evolution of the topic, the issue, the group structure and the group's relationship to the teacher
- Explain why a teacher should facilitate class development and why a teacher should be a change agent
- Identify a group's developmental stage
- Describe strategies to facilitate group development
- Give an example of each strategy in each stage of group development
- Discuss in what stage(s) each of these strategies is most appropriate

A classroom is like all other classrooms.
A classroom is like some other classrooms.
A classroom is like no other classroom.
—D. Lancy (1978)

Every class and every student is unique. As a teacher, though, you also encounter moments you recognise from earlier teaching experiences. No matter how groups and years of students differ, their interactions seem to follow a number of patterns that are recognisable in virtually every group.

For example, one day a student is rude and aggressive to you as well as to everyone else in the gym. In private conversation, however, he has consistently shown himself to be an understanding and friendly person. Or consider this example: You thought that you were very well accepted by the class. However, during the last weeks, they have flooded you with criticism. The class makes jokes throughout the PE lessons and does not show much energy. Or maybe you make a remark to a student about an improvement needed on her technique, and her reaction is extreme, nearly volatile with anger and hostility.

The awareness of patterns of interaction and their development can help you as a physical education teacher to manage your class group and to reach the curriculum goals of the physical education class. This chapter presents a model of group development and some guidelines that follow from them.

Curriculum goals for the physical education class include both physical and socioemotional growth. These goals are interrelated. Facilitating group development serves both. Along with a number of others, the authors conclude that attending to the group's development is an integral part of teaching. Too often classroom management is approached as though it comes on top of the teaching job. Data suggest that both are tightly integrated in the teacher's task. Teaching implies classroom management, and a teacher should be a change agent (Schmuck & Schmuck, 2001).

A good understanding of models of group development requires some knowledge of the context in which they were constructed. This chapter first sheds some light on the origins of contemporary group dynamics and introduces the basic concepts in this tradition.

The model of group development draws on these basic concepts. It describes an evolution of group life on four related levels: what the group is talking about (its **topic**), what the group members are privately dealing with or imply during their conversations (the group's **issue**), the group's internal structure and the group's relation to its leader.

The second part of the chapter offers some guidelines for supporting and directing group development in your class. This part first proposes an approach to identifying developmental stages. This will allow you to situate your class group in its development. The part concludes with a number of suggestions about how to support the group's further growth.

Theoretical Background of Group Dynamics

Group dynamics is the study of people's behaviour in small groups. This section addresses the history and characteristics of group dynamics. It will describe interactions in small groups and a model of group development.

History and Key Characteristics

The origins of group dynamics are commonly situated in the practices of Kurt Lewin and the Research Center for Group Dynamics in the United States, and Wilfred Bion (Rioch, 1975) at the Tavistock Institute in Great Britain, immediately after the second World War (Highhouse, 2002). Since its early history, the field of group dynamics developed a few key characteristics that are relevant for this chapter.

First, the study of group dynamics has always had a practical emphasis. Bion's concern was therapy. Lewin's goal was social change. He and his colleagues were not merely researchers; they were change agents. They studied their groups by working with them. The group therapists and organisational development consultants, whose approaches have their roots in Lewin's training groups and who contributed considerably to group dynamic theory, did so too. Their position is rather similar to a teacher's in this respect: They work with groups to achieve an educational goal, part of which is socioemotional. They help develop the group they observe, and they study the group they change. Their practical perspective is reflected in the fact that theory and guidelines are not strictly separated in this chapter.

Second, the distinction between a task level and a socioemotional level in group functioning has played a major role ever since the early beginnings of group dynamic models. Bion's theory makes a distinction between a group's work, or task, and the basic assumption underlying the group's functioning. A basic assumption is an emotional undercurrent that influences the way the group tackles its task. It is an assumption on which the group seems to base its behaviour. A class can assume, for example, that its teacher should solve all its problems. The students will therefore behave very dependently. They will ask their teacher to deal with the tiniest little inconvenience rather than manage the situation themselves.

In identifying and studying basic assumptions and not focusing on the group's work in great depth, Bion set the tone for the group dynamics field. It is mainly concerned with the socioemotional aspect, and the fit between the socioemotional level and the task level. These concerns are not because group dynamics is not interested in the work being done but because the basic assumptions play an important role in whether the task gets accomplished (Rioch, 1975).

In Lewin's view, **interdependence**, and the group members' awareness of it, is the basis for a group. The difference between a collection of individuals and a group, in other words, is not related to how similar the individuals are or how physically close. Instead, it relies on the degree to which they all depend on each other's actions.

In some definitions, a **group** exists only if the members have a common goal. According to others, a common goal is not a necessary condition. Interdependence can also result from the necessity to share the means needed for individual goals. The common goal then defines the difference between a task group and a **team.** This means that a volleyball game involves two teams competing with each other. The team members' common goal is to make the ball touch the ground in the other team's field. In circuit training, however, stu-

dents merely share the equipment for individual workouts. In this chapter we will therefore refer to students involved in circuit training as 'groups' instead of 'teams'.

Traditionally, group dynamics deals with small groups, which are defined as groups in which members have face-to-face contact. Classes therefore are considered small groups, despite the increasing numbers of students per class.

The dynamic interplay between group and personal identity is one of the driving forces of group development. At the same time, the broader social context in which a group is living (e.g., the school in our case), intergroup relationships (e.g., other classrooms and teams) and outgroup individuals (e.g., teachers, parents) can influence group developmental processes (Arrow, Poole, Henry, Wheelan & Moreland, 2004).

In summary, from a group dynamics point of view, a class is a small group because of the interdependence of its members and their face-to-face interactions. Our primary goal in this field is a better understanding of the personal and relational aspects of the interactions among group members, which may support or interfere with accomplishing the group's task. Although interesting and relevant in group dynamics, intergroup relationships are beyond the scope of this chapter.

Describing the Interactions in Small Groups

In their attempts to describe the socioemotional aspects of group functioning, group dynamics models have interpreted their data in terms of several categories. The following sections describe dimensions for interaction analysis, interaction patterns and the difference between the topic and the issue of an interaction.

Dimensions for Interaction Analysis

Some of the categories of interaction analysis seem more basic than others because they recur in different models. Authors such as Robert Bales (1951, 1970), Timothy Leary (1957) and Paul Hare (1973) have attempted to identify the smallest number of dimensions needed to explain most of the variation in interpersonal behaviour. These dimensions represent aspects of the interactions that seem useful for understanding group phenomena and are presented as bipolar dimensions. The idea is that positioning group members on each of these dimensions presents an accurate view of the group's functioning. The following elaborates the most salient dimensions, which regularly appear in the relevant literature.

The 'in-out' dimension describes people as part or not part of the group. Other terms referring to the same idea are *group membership* or *inclusion*. Students may well sit in the classroom but not be part of the class as a social environment. They are 'out.' They are rejected, or they themselves have rejected the class. The dimension has relevance to issues of students' belongingness within their school (Anderman, 2002), and students' alienation and exclusion from school life (Murdock, 1999).

The 'up-down' dimension describes group members in terms of the influence they exert. Are they dominant, and leaders, or subordinate, and followers? Are they top dogs or underdogs, haves or have-nots? This dimension has been addressed in the literature on students' social status (Pakaslahti, Karjalainen & Keltinkangas-Jarvinen, 2002) and its effect on educational outcomes and students' adjustment (Buhs & Ladd, 2001).

The 'close-far' dimension refers to how tight the links are among group members. Whom do they address themselves to, answer to, hang out with or help?

Students may well sit in the classroom but not be part of the class as a social environment.

© Bob Vincke.

The 'close-far' dimension is sometimes confused with the 'with-against' dimension, which does not refer to whom group members relate to but to the quality of that relation. Is it a relation of agreement, support and fun? Instead, is their interaction characterised by criticism, sarcasm, anger, argument and competition? Group members can be very close in a destructive way! Related studies focused on students' social networks, friendships, social bonds and the quality of their relationships (Wentzel & Caldwell, 1997).

The last basic dimension is 'forward-backward'. Group members can help the group to move on, or they can slow it down. They can play a stimulating role or a stagnating one (Agazarian & Gantt, 2003). What we mean by 'moving on' will become clearer when we describe the stages of group development.

Most teachers have an intuitive understanding of the five dimensions described earlier. The report of an experienced physical education teacher, who described how he usually tries to get a sense of who is who in a new class, is one example of this. He tells how he watches the group walk into the gym hall and change their clothes on the first day. He mainly assesses who the 'ringleaders' are. In terms of the dimensions, he starts by positioning some students on the 'up-down' continuum. While doing this, he decides whether to encourage, neglect or discourage their informal leadership initially. This decision is based on a spontaneous positioning of these 'up' students on the 'forward-backward' dimension. His approach can be recognised in the reports of other teachers or trainers and coaches in team sports.

Realise that these dimensions intend to be descriptive, not evaluative. Neither pole is 'good' or 'bad'. The risk of confusion seems especially real for the 'with-against' dimension, which some authors referred to as positive-negative. The labels merely describe a relationship characterised by agreement or disagreement, by support or by conflict. They do not assume that conflict is bad.

Interaction Patterns

If these dimensions are to help describe group interactions, which relationships should be talked about? In group dynamics, the interactions studied typically centre on the relations among group members, to the leader, to the task, to the organisation and to other groups.

One of the common ways to get an overview on these relations is a **sociogram:** a map in which these relations are drawn with respect to the basic dimensions (see figure 7.1). The map represents the group members, mostly the leader, sometimes the task and occasionally elements in the group's environment, such as other groups, the organisation and so on. Their positions and the relations among them are symbolised by the size of marks, the distance between them, the thickness of lines between them and the symbols + or − next to these lines.

Depending on which dimensions and which relationships are included and how they are symbolised, sociograms take a variety of forms

that are beyond the scope of this chapter. But they seem to have at least one thing in common: If you regularly draw them, patterns emerge. The group shows itself as an evolving network of interconnected relationships.

The group's informal structure that is depicted by such sociograms has an importance in itself, regardless of the group members' characteristics. William Hug and James King (1984) pointed out that the attributes of the individual students determine the friendliness or hostility, apathy or participation of a class far less than do its patterns of relationships. From this perspective one can understand the experience that many teachers have of aggressive, rude students turning out to be

Legend

Group: signified by the large oval

Students: represented by a circle with a name next to it—teachers are not included, only students

Relationships: symbolised by lines between the circles

'In-out': symbolised by the place of the circle, inside or outside the oval

'Up-down': symbolised by the size of the circle

'Close-far': symbolised by the distance between the circles

'With-against': + or − signs next to the lines

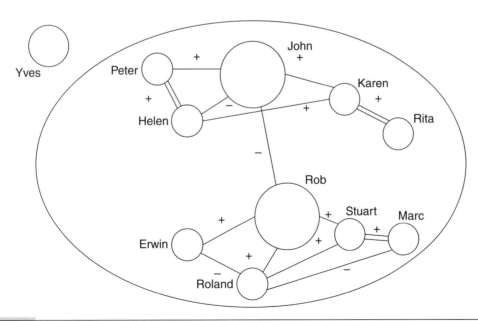

Figure 7.1   Example of a sociogram.

nice, responsible young people in private conversations. During class, they are part of a different relational network. Along the same lines, Richard and Patricia Schmuck (2001) concluded that these informal interaction patterns determine the class interpersonal climate. And this climate evolves along with the structure.

The Topic and the Issue

A final aspect of interaction is the distinction between a group's topic and its issue. The topic is what the group members talk about, what they explicitly address. The issue is their underlying concern; indeed, it is the students' preoccupation.

Depending on the class climate, the topic and the issue may or may not coincide. Students may directly express their concerns, but very often they do not. The issue, then, remains implicit. If, for example, two of the students in your class have a major argument about the way their team should play basketball, the topic may be dribbling or passing, but the issue is being included or left out of the game. The topic may be a player's position on the basketball court, but the issue may be influence and leadership. What is at stake really is not the player's position but the power to decide players' positions.

Discussing dribbling and passing is a lot easier than sharing feelings of being left out. Discussing players' positions is a lot more acceptable than claiming leadership. The group members talk about the topic because they can talk about it. It is available as a topic.

However, they are not necessarily able to discuss the issue. Therefore, group members silently deal with their issue by talking about their topic until the group finally feels safe enough to talk about the issue (Slavin, 2002).

The issue in both basketball examples can be formulated in terms of the five basic dimensions described earlier. In the dribble-or-pass discussion, the issue concerned the 'in-out' dimension. In the conflict about the position on the court, the issue involved the 'up-down' dimension.

A Model of Group Development

Models of group development typically look at a number of the basic dimensions and the relationships summarised previously and describe their evolution in a sequence of stages. Some models focus on what we called the group's issue; others emphasise the group's topic. Still, others attempt to integrate both.

The model of group development in this chapter includes both the issue and the topic in the relationships among students in the class. The model also looks at the shift in the patterns as depicted in a sociogram and pays attention to the issue underlying the class's relationship to the teacher (see figure 7.2).

With regard to the evolution of the issue, our model leans mostly on the basic dimensions 'in-out', 'up-down', and 'close-far', a development first presented by William Schutz (1966) and later elaborated by other authors (Neilsen, 1977). Only Schmuck and Schmuck (2001) referred to adolescents and the development of classes in a school setting.

The description of the topic's evolution requires us to distinguish between the task and socioemotional aspects of group functioning. The task is initially the only available topic; however, as the students get to know each other, it becomes possible to address more emotional and relational matters. Sociograms drawn at different moments in a group's development reflect interaction patterns that evolve from a pool of individuals to an increasingly inclusive group (see figure 7.3).

Finally, the relation of the students to the teacher is understood in terms of these basic dimensions: 'in-out', 'up-down', 'close-far' and 'with-against'.

This section concludes with an overview of trends typically observed in groups. Using first the story of an evolving basketball team, we will indicate the trends typically observed in groups and then summarise them in five stages (see table 7.1). The second part of this chapter will offer a practical approach to situating your class in its development. It will provide a number of ideas on how you can facilitate the group's further evolution.

Stage 1: Task, Inclusion and Dependence

Let us give our theory some substance by looking at a number of young people who get together to play basketball during their time off. They divide into two teams. The chapter will follow one of

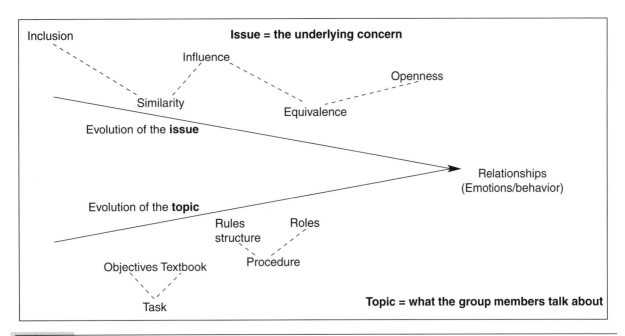

Figure 7.2 In a group, topic and issue gradually converge.

Adapted from J. Hovelynck, 2000, Leidraad in het faciliteren van ervaringsleren [Guidelines to facilitate experimental learning]. Leuven/Belgium: unpublished doctoral dissertation at KULeuven University, Faculty of Psychology and Pedagogical Sciences.

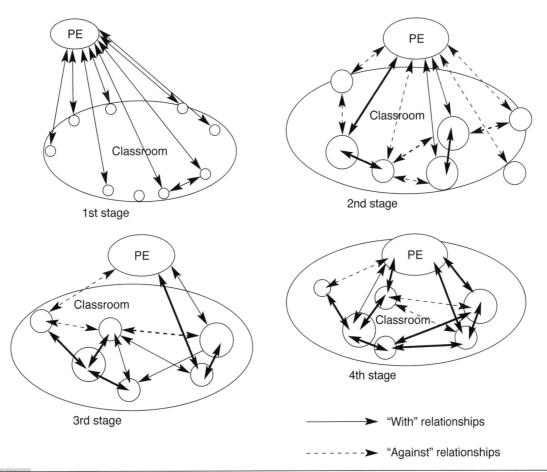

Figure 7.3 A series of sociograms illustrating interaction patterns in the developmental stages: Note that the PE teacher moves in as the classroom develops and that the interactions among students grow stronger (bold lines) and more positive (solid lines).

Table 7.1 Stages of Group Development

Stage 1: Task, inclusion and dependence	• **Topic:** the task and other topics that allow superficial conversation • **Issue:** 'in-out': inclusion; being part of, included or excluded from the class group • **Relation to the class members:** a pool of individuals: relationships remain superficial, and consequently are not clearly 'with' or 'against' • **Relation to the teacher:** dependence: the teacher is 'up' and 'far'; acceptance of instructions and evaluation of performance
Stage 2: Rules, similarity and counter-dependence	• **Topic:** structure and rules needed to accomplish the task • **Issue:** equality/similarity: similar others are included and supported; students are extra sensitive to the uniform application of rules to everyone. • **Relation to the class members:** dyads of students who feel alike in some respect • **Relation to the teacher:** shift toward counterdependence; the teacher remains 'far' and (less high) 'up', and the relationship shifts to 'against'
Stage 3: Roles, influence and interdependence	• **Topic:** roles needed to organize for task achievement • **Issue:** 'up-down': influence; conflict over roles and power in the class • **Relation to the class members:** subgroups, conflicting cliques • **Relation to the leader:** beginning interdependence: the teacher comes back to 'with', comes 'closer', and 'in'; the relation becomes more cooperative.
Stage 4: Behavior, equivalence and continuing interdependency	• **Topic:** includes individual behavior in the class as a topic in the group (as opposed to a topic for gossip dyads) • **Issue:** equivalence; mutual acceptance of interpersonal differences • **Relation to the class members:** spread of effect from the subgroups toward the entire group • **Relation to the teacher:** continuing interdependence
Stage 5: Emotion, openness and continuing interdependence	• **Topic:** includes feelings about the class and achievement, and the relationships among class members; the issue is available as a topic. • **Issue:** 'close-far'; cohesion combined with respect for individual differences • **Relation to the class members:** one group; one tightly interwoven network • **Relation to the teacher:** continuing interdependence

them. Because the new teammates do not really know each other, they will focus on basketball: It is the common interest and a safe topic. Basketball thus defines the single criterion for being a good team and for being a good team member. To gain full membership of the team, one needs to contribute to winning the game. The most obvious way

to do so is by scoring. The result of the members' wishes to be included in the group, therefore, is a general rush to the goal. Group members work simultaneously, rather than together. There is a lot of running around and a lot of chaos.

In such a beginning team, the only person with the authority to address the way the team plays would be the coach. He can impose a zone defence or a man-to-man defence. The coach can assign positions to different players and even decide to take a player out of the game. The player concerned may sigh in disappointment but typically will not oppose the coach's authority.

In a beginning class, students with high social anxiety or a tendency to withdraw are reported to be especially vulnerable (Buhs & Ladd, 2001). They run the risk of having adjustment difficulties, limited classroom participation and schooling problems due to loneliness and low self-esteem.

Stage 2: Rules, Similarity and Counterdependence

Although a coach can help organise a beginning team, the basketball game on the playground does not have a coach. To reduce the chaos, the group's topic must expand from the goals to the game. Players start to address the way they play together by organising the team's efforts. They typically agree to play man defence. This structure allows them to apply the same rule to all the team's players, whereas zone defence would force them to assign different roles.

In organised basketball the coach can expect resistance to his decisions. Team members start to develop an opinion of their own and may confront their coach with it. The player who sighed in disappointment in an earlier stage may now react with an angry 'Why me?' Other group members may join the protest if they believe that the group members are not being treated equally. Bennis and Sheppard (1974) coined the term **counterdependence** to describe this more defiant attitude toward the leader. According to Olweus (1978), teachers' administrative behaviour may trigger such reactions and lead to discipline problems within the classroom. Favouritism is likely to be critiqued heavily.

Stage 3: Roles, Influence and Interdependence

In the long run, organising the game involves different roles. Even if the group chooses to play man defence, they will come to a point at which one team member is better suited to follow a particular opponent than another one is. The topic then shifts from an anonymous 'How do we play?' to 'Who does what?' The group agrees that one

of the players should remain in the back to stop counterattacks and eventually defines a playmaker, forwards and guards. This may take a lot of negotiation. Throughout the process different players establish their influence. Group leaders emerge. As the team develops its own leadership, it becomes less dependent on the leadership of the coach.

Stage 4: Behaviour, Equivalence and Continuing Interdependence

As the team members get to know each other increasingly well, it becomes possible to address the way someone plays her role in the game. The leader is likely to be the first one to get feedback on what she is doing because the leaders' actions have the most impact on the group's performance and experience. Others will follow. If the reactions to feedback are positive and the team members believe that they are equally valued despite their 'unequal' roles, the group will develop further. Alternatively, if the reactions are negative, this may inhibit further development or even trigger a return to earlier stages.

Stage 5: Emotion, Openness and Continuing Interdependence

At this stage members feel accepted as individuals and are therefore able to focus on the group and its task. Concern with the task at this point is very different from the rush to the goal seen in the group's beginning. The players are now genuinely oriented toward the team's goal, whereas before they were driven by the need to prove themselves by scoring. They now call on each others' individual capacities and benefit from the complementarity in the group. Whereas the first stage showed energy, we now see synergy.

Caveats to the Theory

Before describing some guidelines for practice, it seems appropriate to point out some features of the context in which the preceding model was developed, which may affect its significance for practice in different classrooms.

First of all, most models of group development have been based on observations of groups of older adolescents and adults. However, stages in group development obviously interact with stages of personal development. Take counterdependence as an example. This may be a lot nastier in a group of teenagers, who are in a counterdependent age in the first place, than in a group of 10- and 11-year-olds. It is as if one added the group's puberty to the group members' puberty—so to speak.

The same thing occurs in the phase of interdependence, in which the group members treat the teacher as another group member. This obviously takes different forms in preschool and in high school. The developmental psychology perspective is not explicitly included in this chapter.

Second, the evolution in our model starts with a beginning group. Although the model suggests a rather linear development, the reality is more complex. The only times teachers deal with truly new groups are probably the beginning of preschool, the first year at primary school and the start of high school: new classmates, a new school, a different schedule, unknown teachers and so on. In most of the cases, there are carryover effects: Students know each other from the previous academic year and there may be well-developed subgroups within the new class group. When these subgroups have developed to different stages, they may strengthen their boundaries and resist any assimilation within the larger class group. Teachers may also fail to become full, functional members of the PE class group, in part because they may not capture the class's social environment in the same way students do. In addition, teachers may hold different administrative practices and, as a result, may hold different positions within the class group in relation to the 'up-down' and 'close-far' dimensions.

However, a group with a few new members or even an existing group in a new situation is to some extent a beginning group. Members need to get acquainted with each other in this new context. That may require new norms, other roles and different behaviours. Therefore, groups have multiple starts, and, as a consequence, their evolution seems cyclical rather than linear. They will revisit earlier issues using similar topics again. They may do that over and over.

Finally, because of the two points made before, groups may never get to the point at which the issue becomes available as a topic. As a matter of fact, many groups never reach that point. There is no reason to conclude that they are bad groups, however. Rather than considering it a weakness of the group, consider it a caveat to the theory. Eric Neilsen (1977) made the pointed observation that complete group development is never achieved.

Managing Your Group Throughout Its Development

In this section we describe guidelines for managing your group while it develops. It contains three subsections that delve into specifics regarding the topic.

Theory and Practice

Everyone who has ever stepped from educational theory to educational practice has had to adjust both theory and practice to each other. Merely trying to apply others' knowledge to your classroom is often a recipe for failure. That is why, rather than presenting a theory to apply, this chapter hopes to add a perspective to your view of the classroom. How that perspective translates itself into practice seems too context-bound for a textbook to formulate detailed advice. It must happen in the class.

In this part of the chapter, we offer an approach to situating your class in its development as a group. This requires matching your observations in the class to the sequence of typical group characteristics presented in the first part of the chapter. Although using the sociogram as a tool supports this effort, the chapter emphasises listening to relational messages. You must hear the topic and try to understand the issue.

Teachers quickly learn that theory does not always work in practice.

© Bob Vincke.

This part will conclude with some ideas for facilitating group development. This mainly means helping the group deal with its issues. Although simply addressing the issue may sometimes help, the group will not necessarily be ready to talk about it. That is why this part also explores how tasks, task structure, setting rules and personal communication can help the group resolve its issues.

Identifying a Group's Developmental Stage

This section presents an approach to identifying a group's developmental stage. It includes an approach to listening for issues. Sociograms are also described as an additional tool for understanding the issue in its context of group development.

Listening to Relational Messages

Imagine a student who does not excel in sciences or languages but is among the fittest of the class. One day the class works in subgroups of about six students. They take turns on the single bar and help each other. Uncharacteristically, the student seems to sabotage the class. He looks disconnected, does not take his turn, reacts aggressively when others try to get him involved and swears continually about the gymnastics exercises programme.

Listening to relational messages means getting beyond the discussion about gymnastics. When you are in this mode, you assume that the student's discontent is not really about the exercise. You assume that the exercises are just a topic, a vehicle available to express something else.

You may ask, Why not take his remarks at face value instead of suspecting that an issue is hiding under the surface? If you do not listen to relational messages spontaneously, one feature that should catch your attention, and make you switch into listening-for-issues-mode, is the disproportion between the topic and the reaction to it. In this example, the exercise on the bar can hardly account for aggression and continual swearing. The student's reaction is not in proportion to the topic. The intensity of the reaction reflects the issue. We have all seen groups in lively discussions about seemingly worthless details. The disproportion between the reaction and the topic is an indicator of an underlying issue.

Trying to understand the issue, then, requires active listening. This is often hindered by answering. If a student tells you that she believes your grading of students' performances is unfair, the temptation is to try to account for your scores and explain your point of view. Mostly this gets in the way of exploring her point of view. In our gymnastics example, the issue will not be solved by convincing the student that the exercise on the bar is good for him, no matter the issue.

Sometimes the context and the event itself contain the most accessible cues about what the issue might be. You know that the student is a

---

EXERCISE 1: LISTENING TO RELATIONAL MESSAGES

Because tracing the development of a group requires keeping data over a period of time, make written notes of a number of events immediately after the class. What you write down should include the following:

- The date and the class
- Topics you heard students talk about, and the names of the students involved
- Moments that struck you by the disproportion between a topic and the reaction to it, and again the names of the students involved
- Your interpretation of the underlying issue in these moments, and the facts on which this interpretation is based

Take 10 minutes to write these data down weekly during the first month, every two weeks during the second month and monthly afterward.

good sportsperson and appreciated for it. You hear from colleagues that he has difficulty in other classes. You have seen many classes perform the exercise at the bar, and this student would not be the first one to be afraid. You understand from the students' conversations as they came into the sports hall that they had an exam in the class just before yours. You heard the deep sigh when you presented the exercise. Therefore, you can fit all these data into a plausible interpretation of what the issue is. The one way to make sure is to check your interpretation with the student involved. Of course, students are not always open to conversation, either with the teacher or with other students. Asking what the problem is never hurts, but the kind of answer you can expect partially depends on your relationship with the class, and thus on the stage of group development.

Several guidelines will increase your chances of getting a meaningful answer. These include listening and showing your attention by looking at the speaker, asking open-ended questions to stimulate the student to clarify the issue further and checking whether you have interpreted the message correctly. The last part can imply summarising what you heard and asking whether that summary reflects what was said—an approach commonly referred to as paraphrasing.

Making Sociograms

A sociogram can be an interesting means to have a different look at the class. It offers a perspective with hindsight by using a very visual format. We mentioned earlier that sociograms take a variety of forms. We suggest you use the format shown in figure 7.1. Your sketch will then include only the relationships among students and will depict the 'in-out', 'up-down', 'close-far' and 'with-against' dimensions.

The physical education class is a great opportunity to observe such relationships. Because students are not tied down to their seats, they may unconsciously take sociogram positions while they stand together to listen to your instructions. They may reveal the class subgroups when dividing into volleyball teams. Interpersonal attractions may be reflected in the passes in a handball game. Compared to teachers in other subjects, you have the advantage of observing a large field in which such patterns are a lot more visible.

The Student–Teacher Relationship

The only relationship not covered by the exercises so far is the students' relationships to you as a teacher. Even though you are likely to be a recurring topic among your students, you will not likely hear a lot of what they say about you directly. More likely, you will hear remarks about the school and its approach to teaching. Such remarks may be indirect and therefore safer messages to you as the school's representative in this class.

Identifying Your Class's Development Stage

After writing down your class topics and issues and drawing its sociograms for a number of weeks, your data probably show some evolution. If you are interested in situating your class on a developmental continuum, you can try to match your data with the different stages of group development shown in table 7.1.

EXERCISE 2: MAKING SOCIOGRAMS

- After finishing the first exercise, draw a circle to symbolise the group and, without using a class list, position the students in relation to each other. Do not forget to add the date. If in doubt, use the legend from the sociogram in figure 7.1.
- Now compare your sociogram to the class list: A few students may have escaped your attention so far. Check why during the next class: They are probably 'out' or 'down' on the relational dimensions.
- Take another 10 minutes to do this again.
- Do not correct this sociogram after the next class; instead, start a new one.

EXERCISE 3: STUDENT–TEACHER RELATIONSHIPS

After finishing the first two exercises, take another five minutes to combine elements of exercises 1 and 2. Apply this to your own relationship with each of the students, and add the data to the ones you already have. List the following:

- The topics students talked about with you and the names of the students involved
- Reactions to you that struck you as being disproportionate, and again write down names
- The issue(s) revealed by active listening

Under the sociogram, make some notes about how you sense students treat you with regard to the relational dimensions. Do they position you 'in-out', 'close-far', 'with-against'? On the 'up-down' dimension, 'down' is not really an option, but you may have a feeling concerning how high up you are.

EXERCISE 4: SITUATING YOUR CLASS IN ITS STAGE OF DEVELOPMENT AS A GROUP

Match your data with the expectations given by the five stages in table 7.1. Use the descriptions of the different categories of topic, issue and student–teacher relationships to classify what you have written about the subject.

The result of this comparison should give you an approximate idea of where your class can be situated in its development as a group.

You might recall from the introductory quote that 'a classroom is like no other classroom'. Do not try to make your data fit the model! First of all, this chapter grossly simplifies the presentation of the model for the sake of clarity. You will find topics and issues codeveloping, but not quite as simultaneously as the five stages suggest. You will find that some individuals and subgroups develop faster than others and therefore mess up your tidy classification. You will also find sociograms containing a few individuals, some dyads and a subgroup and find yourself wondering where to situate them in our scheme. This will be another reminder that you cannot fit reality into a five-stage model.

Fortunately, the emphasis is not on neatly boxing your class into a category. The exercises are meant to get you started in the discovery of group development, not to help pigeonhole a whole group of people. If the exercises help by adding a relational perspective to your view of the class, they will have met their goal. After all,

even if your class group does not fit any of these categories, facilitating group development still means getting in touch with the class issues and helping the students deal with them!

Facilitating Group Development

Facilitating group development in our view basically means helping the group to deal with its issues. In the remainder of this chapter you will find a number of ideas for doing so. You could categorise them as one of the following approaches: addressing the issue, adapting the task or adjusting the rules and the task setting.

The first approach consists of addressing the issue directly. Actively listening to the student refusing to do the exercise on the single bar may lead to a conversation about his anxiety of failing and losing the recognition of his classmates. In terms of the relational dimensions described earlier, physical education is the only class in which this student has an 'up' position. Being unable to maintain a position that is 'up' and 'with', he shifted to 'against' in an attempt to cope with the expected loss of image. The intensity of his reaction does not relate to the gymnastics exercise, but to his fear of losing face.

An interesting aspect of this example is that it shows how many of us spontaneously interpret this student's behaviour as reflecting a personal problem. The tendency is to think that individual behaviour reflects individual issues. The fact that this student's fear can be described in relational dimensions illustrates that personal emotional safety is a relational issue. Students' behaviour can never be completely understood without situating it in the context of the class and other relationships.

However, addressing the issue directly assumes sufficient group, or subgroup, development for the issue to be a safe topic. As a consequence, this approach is unlikely to be successful during the first few stages previously described.

An alternative can be found in adapting the task. The idea here is to present exercises that allow the group to deal with its issue, rather than taking the task for granted. It will be obvious to any teacher that the opportunities for student interaction in Swedish gymnastics, a dance class or a soccer game are very different. Therefore, some activities may fit better at one point than at another.

The third approach involves manipulating the structure, rules and roles for a given task. It may include a procedure for dividing the class into teams, for example, or a rule that requires the player who scores in a game to switch teams. Such adjustments allow you to influence the social structure of an activity without deviating from the required curriculum.

The following paragraphs present aspects that deserve your attention if you want to facilitate group development at each of the five stages described previously and summarised in table 7.1.

Stage 1: Task, Inclusion and Dependence

A group does not even start to develop if its members do not get the chance to experience themselves as a group. To stimulate your class growth as a group, you need to offer group activities that make students interdependent in a situation that allows them face-to-face contact. Given the interaction between the task and inclusion, we would give special attention to presenting a variety of activities. If the activities call for different strengths, students with different capacities will be able to contribute to task accomplishment. This will give more students an opportunity to become an active part of the physical education class.

Different authors have pointed out the importance of a class setting in which students can see and hear each other (Schmuck & Schmuck, 2001; Stanford, 1977). Although the setting is less stable in a physical education class, you should still pay attention to the underlying concern. Forming a circle stimulates group interaction, whereas traditional lining up does not. Forming circles helps to decentralise communication.

When the students' relationship to the teacher is described as dependent, that implies that you have the power to initially define expectations and norms. You must state as clearly as possible what you expect from your students and what they can expect from you and the physical education class. In doing so, you must realise that nonverbal messages are at least as communicative as verbal ones. What you say may not be heard, but how you say it will come across loud and clear (Neilsen, 1977).

The challenge is to use early classes to model the kind of behaviour you would like to see during the school year. Be aware of students' surprising capacity to read cues about your standards. Subtle evaluations will suffice as hints for someone to feel safe or threatened in your class (Stanford, 1977). You are in a position to set standards; open and appreciative communication will stimulate group development. Examples include adding some personal information about yourself as a teacher to your presentation, calling students by their first names, appreciating effort at least as much as performance and being careful not to discriminate or humiliate.

You are in a position to encourage positive behaviour in your students. We purposefully avoid the word *enforce* here. This is not to say that enforcing rules cannot be part of your job. However, you have the option to speak for yourself instead of presenting the rule. If one student insults another one, you can request politeness—that is the rule. But you could also say, 'If I were addressed that way, I would feel hurt. I do not want people to humiliate each other in my class'. The expectation is equally clear and the message, equally firm. The difference is in how open and personal the communication is. You are now setting the tone for a friendly rather than a polite class.

Failure to satisfy the need to belong and other social goals that students pursue in tandem to academic goals may lead to rejection, decreased participation and a tendency to avoid and even abandon school. Although answering students' questions in the first classes of the semester helps them to gain certainty in a new situation, it makes sense to stop giving the answers to questions that students can answer themselves toward the end of this first stage. This may frustrate them to some extent, but it will stimulate them to become less dependent. One interesting option is to refer students' questions to the class group for an answer.

Stage 2: Rules, Similarity and Counterdependence

After the meeting with the group as a whole, students start looking for classmates with whom they feel comfortable. You can facilitate their search for support by regularly including tasks that allow contact in duos or trios. We suggested earlier that you avoid teaching new and complex skills at this stage that may be important later on in the curriculum. Students tend to be less receptive in this period. Intrinsically rewarding activities are more appropriate at this point.

Indoor climbing walls have started to appear in a number of schools. This is an example of an activity that seems to match the criteria mentioned. It allows working in trios consisting of a climber, a belayer and a backup belayer. For many students, climbing is an intrinsically rewarding activity. The immediate importance of mastering the belaying skills is likely to hold students' attention for the time necessary to teach them.

When defining the rules for the activity, you should recognise students' need for support. Let students choose their own subgroups at this stage. By doing so, you legitimise friendships that are forming and the supportive contact they offer. Gene Stanford (1977) countered this suggestion with his observation that students feel threatened by choosing and being chosen at this stage. He

therefore splits the group at random. We believe that the threat is not in choosing and being chosen, however, but in being forced to choose explicitly. If you just ask your class to divide into four subgroups, the students have a chance to make a number of implicit choices, which they can still claim to be coincidence. In the meantime, they avoid becoming part of an unsafe subgroup.

The hoped-for effect of these self-chosen subgroups would, of course, be annihilated if there were no opportunity for dialogue. Imposing silence would therefore be a counterproductive rule.

Finally, the class feels increased sensitivity to rules and similarity at this stage. Therefore, you may want to pay special attention to respecting the rules you present and applying them to every student equally.

Rewarding group work and appreciating students' common efforts, rather than individual performances, stimulates the group in its growth to independence. Unfortunately, the process of growing independent includes turning away from the teacher in some way. For a lot of teachers, this period is not easy. Although counterdependence in some classes limits itself to a few jokes or riddle-like games that allow students to have more power than their teacher for just one moment, in other classes students seem hostile over long periods of time. However, counterdependence has no quick fix. Trying to discuss things openly is very difficult and is often perceived as self-defence. In the students' eyes you are too powerful for self-defence to be accepted. Negative reaction can lead to very poor teacher–class relationships and recurring episodes of aggressiveness (Neilsen, 1977).

The following reminders have proven helpful for at least some. First of all, do not get paranoid about students' questions: They are not all attacks. Second, do not forget that the concept of counterdependence only explains why all the critical remarks come at the same time and why they sound so negative. It does not imply that the contents of remarks are not relevant or accurate. In other words, you should still actively listen to what students are trying to tell you (Schmuck & Schmuck, 2001; Stanford, 1977). Third, the model interprets part of what you hear as an overreaction in an attempt to gain independence. Therefore, do not take the remarks too personally.

Stage 3: Roles, Influence and Interdependence

After students have gotten to know a few class members really well, tasks in subgroups are likely to facilitate the students' relationships with more class members. The composition of these subgroups can emphasise this move even more. Encourage varying subgroups that regularly include some less known class members. The students should not stick with the class members with whom they have always worked. Rules for choosing or composing subgroups can stimulate this. Several ball sports meet these criteria: volleyball, basketball and so on.

You may need to facilitate or structure some debate among those students who hold different viewpoints on the way their subgroup or the class does things and who try to impose their approach. Remember that they are trying to establish their influence. Students may benefit from your facilitation in the conflict. They achieve better educational outcomes in small groups when they have the opportunity to learn about conflict resolution.

However, they are unlikely to settle their influence issue if you keep the discussion from happening or resolve the conflict for them. We even speculate that **bullying** incidents are more likely in classrooms in which teachers resolve students'conflicts. In our view, **alienation,** aggression and victimisation result from poor interper-

Remember that conflict is often a sign of students' trying to establish their influence.

© Bob Vincke.

sonal relationships because of the unsuccessful development of a classroom. Bullies are more likely to attack those classmates who are the easiest targets: the students who failed to be included in the first stage.

As your relationship with the class opens up and as students feel increasingly confident that they do not need your expertise or permission for every move they make, they start taking responsibility. You can also assign responsibility for later sessions to particular student teams. You are now presented with a valuable opportunity for feedback on your physical education class. At this point you can expect students' responses to your request for feedback about the course to be realistic without being affected by their dependence or counterdependence.

Stage 4: Behaviour, Equivalence and Continuing Interdependence

The competitive urge is over by now, and students feel sufficiently safe in their class to compose subgroups based on task-related criteria, rather than social concerns.

The class should be able to work in student-directed subgroups just fine at this point. Research indicates that such subgroups are preferably mixed-ability groups working toward a common goal. Subgroups should consist of students with different levels of mastery of the task at hand rather than divided based on competence. Within-class grouping based on achievement may have a negative effect on students' understanding and mastery of the course content. It also seems to have a negative impact on class relationships, especially if the teacher labels the subgroups as competence groups and emphasises the differences (Weinstein, 1991). The class as a whole benefits when students with specific abilities present (part of) a class that other students find interesting. In mixed-ability subgroups, these students can often help class members who are less familiar with a particular exercise or sport.

Research also suggests that mixed-gender subgroups should consist of comparable numbers of boys and girls. If this is not possible, not having mixed-gender groups at all may be better (Weinstein, 1991).

As students become interested in you as a person, they may want you to respond to their curiosity about your life beyond being a teacher.

Also, they might expect you to empathise rather than present expert solutions at times.

Stage 5: Emotion, Openness and Continuing Interdependence

At this point the group has reached a stage sometimes referred to as 'mature' because its members accept the responsibility for their group life as well as for their achievement in class (Schmuck & Schmuck, 2001). As a consequence, you can let students choose what sports or exercises they want to do for a few hours if the curriculum allows. You can mostly go along with the spontaneous group structure. The class is able to organise itself.

Debriefing the group's work and condition is a constructive step. Schmuck and Schmuck (2001) suggest having a class discussion about the high points and the low points of the last few days. This may result in problem-solving discussion if need be. Bear in mind that this stage is not an end, but rather a state of readiness for further physical and socioemotional growth.

Purposes of the Model

This chapter has presented a model of group development that may allow you to frame a number of your observations in your classroom. It has also presented some guidelines for daily practice. As mentioned earlier, you cannot expect the complexity of group development to be entirely covered by a five-stage model. Consequently, do not think of the guidelines as a set of fixed rules to be applied unthinkingly. The model can serve several purposes, however.

First of all, this model can serve as a framework for understanding a lot of the findings and advice offered in this book as well as in other sources. We have experienced personally how different bits and pieces of so-called expert information often seem incompatible and how the result is confusion. You may conclude that you'd be better off not believing any of it. Some experts say this, others say the opposite, so what do you do? A lot of seemingly contradictory advice can be integrated by plotting it on a continuum of group development. Take the suggestions on the composition of subgroups as an example. It is not a matter of whether to assign students to subgroups or to let them choose but of *when* to compose the groups

and *when* to let things happen on their own. Guidelines that seem to be mutually exclusive at first may simply apply to different stages in a group's life.

Second, the model and the guidelines combined in this chapter can help you to facilitate a group's evolution. In the introduction we expressed our conviction that both physical and socioemotional education benefit from facilitating group development (the teacher as a change agent). As relational issues are settled to some degree, more energy is available for the physical education task. Groups that evolve to stages of equivalence and intimacy offer crucial opportunities for socioemotional education.

The guidelines are not intended to be recipes. If treated that way, they become a recipe for failure. They need to be backed up by a perspective on and a genuine interest in the issues students deal with. To facilitate group development, one has to wade through the complexity of listening to relational messages. Remember, your classroom is like no other classroom. Consequently, there is no one technique or single right answer for classroom management. Any and all of your actions will be understood in the context of your relationship with the students, which has its ups and downs like any other relationship. However, fully living this relationship and acting accordingly remains the most promising way to create and maintain a healthy learning environment.

This chapter intends to invite you to a new perspective about that learning relationship. Paradoxically, applying the rule for the rule's sake tends not to work. Although a teacher's life would probably be easier if the recipe approach were successful, it sure would make it less interesting.

Summary

Awareness of interaction patterns in the classroom can help the teacher to manage the classroom to reach the curriculum goals and encourage healthy self-concept, skill acquisition and fitness development. Execution of physical education tasks will improve if relational issues are settled to some degree. In contrast with other courses, the format of the physical education class makes a privileged situation to observe and facilitate interactions between students and between students and the teacher.

Facilitating group development means helping the group to deal with its issues. Critical issues arise in each stage; and when the issues are successfully dealt with, the class group moves on. The purpose is to develop a class which is mature, accepts responsibility for group life and group task and is able to organize itself.

Review Questions

1. What are the similarities and the differences between your PE class and a sport team?
2. What exactly is meant by the socioemotional level of a group's functioning?
3. Describe the stages of group development and the key events that characterise each stage of group development.
4. How can you get a view on your PE class's functioning, and identify its developmental stage?
5. What are the primary strategies you can use to facilitate class development? Give an example of each strategy in each stage and discuss under which conditions each of the strategies is most appropriate.

Critical Thinking Questions

1. In what way do phenomena such as aggression (toward the teacher) and bullying (between students) relate to specific changes in relationships between students and their teacher and between students themselves?
2. The teacher of a class is out sick for two months in the middle of an academic year, and you are the replacement. How would you describe your position, and what would you do to manage this class? Justify your answer.
3. You are a teacher at the beginning of a school year, and you want all students to feel included in the class as quickly as possible. What would you do to reach that goal? Justify your answer.

Key Terms

alienation—Students' social withdrawal from school and classroom affairs.

bullying—An umbrella term for all types of aggression between students.

counterdependence—A defiant attitude of group members toward the leader, triggered by the leader's behaviour of setting rules.

group—A collection of people who are interdependent. A common goal is not a necessary condition of a group. Interdependence can also result from the necessity to share the means needed for individual goals.

interdependence—The characteristic of groups that become less dependent on the leadership of their teacher and more dependent on each other's roles and actions.

issue—The underlying concern of group members; individual group members' preoccupation (e.g., feeling left out).

sociogram—A map in which group members, their positions and the relations between them are symbolised.

team—A group in which the members share a common goal.

topic—What group members talk about, what they explicitly address (e.g., dribbling or passing in basketball).

References

Agazarian, Y. & Gantt, S. (2003). Phases of group development: Systems-centered hypotheses and their implications for research and practice. *Group Dynamics: Theory, Research, and Practice, 7,* 238-252.

Anderman, E.M. (2002). School effects on psychological outcomes during adolescence. *Journal of Educational Psychology, 94,* 795-809.

Arrow, H., Poole, M.S., Henry, K.B.,Wheelan, B. & Moreland, R. (2004). Time, change and development: The temporal perspective on groups. *Small Group Research, 35,* 73-105.

Bales, R. (1951). *Interaction process analysis.* Cambridge, MA: Addison-Wesley.

Bales, R. (1970). *Personality and interpersonal behavior.* New York: Holt.

Bennis, W.G. & Shepard, H.A. (1974). A theory of group development. In G. Gibbard, J. Hartman & R. Mann (Eds.), *Analysis of groups* (pp. 127-153). San Francisco: Jossey-Bass.

Buhs, E.S. & Ladd, G.W. (2001). Peer rejection as an antecedent of young children's school adjustment: An examination of mediating processes. *Developmental Psychology, 37,* 550-560.

Hare, P. (1973). Theories of group development and categories for interaction analysis. *Small Group Behavior, 4,* 259-304.

Highhouse, S. (2002). A history of the T-Group and its early applications in management development. *Group Dynamics: Theory, Research, and Practice, 6,* 277-290.

Hovelynck, J. (2000). *Leidraad in het faciliteren van ervaringsleren [Guidelines to facilitate experiential learning].* Unpublished doctoral dissertation: K.U. Leuven, Leuven, Belgium.

Hug, W. & King, J. (1984). Educational interpretations of general systems theory. In R. Bass & C. Dills (Eds.), *Instructional development: The state of the art, part 2* (pp. 18-28). Dubuque, IA: Kendall Hart.

Lancy, D. (1978). The classroom as a phenomenon. In D. Bas-Tal & L. Saxe (Eds.), *Social psychology of education* (pp. 11-132). New York: Ronald.

Leary, T. (1957). *Interpersonal diagnosis of personality.* New York: Ronald.

Murdock, T.B. (1999). The social context of risk: Status and motivational predictors of alienation in middle school. *Journal of Educational Psychology, 91,* 62-75.

Neilsen, E. (1977). Applying a group development model to managing a class. *The Teaching of Organization Behavior, 11*(4), 9-16.

Olweus, D. (1978). *Aggression in the schools: Bullies and whipping boys.* Washington, DC: Hemisphere.

Pakaslahti, L., Karjalainen, A. & Keltinkangas-Jarvinen, L. (2002). Relationships between adolescent prosocial problem-solving strategies, prosocial behavior and social acceptance. *International Journal of Behavioral Development, 26,* 137-144.

Rioch, M. (1975). The work of Wilfred Bion with groups. In A. Colman & W. Bexton (Eds.), *Group relations reader* (pp. 21-33). Sausalito, CA: Grex.

Schmuck, R.A. & Schmuck, P.A. (2001). *Group processes in the classroom.* New York: McGraw-Hill.

Schutz, W. (1966). *The interpersonal underworld.* Palo Alto, CA: Science & Behavior Books.

Slavin, R.L. (2002). Operative group dynamics in school settings: Structuring to enhance educational, social, and emotional progress. *Group, 26,* 297-308.

Stanford, G. (1977). *Developing effective classroom groups.* New York: Hart.

Weinstein, C. (1991). The classroom as a social context for learning. *Annual Review of Psychology, 42,* 493-526.

Wentzel, K.R. & Caldwell, K. (1997). Friendships, peer acceptance, and group membership: Relations to academic achievement in middle school. *Child Development, 68,* 1198-1209.

part three

Promotion of Self-Concept and Cognitive Skills

Dorothee Alfermann

Self-theories are becoming increasingly popular in several psychological disciplines such as developmental, social and, of course, personality psychology. Exercise psychology and sport psychology are no exception to this trend. The increasing emphasis on the self in psychology may reflect a zeitgeist: the tendency in Western culture to overemphasise individualism and individual happiness. During the last two decades or so, exercise psychology has focused on a variety of self variables: self-concept, self-esteem, self-efficacy, body image and physical appearance. The aims of this part are to show that (and how) sport and exercise can influence various aspects of the self and of cognitive skills, and how physical education teachers can help to promote self-concept and cognitive skills in their students. Two of the chapters in this part focus on the self. All three chapters first give short introductions to the respective topics. Afterward they present some studies in more detail. This helps to clarify how and under what conditions sport and exercise would have a positive impact. Finally, examples are given with regard to the physical education setting.

Chapter 8, 'Promotion of a Healthy Self-Concept', by Jeannine Stiller and Dorothee Alfermann, aims to disseminate knowledge about the development and structure of self-concept (including self-esteem and physical self-concept); inform about research results on the influence of exercise on physical self-concept and self-esteem; and suggest ways to improve self-concept through physical education, including the scope and limits of this approach.

Self-concept is conceived as being organised hierarchically with self-esteem at the apex followed by various self-concept dimensions on the domain level that contribute to self-esteem. Since its inception, the multidimensional, hierarchical model of self-concept has been tested in numerous studies focusing on academic self-concept. However, since the 1990s, there has been a growing interest in studying other aspects of self-concept as well, physical self-concept in particular.

Chapter 9, 'Self-Regulation and Strategic Learning: The Role of Motivational Beliefs and the Learning Environment in Physical Education', by Yngvar Ommundsen and Pierre-Nicolas Lemyre, gives an overview of the role of achievement-related beliefs on young people's self-regulation of their learning in physical education. The chapter first presents a theoretical framework blending perspectives on motivation self-regulation. In the second part, this framework is backed up by empirical findings on motivation and self-regulation within the general education domain. In the third part of the chapter the authors review the results of Norwegian studies examining differential achievement beliefs including implicit theories of ability, achievement goals and motivational climate perceptions in relation to pupils' self-regulation in physical education classes. Results from these studies add to those from the general education domain by revealing that optimistic and personally controllable self-beliefs regarding the ability to learn are associated with adaptive self-regulation also in the physical-motor domain of physical education. In contrast, avoidance-oriented and fixed-achievement self-beliefs reflecting a lack of personal control over one's ability to learn seem to negatively affect adaptive self-regulation and predict the use of self-handicapping strategies. Also, a motivational climate that is perceived to emphasise competition and social comparison seems to induce fixed-ability beliefs, whereas a mastery climate, partly mediated by task goals and performance-approach goals, generates adaptive forms of self-regulation. The pattern of results from these studies underscores the importance of studying social-cognitive factors in order to understand pupils' self-regulation in the gym. Finally, practical implications for the PE teacher are forwarded.

Chapter 10 is 'Interdisciplinary Teaching, Multiple Goals and Self-Concept', by Dimitris Milosis and Athanasios Papaioannou. According to the multidimensional model of goal orientations, the adoption of a personal development goal in life and its implementation in different life settings, such as school and sport, leads to adaptive cognitions, affect and behavioural outcomes. Based on this assumption, a six-month intervention study was conducted in four physical education classes, which aimed to boost the creation of personal development goals in life, physical activity, academic and family settings. The control group comprised eight classes in three different geographical locations in the same city. Questionnaires were administered before and immediately after the intervention. The implementation of the intervention is presented in detail. In addition to the strategies aiming to create a task-involving climate in physical education, this intervention attempted to transfer the value of personal development and self-regulation strategies such as goal setting, self-monitoring, self-talk and imagery from physical education to math, Greek language and family settings. The intervention had positive effects on task-involving climate in physical education; personal development goals and intrinsic motivation in physical education, math, Greek language and life in general; self-esteem (sport, math, verbal, emotional stability, parent relations and general); and grades in Greek language. The findings are discussed in light of recent educational policies in Greece aiming to promote integrated curricula in primary and secondary education. The common and distinct elements between existing cross-disciplinary curriculum models and the present model are delineated.

chapter eight

Promotion of a Healthy Self-Concept

Jeannine Stiller
Dorothee Alfermann
University of Leipzig, Germany

After reading this chapter, you will be able to do the following:

- Define self-concept
- Describe the components and hierarchical structure of self-concept
- Consider peculiarities in the development of self-concept
- Describe the physical self
- Understand the relationship between the physical self and behaviour
- Detail useful guidelines for nurturing a positive physical self-concept through sport and exercise

Miriam is an enthusiastic eight-year-old soccer player. She is living in a small community and is a member of a mixed-gender team in a local soccer club, the Winden Lions. She is playing as a striker and scores one or two goals every match. Because of her success and the encouragement of her parents and the coach, she is convinced that she is a talented player with the necessary physical abilities and tactical knowledge and that she will make it to the national team.

When Miriam grows older, the team has to dissolve because of the regulations of the soccer federation that girls and boys are no longer allowed to play on the same team when they reach the age of 10. Only a few girls are left, and they now have to find more teammates to continue as a team in the U12 female soccer league. Unfortunately, there are not enough female players of her age in her club. She has two alternatives: either to play with older teammates in the U14 league or to leave her club and try to find another one. After a long debate with her former coach and teammates, she continues playing with the Winden Lions on a U14 team. But many of the players are taller, faster and tougher than Miriam is. She is no longer able to score as many goals as she did on her former team. She is developing doubts about her physical competence and wonders whether she should continue playing soccer, although her parents are still encouraging her.

Like Miriam, we all develop an inner feeling about our strengths and weaknesses; we get feedback about our competence from the results of our actions and from significant others. Miriam learned a lot about her physical abilities from playing soccer on a team. Compared to the others she was very good and therefore had a positive **physical self-concept** (PSC), but it was very dependent on her success in competitions. When she changed teams, she also changed her reference group. Compared to her older teammates and opponents, she now feels less competent and talented. She is not considering the differences in physical strength and condition due to different levels of physical maturity.

How do we develop self-concept and physical self-concept? What are the critical influences? And how do our sense of self-concept and our actions interact? Do sport and exercise contribute to self-concept and vice versa? In this chapter we introduce you to the topic of self-concept, its structure and influence.

What Is Self-Concept?

A main research area of psychology is focused on the structure and development of **self-concept** in childhood, youth and adolescence (Bracken & Lamprecht, 2003; Fox, 1997; Harter, 1999; Marsh & Hattie, 1996). Developing a positive and healthy self-concept is regarded as one of the most important developmental tasks of human beings (Bracken & Lamprecht, 2003; Erikson, 1980). A healthy self-concept includes being self-confident, sociable and competent, as well as having a positive attitude toward one's body. Though *self-concept* is a very popular term, its meaning is by no means unequivocal (see the sidebar on page 125). In their state-of-the-art review, Bracken and Lamprecht (2003, p. 104) summarised the self-concept research as a 'chaotic state of the professional literature' because sophisticated self-concept instruments, though existent, are often not used but replaced instead by less elaborated measures of questionable validity, such as single-item scales or ad hoc developed instruments. Apart from these methodological concerns, we agree that developing a healthy, positive self-concept is an important developmental task and life goal. Parents, teachers and other educators should therefore be sensitive in fostering a positive self-concept, particularly in children and adolescents (see also Marsh, 1990).

In this chapter we will do the following:

- Summarise knowledge about the development and structure of self-concept (including self-esteem and physical self-concept).

- Review research results about the influence of exercise on physical self-concept and self-esteem.

- Suggest methods for improving self-concept through physical education, including the scope and limits of this approach.

Development and Structure of Self-Concept

In this section we will introduce the process of self-concept development, list its primary determinants and discuss structural models of self-concept.

A PROPER DEFINITION OF SELF-CONCEPT

When scanning the literature on self-concept, you may find several terms and definitions. For example, Bracken and Lamprecht (2003) proposed to use the terms *self-concept, self-esteem* or *self-image* interchangeably, whereas Dusek and McIntyre (2003) saw differences. In their view self-concept refers to 'the dimensions or categories along which we view the self', whereas **self-esteem** refers to 'our evaluation or assessment of our self' (p. 290).

In this chapter we distinguish between a global conceptualisation of self-concept and a more differentiated one. The global conceptualisation involves a general evaluation of oneself derived from a knowledge and evaluation of competencies and skills in different areas such as social relationships, academic subjects and physical tasks. This general evaluation of the self is called self-esteem. But the term *self-concept* encompasses more than that. In addition, it comprises self-knowledge and self-evaluation on several dimensions of competence and skills. Bracken and Lamprecht (2003) proposed six dimensions; namely, physical, family, academic, social, affect and competence (see figure 8.1). Shavelson, Hubner and Stanton (1976) were the first to suggest a hierarchical model with self-esteem on the apex and several dimensions (similar to those of Bracken and Lamprecht) on the second level. Their model received considerable attention in the psychological literature. Therefore, a proper definition of self-concept should include several aspects: 'Seven features can be identified as critical to the construct definition. Self-concept may be described as: organized, multifaceted, hierarchical, stable, developmental, evaluative, differentiable' (Shavelson, Hubner & Stanton, 1976, p. 411).

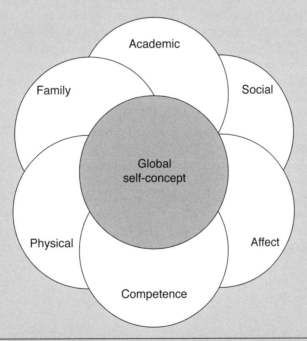

Figure 8.1   A multidimensional self-concept model. The Venn diagram offers a hierarchical model of self-concept with global self-concept on the apex and somewhat overlapping dimensions below.

Reprinted, by permission, from B.A. Bracken and M.S. Lamprecht, 2003, "Positive self-concept: An equal opportunity construct," *School Psychology Quarterly* 18: 103-121.

Developmental Characteristics

Psychological research from different disciplines contributes to a better understanding of the self and the development of self-concept. Starting with William James' legendary proposal in 1890 that self-esteem is a result of *the relationship between one's presumed abilities and one's actual accomplishments,* psychological research in the past hundred years or so relied heavily on his model of a cognitive-affective self-system that contributes to the development of self-concept (James, 1981). James considered external factors as less determinant; namely, the social environment and external stimuli. A more recent version of the self-system was proposed by Susan Harter (1999), who spoke of the self in terms of 'self-representations, self-perceptions and self-descriptions' (p. 3) with an emphasis on the social-*cognitive* meaning of self. Though she accepts the distinction between descriptive (cognitive) and evaluative self-representations, in her opinion self-descriptions are more or less automatically combined with evaluative judgments of good or bad. If this evaluation is more global, it corresponds to self-esteem; if descriptions or evaluations are more domain specific, they include aspects of self-concept. In line with cognitive-developmental theories, the construction of the self is regarded as inevitable and necessary in order to make meaning of one's experiences and of the world. In this sense the self is regarded as a cognitive construction.

Apart from the cognitive construction of the self-system, Susan Harter also emphasised the developmental influences on this system. Because these influences are mainly social influences, besides internal factors of biological maturity and cognitive development, the self is also a social construction. Social influences, such as information and evaluative feedback from caregivers, teachers or peers shape our self-concept. It is neither a looking-glass self, reflecting only what others want us to be, nor an individual self, constructed only by our cognitive-evaluative abilities. Instead, the development of self-concept depends on our ability to build, interpret and organise information and experiences as well as on environmental feedback. More than one hundred years after James' pioneering analysis of the self, as the result of a social-cognitive construction process, psychology now sees the development of self-concept as the result of an interaction between the developing person's cognitive construction processes and environmental shaping. *Therefore, the self is a both a cognitive and a social construction.*

In the beginnings of empirical self-concept research, the prevalent model of self relied on the assumption of a unidimensional structure with no distinction between different dimensions or hierarchical levels (Marsh & Hattie, 1996). In 1976, Shavelson and colleagues (1976) were the first to suggest that self-concept is multidimensional and hierarchical and undergoes a developmental process. It becomes more and more differentiated during ontogenesis (see also Harter, 1996). The structure of physical self-concept is supposed to undergo changes during the life span as well. Children at a younger age should be less able to differentiate between specific subdomains such as strength, coordination or flexibility than older people (Harter, 1996). They should perceive their own physical abilities in a more global way—for example, being good at sport—without further differentiation. Adolescents and middle-aged adults, whose cognitive and physical abilities are fully developed, should be better at recognising their own physical abilities in a more detailed manner. At this developmental stage, they should distinguish between different subdomains of physical abilities.

According to developmental psychology, the transition from childhood to adolescence (maturity) is one of the most important biological changes leading up to and through the growth-spurt years. It typically starts at the age of 10 to 12 for girls, and two years later for boys. The changes lead to a massive physical development, accompanied by cognitive, emotional and social developmental processes that all are related to the development of self-concept, including self-esteem. Bracken and Lamprecht (2003) pointed out that with increasing age and maturity, self-concept development can be described as an increase of refinement within individual self-concept dimensions and at the same time as an increase of differentiation across these dimensions.

Dusek and McIntyre (2003) reviewed moderating influences on the development of self-concept and emphasised the early or late maturation that can be troublesome for adolescents. Those who mature especially early tend to become involved in activities or roles with which they don't have the skills or abilities to cope (Dusek & McIntyre,

2003). Other powerful influencing variables are socialisation agents; for example, the school environment is influential because students spend much of the day at school. Another example is the relationship with parents. And the peer group presumably plays an important role in self-concept development. All three—school, parents and peers—have a high impact on the development of the self, but a discussion of these would go beyond the scope of this chapter. For an overview we recommend Dusek and McIntyre (2003).

Structure

As noted earlier, Shavelson and colleagues (1976) developed a hierarchically organised, multidimensional model of self-concept. They portrayed a self-concept structure that is similar to a hierarchically based personality structure and can be tested empirically. Further, it is thought to represent global perceptions of the self, with general self-concept at the apex and actual behaviour at the base. Moving from top to bottom, the self-concept structure is assumed to be more and more differentiated. In particular, general self-concept should split into two parts: academic and nonacademic. These two parts should then split into several dimensions at the next level,

such as social, emotional and physical. These dimensions should differentiate even further, and so on. Because the structure of self-concept is multidimensional, it should be kept in mind that the various dimensions are distinct and more or less independent. They are measurable and empirically testable. The hierarchical nature of self-concept implies that the correlations between adjacent levels of the hierarchy are higher than those between the more remote levels (Marsh, 1997; Marsh & Shavelson, 1985).

The model of Shavelson and colleagues (1976) represents a typical multidimensional self-concept model. Many more exist. Models that assume that self-concept is critical for structuring and guiding behaviour are not without critics. For example, behavioural theories stress the fact that behaviour is observable, whereas self-concept is obviously a hypothetical construct. 'From a behavioral perspective the "self" might be conceived of as a pattern of behavior that is sufficiently unique to an individual to be identified as the core of that individual' (Bracken & Lamprecht, 2003, p. 105). Others have pointed out that self-concept has not been adequately tested empirically because of its complexity (Marsh & Hattie, 1996). Table 8.1 shows further theories and models that are discussed in the self-concept literature.

Table 8.1 Theories and Models of Self-Concept in the History of Psychological Self-Concept Research

Author(s)	Content
Coopersmith (1967)	*Unidimensional*, general factor model: As in former intelligence theories, self-concept is dominated by a general factor; it is not possible to differentiate self-concept from other factors.
Soares and Soares (1977)	*Taxonomic* model: Inspired by Guilford's intelligence model, this model assumes that the dimensions of the self reflect the connection of two or more facets.
Marx and Winne (1978)	*Compensatory* model: This model proposes a global self-concept factor and multiple lower-order factors (e.g., social, academic, physical).
Marsh (1986)	*Internal/external frame of reference* model: This model focuses on correlations among several self-concepts. People create their self-concept in a particular dimension by comparing their own competence with the perceived competence of others in the same and other dimensions.
Bracken (1992)	*Multidimensional, hierarchical* model: Global self-concept is at the centre, and specific domains overlap equally with global self-concept.

Adapted from H.W. Marsh and J. Hattie, 1996, Theoretical perspectives on the structure of self-concept. In *Handbook of self-concept. Developmental, social, and clinical considerations*, edited by B.A. Bracken (New York: John Wiley & Sons, Inc.), 38-90.

Physical Self: Structure and Measurement

Since its inception, the structural model of self-concept has been tested in numerous studies, with the focus of research directed primarily toward academic self-concept (for an overview, see Byrne, 1996; Marsh, 1990; Marsh & Hattie, 1996). However, since the 1990s, there has been a growing interest in studying other aspects of self-concept as well, such as social (Byrne & Shavelson, 1996) and, in particular, physical self-concept. These facets of self-concept have been shown to be multifaceted too. Fox and Corbin (1989) were the first to present a hierarchical and multidimensional model of physical self-concept with self-esteem at the apex, physical self-worth at the domain level and several subdimensions on the subdomain level. They also developed a measuring instrument for physical self-concept, the *Physical Self-Perception Profile (PSPP)*. Both the model and the instrument made important contributions to a better understanding of the dynamics between physical self-concept and physical activity. The *PSPP* was used in several studies that tested the effects of exercise on self-concept.

The *PSPP* is not the only questionnaire for measuring physical self-concept. Marsh and Redmayne (1994) developed a six-dimensional scale for adolescents that taps the more global perception of physical ability and physical appearance at the domain level, and several subdimensions of physical ability (namely, endurance, flexibility, strength and balance) at the subdomain level. Physical ability and physical appearance were assumed to be independent of each other but were actually positively correlated (Marsh & Redmayne, 1994; Marsh, Richards, Johnson, Roche & Tremayne, 1994). Marsh and colleagues (1994) presented an expanded version of the scale, the *Physical Self-Description Questionnaire (PSDQ)*, which consists of 11 scales showing reasonable congruent and discriminant validity. The *PSDQ* has now been translated into several languages and is available to teachers and researchers from non-English-speaking countries. An advantage of Marsh's instruments is that they measure more subdimensions of physical ability than the *PSPP* does, whereas an advantage of the *PSPP* is its greater age range of target groups.

What about cultural differences in the structure of physical self-concept? The hierarchical models were developed in Anglo-American and Australian contexts. Less is known about the applicability of the model to other, non-English-speaking nations and cultures. But the *PSDQ* was successfully replicated in France (Guérin, Marsh & Famose, 2004), Turkey (Marsh, Aşçi & Thomás, 2002), Israel (Richards, Marsh, Bar-Eli & Zach, 2005) and Germany (Stiller & Alfermann, 2004). With a sample of Finnish adolescents, Lintunen (1995) successfully replicated the factor structure of physical self-concept as suggested by Marsh and colleagues (1994), but at the same time found significant gender differences in the relationship between physical self-concept and physical fitness. Stiller and Alfermann (2004) and Aşçi, and Çağlar (2005) likewise found gender differences, with girls scoring lower than boys on most self-concept dimensions. Brettschneider and Heim (1997), using Marsh's *Self-Description Questionnaire (SDQ II)*, an inventory measuring academic and nonacademic self-concept, found a comparable factor structure with the original instrument in German adolescents. These results seem to indicate that within the Western culture the structure of self-concept follows similar guidelines, but there might be differences within the hierarchical levels between subcultures (such as gender) and nations. But other authors cited evidence *against* the hierarchical model. Kowalski, Crocker, Kowalski, Chad and Humbert (2003) investigated the development of physical self-concept in adolescent girls and found no evidence for a hierarchical structure. More cross-national and cross-cultural comparison studies are needed to gain insights into the universality or specificity (or both) of the structure and the relationships among different components of self-concept.

Sport, Exercise and Physical Self-Concept: Reciprocal Effects

Physical self-concept has only recently received major attention from exercise researchers (Sonstroem, 1997a, 1997b). Besides measurement and construct issues, the main focus of research was directed toward the relationship between the physical self and sport and exercise. For example, in a meta-analysis, Gruber (1986) demonstrated that physically active children exhibited higher self-esteem than inactive children. In another meta-analysis, McDonald and Hodgdon (1991) likewise found significant differences in self-concept measures of exercisers and nonexercisers regardless of age and gender, though it must be taken into consideration that the majority of these studies were done with younger age groups and were survey studies that are not able to reveal *causal* relationships. Exercisers showed a more positive physical self-concept and self-esteem than did nonexercisers, but it remains unclear from these studies whether exercise heightens physical self-concept or vice versa. An early study by Guyot, Fairchild and Hill (1981) focused on the relationship among physical fitness, sport participation and self-concept, including body image in childhood. They found that boys and girls in the high physical fitness group scored higher than boys and girls in the low physical fitness group. Also, Smith (1986) pointed out that children who participate in sports may have a higher self-concept than nonparticipants.

In the last 20 years or so, an increasing number of studies have addressed the relationship between sport and exercise and self-concept, which has expanded our knowledge base. From the accumulated results of these studies, there is now ample evidence that exercise is able to improve physical self-concept, whereas mixed results are found for self-esteem (Fox, 2000). A recent meta-analysis with adult samples showed a small but consistently positive effect of exercise on self-esteem (Spence, McGannon & Poon, 2005). In addition, there is no one-way causal path from exercise to self-esteem, but instead a reciprocal relationship has to be considered. Sport or exercise and self-concept are mutually related and influence each other.

The *Exercise and Self-Esteem Model* of Sonstroem and Morgan (1989), which was later revised into an expanded *EXSEM* (Sonstroem, Harlow & Josephs, 1994; see also Sonstroem, 1997b, 1998), postulates a direct causal path from exercise to self-concept. It assumes that exercise first influences physical self-concept (PSC) in such a way that people develop a higher degree of physical competence and physical acceptance. This subsequently should lead to heightened feelings of global self-esteem (SE). The path from exercise to self-esteem corresponds to the skill development hypothesis. Improving physical competence and performance should lead to a more positive self-concept. In consequence, fostering a healthy self-concept means improving physical competence first and self-concept second.

At the same time, however, the self should also influence physical activity and performance. The pathway from self to activity and performance corresponds to the widely shared assumption that we behave according to our self-concept. If this is true, then our self-concept should influence our (perception of) performance and shape our behaviour within the environment. This pathway corresponds to the self-enhancement hypothesis (Sonstroem, 1998, p. 134), which states that fostering a positive physical self-concept will result in greater efforts toward increasing physical performance and sport or exercise participation. Both causal pathways (from SE and PSC to the environment and vice versa) represent the bidirectional influence of self-concept and behaviour. Self-concept is not only influenced by performance and success or failure, but is a causal agent itself. Thus, not only can physical activity improve perceived physical competence and thus, in turn, self-esteem (the skill development hypothesis), but self-esteem and physical self-concept can also influence physical activity (Sonstroem, 1998).

Improving physical competence and performance should lead to a more positive self-concept.
© Bob Vincke.

The earlier and later versions of the *Exercise and Self-Esteem Model* (see Sonstroem, 1997b) have been tested in several studies since their publication, mostly with adult participants. Sonstroem, Harlow and Salisbury (1993) tested the model in a longitudinal study with male swimmers. Participants were administered a test battery with a self-esteem scale, a physical competence scale and a study-developed swimming skills scale at three points of measurement. Significant increases were found in SE, in PSC and in perception of skills over time.

The expanded *EXSEM* represents a hierarchical, four-level model with self-efficacy and physical activity at the lowest (behavioural) level, physical competence as a multidimensional construct at the subdomain level, physical self-worth at the next highest (domain) level and self-esteem at the highest level (see also Fox & Corbin, 1989). Caruso and Gill (1992) conducted two intervention studies with male and female students. The correlation patterns in both studies between the various self-concept measures offered some support for the hierarchical *EXSEM*. Sonstroem and Potts (1996) analysed the relationship between physical self-concept and life adjustment indexes in a sample of male and female university students. Using regression analyses, the authors showed that self-perceptions of PSC significantly improved associations with life adjustment. These relationships were robust across genders. Using a multidimensional physical self-concept instrument in three experiments with middle-aged and older adults, Alfermann and Stoll (2000; Stoll & Alfermann, 2002) found support for the assumption that exercise may improve physical self-concept, whereas the influence on self-esteem remained equivocal.

Marsh and colleagues tested the impact of sport and exercise on physical self-concept and vice versa in a number of studies. With top-ranked elite swimmers from 30 countries, they were able to show that the athletes' physical self-concept contributed to swimming performance in a championship competition above and beyond the swimmers' previous personal-best result (Marsh & Perry, 2005). This means that athletes with a positive self-concept improved their swimming performance more than those with a less positive one, showing clear evidence of a self-enhancement model. But, as explained earlier, assuming an exclusively unidirectional influence

of self-concept on behaviour is oversimplistic. Instead, the mutual impact of self-concept and behaviour has to be considered. Methodologically this should lead to longitudinal studies with at least two points of measurement in both sets of variables.

Papaioannou, Marsh and Theodorakis (2004) collected data on exercise behaviour and physical self-concept from a Greek sample of 200 physical education classes early (T1) and late (T2) in the school year. Supporting a reciprocal effects model of self-concept and behavioural achievement, the results clearly showed an influence of T1 self-concept on T2 physical activity and of T1 physical activity on T2 physical self-concept.

In a study with 20 gymnastics classes, grades seven to nine, self-concept and performance measures were collected over a 10-week period (Chanal, Marsh, Sarrazin & Bois, 2005). Similar to the results of Papaioannou and colleagues, self-concept and achievement were mutually related—with self-concept influencing achievement and vice versa. Results showed in addition that self-concept was *positively* related to individual skill level, whereas the group's average skill level was *negatively* related to self-concept. Both correlations increased over time. This result can be interpreted as corroborating the big-fish-little-pond effect. Individuals compare their achievement with those of their respective groups (e.g., in classrooms or in teams). The more selective the group is, the higher the average performance will be, and the more likely it is that the effect on self-concept will be negative. Marsh and Hau (2003) showed this effect in the academic domain in a 26-nation study. The negative effect of the group's average skill level on self-concept is a very robust and universal finding, and, as Chanal and colleagues showed, it exists not only in the academic domain but also in an exercise setting such as physical education.

What are the implications of the empirical findings on self-concept and behaviour or achievement? First of all, because a healthy self-concept is a determinant of achievement and exercise behaviour, it is important to promote self-concept. But because the relationship is reciprocal, performance enhancement itself should contribute to a positive self-concept. Teaching students how to improve their skills, and giving them opportunities to experience success, should result in a higher self-concept (Chanal et al., 2005; Papaioannou et al., 2004). But the effect is dependent on context factors, one of which is the placement of participants within a group. Both gifted students who are placed in groups for the specially talented, and low achievers who are placed in regular classes, show a decrease in self-concept (Marsh & Hau, 2003). Though students may increase in achievement and experience some success, overall the result is negative, and the reasons are the comparison processes of individual group members with the group average. Overall, this leads in many cases to a loss of positive self-concept. Selective groups and schools are therefore a double-edged sword. On the one hand, they may be more apt to enhance performance and skills. On the other hand, they are detrimental to the students' self-concept, which in the long run may negatively influence performance.

Development of Physical Self-Concept in Adolescence: A Cross-Sectional Study

Earlier in this chapter we emphasised the gradual differentiation of self-concept during childhood and adolescence. Less is known about the development of physical self-concept. In this section we present a cross-sectional study that sought to investigate the structure and development of physical self-concept during adolescence.

We translated a former version of the *PSDQ* (Marsh & Redmayne, 1994; Marsh et al., 1994), which measures six dimensions; namely, physical appearance and physical ability at the domain level, and four dimensions of physical ability at the subdomain level (strength, endurance, flexibility and coordination). Additionally, we developed a fifth domain level with regard to a complete representation of physical abilities; namely, speed (see Stiller, Würth & Alfermann, 2004). With this instrument we were able to expand the model of Fox and Corbin (1989) and to test the structure of physical self-concept in people of various ages, following the expanded *EXSEM* as well as the model of Marsh and colleagues (1994). With self-esteem at the apex, we assumed that physical self-worth, which was postulated by Fox and Corbin (1989) to be located at the domain level, could best be described by two dimensions: (1) physical ability (sport competence) and (2) physical appearance. Furthermore, physical ability should be multidimensional as well: Coordination, strength, flexibility, endurance and speed are the classical five subdomains of physical ability.

Perceived physical appearance and perceived physical ability are supposed to be independent (see figure 8.2). Moreover, the structure of physical self-concept is supposed to undergo changes during the life span (Alfermann & Stiller, 2001). Young adolescents should be less able to differentiate

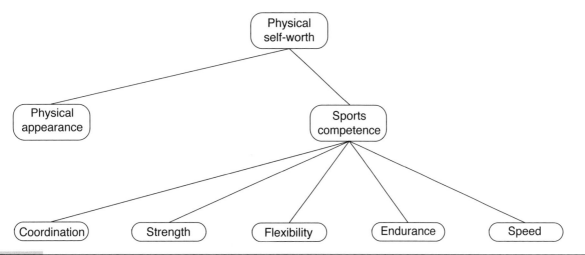

Figure 8.2 Hypothetical model of physical self-concept.

Adapted from J. Stiller, S. Würth and D. Alfermann, 2004, Die Messung des physischen Selbstkonzepts—Zur Entwicklung der PSK-Skalen für Kinder, Jugendliche und junge Erwachsene. [The measurement of physical self-concept—On developing the PSK-scales for children, adolescents, and young adults]. *Zeitschrift für Differentielle und Diagnostische Psychologie, 25*, 239-257.

between specific subdomains (such as strength, coordination and flexibility) than individuals at later ages are (Harter, 1996). They should perceive their own physical abilities in a more global way—for example, to be good at sport, without further differentiation. Late adolescents whose cognitive and physical abilities are fully developed should be better able to recognise their own physical abilities in a more detailed manner. In this developmental stage they should be able to distinguish among different subdomains of physical ability. Because of the physical changes that occur during adolescence, which may lead to concomitant feelings of physical distress (though transient), we expected that children and late adolescents would score higher on physical self-concept scales than early adolescents would.

Measures

Physical self-concept was measured with five subscales of the *PSDQ* (Marsh & Redmayne, 1994); namely, strength (e.g., 'I am good at lifting heavy objects'), endurance ('I think I could run a long way without getting tired'), flexibility ('I am quite good at bending, twisting and turning my body'), coordination ('I am graceful and coordinated when I do sports and activities') and sport competence, a global measure of physical ability ('I have good sport skills'). The scales had been translated into German and tested extensively with German adolescents. In addition, we developed a scale measuring speed ('I can run short distances very fast') because speed is an important dimension of physical ability. Physical appearance ('I am proud of my body') was assessed with a German scale developed in our lab. Cronbach alpha coefficients for the seven scales range from .79 to .92, thus showing high internal consistency. Retest coefficients are also highly acceptable, ranging from .73 to .93. All scales were published in Stiller and colleagues (2004), where more details about their development and validation are available.

Self-esteem (SE) was assessed with two subscales of a German self-concept inventory (Deusinger, 1986). One scale (*FSAL*) measures global SE based on success in life ('If I set a goal, I can accomplish it'). The other scale (*FSKU*) measures social SE, based on social approval ('I easily make contact with other people'). All items were rated on either four- or six-point Likert-type scales ranging from 1 (*strongly disagree*) to 4 and 6, respectively (*strongly agree*).

Participants

To test the hypothesis that physical self-concept differs according to age and gender, data were collected with participants ($n = 914$) representing 12 age groups across childhood and adolescence (see table 8.2). Overall, participants' age ranges from 10 to 25 years ($M = 16.15$; $SD = 3.63$; $n = 384$ boys; $n = 530$ girls). The majority of the participants took part in various sport programmes, either in competitive sports or in leisure sports.

Results

To test the differences between age and gender, several two-way analyses of variance were conducted with age and gender as independent variables. The dependent variables were represented by (1) the five dimensions of physical ability (strength, flexibility, endurance, speed and coordination), (2) the higher-order dimensions of physical appearance and sport competence and (3) the two scales of self-esteem.

Results revealed significant age × gender interaction effects for all five dimensions of physical self-concept ($mF = 2.67$, $p < .001$; $\eta^2 = .03$) and physical appearance, whereas the results for sport competence, as well as global and social SE, were nonsignificant (self-esteem: $mF = 0.87$; $p =$ n.s.; $\eta^2 = .02$; see table 8.3). As figure 8.3 shows, female adolescents aged 15 to 17 years old scored lowest on coordination, endurance, speed and

Table 8.2　Number of Participants Divided by Age and Gender

Age (years)	10 and 11	12	13	14	15	16	17	18	19	20	21 to 25	All
Male (*n*)	41	51	29	14	26	37	20	25	34	38	33	384
Female (*n*)	49	55	50	54	46	51	32	39	69	41	20	530
All (*n*)	90	106	79	68	72	88	52	64	103	79	113	914

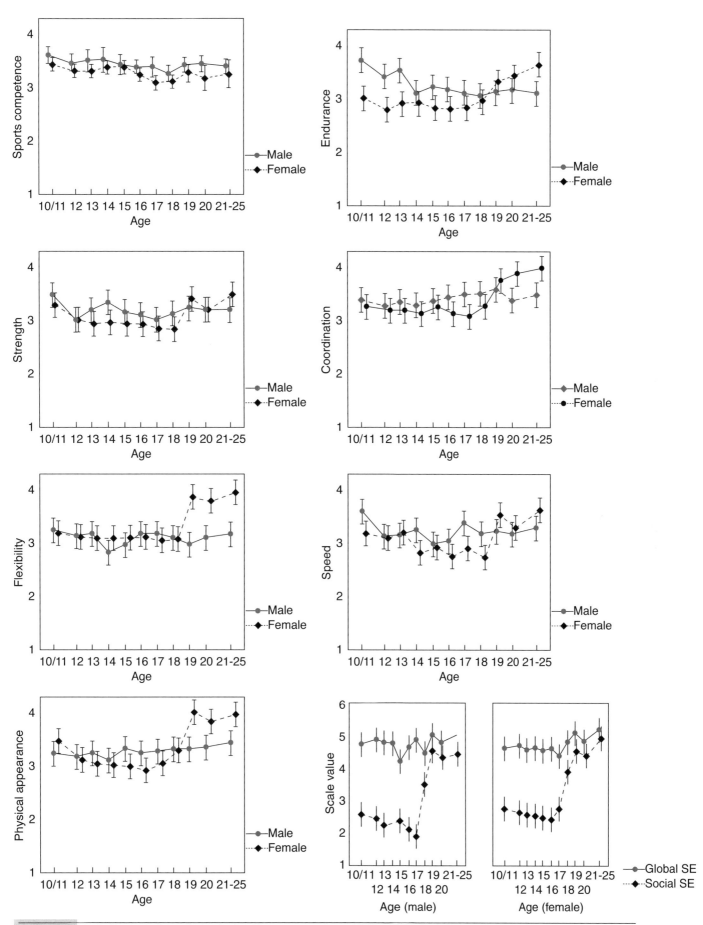

Figure 8.3   Self-perception of physical self-concept across childhood and adolescence.

Table 8.3 Results of 2 (gender) × 11 (age) Analyses of Variance (between subjects)

Source	Endurance	Flexibility	Coordi-nation	Strength	Speed	Compe-tence	Appearance	Global SE	Social SE
Gender (G) $df = 1$	2.75	18.24[c]	.09	2.68	2.42	17.64[c]	.67	2.28	3.03
η^2	.00	.02	.00	.00	.00	.02	.00	.01	.01
Age (A) $df = 10$	4.79[c]	7.33[c]	13.03[c]	6.43[c]	4.50[c]	2.02[a]	11.02[c]	3.42[c]	81.48[c]
η^2	.05	.08	.13	.06	.07	.03	.11	.07	.66
G × A $df = 10$	4.11[c]	7.01[c]	6.16[c]	2.11[a]	2.92[c]	.45	6.66[c]	.62	.45
η^2	.05	.07	.07	.02	.03	.00	.07	.01	.02

[a]$p < .05$, [b]$p < .01$, [c]$p < .001$; SE = self-esteem

physical appearance, whereas the 19- to 25-year-old females scored highest. The males' scores on these dimensions stayed relatively stable across age. The interaction effect for flexibility is due to the fact that female late adolescents have a higher self-concept of flexibility than their male counterparts have.

In addition to the interaction effects, the primary effects of age were revealed for the dimensions of sport competence, as well as global and social SE. Whereas 10-year-olds had the highest scores for sport competence, those in the oldest age group (19- to 25-year-olds) had higher scores for self-esteem. This was especially true for social self-esteem. Additional effects of gender occurred for sport competence, with males scoring higher than females did.

Conclusions

Our data showed that on five of the nine dimensions (mostly physical abilities), neither age nor gender alone contribute to differences in physical self-concept and self-esteem. Instead, both variables have to be taken into account. This means that physical self-concept may develop differently for boys and girls across age. Our results revealed that male adolescents show a relatively stable development in their self-concept of physical abilities, with higher scores than females until the age of 16 or 17. Females outscore males in late

adolescence as a result of a high increase of self-concept from 18 years onward. This is especially noticeable in flexibility, coordination, endurance, strength and physical appearance.

Whereas global self-esteem develops quite similarly for boys and girls and across age, social self-esteem is relatively low in early and middle adolescence but shows a remarkable increase from 18 years onward—independent of gender. Sport competence, which is a more global self-attribution of physical ability, is relatively uninfluenced by age but more by gender, with boys making higher self-attributions of sport competence.

How to Acquire Self-Concept

How do we acquire our self-concept? How is the information about ourselves learned, processed and integrated into different dimensions? Bracken and Lamprecht (2003) described how people acquire self-concept as a consequence of their interactions with their environment. Feedback from the environment is either received directly (e.g., through personal experiences such as success or failure) or indirectly from other people within the environment. The feedback can then be compared against four standards: absolute, comparative, ipsative and ideal (see figure 8.4).

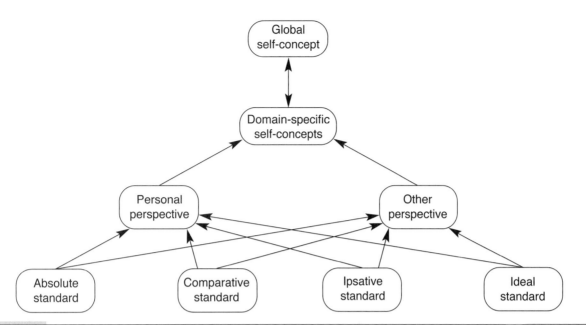

Figure 8.4 Self-concept behavioural acquisition model.

Adapted, by permission, from B.A. Bracken and M.S. Lamprecht, 2003, "Positive self-concept: An equal opportunity construct," *School Psychology Quarterly* 18, 103-121.

An absolute standard reflects a fairly objective personal evaluation based on directly observable attributes, characteristics or behaviours (Bracken & Lamprecht, 2003, p. 108). Motor performance or exercise behaviours are typical examples in which absolute standards are applicable. Behavioural results give direct feedback about successful or unsuccessful performances. The self-concept of physical abilities is influenced by these results. For example, feedback about endurance or speed performance may directly influence the self-concept of endurance and speed skills, respectively.

'The comparative standard is employed when an individual's behavior or personal characteristics are compared to those of other persons' (Bracken & Lamprecht, 2003, p. 108). Sport competitions or any other kind of implicit or explicit social comparison process for evaluating physical performance rely heavily on the comparative standard. The comparative evaluation (better or worse than classmates, one's age group, other boys, etc.) can be done using external sources such as teachers, peers or classmates, or by oneself. Though the comparative standard is quite popular in sports, results about goal orientations in youth sports clearly show that the comparative standard should be used with care and only occasionally. Otherwise, intrinsic motivation may be under-

mined, and physical self-concept may become too dependent on external information.

'Ipsative standards are used when students evaluate one behavior or personal characteristic in light of other individual behaviors or personal characteristics' (Bracken & Lamprecht, 2003, p. 109). The ipsative standard relies on individual comparison processes in which students evaluate their physical abilities, such as strength, in light of other abilities, such as coordination or endurance. Better performance in one area may compensate for lesser performance in another area. If a young woman believes that she is not good at sports but is good looking, this may heighten her self-esteem if she places a higher emphasis on physical attractiveness than on physical abilities.

'Ideal standards are employed when some ideal level of accomplishment is set as the goal or standard of comparison' (Bracken & Lamprecht, 2003, p. 109). This standard is similar to the person's aspiration level in achievement situations. Goals that are set as standards of accomplishment should be realistic and challenging at the same time. Achievement motivation theories and goal-setting approaches conclude unanimously that task difficulty should be intermediate, which corresponds to a probability level of about .50. This means that the probability of success is as high as the probability of failure. High achievers tend to choose goals of intermediate task difficulty and to attribute success to their abilities and failure to a lack of effort. In addition, they more easily remember success than failure. Therefore, high achievers should develop a positive and healthy self-concept because of their success history and their pattern of attribution. In contrast, low achievers, apart from their preference to choose either very difficult or very easy tasks, prefer to attribute success to external causes and failure to a lack of ability. Their self-concept of physical abilities may therefore be impaired because of a biased memory for failures and an attribution pattern that downgrades their physical competence.

How to Improve Self-Concept Through Physical Education

All standards of evaluation come into play in physical education. Apart from the comparative standard that should be introduced only occasionally, the other three standards for evaluating physical and motor performance may be used interchangeably. A predominantly intermediate task difficulty, an attribution of success to one's own ability and of failure to a lack of effort, and a standard of evaluation that emphasises one's own improvements and accomplishments (i.e., a task-involving motivational climate) should contribute to a healthy self-concept.

Some have argued that self-concept research doesn't go beyond the theoretical model, its structure and methodologies. This would mean that self-concept research is still satisfied with solving measurement problems and describing self-concept. Whereas it is fully acknowledged that progress in physical self-concept research and application relies heavily on a sophisticated theoretical model and on measures that meet the relevant test criteria, we should at the same time be aware that fostering a positive physical self-concept is a crucial task for all those who are involved in physical education. Of course, school is not the only source of influence. Three important sources may be relevant in adolescence: pubertal growth, the school (including physical education) and the social environment, especially

family, peers and coaches. Improving physical self-concept and self-esteem is regarded as an important goal of physical education. Healthy self-esteem may even be regarded as a national task (Bracken & Lamprecht, 2003). If sport and exercise can improve the physical self and may influence self-esteem, as we noted earlier, then physical education should be helpful in improving self-concept as well.

How can physical education improve students' self-concept? In principle, there are two possible ways (Calsyn & Kenny, 1977). One is the self-enhancement strategy, in which efforts focus directly on self-esteem (e.g., through praise and support). The other strategy is the skill development strategy, which focuses on competence. As previously discussed, self-concept is the result of cognitive and social construction processes. Attempts at enhancing self-concept directly were not as successful as those that focused on enhancing competence. The best way to influence self-concept is by improving competence and supporting experiences of success. Intervention strategies may be directed toward either cognitive determinants or social determinants of self-concept (Dweck, 1999). Any effort is virtuous that is directed toward improving skills, teaching criteria for skill evaluation, choosing problems that can be solved and making internal attributions. Self-concept can best be improved by teaching and improving motor skills.

Summary

After reading this chapter, you should understand the concept of self-concept, why it is an important agent of behaviour and at the same time its result. Self-concept can be conceptualised as more global or more differentiated. Global self-concept is defined as the general evaluation of oneself based on a knowledge and evaluation of one's competencies and skills. This general evaluation is called self-esteem. The differentiated self-concept comprises not only global self-esteem but also a differentiated structure of self-knowledge and self-evaluation on various dimensions of competencies and skills. The development of self-concept relies on biological factors (for example, maturity), cognitive factors (such as information integration) and social factors (particularly informational and evaluative feedback from social agents). Thus, self-concept is the result of a cognitive and social construction process. This is why motor tests indicate only a moderate relationship between physical abilities and self-concept.

Physical self-concept is only one facet of the self and is of particular importance in sport and physical education. It is said to be influenced by the results and accomplishments in exercise and sport. This is mainly dependent on student's interpretations and social feedback, for example, from teachers and other students. The resulting self-concept also relies heavily on social comparison processes. This means that the reference group and the class environment contribute to the developing self-concept. Helping students to learn motor skills and to improve their competence may also improve their physical self-concept, but a task-involving motivational climate will be most helpful.

In addition, physical self-concept may itself influence behaviour and thus determine, for example, the student's initiative, motivation and goal setting in PE. This reciprocal relationship between exercise and the (physical) self should be considered in PE lessons.

Self-concept, including the physical domain, develops over the life span. In adolescence it becomes more and more differentiated, depending on the person's cognitive, physical and social development.

Review Questions

1. What is self-concept?
2. Give an example of a multidimensional model of physical self-concept and its measurement.
3. How is sport or exercise related to self-concept? Give examples.
4. How is the life span related to physical self-concept?
5. Describe the four comparison standards that help to integrate external feedback into self-concept.
6. Give an example of a skill development strategy to enhance physical self-concept through physical education.

Critical Thinking Questions

1. Physical education should not only increase sport competence, but also improve physical self-concept. Design a series of PE lessons to reach the goal of improved physical self-concept.
2. During the school year an increasing number of children want to take part in your extracurricular exercise programme. You recognise the heterogeneous skill level of the group. What could you do to encourage each of them and to promote their physical self-concept?
3. You are working as a coach doing exercise activities with children aged 10 to 12 once a week. What would you do to promote self-esteem? Is working with adolescents different from working with younger children?

Key Terms

physical self-concept—Self-knowledge and self-evaluation on several dimensions of physical competence and skills.

self-concept—Self-knowledge and self-evaluation on several dimensions of competence and skills.

self-esteem—A general evaluation of oneself.

References

Alfermann, D. & Stiller, J. (2001). Physical self-concept across the life-span. In M.M. Mboya (Ed.), *Self-concept theory, research and practice: International perspectives* (pp. 230-248). Pretoria, South Africa: Ilitha.

Alfermann, D. & Stoll, O. (2000). Effects of physical exercise on self-concept and well-being. *International Journal of Sport Psychology, 31,* 47-65.

Aşçi, F.H. & Çağlar, D.H. (2005, August). *Physical self-concept of Turkish late adolescents and early adults.* Paper presented at the Xth World Congress of Sport Psychology, Sydney, Australia.

Bracken, B.A. (1992). *Multidimensional Self-Concept Scale.* Austin, TX: Pro-Ed.

Bracken, B.A. & Lamprecht, M.S. (2003). Positive self-concept: An equal opportunity construct. *School Psychology Quarterly, 18,* 103-121.

Brettschneider, W.D. & Heim, R. (1997). Self-esteem in children and youth: The role of sport and physical education. In K.R. Fox (Ed.), *The physical self: From motivation to well-being* (pp. 205-227). Champaign, IL: Human Kinetics.

Byrne, B.M. (1996). *Measuring self-concept across the life span: Issues and instrumentation.* Washington, DC: American Psychological Association.

Byrne, B.M. & Shavelson, R.J. (1996). On the structure of social self-concept for pre, early, and late adolescents: A test of the Shavelson, Hubner, and Stanton (1976) model. *Journal of Personality and Social Psychology, 70,* 599-613.

Calsyn, R.J. & Kenny, D.A. (1977). Self-concept of ability and perceived evaluation of others: Cause or effect of academic achievement? *Journal of Educational Psychology, 69,* 136-145.

Caruso, C.M. & Gill, D.L. (1992). Strengthening physical self-perceptions through exercise. *Journal of Sports Medicine and Physical Fitness, 32,* 416-427.

Chanal, J.P., Marsh, H.W., Sarrazin, P.G. & Bois, J.E. (2005). Big-fish-little-pond effects on gymnastics self-concept: Social comparison processes in a physical setting. *Journal of Sport & Exercise Psychology, 27,* 53-70.

Coopersmith, S. (1967). *The antecedents of self-esteem.* San Francisco: Freeman.

Deusinger, I. (1986). *Die Frankfurter Selbstkonzeptskalen (FSKN) [The Frankfurt self-concept scales (FSKN)].* Göttingen, Germany: Hogrefe.

Dusek, J.B. & McIntyre, J.G. (2003). Self-concept and self-esteem development. In G.R. Adams & M. Berzonsky (Eds.), *Blackwell handbook of adolescence* (pp. 290-309). Malden, MA: Blackwell.

Dweck, C.S. (1999). *Self-theories: Their role in motivation, personality, and development.* Philadelphia: Taylor & Francis.

Erikson, E.H. (1980). *Identity and the life cycle.* New York: Norton (originally published in 1959).

Fox, K.R. (1997). *The physical self: From motivation to well-being.* Champaign, IL: Human Kinetics.

Fox, K.R. (2000). The effects of exercise on self-perception and self-esteem. In S J.H. Biddle, K.R. Fox & S.H. Boutcher (Eds.), *Physical activity and psychological well-being* (pp. 88-117). London: Routledge.

Fox, K.R. & Corbin, C.B. (1989). The physical self-perception profile: Development and preliminary validation. *Journal of Sport & Exercise Psychology, 14,* 1-12.

Gruber, J.J. (1986). Physical activity and self-esteem development in children: A meta-analysis. In G. Stull & H. Eckert (Eds.), *Effects of physical activity on children* (pp. 30-48). Champaign, IL: Human Kinetics and American Academy of Physical Education.

Guérin, F., Marsh, H.W. & Famose, J.-P. (2004). Generalizability of the PSDQ and its relationship to physical fitness: The European French connection. *Journal of Sport & Exercise Psychology, 26,* 19-38.

Guyot, G.W., Fairchild, L. & Hill, M. (1981). Physical fitness, sport participation, body build, and self-concept of elementary school children. *International Journal of Sport Psychology, 12,* 105-116.

Harter, S. (1996). Causes, correlates, and the functional role of global self-worth: A lifespan perspective. In R.J. Sternberg & J. Kolligian, Jr. (Eds.), *Competence considered* (pp. 67-97). New Haven: Yale University Press.

Harter, S. (1999). *The construction of the self: A developmental perspective.* New York: Guilford.

James, W. (1981). *The principles of psychology.* Cambridge, MA: Harvard University Press (originally published in 1890).

Kowalski, K.C., Crocker, P.R.E., Kowalski, N.P., Chad, K.E. & Humbert, M.L. (2003). Examining the physical self in adolescent girls over time: Further evidence against the hierarchical model. *Journal of Sport & Exercise Psychology, 25,* 5-18.

Lintunen, T. (1995). Self-perceptions, fitness, and exercise in early adolescence: A four-year follow-up study. *Studies in Sport, Physical Education, and Health, 41.* Jyväskylä, Finland: University of Jyväskylä.

Marsh, H.W. (1986). Global self-esteem: Its relation to specific facets of self-concept and their importance. *Journal of Personality and Social Psychology, 51,* 1224-1236.

Marsh, H.W. (1990). A multidimensional, hierarchical model of self-concept: Theoretical and empirical justification. *Educational Psychological Review, 2,* 77-172.

Marsh, H.W. (1997). The measurement of physical self-concept: A construct validation approach. In K.R. Fox (Ed.), *The physical self: From motivation to well-being* (pp. 27-58). Champaign, IL: Human Kinetics.

Marsh, H.W., Aşçi, F.H. & Tomás, I.M. (2002). Multitrait-multimethod analyses of two physical self-concept instruments: A cross-cultural perspective. *Journal of Sport & Exercise Psychology, 24,* 99-119.

Marsh, H.W. & Hattie, J. (1996). Theoretical perspectives on the structure of self-concept. In B.A. Bracken (Ed.), *Handbook of self-concept: Developmental, social, and clinical considerations* (pp. 38-90). New York: Wiley.

Marsh, H.W., & Hau, K.T. (2003). Big-fish-little-pond effect on academic self-concept: A cross-cultural (26-country) test of the negative effects of academically selective schools. *American Psychologist, 58,* 364-376.

Marsh, H.W. & Perry, C. (2005). Self-concept contributes to winning gold medals: Causal ordering of self-concept and elite swimming performance. *Journal of Sport & Exercise Psychology, 27,* 71-91.

Marsh, H.W. & Redmayne, R.S. (1994). A multi-dimensional physical self-concept and its relations to multiple components of physical fitness. *Journal of Sport & Exercise Psychology, 16,* 43-55.

Marsh, H.W., Richards, G.E., Johnson, S., Roche, L. & Tremayne, P. (1994). Physical self-description questionnaire: Psychometric properties and a multitrait-multimethod analysis of relations to existing instruments. *Journal of Sport & Exercise Psychology, 16,* 270-305.

Marsh, H.W. & Shavelson, R.J. (1985). Self-concept: Its multifaceted, hierarchical structure. *Educational Psychologist, 20,* 107-125.

Marx, R.W. & Winne, P.H. (1978). Construct interpretations of three self-concept inventories. *American Educational Research Journal, 15,* 99-108.

McDonald, D.G. & Hodgdon, J.A. (1991). *Psychological effects of aerobic fitness training: Research and theory.* New York: Springer.

Papaioannou, A., Marsh, H.W. & Theodorakis, Y. (2004). A multilevel approach to motivational climate in physical education and sport settings: An individual or a group level construct? *Journal of Sport & Exercise Psychology, 26,* 90-118.

Richards, G.E., Marsh, H.W., Bar-Eli, M. & Zach, S. (2005, August). *A multitrait-multimethod evaluation of three physical self-concept measures: A cross-national comparison of Australian and Israeli responses.* Paper presented at the Xth World Congress of Sport Psychology, Sydney, Australia.

Shavelson, R.J., Hubner, J.J. & Stanton, G.C. (1976). Self-concept: Validation of construct interpretations. *Review of Educational Research, 46,* 407-441.

Smith, T.L. (1986). Self-concepts of youth sport participants and nonparticipants in grades 3 and 6. *Perceptual and Motor Skills, 62,* 863-866.

Soares, L.M. & Soares, A.T. (1977). *The self-concept: Mini, maxi, multi.* Paper presented at the annual meeting of the American Educational Research Association, New York.

Sonstroem, R.J. (1997a). Physical activity and self-esteem. In W.P. Morgan (Ed.), *Physical activity and mental health* (pp. 127-143). Washington, DC: Taylor and Francis.

Sonstroem, R.J. (1997b). The physical self-system: A mediator of exercise and self-esteem. In K.R. Fox (Ed.), *The physical self: From motivation to well-being* (pp. 3-26). Champaign, IL: Human Kinetics.

Sonstroem, R.J. (1998). Physical self-concept: Assessment and external validity. *Exercise and Sport Sciences Reviews, 26,* 133-144.

Sonstroem, R.J., Harlow, L.L. & Josephs, L. (1994). Exercise and self-esteem: Validity of model expansion and exercise associations. *Journal of Sport & Exercise Psychology, 16,* 29-42.

Sonstroem, R.J., Harlow, L.L. & Salisbury, K.A. (1993). Path analysis of a self-esteem model across a competitive swim season. *Research Quarterly in Exercise and Sport, 64,* 335-342.

Sonstroem, R.J. & Morgan, W.P. (1989). Exercise and self-esteem: Rationale and model. *Medicine and Science in Sports and Exercise, 21,* 329-337.

Sonstroem, R.J. & Potts, S.A. (1996). Life adjustment correlates of physical self-concepts. *Medicine and Science in Sports and Exercise, 28,* 619-625.

Spence, J.C., McGannon, K.R. & Poon, P. (2005). The effect of exercise on global self-esteem: A quantitative review. *Journal of Sport & Exercise Psychology, 27,* 311-334.

Stiller, J. & Alfermann, D. (2004, August). *Testing a German version of the Physical Self-Description Questionnaire (PSDQ).* Paper presented at the SELF research conference, Berlin, Germany.

Stiller, J., Würth, S. & Alfermann, D. (2004). Die Messung des physischen Selbstkonzepts: Zur Entwicklung der PSK-Skalen für Kinder, Jugendliche und junge Erwachsene. [The measurement of physical self-concept: On developing the PSK-scales for children, adolescents, and young adults]. *Zeitschrift für Differentielle und Diagnostische Psychologie, 25,* 239-257.

Stoll, O. & Alfermann, D. (2002). Effects of physical exercise on resources evaluation, body self-concept and well-being among older adults. *Anxiety, Stress and Coping, 15,* 311-319.

chapter nine

Self-Regulation and Strategic Learning: The Role of Motivational Beliefs and the Learning Environment in Physical Education

Yngvar Ommundsen
Pierre-Nicolas Lemyre
The Norwegian School of Sport Sciences, Norway

After reading this chapter, you will be able to do the following:

- Define and understand the concept of self-regulation and self-regulation strategies

- Understand the importance of self-regulation strategies for pupils' learning and performance in physical education

- Understand the role of motivational aspects of the learning environment and motivational beliefs for pupils' self-regulation

- Be knowledgeable about research on environmental and personal influences on pupils' self-regulation in academics and physical education

- Describe ways of building self-regulation skills in physical education

Peter and Carol are two 12-year-old pupils taking part in school physical education every week. They are in different classes and have different physical education teachers.

Carol likes being in a class in which the teacher emphasises learning and improvement. In this class, effort and the exploration of different strategies and ways of approaching the learning tasks are valued. Carol has a sense that she is able to learn a lot through hard work and effort, and she feels a sense of mastery when she has finished her tasks and done her best. She loves the 'gym' lessons, she is eager to learn and she approaches the learning tasks with a high amount of concentration. She is clever at monitoring her progress. When faced with a new task, she sets process goals, regulates her effort in the face of challenges and difficulties and asks her teacher or her fellow students for help when she needs it.

Peter likes being in a class that is very competitive. The teacher often underscores the value of competition, and social comparisons are often being made between pupils' performances and achievements. Peter has a sense that the teacher is preoccupied with the high physical-motor achievers in the class. Peter has started to question whether he is learning much in PE. He usually compares his achievements with those of others in class, he quickly sets outcome goals when faced with a new task and he feels satisfied only when he performs better than the others. Recently, he has not done as well as others in the class. He would like to be among the high achievers, but he often feels frustrated when his aspirations do not match his achievements. Although Peter is often eager to start the lessons, he often quickly withdraws his efforts when confronted with difficulties. Peter has a hard time focusing on the learning tasks, he is easily distracted and he is unaware of his progress and whether he has learned anything. He avoids asking for help when he clearly would benefit from it. Recently, Peter's enjoyment of PE has declined, and he has started to avoid turning up to some of the PE classes, in particular when the teacher arranges tests of physical-motor skills and athletic skills. He often has excuses for not having been able to practise much before taking the tests.

These two pupils are seemingly very different in their approaches and attitudes toward physical education lessons and learning tasks. Why do they feel, think and behave differently in these two different physical education contexts? The contrasting stories identify the two students as very different in terms of the way they approach, interpret and react to learning and practice situations in PE. It would be easy to label Carol as having reached the stage of a self-regulated learner and Peter as less able to take responsibility for his own learning. He focuses on skills relative to others, and he does not seem to have acquired the skills to monitor his own progress, reflect on his work, change his strategies when needed, manage his emotions and ask for help when needed. He clearly needs to enhance his motivation and become more self-directed in his approach to learning.

This chapter focuses on important personal and environmental factors that influence pupils' **self-regulation** of their learning and performance in PE. First, the role and value of self-regulation skills in physical education is briefly sketched out. Second, we present conceptual dimensions of self-regulated learning and review theory and research on the role of personal and environmental factors that have been found to enhance young pupils' ability to become self-regulated learners in school physical education. Specifically, the chapter includes (1) definitions and categorisations of self-regulated learning; (2) a social-cognitive view of the development of self-regulatory skills; (3) a motivational model of self-regulation; (4) a short description of the concepts of learning environment, achievement goals and implicit theories of ability that are seen as the motivational driving forces of self-regulation; (5) empirical findings regarding self-regulation in the academic and physical education realm, including recent Norwegian findings on self-regulation in physical education; and (6) lessons from research, perspectives, conclusions and practical implications for the PE teacher.

Developing Lasting Involvement in Physical Activity

PE is an important component of the school's general education programme. As school professionals, physical educators have a duty to educate the whole (thinking, feeling, moving) pupil. Physical education allows for the simultaneous stimulation of students' minds and bodies. As providers of this unique learning context, physical educators fulfil the complex task of energising students through sport and exercise activities. Successful physical educators are often required to combine many distinctive roles to provide students with the appropriate learning context. PE offers students the opportunity to learn, to progress and to develop in a context in which synchrony of the body and mind is a requirement to better understand, reproduce and perform the challenging tasks involved in sport and exercise activities.

Many now see PE in the school curriculum as a marketing tool to promote a long-lasting, healthy lifestyle that includes regular leisure-time physical activities (O'Sullivan, 2004). Some conditions necessary to achieve this goal are the identification and understanding of the dispositional and contextual factors influencing the students' learning experience of PE lessons. Current social-cognitive perspectives on education and sport participation (Biddle, Soos & Chatzisarantis, 1999; Standage, Duda & Ntoumanis, 2003) suggest that the promotion of exercise and sport participation among young people both inside and outside the educational context of school should emphasise the development of positive affect and intrinsic motivation to participate in physical activity. To promote long-lasting, successful learning and behaviour change, some have proposed that shaping **motivational beliefs** by intervening through the **learning environment** around the students is an effective strategy to positively influence

Physical education allows for the simultaneous stimulation of students' minds and bodies.
© Bob Vincke.

their motivation and emotional experiences in PE lessons (Ommundsen, 2001a; Standage et al., 2003).

Role of Physical-Motor Competence

PE research has shown that pupils who perceive their PE classes positively are more intrinsically motivated and involved in out-of-school participation in physical activities than those who do not (Hagger, Chatzisarantis, Culverhouse & Biddle, 2003). In particular, evidence suggests that those who enjoy PE are more physically active during leisure time, perceive themselves as competent in physical education and are task involved (Ommundsen & Eikanger Kvalø, 2007; Telema, Nupponen & Pieron, 2005).

Nevertheless, findings regarding the influence of PE programmes on after-school physical activity in the longer term are less definite (Stone, McKenzie, Welk & Booth, 1998). Further, there is little research evidence of a strong tracking effect of physical activity motivation and involvement from childhood and adolescence into adult life (Boreham et al., 2004; Campbell et al., 2001). Moreover, the pervasive public health message reinforcing the necessity of enhanced physical activity for health has generally induced a curriculum based on a fitness and health ideology in school physical education. This has been done at the expense of developing movement abilities (Kirk & Tinning, 1994), which may easily lead to a marginalisation of the value of motor learning and skill development as well as of critical, reflexive thinking ability (Tinning, Kirk, Evans & Glover, 1994).

Thus, although higher physical activity levels within PE lesson participation may have instant beneficial effects in terms of childhood physical fitness, motivation and health, physical activity involvement in and of itself and situational motivation in PE (or in other contexts of physical activity in youth) may not generate persistent motivation to remain involved in physical activity, exercise or sport into adulthood.

Explicit educational objectives that clearly enhance motor and cognitive learning can only be provided by systematic curricula delivered by competent physical educators (Tinning, 1997). To obtain the necessary recognition in schools, physical educators may need to set forth clear curricular goals that go beyond the enhanced physical fitness of students, rather emphasising the preeminence of motor skills as the main educational objective (Arnold, 1991; Kirk, 2005). Accordingly, enhancing our knowledge of factors that contribute to students' motor-cognitive learning and skill development in PE seems warranted. In this chapter we take as a starting point research findings showing that the development of pupils' optimal competence requires more than basic talent and high-quality instruction; it involves self-regulatory skill, accompanying self-motivational beliefs and a constructive learning environment (Ames & Archer, 1988; Pintrich 2000a, 2000b; Zimmerman & Kitsantas, 2005).

Self-Regulatory Processes, Learning and Achievement in Physical Education

Current perspectives on the self-regulation of learning (i.e., Pintrich 2000a, 2000b) suggest that students who develop into self-regulated learners are more successful at developing academic skills and knowledge. Also, motor learning and performance embrace adaptive cognition and motivation (Zimmerman, 2000; Zimmerman & Kitsantas, 2005). Motor learning and performance are likely to be influenced by cognitive and motivational self-regulation, including the use of task-pertinent learning strategies (e.g., Clark, 1995; Glencross, 1994; Lavisse, Deviterne & Perrin, 2000; Lidor, 2004; Lidor, Tennant & Singer, 1996; Luke & Hardy, 1999b; Masson, 1990; Singer, Flora & Abourezk, 1989; Zimmerman & Kitsantas, 1996).

Lee, Landin and Carter (1992) investigated the role of cognitive strategy use among students during tennis motor skill instruction. They found that students who experienced a high level of success were able to articulate specific strategies they employed to improve their performance. Low-success students, on the other hand, were more concerned with their inability to perform the skill than with implementing strategies to improve their skill.

Zimmerman and Kitsantas (1996) studied the effects of monitoring and goal setting on dart-throwing performance among novice adolescent dart throwers. The 50 sixteen-year-old female physical education students were randomly assigned to one of five conditions: (1) set a product goal and did not monitor; (2) set a product goal and monitored; (3) set a process goal and did not monitor; (4) set a process goal and monitored; and (5) control—did not set goals and did not monitor. Results revealed that both goal setting and monitoring improved performance. Moreover, goal setting was most effective in improving performance, and monitoring had a stronger influence on self-efficacy.

Apparently, students need to be actively and strategically involved in their own learning process. When they are self-regulated learners, they typically use more efficient metacognitive strategies, they are able to learn material and motor tasks faster, they understand the curriculum content better and they retain the learned information longer (Luke & Hardy, 1999a). An increase in self-regulation influences students' perception of control and responsibility over their own learning processes (Nisbet & Schucksmith, 1986).

Together, these findings clearly support the assertion that efficient and adaptive learning strategies can facilitate learning and performance in PE classes. Hence, factors that may facilitate cognitive and motivational self-regulation in student learning and performance in PE seem important to identify. The following sections provide definitions of self-regulation and an overview of motivational factors known to be important for developing self-regulation.

Self-Regulated Learning

A general working definition of self-regulation, or self-regulated learning, is that it is an active, constructive process whereby students have learned to set goals for their learning and then attempt to monitor, regulate and control their cognition, motivation, affect and behaviour, guided or constrained by their goals and the contextual features of the environment. Self-regulation embraces self-initiated personal, behavioural and environmentally focused processes designed to attain personal goals. These self-regulatory activities are assumed to mediate the relationship between students' learning environment, cognitions and beliefs on the one hand, and their affective reactions, motivation and behaviour on the other. Affective reactions, motivation and achievement behaviour then, in turn, determine their overall learning and achievements (Pintrich, 2000b; Zimmerman, 2000; Zimmerman & Kitsantas, 2005). Taking a constructive perspective, self-regulated learning also embraces a fundamental change in knowledge structures or mental models critical for pupils' understanding and knowledge development (Ennis, 2006).

By creating a motivationally adaptive educational environment coupled with adequate teaching methods that also foster self-regulation, teachers may help pupils to develop motivational beliefs and the necessary self-regulatory skills (Pintrich, 2000a, 2000b; Zimmerman & Kitsantas, 2005). Such motivational beliefs and self-regulatory skills are seen to help increase pupils' perceived control over learning processes and help them take an active part in their own learning (become self-regulated learners). As a result, motor skill learning and performance can be enhanced, and many learning disabilities found among low-achieving students can be alleviated. In some instances, however, maladaptive motivational self-regulation activities may result. In the following sections we describe both adaptive and maladaptive self-regulation strategies.

Adaptive Self-Regulation Strategies

Adaptive strategies comprise several cognitive-behavioural and motivational facets that are thought to enhance students' learning as well as skill development and acquisition. Most models of self-regulation include a description of three distinct concepts: cognitive self-regulation, metacognitive self-regulation and the self-regulation of motivation and behaviour (Wolters, 2003b).

Cognitive Self-Regulation

Cognitive self-regulation strategies include rehearsal, elaboration and organisational strategies. Rehearsal strategies may help students select important information regarding various elements embedded in the activity and keep it stored in memory. Elaboration and organisational strategies represent more deep-level processing strategies, including summarising activity material and creating analogies between activities, reorganising and connecting ideas. One example would be solving related but dissimilar movement problems (Weinstein & Mayer, 1986).

Metacognitive Self-Regulation

Metacognitive self-regulation reflects a dynamic and ongoing awareness, judgment and monitoring of various aspects of cognition that students may engage in as they perform a motor-physical task. It encompass the covert regulation of cognition in which students monitor, control or adjust their cognitive processing in response to shifting demands or conditions (Corno, 1986; Wolters, 2003b; Zimmerman & Martinez-Pons, 1986). Included are activities such as **planning, monitoring** and regulating that they may engage in to control and adjust their cognition (Pintrich, 2000b; Pintrich & Schrauben, 1992).

Planning is a process whereby goal setting and task analysis help activate or prime relevant aspects of prior knowledge, thus making organising and comprehending material and motor tasks easier.

Monitoring involves tracking one's attention as one performs a motor task; it includes self-testing and self-questioning to assist in understanding and integrating the tasks with prior tasks and motor learning activities.

Regulating cognitive activities refers to fine-tuning and continuously adjusting one's cognitive activities while performing learning tasks and activities. Regulating may improve achievement and learning by helping students check and correct their behaviours as they practise their learning tasks and activities (Pintrich, Smith, Garcia & Mckeachie,1993).

Self-Regulation of Motivation and Behaviour

Regulation of motivation and behaviour is the third distinctive aspect of self-regulation. Regulation of motivation takes place when students initiate, maintain and complete particular activities or behaviours in order to reach their goals (Wolters, 2003b). Two often-mentioned aspects include **regulation of effort** and help seeking.

Regulation of effort   Regulation of effort refers to students' attempts to control their effort; it has also been described as resource management (Garcia & Pintrich, 1994; Wolters, 2003b). Regulation and management of effort are important motivational aspects of self-regulation. For example, it is important to be able to persist in the face of difficult or less interesting learning tasks (Corno, 1986; Kuhl,

2000). Effort management reflects a commitment to completing one's goals, even when there are difficulties or distractions in the physical education context. Effort management is important for motor learning and performance because it signifies not only motivation and commitment, but also the continued use of other learning strategies (Pintrich et al., 1993).

Help seeking   Seeking assistance or help when really needed is a necessary component of students' regulation of their behaviour (Newman, 1994, 1998). Students will inevitably encounter ambiguity or difficulty when faced with motor learning tasks and need assistance. When they face difficulties in the process of learning that they cannot overcome on their own, seeking help from teachers and knowledgeable peers serves a very adaptive purpose (McCaslin & Good, 1996). Newman (1994) labeled this adaptive strategy 'help seeking'. Indeed, help seeking is an important behavioural-motivational self-regulatory strategy that contributes to student learning and performance (Newman, 1994, 1998; Zimmerman & Martinez-Pons, 1988). Adaptive help seeking should be differentiated from executive or expedient help seeking, which involves asking for help before even trying the activity in an attempt to avoid work (Karabenick, 2004; Newman, 2000).

Maladaptive Self-Regulation Strategies

Three maladaptive self-regulation strategies that are described in the literature are **self-handicapping,** defensive pessimism and self-affirmation. They are all thought to relate negatively to adaptive learning strategies, achievement and learning (Garcia & Pintrich, 1994). Our focus in this chapter will be on self-handicapping.

Self-Handicapping

Self-handicapping comprises excuse making and generally involves engaging in purposeful action to create some explanation for a potential poor performance that is external to the students themselves (Jones & Berglas, 1978). As such, self-handicapping is a motivational self-regulatory strategy designed by students to regulate their affective response to poor performance.

By making use of self-handicapping, students may be able to protect or maintain their self-worth by avoiding looking stupid when faced with potential poor performance or failure (Rhodewalt & Vohs, 2005). Clearly, self-handicapping represents a form of avoidance behaviour in that it often involves a reduction of effort and an undermining of performance (Covington, 1992; Urdan, Ryan, Anderman & Gheen, 2002). Figure 9.1 illustrates

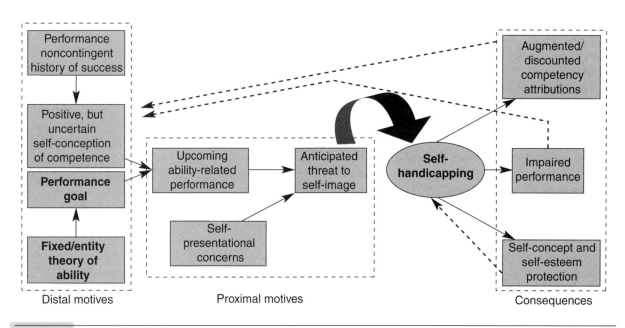

Figure 9.1   A self-handicapping self-regulation cycle.

Adapted, by permission, from F. Rhodewalt and Tragakis, 2002, Defensive strategies, motivation, and the self. In *Handbook of competence and motivation,* edited by A.J. Elliot and C.S. Dweck (New York: Guilford Press).

the self-handicapping self-regulation cycle. Motivational antecedents of self-handicapping, as well as consequences in the form of impaired performance and less functional attributions, relate to one's own performance, which in turn feed back to one's distal motives including motivational beliefs.

An Alternative Categorisation of Self-Regulation

Zimmerman (2000) created a somewhat different division of self-regulation strategies. He described three forms that are partly embedded in those already presented: behavioural self-regulation, environmental self-regulation and covert self-regulation. Pupils who use *behavioural self-regulation* observe their own performances and learning outcomes to make adjustment in their strategies. One example would be seeking help, as already discussed. In *environmental self-regulation,* self-observations are followed by adjustments to different situations, and social feedback takes place. One example would be pupils who change the place where they practise their skills to avoid being disturbed by external influences. *Covert self-regulation* involves monitoring one's own strategies and how one feels and thinks about the process. One example of covert

self-regulation that has already been mentioned is metacognitive self-regulation.

Fundamentally, then, self-regulation seems to imply that (1) pupils develop strategies based on their beliefs (Can I do this? What is my purpose?), and (2) strategies may be reinforced by external sources (the environment) as well as internal sources (covert self-regulation, which includes monitoring how one thinks and feels) as pupils progress toward their goals. According to Zimmerman (2000), self-regulation typically involves processes that are typically cyclical in nature.

Cyclical Nature of Self-Regulation

Zimmerman and coworkers divided the process of self-regulation into three distinct phases making a cycle: the **forethought phase,** the **performance phase** and the **self-reflection phase** (Zimmerman, 2000; Zimmerman & Kitsantas, 2005). Within these phases he also included some self-regulatory processes that supplement those already accounted for earlier. These will also be dealt with in presenting the different phases. The cyclical nature of these phases, with their subprocesses of self-regulation, is illustrated in figure 9.2.

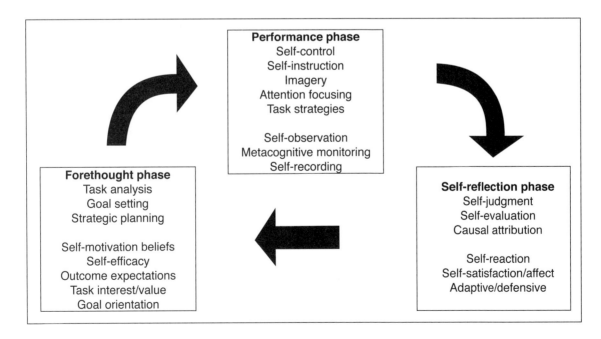

Figure 9.2   Phases and subprocesses of self-regulation.

Adapted, by permission from B.J. Zimmermann and A. Kitsantas, 2003, The hidden dimension of personal competence—self-regulated learning and practice. In *Handbook of competence and motivation,* edited by A.J. Elliot and C.S. Dweck (New York: Guilford Press).

Forethought Phase

The forethought phase of self-regulation involves the influential processes that precede the effort to act and set the stage for it (Zimmerman, 2000). This phase comprises self-regulatory processes and beliefs that fall into two categories: task analysis (including goal setting, strategic planning and activation of perceptions) and knowledge of the task. In addition, the self in relation to the task is activated by means of self-motivational beliefs. These include self-efficacy, outcome expectations, an interest in and valuing of the task and achievement goal orientations. In this chapter selected self-motivational beliefs included in the forethought phase will be used as exemplars to theoretically and empirically introduce the reader to the area of self-regulation in PE (see figure 9.3, page 150).

Performance Phase

The performance phase of self-regulation includes processes that occur during motor efforts and affect one's attention and action. Two major classes of processes are involved: strategy use and self-observation. Strategy use comprises self-instruction, imagery, environmental structuring and attention-focusing strategies. Self-observation comprises metacognitive monitoring and physical record keeping of specific aspects of one's performance, the conditions that surround it and the effects that it produces. Thus, except for planning and goal setting, which are embedded in the forethought phase, it is during the performance phase that pupils make use of what we have typically labeled as different adaptive or less adaptive self-regulation strategies (see figure 9.3, page 150).

Self-Reflection Phase

The self-reflection phase involves processes that occur after performance efforts and influence pupils' response to that experience. The phase consists of two main subprocesses: self-judgments and self-reactions. Self-judgments involve evaluating one's performance and attributing causes to attained outcomes. Self-reactions have two key forms: self-satisfaction and adaptive inferences on the one hand, and maladaptive, or defensive, strategies on the other. Adaptive strategies involve deciding what needs to be done to do better; defensive strategies involve task avoidance, disengagement or self-handicapping. The self-reflections and reactions in this phase cyclically influence forethought regarding subsequent learning efforts (Zimmerman & Kitsantas, 2005). Self-handicapping may represent a good example: Poorly self-regulated learners in PE may react with anxiety and become emotionally defensive when faced with failure experiences. In turn, maladaptive attribution (i.e., attributions to uncontrollable causes) may lead to the use of self-handicapping strategies prior to new learning situations in PE (e.g., during a new forethought phase) (see figure 9.3, page 150). Alternatively, self-handicapping elicits attributions that in turn influence the forethought phase (e.g., distal motives in figure 9.1).

Developmental Levels of Self-Regulation

How do socially conveyed skills, whether they are motor or cognitive in nature, become self-regulated? Zimmerman (2000) argued that when pupils are approaching new motor skills and trying to learn them, they typically acquire self-regulatory skills through four developmental levels: the **observation level, emulation level, self-control level** and **self-regulation level.** Advancement through each of the four developmental levels occurs by means of forethought, performance and self-reflection phases in which all subprocesses described earlier are activated.

Pupils learn to self-regulate by observing competent models performing the skill. Models may also convey associated self-regulatory processes, such as adherence to performance standards, implicit theories of ability, achievement goal orientations, self-efficacy beliefs and sustained effort in the face of challenges and hindrances. At this level of self-regulatory skill development, pupils rely heavily on social guidance by observing the teacher or other models in class perform and self-regulate. At this level pupils respond *reactively* to goal setting and strategy use by social models. As such, regulation is social in nature, rather than self-regulated at this stage (Zimmerman, 2000).

Emulation takes place when pupils begin to imitate a model with the assistance of guidance, social feedback and reinforcement during practice. At this level, self-regulatory skills are achieved as the pupils' use of strategies begins to look more like that of the model they are trying to emulate. At this level social feedback by the PE teacher or other models in class serves an important motivational role. The source of learning of self-regulatory skills is primarily social at these two first levels.

At the self-control level of self-regulation, pupils begin to use self-directed, deliberate practice. This implies an independent display of the model's skill using internal images (a personal standard). At this level pupils rely on monitoring and process goals rather than social feedback. The loci of sources of learning now shift from the social domain to the self. At this level pupils typically practise motor tasks individually, either in PE class or on their own, without the presence of models, guidance and social feedback.

The self-regulation level implies that pupils are capable of adapting to different situations and coping with environmental and personal demands as they perform a skill. Pupils may now be able to choose a strategy and adapt its features with little or no residual dependence on models (Zimmerman, 2000), thus acting *proactively* to regulate both internal processes and external forces. To sustain this level of self-regulation, pupils must have developed optimistic motivational beliefs. At this level, they may do less process monitoring (e.g., focusing on the execution of their badminton serve) and instead enjoy outcome goals such as placing the serve where it is likely to result in a point in a game. Research has shown that at this level pupils may learn more and perform better if they shift from process to outcome goals (Zimmerman, 2000) (process versus outcome goals are discussed later in this chapter).

According to Zimmerman and Kitsantas (2005), these four levels of acquiring self-regulatory competence may be used didactically as a social-cognitive training programme to enhance pupils' skills at self-regulating their physical-motor learning. Some of these didactical implications are dealt with in the practical implication section at the end of the chapter.

A Motivational Self-Regulation Framework

In the last two decades, numerous theories and models have tried to identify processes that intervene in self-regulated learning and to establish relations between these processes and cognitive and motor outcomes. These models include Boekaerts' model of adaptable learning (Boekaerts & Niemivirta, 2000), Pintrich's general framework for self-regulated learning (Pintrich, 2000b), Winne's four-stage model of self-regulated learning (Winne & Perry, 2000) and finally, Zimmerman's social-cognitive model of self-regulation (Zimmerman, 2000; Zimmerman & Schunk, 2004). Although these models differ in terms of theoretical origin, they all share some general assumptions and features. Similarities include the definition of self-regulation and components included in the models. The Pintrich and Zimmerman models differ from the other models in their emphasis on a goal-oriented definition of self-regulated learning, as well as on social-environmental influences on self-regulation.

In this section we will illustrate and make use of the Pintrich (2000b) model supplemented with aspects of Zimmerman's social-cognitive model of self-regulation (Zimmerman, 2000; Zimmerman & Kitsantas, 2005) as a heuristic device in organising our thinking and research on self-regulated learning in PE. This heuristic device is further supplemented with theoretical reasoning on the role of implicit theories of ability (Dweck, 1991; Dweck & Leggett, 1988). We will use the social-cognitive motivational model of self-regulation (Pintrich, 2000b) as an exemplar to illustrate how motivational factors interrelate with students' metacognitive and motivational self-regulation of their learning. The Pintrich model supplemented with Zimmerman's phases seems particularly useful because it invites a merging of theoretical perspectives on motivation and self-regulation. We therefore present a modified version of Pintrich's model that also includes implicit theories as part of the motivational beliefs and Zimmerman's phases. The model is presented in figure 9.3.

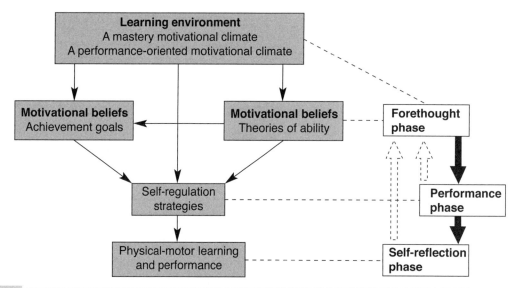

Figure 9.3 A social-cognitive-based motivational model of self-regulation in physical education including Zimmerman's concept of cyclical self-regulatory phases (Zimmerman & Kitsantas, 2005). Dotted arrows between phases represent feedback loops.

Pintrich's goal-oriented definition of self-regulation implies that monitoring, regulating and controlling one's own learning in PE includes cognitive, motivational, emotional and social factors. The motivational aspect of self-regulation seems particularly important because knowledge of cognitive and self-regulatory strategies is usually not enough to promote student learning and achievement. Students must also possess adaptive self-motivational beliefs and be surrounded by a constructive learning environment that motivates them to use adaptive self-regulation strategies (Pintrich, 2000b). This is reflected in figure 9.3. The model reveals that **motivational climates** and motivational beliefs are seen as the primary personal and environmental driving forces for pupils' self-regulation strategies.

The key characteristic of a self-regulated learner is the ability to exercise control over how one thinks, acts and feels as one attempts to attain one's goals (Zimmerman, 2000). According to Zimmerman, these strategies develop through self-reinforcing cycles in which pupils obtain internal feedback from monitoring their mastery attempt and learning efforts (covert self-regulation) as well as through the social feedback they receive from contextual features embedded in their environment. As revealed in figure 9.3, the climate (social feedback characteristics) influences self-regulation strategy use, and feedback from the self-regulation itself loops back into the forethought phase, of which regulative motivational beliefs are a part (see dotted, nonfilled arrows).

Pintrich's general framework rests on the following four premises:

1. *Students are active, constructive participants in the learning process (self as agent).* Students are assumed to actively construct their own meanings, implicit theories of ability, goals and strategies from the information available in the external environment as well as in their own minds (internal environment). Thus, learners are not just passive recipients of the ideas of teachers and others, but rather active, constructive meaning makers as they go about learning (Pintrich, 2000b).

2. *Students can monitor, control and regulate certain aspects of their cognition, motivation and behaviour.*

3. *Students are goal-directed learners, having some standard or criteria against which they monitor and regulate their learning endeavours.* Thus, students are assumed to set standards or goals to strive for in their learning, monitor their progress toward these goals and adapt and regulate

their cognition, motivation and behaviour to reach their goals. Dweck argued that students' implicit theories of ability fuel these goals differentially (Dweck & Leggett, 1988).

4. *Self-regulatory activities are mediators between personal and contextual characteristics and actual achievement and learning outcomes* (Pintrich, 2000b). Put differently, students' cultural, demographic or personality characteristics, or contextual characteristics of the PE environment, do not directly shape achievement or influence learning. Rather, students' self-regulation of their cognition, motivation and behaviour mediate the relationships among the person, learning environment and subsequent achievement and learning outcomes.

The addition of Zimmerman's concept of cyclic phases of self-regulation to the models invites a fifth assumption:

5. The self-reflections emanating from students' learning experiences and performance outcomes (self-reflection phase), as well as the strategies they use (performance phase), feed directly back into the forethought phase, influencing their motivational beliefs, thus completing a self-regulatory cycle (see dotted arrows in figure 9.3).

Defining the Learning Environment

The learning environment includes how the teacher interacts psychologically with students and how the teacher communicates content, educational values and curriculum priorities. The learning environment enhances or constrains pupils' learning outcomes in terms of cognition, motivation affect, behaviour in general and achievement.

Current views on the interrelationship of motivation and cognition stress the ability of the psychological learning environment to enhance or constrain cognition and motivation. Hence, what teachers communicate in terms of educational effort influences students' self-regulation (Pintrich, 2003; Zimmerman, 2000). According to Pintrich's and Zimmerman's frameworks of self-regulation, students' own cognitions and their perceptions of contextual features prime their motivational beliefs as well as cognitive and motivational self-regulatory activities, thereby mediating their learning achievements (Pintrich, 2000b). Clearly, strong environmental influences in the form of teacher behaviours and regulations can influence students to hold different motivational beliefs than the ones they would normally or chronically hold (Pintrich, 2000c).

According to the achievement goal perspective embedded in Pintrich's motivational model of self-regulation, motivational climates may facilitate or constrain pupils' self-regulation, either directly via generally effective teacher communication including social feedback and evaluation structures, or indirectly by influencing pupils' motivational beliefs, which in turn set the stage for pupils' self-regulation strategy use (see figure 9.3). This perspective bears similarities to Zimmerman's social-cognitive perspective on self-regulation, in which the social and physical environments are seen as resources for self-enhancing forethought (for example, self-efficacy beliefs, inducing a task **achievement goal orientation**), performance or volitional control and self-reflection. Zimmerman argued that through instruction, modelling, setting goals for pupils and monitoring their work and giving feedback, teachers socially convey self-regulatory skills, such as goal-setting skills, monitoring, persistence or effort regulation and help seeking. Hence, according to Zimmerman (2000), the learning environment plays an important role in the early levels of development of self-regulation (observation and emulation levels).

Taking into consideration the influence of environment and motivational beliefs on self-regulated learning may help us understand why Carol and Peter, discussed at the beginning of this chapter, deal with self-regulation so differently. In the following sections we will discuss the influence of motivational climates and the motivational beliefs pupils hold on self-regulation.

Perceived Motivational Climate

Most researchers have focused on two types of achievement climates or goal structures in achievement settings: mastery or task oriented and performance oriented.

A mastery-oriented, or task-oriented, climate or goal structure describes an environment in which instructional practices, policies and norms convey to students that learning is important, that all students are valued, that trying hard is important and that all students can be successful, learn and develop if they work hard (Ames, 1992; Midgley et al., 1998; Ommundsen, 2001b; Ommundsen, Roberts & Kavussanu, 1998). Such a climate should be seen as filled with learning opportunities and may be conducive to the development of adaptive self-regulation. Such a climate should also prevent students from using dysfunctional motivational strategies to protect their self-esteem.

A performance-oriented climate or goal structure describes an environment comprising normative grading practices that communicate to students that being successful means getting extrinsic rewards, demonstrating high ability and doing better than others. Such a climate usually also communicates that teacher attention depends on student performances so that the less able get less attention and are less supported in class (Ames, 1992). Clearly, such constraining features of students' psychological working environment may generate self-protection behaviours and do little to stimulate self-regulated learning (Randi & Corno, 2000).

Motivational Beliefs

Motivational beliefs are a set of interrelated beliefs that include thoughts about one's ability to learn and perform, epistemological theories including beliefs about the certainty and simplicity of knowledge and skills, efficacy-competence judgments, goal orientation, outcome expectations and the value of the learning task (Pintrich, 2000a, 2000b; Zimmerman, 2000). Given space considerations, in this chapter we will restrict our focus to achievement goal orientations and implicit theories of ability to illustrate motivational beliefs. Motivational beliefs represent the agency aspect

of self-regulation in that motivational beliefs are regarded as driving forces in pupils' motivation to self-regulate. Hence, the agency perspective explains why Carol and Peter are so different in terms of their motivation and willingness to make use of adaptive self-regulation practices.

According to Zimmerman's self-regulation perspective (Zimmerman, 2000), the self-motivational beliefs are embedded in the forethought phase of self-regulated learning. These beliefs prepare pupils to learn, setting the stage for how they cognitively and motivationally approach learning situations (e.g., task analysis and goal setting), how they strategically respond to them (e.g., strategic planning) and how they reflect on them in the self-reflecting phase.

Goals

As noted previously, self-regulation is driven by goal-directed behaviour comprising a standard, criteria or reference value that serves to guide self-regulatory processes (Zimmerman & Schunk, 2004). In self-regulated learning research, two general classes of goals have been discussed under various names, such as target goals and purpose goals, or task-specific goals and goal orientations. Our focus will be on goal orientations.

Purpose Goals Versus Task-Specific Goals

Purpose goals, or goal orientations, reflect the more general reasons students perform a task and are more related to the research on achievement motivation (Ames, 1992; Dweck, 1986; Duda, 2001; Elliot, 1997; Nicholls, 1989). Purpose goals reflect a general orientation or schema or theory for approaching the task, doing the task and evaluating the performance of the task. As Zimmerman and Schunk (2004) argued, 'Goal orientation measures do not focus on attaining a particular goal within a particular time frame, but rather on a general valuing of learning competence (i.e., the means) or performance outcomes (i.e., the ends)' (p. 332). Central to the goal orientation perspective is that these orientations represent the driving force of pupils' self-regulation practices.

In contrast to goal orientations, Zimmerman and Schunk (2004), in their social-cognitive approach, differentiated between time-framed task-specific process and outcome goals. Task-specific goals may represent *outcome goals* or *process goals*. Outcome goals represent the specific outcome students are attempting to accomplish— for example, placing the tennis serve so as to win a game point (Locke & Latham, 2002). Such a goal focuses on the attainment of a specific outcome, whether this outcome is the mastery of a specific skill or performing the skill better than others. Process goals, in contrast, focus on strategic steps to obtain an outcome goal, such as focusing on follow-through, or hitting the ball over the net or into a certain zone in volleyball. Process goals are activated in the forethought phase through the subprocess of goal setting.

Zimmerman and coworkers further argued that assigned task-specific, learning-focused goals (process goals) may even neutralise pupils' initial goal orientations. Finally, as previously mentioned, Zimmerman and coworkers argued that shifting from process goals to outcome goals when pupils reach the self-regulation level may result in performance enhancements.

Types of Achievement Goal Orientations

Achievement goal orientations are cognitive schemas or predispositions to act in an ego-involved (approach or avoidance oriented) or task-involved manner (Elliot & Harackiewicz, 1996; Roberts, 2001). They concern pupils' own purposes for pursuing achievement-related tasks and the criteria for success they use. Three types of achievement goal orientations are generally dealt with in the literature: mastery or task goals, performance-approach goals and performance-avoidance goals (Elliot & Harackiewicz, 1996; Ommundsen, 2004, 2006; Skaalvik, 1997). Indeed, a task approach-avoidance distinction has recently also been proposed in the literature. However, this distinction will not be dealt with in this chapter.

Mastery, or task, goals reflect a desire to develop competence, improve skills and further one's understanding in achievement endeavours. A task goal orientation focuses on learning for its own sake. Hence, task-oriented pupils make use of an undifferentiated conception of ability in which progress, effort and new learning equal success and mastery.

Performance-approach goals (originally labeled performance goals) reflect a concern with demonstrating competence and are often defined in social-comparative terms. The individual strives to demonstrate competence by achieving better than others and outperforming them. Hence, performance-oriented pupils make use of a differentiated conception of ability, in which being better than others and winning equals success and mastery. Such goals have also been labeled performance goals, ego goals or self-enhancing goals (Dweck & Leggett, 1988; Nicholls, 1989; Skaalvik, 1997). Performance-approach goals represent an approach form of motivation driven by a motive to attain success (Elliot & Harackiewicz, 1996).

Performance-avoidance goals are also often described in social-comparative terms. However, they represent the goal of avoiding appearing incompetent or less competent than others. Performance-avoidance goals represent a withdrawal from achievement situations, which is driven by a motive to avoid failure (Elliot & Harackiewicz, 1996).

Task-oriented students are highly motivated.
© Bob Vincke.

Implicit Theories of Ability

Implicit theories of ability are forms of a self-theory comprising students' beliefs about the fixedness or malleability of their personal qualities, such as their abilities, which influence their perceived ability or potential to learn and achieve (Dweck, 1991). According to Dweck and colleagues (Dweck & Leggett 1988; Hong, Chiu & Dweck, 1995), pupils differ in the degree to which they see ability as a fixed, unchangeable entity generated by talent. Some pupils do not believe in the role of effort, whereas others believe that knowledge and skills increase incrementally with practice and effort. The former has been referred to as an entity or fixed theory of ability and the latter as an incremental theory. This constellation of means–ends beliefs (Skinner, 1995) or beliefs about the nature of knowledge (Schommer, 1990) has later been expanded to include propositions that ability can also be viewed as stable over time, and general (see Sarrazin et al., 1996, and Stipek & Gralinski, 1996, for further details). The two theories are defined next.

Fixed theories of ability encompass a mind-set in which pupils believe their ability is fixed and cannot be changed. You have a certain amount of talent for physical-motor tasks and that's that (Dweck & Molden, 2005). A fixed mind-set represents a pessimistic view of learning in that learning may be perceived as impossible, leading to lowered expectations and reduced self-efficacy beliefs.

An incremental theory of ability encompasses a belief that one's abilities can be changed, cultivated and developed through effort and learning. Pupils holding an incremental theory of ability don't deny the differences between them—that some may be able to learn faster or even have more natural facility in PE. However, they focus on the idea that everybody can get better over time (Dweck & Molden, 2005). Clearly, an incremental theory of ability raises expectations for learning and reinforces personal beliefs about self-efficacy (Jourden, Bandura & Banfield, 1991).

Dweck and colleagues further argued that the two theories of ability set up different mind-sets and lead pupils to pursue and value different achievement goals. Indeed, an entity theory, with its idea of fixed ability, has been found to make students concerned with how much ability they have and showing they are smart. That is,

they hold a performance goal in which ability as compared to others is important. By contrast, an incremental theory of ability has been found to foster a task or learning goal orientation in which students focus on improvement, learning and developing new skills. In line with Pintrich's framework of self-regulated learning (Pintrich, 2000b), Dweck and colleagues further argued that differential achievement goals in turn lead to different achievement-related cognition, affect and behaviours (Dweck & Leggett, 1988).

In terms of self-regulation, Dweck and Leggett hold that implicit theories of ability influence students' self-regulated learning by setting up differential goals affecting their self-regulation strategies, which in turn influences motor learning and achievement (Dweck & Leggett, 1988).

Beliefs, Climates and Self-Regulation in Physical Education

According to the model presented in figure 9.3, students' implicit theories of ability, their adoption of different goal orientations as well as their perceptions of the goal structure or the motivational climate are thought to have important implications for cognitive and motivational engagement during learning experiences in physical education classes. With respect to achievement goals, two lines of reasoning become relevant as to how goals influence self-regulation. First, goals signal reasons pupils pursue tasks and activities; and second, sources of motivation influence behaviour. These two aspects are handled next.

Motivation to Pursue Learning Tasks

The inclusion of the reasons students are pursuing a learning task allows for an integration of the achievement motivation perspective into models of self-regulated learning. According to achievement goal theory, people strive to achieve a variety of goals for different purposes and hold different criteria for perceiving their achievement strivings as successful. Further, different purposes behind achievement behaviours, as reflected in different achievement goals, are believed to lead to different outcomes. In this regard, goal orientations have been described with respect to their interactions with cognitive, affective and motivational variables, suggesting that the goals pursued by students or athletes elicit different motivational patterns that contribute to qualitatively different motivational and cognitive forms of self-regulation in academic and motor tasks (Pintrich, 2000a; Zimmerman & Kitsantas, 1996; Zimmerman & Schunk, 2004).

Sources of Motivation Inform Behaviour

By considering what motivates students, we can discover the kinds of learning tasks they will pursue (Meece, 1994). For example, if students are motivated to master a motor learning task and learn the techniques connected to the task, then they should orient their monitoring processes to cues that show progress in learning and invoke certain types of cognitive strategies for learning (e.g., deep processing strategies) so as to make progress toward their goal of learning and mastery. In contrast, if they are oriented toward demonstrating their superiority over others in terms of better performances and quicker learning results, or toward avoiding demonstrating inability, then their monitoring and control processes may be qualitatively different because they monitor others' work and results and attempt to regulate their motivation and cognition to demonstrate their superiority or avoid feelings of inferiority.

Achievement Goal Orientations and Self-Regulation

A number of studies in the academic domain (but fewer in the physical-motor domain) have shown that different achievement goals can lead to different patterns of cognitive and motivational engagement and achievement (Lochbaum & Roberts, 1993; Meece, 1994; Meece, Blumenfeld & Hoyle, 1988; Pintrich, 2000a, 2000b; Roberts & Ommundsen, 1996). For example, a focus on mastery, or task, goals appears to result in deeper cognitive processing on academic tasks, as well as on effort regulation and help seeking, than does a focus on performance goals (Elliot, McGregor &

Gable, 1999; Ryan & Pintrich, 1997). A focus on performance goals (grades, besting others), in contrast, seems to result in more surface processing and less overall cognitive engagement than does a focus on mastery goals (Dweck & Leggett, 1988; Nolen, 1988; Pintrich & De Groot, 1990).

In elementary science classrooms, pupils who adopted a task-oriented, or mastery-oriented, goal were more likely to use cognitive and metacognitive strategies (Meece et al., 1988). Several other studies have also found a positive relation between adopting mastery, or task, goals and students' reported use of adaptive self-regulatory strategies (Elliot, McGregor & Gable, 1999; Middleton & Midgley, 1997; Miller, Behrens, Greene & Newman, 1993; Pintrich, 2000a, 2000b), as well as persistence and effort regulation (Miller, Greene, Montalvo, Ravindran & Nicols, 1996). In the physical-motor domain, Roberts and Ommundsen (1996) found that a focus on mastery, or learning, goals was associated with positive effort regulation in a group of university students engaged in sport activity tasks.

Research has also shown, however, that the relationship between performance goals and students' cognitive engagement is ambiguous. For example, some studies have found a performance goal to be related to more frequent use of some learning strategies (i.e., Greene & Miller, 1996; Vermetten, Lodewijks & Vermunt, 2001). Others, by contrast, have either failed to find any clear evidence linking students' endorsement of performance goals and their use of cognitive, metacognitive or self-regulatory strategies (i.e., Archer, 1994; Miller et al., 1996; Pintrich & Garcia, 1991), or have found performance goals to be associated with withdrawal of effort and less overall cognitive engagement when facing difficulties in physical-motor activities (Roberts & Ommundsen, 1996).

Performance-Approach and Performance-Avoidance Goals and Self-Regulation

In research that has differentiated between performance-approach and performance-avoidance goals, a clear and consistent pattern of results for performance-approach goals has failed to emerge in some studies. Some studies have revealed a positive relation between performance-approach goals and cognitive strategies in secondary school students (Pintrich, 2000a, 2000b; Wolters, Yu & Pintrich, 1996). In younger students Elliot and colleagues (1999) found that a performance-approach goal was positively related to effort and persistence and surface processing of information in the form of rehearsal. On the other hand, a performance-avoidance goal was a negative predictor of deep processing, a positive predictor of surface processing and unrelated to effort regulation and persistence. This latter finding supported additional research showing that, as opposed to a performance-approach orientation, a performance-avoidance orientation is associated with maladaptive cognitive outcomes with no evidence of positive self-regulation effects (Elliot, 1999; Pintrich, 2000b).

Performance-Approach and Performance-Avoidance Goals and Help Seeking

In terms of help seeking, Middleton and Midgley (1997) studied the role of performance-approach and performance-avoidance goals and found that the avoidance component emerged as a predictor of avoiding help seeking, whereas the approach component did not, when both were included in the same model. Ryan and Pintrich (1997) found that an orientation to performance-approach goals positively predicted avoiding seeking academic help in the classroom but was unrelated to adaptive help seeking. In a study among ninth-grade Japanese students, Tanaka and colleagues (Tanaka, Murakami, Okuno & Yamauchi, 2001) found that performance-approach goals had a direct positive relation with adaptive help seeking and a negative relation with the avoidance of help seeking. Performance-avoidance goals were related to perceived threats, in turn being positively related to the avoidance of help seeking and negatively related to adaptive help seeking.

Performance-Approach and Performance-Avoidance Goals and Self-Handicapping

Differentiating between performance-approach and performance-avoidance goals, Midgley and Urdan (2001) found that self-handicapping was predicted by a performance-avoidance goal but not by a performance-approach goal. Furthermore, Wolters (2003a) found a positive relationship between a performance-approach goal and self-handicapping in the form of procrastination. Differentiating between performance-approach and performance-avoidance orientations, Urdan (2004), as well as Elliot and Church (1997), found that performance-approach goals were negatively related to self-handicapping, whereas performance-avoidance goals related positively.

Implicit Theories of Ability and Self-Regulation

The evidence suggests that incremental theories of ability are conducive to the development of adaptive motivational patterns, including persistence when confronted with difficulty, the use of strategies likely to lead to problem solution and asking for help when needed (Elliott & Dweck, 1988; Kasimatis, Miller & Marcussen, 1996). By contrast, those holding a fixed theory of ability seem more apt to display maladaptive behaviours and ineffective achievement strategies, such as an unwillingness to exert effort when task demands are high and a tendency to avoid challenge and make use of self-handicapping strategies. This may be particularly so for people who doubt their own abilities (Cury, Biddle, Sarrazin & Famose, 1997; Hong et al., 1995; Nicholls, 1989).

Differential Motivational Beliefs and Self-Regulation in Norwegian Physical Education

Ommundsen (2004) examined the relationships between achievement goals (task, performance-approach, performance-avoidance) and self-handicapping among ninth-graders in the area of secondary school physical education. Results revealed that task goals and a performance-approach goal were negatively related to self-handicapping, whereas a performance-avoidance goal related positively to self-handicapping. Apparently, a performance-avoidance goal more strongly deserved being labeled the 'bad guy' in terms of generating self-handicapping. A performance-approach goal, in contrast, was more readily characterised as a double-edged sword, able to facilitate as well as hinder self-handicapping.

In a recent study, Ommundsen (2003) examined the relationships between ninth-grade students' implicit theories of ability and their self-regulated learning in PE. A learning, or incremental, conception of ability strongly predicted students' use of metacognitive, or elaboration, strategies when faced with learning tasks in PE. These students also modulated their effort efficiently and asked for help when needed.

In contrast, a stable conception of ability, unaffected by effort, was strongly and negatively associated with optimal modulation of effort in the face of learning tasks. The results underscore the educational value of instilling in pupils a belief in the modifiability of ability through effort, hard work and learning. The findings further illustrate the importance of linking the motivational and cognitive characteristics of students to provide a fuller understanding of young peoples' self-regulation of their learning in physical education.

In another cross-sectional study of Norwegian ninth-graders, Ommundsen (2001b) investigated the role of implicit theories of ability and achievement goals on self-handicapping strategies in physical education classes. Results revealed that a fixed theory of ability had a direct, positive effect on students' self-handicapping in physical education classes. The effects of an incremental implicit theory of ability on self-handicapping were negative and mediated by a task orientation. As revealed in figure 9.4, high perceived competence in PE was found to buffer the aversive affect of holding a stable theory of ability on self-handicapping. Clearly, theories of ability seem to generate self-handicapping strategies among students in PE.

Motivational Climate and Adaptive Self-Regulation

The body of research linking motivational climates to students' adaptive learning strategies is limited. In the academic domain, Wolters (2004) found that students who perceived their classroom as having more of an emphasis on learning and improving their ability in mathematics tended to report more adaptive motivational engagement (e.g., enhanced persistence, effort and choosing additional mathematic courses in the future) than students who did not report their classrooms as strongly emphasising mastery goals. Students who viewed the instructional practices and policies

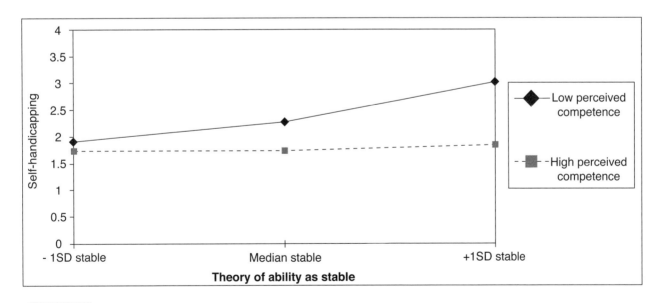

Figure 9.4 The interaction of perceived competence and a theory of ability as stable in the reported use of self-handicapping strategies.

in their classroom as stressing competition and demonstrating ability reported disengaging from their academic tasks when they faced difficulty or boredom.

Xiang and Lee (2002) found that a mastery-oriented motivational climate related positively to students' reporting of mastery behaviours in physical education such as focusing on effort while working on motor tasks, seeking challenging tasks and persisting in the face of difficulty. Importantly, in a recent longitudinal study of college students, Gano-Overway and Ewing (2004) were able to show that aspects of the task-involving climate predicted practice strategies throughout several 16-week physical activity classes.

Motivational Climate and Help Seeking

Butler and Neuman (1995) found that young Israeli students who worked under a salient-task goal structure were more likely to request help and explain help avoidance as guided by strivings for independent mastery than were students working in an ego-focused condition. This latter group also explained help avoidance in terms of masking incapacity. In a similar vein, Ryan, Gheen and Migley (1998) found that in mastery-oriented classrooms students were less likely to avoid seeking help when needed than were students in classrooms having a focus on competition and proving one's ability. Recently, Karabenick (2004) found that college students' self-reports of adaptive help seeking were related to their perception of class goals as mastery oriented and receptive of asking for help when needed.

Motivational Climate and Maladaptive Self-Regulation

In a recent study, Urdan (2004) found that a performance-oriented class climate elicited self-handicapping, mediated by performance-avoidance goals. It is suggested that a performance-oriented situational goal structure seems to encourage maladaptive learning strategies and various forms of behaviours signalling self-protection and motivational disengagement.

Indeed, there is accumulating evidence that classroom discourse and instructional practices that force students to demonstrate ability or avoid demonstrating inability (Nicholls, 1989), encourage the use of social reference norms (Ames, 1992) or emphasise evaluation procedures (Urdan et al., 2002) automatically increase a self-focus (Turner et al., 2002). This elicits a coping mode in which the learner becomes primarily concerned with ego protection, emotion control and preventing loss of resources (Boekaerts & Niemivirta, 2000; Covington, 1992). One such ego-protection strategy or form of emotion control is self-handicapping.

Motivational Climate and Self-Regulation Within Norwegian Physical Education

Ommundsen (2006) examined the joint role of motivational goal structures, or climate, and differential achievement goals on secondary school physical education students' adaptive and maladaptive learning strategies. As depicted in figure 9.5, analyses revealed that a mastery climate positively influenced pupils' metacognitive strategies, effort regulation and help seeking by facilitating a task goal. A mastery climate also directly influenced pupils' use of metacognitive strategies and effort regulation unmediated by a task goal (see figure 9.5) and by a performance-approach goal (see figure 9.6). Also, a performance climate influenced self-handicapping directly and positively, as well as indirectly (mediated by a performance-avoidance goal) (see figure 9.6).

There was also some support for interaction effects among the personal and contextual predictors in that a strong performance-avoidance goal seems to override the beneficial effect of a strong mastery climate on adaptive effort regulation. This is shown in figure 9.7.

Research results attest to the importance of including both aspects of achievement goal theory when examining personal and situational goal influences on students' self-regulation. The findings show that both motivational climate and personal goal orientations independently affect students' self-regulation strategies in PE. Further, task goals strongly mediate the positive influence of a mastery motivational climate on students' self-regulation strategies as measured by metacognitive strategies and effort regulation.

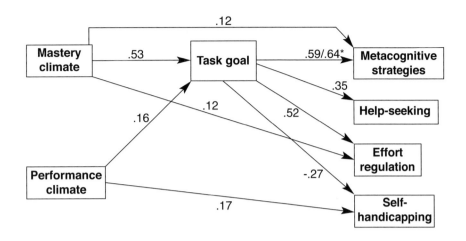

*Mastery and performance climate, respectively

Figure 9.5 Direct and indirect climate effects (mediated by a task goal) on self-regulation strategies. Significant paths shown.

From Y. Ommundsen, 2006, "Pupils' self-regulation in physical education: The role of motivational climates and differential achievement goals," *European Physical Education Review* 12(3): 289-315.

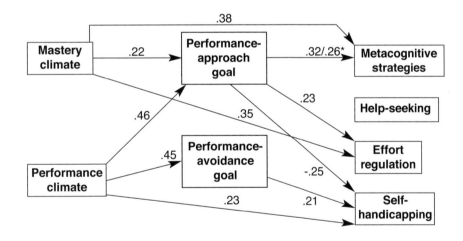

*Mastery and performance climate, respectively

Figure 9.6 Direct and indirect climate effects (mediated by performance-approach and performance-avoidance goals) on self-regulation strategies. Significant paths shown.

From Y. Ommundsen, 2006, "Pupils' self-regulation in physical education: The role of motivational climates and differential achievement goals," *European Physical Education Review* 12(3): 289-315.

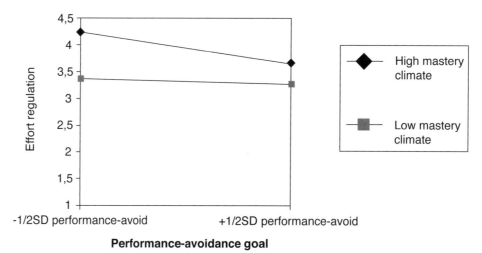

Figure 9.7   The interaction of mastery climate and a performance-avoidance goal in the reported use of effort regulation.

From Y. Ommundsen, 2006, "Pupils' self-regulation in physical education: The role of motivational climates and differential achievement goals," *European Physical Education Review* 12(3): 289-315.

Lessons From Research

Findings from different samples of Norwegian secondary school students support findings obtained primarily in the academic domain. Results indicate that motivational beliefs and the motivational climate both influence students' self-regulation strategies in physical education. Consistent relationships between contextual and personal motivational factors represented by motivational climates, implicit theories of ability and achievement goals, and students' adaptive as well as dysfunctional self-regulation of their learning, were also observed in the physical-motor domain of school physical education.

Generally, the consistent pattern of findings that emerge are in line with Dweck's theoretical predictions (Dweck & Leggett, 1988) and Pintrich's general model of self-regulation (Pintrich, 2000a, 2000b) developed within the academic domain. Pintrich's model, backed up by several findings, sensitises us to the fact that pupils' perception of the motivational climate, as well as their motivational beliefs, elicits differential forms of self-regulation in PE. Findings also concur with Zimmerman and coworkers' notion of self-regulation phases. As revealed, students' motivational beliefs, elicited by the motivational climate, seem to correspond to the forethought phase that set in motion their adoption of adaptive or less adaptive self-regulation practices, which is indicative of the performance phase of self-regulation.

Climate, Goals and Self-Regulation

A mastery climate may facilitate incremental theories and task goals leading to students' positive interpretation and appraisals of the ongoing learning episodes (Ommundsen, 2001c, 2006). This may lead them into a nonthreatening mastery mode of task engagement (Boekaerts & Niemivirta, 2000), facilitating metacognitive self-regulation, adaptive regulation of effort and seeking help when needed (Butler & Neuman, 1995; Karabenick, 2004; Newman, 1998; Ryan et al., 1998; Wolters, 2004). Research seems to support that the opposite consequences may result when teachers activate a performance-oriented climate. Apparently, a task goal orientation generates a greater sense of control over the learning situation among pupils, which facilitates their development and use of adaptive self-regulation strategies.

In terms of goals, a task orientation seems to prevent dysfunctional, motivationally based self-regulation strategies and promote positive affective experiences that may reinforce adaptive self-regulation strategies among students in physical education classes.

Performance-avoidance goals, in contrast, are basically grounded in aversive motivation (Elliot, 1999). Thus, such goals should be expected to generate threat appraisals constraining adaptive self-regulation, instead activating ego-protective tactics such as self-handicapping and hindering other forms of adaptive regulation. This was observed in several studies. For example, performance-avoidance goals were also negatively related to effort regulation. Apparently, students holding such goals may develop self-protective strategies that keep them from the adaptive effort regulation that leads to learning and achievement.

Performance-approach goals were found to be positively unrelated to self-handicapping and positively related to effort regulation. According to a normative, traditional achievement goals perspective (e.g., Ames, 1992; Dweck & Leggett, 1988; Nicholls, 1989), a performance goal is regarded unconditionally as detrimental in terms of cognitive, affective and behavioural self-regulation. Our pattern of findings conflicts with this view. Rather, adopting performance-approach goals may not necessarily be detrimental in terms of adaptive self-regulation in physical education (Cury, Elliot, Sarrazin, Da Fonseca & Rufo, 2002; Harackiewicz, Barron, Pintrich, Elliot & Thrash, 2002; Ommundsen, 2004; Wolters, 2004). In fact, research provides stronger support for a revised achievement goal perspective. According to this perspective, the decisive factors seem to be whether students are task oriented and whether they are focused on fear of failure, as embedded in performance-avoidance goals, rather than focused on expectations of normative success as embedded in performance-approach goals (Elliot, 1999).

Importantly, however, performance-approach goals also appear to carry with them some risks and vulnerabilities. Thus, although the empirical message in several instances is positive, performance-approach goals are neither good nor bad; rather, they represent valuable, yet vulnerable forms of regulation (Elliot & Moller, 2003). Clearly, in physical education, as in the classroom and in sport, young people learn that normative competence (being better than others) is highly valued. Hence, teachers and parents often guide pupils, in both explicit and implicit ways, toward the pursuit of performance-approach goals. However, under these conditions, performance-approach goals are often misunderstood; they become tools for pleasing others, validating one's worth and demonstrating positive characteristics rather than for acquiring competence information per se (Elliot & Moller, 2003). When this is the case, performance-approach goals may develop into a vulnerable goal orientation generating maladaptive forms of self-regulation.

Implicit Theories of Ability and Self-Regulation

An entity theory of ability seems to increase evaluative concerns about performance and diminish adaptive regulation because performance is considered diagnostic of physical, or motor, capacity, which seems to be general and not changeable through effort (Stipek & Gralinski, 1996). In this case, students may, for example, come to see effort as a 'double-edged sword' (Covington, 1992) and feel at risk because trying hard and failing is clear evidence of low ability (Kun, 1977; Kun & Weiner, 1973). By not trying, they can obscure the causes of failure and avoid revealing their low ability, thus avoiding negative emotions and protecting their self-esteem (Covington, 1992).

A strong belief that ability is a stable entity unaffected by effort may reinforce external control beliefs among students (Pintrich & Schrauben, 1992; Skinner, 1995) and generate low perceived self-efficacy (Lirgg, Chase, George & Ferguson, 1996). Externally referenced control beliefs and low self-efficacy may leave students with little optimism for the possibility of learning new motor tasks by means of effort and hard work. As a consequence, students' cognitive engagement may decrease, and they may not adopt self-regulatory strategies, such as planning, monitoring their understanding and changing their approach to the learning tasks, when needed. The external control beliefs reflected in a stable conception of ability may also lead students to set low and diffuse goals. Moreover, they may not spontaneously visualise sequential action steps in the learning tasks (Skinner, 1995). Consequently, their views of each achievement task confronting them may be disorganised and truncated and contain few means–ends or strategy, beliefs (Skinner, 1995).

Students who endorse an incremental, or learning, theory of ability, in contrast, were more likely to plan, monitor and regulate their cognition while working with different learning tasks in PE than were those with low incremental beliefs. Students who believe in the role of effort, hard work and their capability to learn in PE seem to perceive themselves as being more in control of their own learning (Skinner, 1995). Thus, they seem better equipped to set goals for themselves and monitor or check their comprehension as they go through different motor tasks to reach those goals. Students who are in control of their own learning may also be more likely to adapt and revise action plans in the lessons to match existing conditions when actions do not initially result in success (Skinner, 1995).

Also, a high perception of internal control and a belief in the utility of effort may enable students to fully focus their attention on their action plans and make use of elaboration. Thus, they can fully use their cognitive resources, which will result in deeper information processing (Weinstein & Mayer, 1986). In terms of effort regulation, holding a strong, stable conception of ability, as opposed to holding an incremental one, may generate a belief among students that effort does not pay off.

An incremental, or learning, conception of ability also seems to facilitate help seeking, whereas general as well as stable theories were negatively associated with seeking help from the teacher and from peers. Motivational theorists view help seeking as a way of achieving environmental control in the learning process. Help seeking is a volitional strategy that can protect one's intentions to learn when faced with competing action tendencies, such as giving in to distraction, self-handicapping or giving up (Kuhl, 2000; Ommundsen, 2001c). Relying on assistance from peers or teachers is a type of task engagement that is much preferred to dysfunctional perseverance (Newman, 1994).

Applications for Teaching

Previous studies in the context of health-related physical activity have underscored the importance of students' affect and cognitions for their achievement strivings, learning outcomes and subsequent physical activity behaviour priorities in school and leisure time. Despite short-term motivational effects on physical activity, however, there is little evidence to date that physical education classes contribute to sustained motivation into adulthood (Kirk, 2005). In fact, as we have shown in this chapter, unless steps are taken to ensure that PE teachers emphasise not only fitness, physical activity and enjoyable experiences, but also explicit learning experiences, in which students develop into self-regulated learners, PE in school will contribute only marginally to young peoples' preference for staying physically active into adulthood. In light of this, the theory and research on self-regulation seems important because it sheds light on the motivational pre-

PE teachers must emphasise not only fitness, physical activity and enjoyable experiences, but also explicit learning experiences in which students develop into self-regulated learners.
© Bob Vincke.

requisites for adaptive self-regulation of learning. Becoming a self-regulated learner in PE is important if students are to benefit from learning experiences that enhance motor learning and achievement. Such experiences may result in their selecting motor activities that they can continue to engage in into adulthood.

Taking an educational psychological perspective, the main focus of this chapter has been on the role of the psychological environment in PE classes to facilitate or constrain pupils' self-regulated, strategic learning, either directly or indirectly, by influencing their motivational beliefs. Enhancing students' self-regulated learning through the psychological environment may not be enough, however. In terms of the enacted curriculum, it would seem important that PE teachers ensure that their curricular priorities not only focus on motor skills, but also harmonise with students' different backgrounds and situational interests, and that the learning task be culturally, developmentally and gender sensitive (Ennis, 1999; Kirk, 2005; Van Wersch, Trew & Turner, 1992). In particular Ennis (2006) asserted that to stimulate strategic learning and help pupils become self-regulated learners, teachers must develop and implement coherent physical education curricula in which pupils perceive visible linkages between educational purposes and their lived experiences. Pupils must see themselves as agents in learning, with ownership in the learning process.

Consider an example with gender relevance: The belief that certain activities in PE are not appropriate for girls may reinforce fixed conceptions of ability and performance-avoidance goals, leading to lower levels of task self-efficacy and reducing the possibility that girls will become self-regulated learners in PE (Solomon, Belcher, House & Wells, 2003).

To stimulate self-regulated, strategic learning, the curriculum must be structured so that pupils perceive programme sequencing over the course of their school years. Indeed, structuring the programme activities as meaningful wholes that build on each other and in which subparts are seen as naturally connected would also help facilitate pupils' cognitive, metacognitive and motivational involvement in the learning process. Several curriculum models have been forwarded in the pedagogy literature to this end; examples are the sport education model and teaching games for understanding (Kirk, 2005). Indeed, the development of self-regulated, strategic learning in PE depends on strategic didactical and psychological decision making and acting on the part of learners, teachers, schools and curriculum makers.

Conclusions

We began this chapter by positing that adaptive motivational and cognitive self-regulation strategies seem important for motor learning and achievement. Apparently, by reinforcing a positive mastery-oriented learning climate and developing incremental conceptions of ability and task goals, PE teachers may develop self-efficacy in pupils and make it easier for them to become self-regulated learners. This seems important in order for them to participate and function optimally in their present and future movement cultures. In terms of achievement goals and self-regulation, results in the context of physical education support previous ones in the academic field. Despite the ability of performance-approach goals to enhance students' regulation of their effort, we would not advise teachers to use performance goals to generate self-regulated learners in PE. The message that task involvement is preferable still clearly holds true. With this in mind we offer some practical suggestions for how PE teacher may be able to facilitate adaptive motivational and cognitive self-regulation among students in physical education classes. Included are several didactical implications that naturally follow from Pintrich's motivational framework and Zimmerman's social-

cognitive approach to self-regulation. Admitting also the importance of curriculum approaches to facilitate self-regulated learning (Ennis, 2006), we also offer examples of implications emanating from the curriculum perspective.

- Teachers should provide students with opportunities to meet challenges successfully by providing choices and different difficulty levels to match students' skill levels and opportunities.

- Teachers can build learning 'communities' in their classrooms by teaching students cooperative and group learning skills, emphasising respect for others' ideas and dividing responsibility when students are working in groups. By encouraging shared responsibility for learning, teachers can help students focus on progress and mastery, thereby decreasing social comparison and self-derogatory thought processes that impede learning.

- Peers can provide additional feedback and also serve as expert models with whom students can identify. Peer modelling can enhance incremental theories of ability and self-efficacy expectations that may enhance the use of self-regulation strategies among others in the class.

- Teachers should provide students with explicit strategy guidance based on scaffolding and fading principles. They could begin by giving students good examples of how to monitor certain elements of motor tasks. They then help students self-monitor, providing examples of essential movement corrections to raise the quality of students' skills on the task. The goal is for students to be able to make independent use of monitoring and task correction when working on different motor tasks in PE.

- Students should be given opportunities to evaluate their learning efforts against predetermined criteria (short-term, realistic and specific teacher- or self-set goals), and teachers should emphasise specific qualitative feedback targeting improved performance.

- Teachers can also encourage self-monitoring among students by offering examples of self-set goals and combining this with feedback from students themselves in terms of self-talk.

- Teachers can encourage students to self-monitor their skill-learning process by keeping logs of aspects related to the learning activities. Logs can include notes on important elements to remember when executing a particular motor skill, or specific challenges or difficulties that the student has to overcome to proceed to a higher efficiency level.

- Teachers may use video or digital recording when teaching motor skills and tactical strategies in games. Such recordings can provide relevant feedback that may guide students' efforts to achieve future goals.

- Teachers should help students set goals by providing cues regarding essential aspects of a motor task, by modelling difficult procedures or rhythm of movements and by helping and problem solving with students when they face difficulties. PE teachers should emphasise process goals at early levels of self-regulation, while encouraging outcome goals when pupils have attained a higher level of self-regulation in their learning.

- Teachers may take advantage of an apprenticeship model of teaching in which they help students acquire knowledge and skills by appropriately structuring learning activities and by working alongside students as coparticipants and facilitators. By letting students become co-decision makers in the learning process, teachers demonstrate confidence in their students, which can lead students to deeper cognitive and motivational engagement and self-regulation.

- Teachers should organise instruction and learning activities around cognitive and metacognitive strategies. For example, teachers can encourage students to engage in self-regulatory processes by giving them opportunities to initiate and direct their own learning in PE. When teachers do this, students are less likely to believe that their learning is controlled by others. More specifically, students should be given a sense of self-determination, autonomy and choice by allowing them to ask questions, discuss their understanding of the learning tasks, choose learning partners in class and decide the order in which to complete their work in class.

- Teachers should provide clear and accurate feedback regarding competence and self-efficacy, focusing on the development of competence, expertise and skill. Feedback should stress the process nature of learning, including the importance of effort combined with good strategies and the potential self-control of learning. This may enhance pupils' incremental conceptions of ability.

- Teachers should use organisational and management structures that encourage personal and social responsibility and provide a safe and predictable learning environment.

- The classroom discourse of PE classes should always focus on mastery, learning, effort, progress and an understanding of tasks and motor learning activities. This should also be reflected in task, reward and evaluation structures. Students are more likely to adopt a task, or mastery, involvement that supports self-regulated learning when they are given opportunities to improve their skills, are rewarded for self-improvement, have a choice of evaluation methods and are not compared with other students. By creating a mastery-oriented motivational climate, PE teachers seem to facilitate an incremental theory of ability and a task goal orientation that appears to benefit students' metacognition, their adaptive help seeking from teachers and peers and their regulation of effort when facing obstacles in motor learning tasks and activities.

- Teachers should provide content material and learning tasks that are personally meaningful, relevant and interesting to the students and that contain some variety and novelty. Articulating the role of the learning activity in relation to students' personal goals may foster a sense of relevance, support autonomy and facilitate deeper motivational and cognitive engagement.

- Teachers should make sure that students have a good understanding of the task and the structure of practice. If students lack metacognitive knowledge of task variables or do not understand the purpose of tasks and motor learning activities, even with time and effort, efficient learning may not occur.

- Schools should provide coherent curricula that are culturally, socially and gender sensitive so pupils will perceive their education as relevant. Evidence reveals that students of different cultural and social backgrounds, and of different genders, have different physical activity, sport and movement interests.

- Schools also need to be more aware of the importance of implementing a structured curriculum across grade levels to facilitate the sequencing and reinforcement of already coherent and meaningful activity components.

Summary

This chapter defined the concept of self-regulation and explained self-regulation strategies. Self-regulation promotes physical-motor learning and achievement by having pupils focus on the learning tasks, monitor their progress, change strategies and ask for help when needed. We also discussed the psychological environment and how pupils' motivational beliefs affect the self-regulation of their learning. A mastery climate, incremental theories of ability and task-oriented achievement goals seem to promote self-regulated learning. We also addressed ways of building self-regulation skills in physical education. One way is to provide pupils with clear-cut and accurate feedback regarding competence and self-efficacy, focusing on the development of competence, expertise and skill. Feedback should stress the process nature of learning, including the importance of effort combined with good strategies, and the potential self-control of learning.

Review Questions

1. What do we mean by self-regulation?
2. Why are self-regulation skills important in PE?
3. In which phase of self-regulation are motivational beliefs most important?
4. Describe the subprocesses comprising metacognitive self-regulation.
5. Give a PE example in which the use of metacognitive skills may be important.
6. Why might some students choose not to ask for help when needed?
7. What is the difference between goal orientations and situation- or task-specific goals?
8. Discuss the self-regulation characteristics of a student scoring high on an incremental theory of ability.
9. Describe the relationship among motivational climates, theories of ability, achievement goal orientations and self-regulation skills.
10. Why might a performance-approach goal orientation be considered a 'double-edged sword' in terms of self-regulation consequences?
11. Name three ways to build pupils' adaptive self-regulation skills in physical education.

Critical Thinking Questions

1. Using figure 9.3, make your own cognitive map of the key content as you perceive it in this chapter.
2. Relate the concept of self-regulation to other educational purposes; for example, the social-emotional domain. Do you see any relationship between pupils' ability to self-regulate and the development of their social competence? What about pupils' self-regulation of their emotions?

3. You are a PE teacher in the sixth grade preparing a lesson in badminton. You are already aware that your pupils have little experience with this game. How would you approach the lesson to develop your pupils' self-regulation skills?

Key Terms

achievement goal orientations—Cognitive schemas or predispositions to act in an ego-involved (approach- or avoidance-oriented) or task-involved manner.

emulation level—The second level of self-regulation, in which pupils imitate a model with the assistance of guidance, social feedback and reinforcement during practice.

forethought phase—The phase of self-regulation that involves influential processes that precede the effort to act and set the stage for it.

implicit theories of ability—Forms of a self-theory comprising students' beliefs about the fixedness or malleability of their personal qualities, such as their abilities, which influence their perceived ability or potential to learn and achieve.

learning environment—The instructive environment that includes how the teacher interacts psychologically with students and how the teacher communicates content, educational values and curriculum priorities. The learning environment enhances or constrains pupils' learning outcomes in terms of cognition, motivation affect, general behaviour and achievement.

monitoring—Tracking one's attention as one performs a motor task; includes self-testing and self-questioning to assist in understanding and in integrating the tasks with prior tasks and motor learning activities.

motivational beliefs—A set of interrelated beliefs that include thoughts about one's ability to learn and perform, epistemological theories including beliefs about the certainty and simplicity of knowledge and skills, efficacy-competence judgments, goal orientation, outcome expectations and the value of the learning task.

motivational climates—Learning climates that shape, facilitate or constrain students' motivational, behavioural and cognitive self-regulation.

observation level—The first level of self-regulation, in which pupils observe competent models performing the skill.

performance phase—The phase of self-regulation that includes processes that occur during motor efforts, which affect attention and action. Two major classes of processes are involved: strategy use and self-observation.

planning—A process whereby goal setting and task analysis help activate or prime relevant aspects of prior knowledge, thus making organising and comprehending material and motor tasks easier.

regulation of cognitive activities—The fine-tuning and continuous adjustment of one's cognitive activities while performing learning tasks and activities.

regulation of effort—Students' attempts to control their effort; also described as resource management.

self-control level—The third level of self-regulation, in which pupils begin to use self-directed, deliberate practice. They are able to perform the skill correctly using internal images (a personal standard).

self-handicapping—A self-protective mechanism that is maladaptive for learning and achievement; involves excuse making and engaging in purposeful action to create some explanation for a potential poor performance.

self-reflection phase—The phase of self-regulation that involves processes that occur after performance efforts and influence pupils' response to that experience. The phase consists of two main subprocesses: self-judgments and self-reactions.

self-regulation—An active, constructive process whereby students have learned to set goals for their learning and then attempt to monitor, regulate and control their cognition, motivation, affect and behaviour, guided or constrained by their goals and the contextual features of the environment.

self-regulation level—The final level of self-regulation, in which pupils are capable of adapting to different situations and coping with environmental and personal demands as they perform a skill. Pupils are now able to choose a strategy and adapt its features with little or no residual dependence on models.

References

Ames, C. (1992). Achievement goals, motivational climate and motivational processes. In G.C. Roberts (Ed.), *Motivation in sport and exercise* (pp. 161-176). Champaign, IL: Human Kinetics.

Ames, C. & Archer, J. (1988). Achievement goals in the classroom: Students' learning strategies and motivational processes. *Journal of Educational Psychology, 80,* 260-267.

Archer, J. (1994). Achievement goals as a measure of motivation in university students. *Contemporary Educational Psychology, 19,* 430-446.

Arnold, P. (1991). The pre-eminence of skill as an educational value in the movement curriculum. *Quest, 43,* 66-77.

Biddle, S., Soos, I. & Chatzisarantis, N. (1999). Predicting physical activity intentions using a goal perspectives approach: A study of Hungarian youth. *Scandinavian Journal of Medicine & Science in Sports, 9,* 353-357.

Boekaerts, M. & Niemivirta, M. (2000). Self-regulated learning: Finding a balance between learning goals and ego-protective goals. In M. Boekaerts, P. Pintrich & M. Zeidner (Ed.), *Handbook of self-regulation* (pp. 417-451). New York: Academic Press.

Boreham, C., Robson, P., Gallagher, A.M., Cran, G.W., Savage, J.M. & Murray, L.J. (2004). Tracking of physical activity, fitness, body composition and diet from adolescence to young adulthood: The Young Hearts Project, Northern Ireland. *The International Journal of Behavioral Nutrition and Physical Activity, 1,* 1-14.

Butler, R. & Neuman, O. (1995). Effects of task and ego achievement goals on help-seeking behaviours and attitudes. *Journal of Educational Psychology, 87,* 261-271.

Campbell, P.T., Katzmarzyk, P.T., Malina, R.M., Rao, D.C., Preusse, L. & Bouchard, I.C. (2001). Prediction of physical activity and physical work capacity in young adulthood from childhood and adolescence with consideration of parental measures. *American Journal of Human Biology, 13,* 190-196.

Clark, J.E. (1995). On becoming skillful: Patterns and constraints. *Research Quarterly for Exercise and Sport, 66,* 173-183.

Corno, L. (1986). The meta-cognitive control components of self-regulated learning. *Contemporary Educational Psychology, 11,* 333-346.

Covington, M. (1992). *Making the grade: A self-worth perspective on motivation and school reform.* New York: Cambridge University Press.

Cury, F., Biddle, S., Sarrazin, P. & Famose, J.P. (1997). Achievement goals and perceived ability predict investment in learning a sport task. *British Journal of Educational Psychology, 67,* 293-309.

Cury, F., Elliot, A., Sarrazin, D., Da Fonseca, D. & Rufo, M. (2002). The trichotomous achievement goal model and intrinsic motivation: A sequential mediational analysis. *Journal of Experimental Social Psychology, 38,* 473-481.

Duda, J.L. (2001). Achievement goal research in sport: Pushing the boundaries and clarifying some misunderstandings. In Roberts, G.C. (Ed.), *Advances in motivation in sport and exercise* (pp. 129-182). Champaign, Illinois: Human Kinetics.

Dweck, C.S. (1986). Motivational processes affecting learning. *American Psychologist, 41,* 1040-1048.

Dweck, C.S. (1991). Self-theories and goals: Their role in motivation, personality and development. In R. Dienstbier (Ed.), *Perspectives on motivation, Nebraska symposium on motivation 1990, Vol. 38* (pp. 200-235). Lincoln/London: University of Nebraska Press.

Dweck, C.S. & Leggett, E.L. (1988). A social-cognitive approach to motivation and personality. *Psychological Review, 95,* 256-273.

Dweck, C.S. & Molden, D.C. (2005). Self-theories: Their impact on competence motivation and acquisition. In A.J. Elliot & C.S. Dweck (Eds.), *Handbook of competence and motivation* (pp. 122-140). New York: Guilford Press.

Elliot, A.J. (1997). Integrating the "classic" and "contemporary" approaches to achievement motivation: A hierarchical model of approach and avoidance achievement motivation. In M.L. Maehr & P.R. Pintrich (Eds.), *Advances in motivation and achievement* (pp. 143-179). Greenwich, CT: JAI Press.

Elliot, A.J. (1999). Approach and avoidance motivation and achievement goals. *Educational Psychologist, 34,* 169-189.

Elliot, A.J. & Church, M.A. (1997). A hierarchical model of approach and avoidance achievement motivation. *Journal of Personality and Social Psychology, 54,* 218-232.

Elliot, A.J. & Harackiewicz, J.M. (1996). Approach and avoidance achievement goals and intrinsic motivation: A mediational analysis. *Journal of Personality and Social Psychology, 70,* 461-475.

Elliot, A.J., McGregor, H.A. & Gable S. (1999). Achievement goals, study strategies and exam performance: A mediational analysis. *Journal of Educational Psychology, 91,* 549-563.

Elliot, A.J. & Moller, A.C. (2003). Performance-approach goals: Good or bad forms of regulation? *International Journal of Educational Research, 39,* 339-356.

Elliott, E.S. & Dweck, C.S. (1988). Goals: An approach to motivation and achievement. *Journal of Personality and Social Psychology, 54,* 5-12.

Ennis, C.D. (1999). Creating a culturally relevant curriculum for disengaged girls. *Sport, Education and Society, 4,* 31-49.

Ennis, C.D. (2006). Curricular coherence: A key to effective physical activity programs. In P. Heikinaro-Johansson & E. McEvoy (Eds.), *The role of physical education and sport in promoting physical activity and health* (pp. 134-136). Jyväskylä, Finland: Department of Sport Sciences, University of Jyväskylä.

Gano-Overway, L.A. & Ewing, M E. (2004). A longitudinal perspective of the relationship between perceived motivational climate, goal orientations, and strategy use. *Research Quarterly for Exercise and Sport, 75,* 315-325.

Garcia, T. & Pintrich, P.R. (1994). Regulating motivation and cognition in the classroom. The role of self-schemas and self-regulatory strategies. In D.H. Schunk & B.J. Zimmerman (Eds.), *Self-regulation of learning and performance: Issues and educational applications* (pp. 127-153). Hillsdale, NJ: Erlbaum.

Glencross, D.J. (1994). Human skill and motor learning: A critical review. *Sport Science Review, 1,* 65-78.

Greene, B.A. & Miller, R.B. (1996). Influences on achievement: Goals, perceived ability, and cognitive engagement. *Contemporary Educational Psychology, 21,* 181-192.

Hagger, M.S., Chatzisarantis, N.L.D., Culverhouse, T. & Biddle, S.J.H. (2003). The processes by which perceived autonomy support in physical education promotes leisure-time physical activity intentions and behaviour: A trans-contextual model. *Journal of Educational Psychology, 95,* 784-795.

Harackiewicz, J.M., Barron, K.E., Pintrich, P.R., Elliot, A.J. & Thrash, T.M. (2002). Revision of achievement goal theory: Necessary and illuminating. *Journal of Educational Psychology, 94,* 638-645.

Hong, Y., Chiu, C. & Dweck, C.S. (1995). Implicit theories of intelligence: Reconsidering the role of confidence in achievement motivation. In M. Kernis (Ed.), *Efficacy, agency and self-esteem* (pp. 197-216). New York: Plenum Press.

Jones, E.E. & Berglas, S. (1978). Control of attributions about self through self-handicapping strategies: The appeal of alcohol and underachievement. *Personality and Social Psychology Bulletin, 4,* 200-206.

Jourden, F.J., Bandura, A. & Banfield, J.T. (1991). The impact of conception of ability on self-regulatory factors and motor skill acquisition. *Journal of Sport and Exercise Psychology, 13,* 213-226.

Karabenick, S.A. (2004). Perceived achievement goal structure and college student help seeking. *Journal of Educational Psychology, 96,* 569-581.

Kasimatis, M., Miller, M. & Marcussen, L. (1996). The effects of implicit theories on exercise motivation. *Journal of Research in Personality, 30,* 510-516.

Kirk, D. (2005). Physical education, youth sport and lifelong participation: The importance of early experiences. *European Physical Education Review, 11,* 239-255.

Kirk, D. & Tinning, R. (1994). Embodied self-identity, healthy lifestyles and school physical education. *Sociology of Health and Illness, 16,* 600-625.

Kuhl, J. (2000). A functional-design approach to motivation and self-regulation: The dynamics of personality systems interactions. In M. Boekaerts, P. Pintrich & M. Zeidner (Eds.), *Handbook of self-regulation* (pp.111-169). New York: Academic Press.

Kun, A. (1977). Development of the magnitude-covariation and compensation schemata in ability and effort attributions of performance. *Child Development, 48,* 862-873.

Kun, A. & Weiner, B. (1973). Necessary versus sufficient causal schemata for success and failure. *Journal of Research in Personality, 7,* 197-207.

Lavisse, D., Deviterne, D. & Perrin, P. (2000). Mental processing in motor skill acquisition by young subjects. *International Journal of Sport Psychology, 31,* 364-375.

Lee, A.M., Landin, D.K. & Carter, J.A. (1992). Student thoughts during tennis instruction. *Journal of Teaching in Physical Education, 11,* 256-267.

Lidor, R. (2004). Developing metacognitive behaviour in physical education classes: The use of task-pertinent learning strategies. *Physical Education and Sport Pedagogy, 9,* 55-71.

Lidor, R., Tennant, K.L. & Singer, R. (1996). The generalizability effect of three learning strategies across motor task performances. *International Journal of Sport Psychology, 27,* 23-36.

Lirgg, C.D., Chase, M.A., George, T.R. & Ferguson, R.H. (1996). Impact of conception of ability and sex-type of task on male and female self-efficacy. *Journal of Sport & Exercise Psychology, 18,* 426-434.

Lochbaum, M.R. & Roberts, G.C. (1993). Goal orientations and perceptions of the sport experience. *Journal of Sport and Exercise Psychology, 84,* 290-299.

Locke, E.A. & Latham, G.P. (2002). Building a practically useful theory of goal setting and task motivation: A 35-year odyssey. *American Psychologist, 57,* 705-717.

Luke, I. & Hardy, C. (1999a). Students' metacognition and learning. In C.A. Hardy & M. Mawer (Eds.), *Learning in physical education* (pp. 38-58). London: Falmer Press.

Luke, I. & Hardy, C. (1999b). Cognitive strategies. In C.A. Hardy & M. Mawer (Eds.), *Learning in physical education* (pp. 59-79). London: Falmer Press.

Masson, M.E.J. (1990). Cognitive theories of skill acquisition. *Human Movement Science, 9,* 221-239.

McCaslin, M. & Good, T.L. (1996). The informal curriculum. In D. Berliner & R. Calfee (Eds.), *Handbook of educational psychology* (pp. 622-670). New York: Macmillan.

Meece, J. (1994). The role of motivation in self-regulated learning. In D.H. Schunk & B. Zimmerman (Eds.), *Self-regulation of learning and performance: Issues and educational applications* (pp. 25-44). Hillsdale, NJ: Erlbaum.

Meece, J.L., Blumenfeld, P.C. & Hoyle, R.H. (1988). Students' goal orientations and cognitive engagement in classroom activities. *Journal of Educational Psychology, 80,* 514-523.

Middleton, M.J. & Midgley, C. (1997). Avoiding the demonstration of lack of ability: An underexplored aspect of goal theory. *Journal of Educational Psychology, 89,* 710-718.

Midgley, C., Kaplan, A., Middleton, M., Maehr, M., Urdan, T. & Anderman, E. (1998). The development and validation of scales assessing students' achievement goal orientations. *Contemporary Educational Psychology, 23,* 113-131.

Midgley, C. & Urdan, T.C. (2001). Academic self-handicapping and achievement goals: A further examination. *Contemporary Educational Psychology, 26,* 61-75.

Miller, R.B., Behrens, J.T., Greene, B.A. & Newman, D. (1993). Goals and perceived ability: Impact on student valuing, self-regulation, and persistence. *Contemporary Educational Psychology, 18,* 2-14.

Miller, R.B., Greene, B.A., Montalvo, G.P., Ravindran, B. & Nicols J.D. (1996). Engagement in academic work: The role of learning goals, future consequences, pleasing others, and perceived ability. *Contemporary Educational Psychology, 21,* 388-422.

Newman, R.S. (1994). Adaptive help seeking: A strategy of self-regulated learning. In D. Schunk & B. Zimmerman (Eds.), *Self-regulation of learning and performance: Issues and educational applications* (pp. 283-301). Hillsdale NJ: Erlbaum.

Newman, R.S. (1998). Students' help seeking during problem solving: Influences of personal and contextual achievement goals. *Journal of Educational Psychology, 90,* 644-658.

Newman, R.S. (2000). Social influences on the development of children's adaptive help-seeking: The role of parents, teachers, and peers. *Developmental Review, 20,* 350-404.

Nicholls, J. (1989). *The competitive ethos and democratic education.* Cambridge, MA: Harvard University Press.

Nisbet, J. & Shucksmith, J. (1986). *Learning strategies.* London: Routledge and Keagan Paul.

Nolen, S. (1988). Reasons for studying: Motivational orientations and study strategies. *Cognition and Instruction, 5,* 269-287.

Ommundsen, Y. (2001a). Students' affective responses in PE: The influence of implicit theories of the nature of ability and achievement goals. *European Physical Education Review, 7,* 219–240.

Ommundsen, Y. (2001b). Self-handicapping strategies in physical education classes: The influence of implicit theories of the nature of ability and achievement goals. *Psychology of Sport & Exercise, 2,* 139-156.

Ommundsen, Y. (2001c). The role of the motivational climate on students' implicit theories of ability. *Learning Environment Research, 4,* 139-158.

Ommundsen, Y. (2003). Implicit theories of ability and self-regulation strategies in physical education classes. *Educational Psychology, 23,* 141-157.

Ommundsen, Y. (2004). Self-handicapping related to task and performance-approach and avoidance goals in physical education. *Journal of Applied Sport Psychology, 16,* 183-197.

Ommundsen, Y. (2006). Pupils' self-regulation in physical education: The role of motivational climates and differential achievement goals. *European Physical Education Review, 12,* 289-315.

Ommundsen, Y. & Eikanger Kvalø, S. (2007). Autonomy-mastery supportive or controlling: Differential teacher behaviours and pupils' outcomes of physical education. In *Scandinavian Journal of Educational Research, 51*(5) [in press].

Ommundsen, Y., Roberts, G.C. & Kavussanu, M. (1998). Perceived motivational climate and cognitive and affective correlates among team sport athletes. *Journal of Sport Sciences, 16,* 153-164.

O'Sullivan, M. (2004). Possibilities and pitfalls of a public health agenda for physical education. *Journal of Teaching in Physical Education, 23,* 392-404.

Pintrich, P. (2000b). The role of goal orientation in self-regulation. In M. Boekaerts, P. Pintrich & M. Zeidner (Eds.), *Handbook of self-regulation* (pp. 452-502). New York: Academic Press.

Pintrich, P. (2000c). An achievement goal theory perspective on issues in motivation, terminology, theory and research. *Contemporary Educational Psychology, 25,* 92-104.

Pintrich, P. (2003). A motivational science perspective on the role of student motivation in learning and teaching contexts. *Journal of Educational Psychology, 45,* 667-686.

Pintrich, P. & De Groot, E. (1990). Motivational and self-regulated learning components of classroom academic performance. *Journal of Educational Psychology, 82,* 33-40.

Pintrich, P. & Garcia, T. (1991). Student goal orientation and self-regulation in the college classroom. In M.L. Maehr & P. Pintrich (Eds.), *Advancement in motivation and achievement: Goals and self-regulatory processes* (pp. 371-402). Greenwich, CT: JAI Press.

Pintrich, P. & Schrauben, B. (1992). Students' motivational beliefs and engagement in classroom academic tasks. In D. Schunk & J. Meece (Eds.), *Student perceptions in the classroom* (pp. 149-183). Hillsdale, NJ: LEA Press.

Pintrich, P., Smith, D., Garcia, T. & Mckeachie, W. (1993). Predictive validity and reliability of the Motivated Strategies for Learning Questionnaire (MLSQ). *Educational and Psychological Measurement, 53,* 801-813.

Pintrich, P.R. (2000a). Multiple goals, multiple pathways: The role of goal orientations in learning and achievement. *Journal of Educational Psychology, 92,* 544-555.

Randi, J. & Corno, L. (2000). Teacher innovations in self-regulated learning. In M. Boekaerts, P. Pintrich & M. Zeidner (Eds.), *Handbook of self-regulation* (pp. 651-685). New York: Academic Press.

Rhodewalt, F. & Tragakis, M. (2002). Self-handicapping and the social self: The costs and rewards of interpersonal self-construction. In J.P. Forgas & K.D. Williams (Eds.), *The social self: Cognitive, interpersonal, and inter-group perspectives* (pp. 121-140). New York: Psychology Press.

Rhodewalt, F. & Vohs, C.K. (2005). Defensive strategies, motivation, and the self. In A.J. Elliot & C.S. Dweck (Eds.), *Handbook of competence and motivation* (pp. 548-565). New York: Guilford Press.

Roberts, G.C. (2001). Understanding the dynamics of motivation in physical activity: The influence of achievement goals on motivational processes. In G.C. Roberts (Ed.), *Advances in motivation in sport and exercise* (pp. 1-50). Champaign, IL: Human Kinetics.

Roberts, G.C. & Ommundsen, Y. (1996). Effect of goal orientation on achievement beliefs, cognition and strategies in team sport. *Scandinavian Journal of Medicine & Science in Sports, 6,* 46-56.

Ryan, A.M., Gheen, M. & Migley, C. (1998). Why do some students avoid asking for help? An examination of the interplay among students' academic efficacy, teachers' social-emotional role, and classroom goal structure. *Journal of Educational Psychology, 90,* 528-535.

Ryan, A.M. & Pintrich, P. (1997). "Should I ask for help?" The role of motivation and attitudes in adolescents' help seeking in math class. *Journal of Educational Psychology, 89,* 329-341.

Sarrazin, P., Biddle, S., Famose, J.P., Cury, F., Fox, K. & Durand, M. (1996). Goal orientations and conceptions of the nature of sport ability in children: A social cognitive approach. *British Journal of Social Psychology, 35,* 399-414.

Schommer, M. (1990). Effect of beliefs about the nature of knowledge on comprehension. *Journal of Educational Psychology, 82,* 498-504.

Singer, R., Flora, L.A. & Abourezk, T. (1989). The effect of a five-step cognitive learning strategy on the acquisition of a complex motor task. *Journal of Applied Sport Psychology, 1,* 98-108.

Skaalvik, E.M. (1997). Self-enhancing and self-defeating ego orientation: Relations with task and avoidance orientation, achievement, self-perceptions, and anxiety. *Journal of Educational Psychology, 89,* 71-81.

Skinner, E.A. (1995). *Perceived control, motivation and coping.* Thousand Oaks, CA: Sage.

Solomon, M., Belcher, D., House, L., Jr. & Wells L. (2003). Beliefs about gender appropriateness, ability and competence in physical activity. *Journal of Teaching in Physical Education, 22,* 261-279.

Standage, M., Duda, J.L. & Ntoumanis, N. (2003). A model of contextual motivation in physical education: Using constructs from self-determination and achievement goal theories to predict physical activity intentions. *Journal of Educational Psychology, 95,* 97-110.

Stipek, D. & Gralinski, J.H. (1996). Children's beliefs about intelligence and school performance. *Journal of Educational Psychology, 88,* 397-407.

Stone, E.J., McKenzie, T.L., Welk, G.J. & Booth, M.L. (1998). Effects of physical activity interventions in youth. *American Journal of Preventive Medicine, 15,* 298-315.

Tanaka, A., Murakami, Y., Okuno, T. & Yamauchi, H. (2001). Achievement goals, attitudes toward help-seeking behaviour in the classroom. *Learning and Individual Differences, 13,* 23-35.

Telema, R., Nupponen, H. & Pieron, M. (2005). Physical activity among young people in the context of lifestyle. *European Physical Education Review, 11,* 115-137.

Tinning, R. (1997). Performance and participation discourses in human movement: Toward a socially critical physical education. In J.M. Fernandez-Balboa (Ed.), *Critical postmodernism in human movement, physical education and sport* (pp. 99-119). New York: State University of New York Press.

Tinning, R., Kirk, D., Evans, J. & Glover, S. (1994). School physical education: A crisis of meaning. *Changing Education: A Journal for Teachers and Administrators, 1,* 13-15.

Turner, J.C., Midgley C., Meyer, D.K., Gheen, M., Anderman, E.M., Kang, Y. & Patrick, H. (2002). The classroom environment and students' reports of avoidance strategies in mathematics: A multimethod study. *Journal of Educational Psychology, 94,* 88-106.

Urdan, T. (2004). Predictors of academic self-handicapping and achievement: Examining achievement goals, classroom goal structures, and culture. *Journal of Educational Psychology, 96,* 251-264.

Urdan, T., Ryan, A.M., Anderman, E.M. & Gheen, M.H. (2002). Goals, goal structures, and avoidance behaviours. In C. Midgley (Ed.), *Goals, goal structures, and patterns of adaptive learning* (pp. 55-83). Hillsdale, NJ: Erlbaum.

Van Wersch, A., Trew, K. & Turner, I. (1992). Post-primary school students' interest in physical education: Age and gender differences. *British Journal of Educational Psychology, 62,* 56-72.

Vermetten, Y.J., Lodewijks, H.G. & Vermunt, J.D. (2001). The role of personality traits and goal orientations in strategy use. *Contemporary Educational Psychology, 26,* 149-170.

Weinstein, C.E. & Mayer, R.E. (1986). The teaching of learning strategies. In M. Wittrock (Ed.), *Handbook of research on teaching* (pp. 315-327). New York: Macmillan.

Winne, P.H. & Perry, N.E. (2000). Measuring self-regulation. In M. Boekaerts, P. Pintrich & M. Zeidner (Eds.), *Handbook of self-regulation* (pp. 532-566). New York: Academic Press.

Wolters, J. (2003a). Understanding procrastination from a self-regulated learning perspective. *Journal of Educational Psychology, 95,* 179-187.

Wolters, J. (2003b). Regulation of motivation: Evaluating an underemphasized aspect of self-regulated learning. *Educational Psychologist, 38,* 189-205.

Wolters, J. (2004). Advancing achievement goal theory: Using goal structures and goal orientations to predict students' motivation, cognition, and achievement. *Journal of Educational Psychology, 96,* 236-250.

Wolters, J., Yu, S. & Pintrich, P. (1996). The relation between goal orientations and students' motivational beliefs and self-regulated learning. *Learning and Individual Differences, 8,* 211-238.

Xiang, P. & Lee, A. (2002). Achievement goals, perceived motivational climate, and students' self-reported mastery behaviors. *Research Quarterly for Exercise and Sport, 73,* 58-65.

Zimmerman, B. (2000). Attaining self-regulation: A social cognitive perspective. In M. Boekaerts, P. Pintrich & M. Zeidner (Eds.), *Handbook of self-regulation* (pp. 13-39). New York: Academic Press.

Zimmerman, B. & Campillo, M. (2003). Motivating self-regulated problem solvers. In J.E. Davison & R.J. Sternberg (Eds.), *The nature of problem solving* (pp. 233-262). New York: Cambridge University Press.

Zimmerman, B.J. & Kitsantas, A. (1996). Self-regulated learning of a motor skill: The role of goal setting and monitoring. *Journal of Applied Sport Psychology, 8,* 69-84.

Zimmerman, B.J. & Kitsantas, A. (2005). The hidden dimension of personal competence: Self-regulated learning and practice. In A.J. Elliot & C.S. Dweck (Eds.), *Handbook of competence and motivation* (pp. 509-526). New York: Guilford Press.

Zimmerman, B. & Martinez-Pons, M. (1988). Construct validation of a strategy model of student self-regulated learning. *Journal of Educational Psychology, 80,* 284-290.

Zimmerman, B.J. & Schunk, D.H. (2004). Self-regulating intellectual processes and outcomes: A social cognitive perspective. In D. Yun Dai & R.J. Sternberg (Eds.), *Motivation, emotion and cognition: Integrative perspectives on intellectual functioning and development* (pp. 323-349). Mahwah, NJ: Erlbaum.

chapter ten

Interdisciplinary Teaching, Multiple Goals and Self-Concept

Dimitris Milosis
Democritus University of Thrace, Greece

Athanasios G. Papaioannou
University of Thessaly, Greece

After reading this chapter, you will be able to do the following:

- Explain why an intervention based on the multidimensional model of goal orientations (MMGO) is different from previous interventions aiming to affect motivational climate

- Explain why an intervention based on the MMGO can affect multidimensional self-concept

- Describe the targets of the intervention described in this chapter according to the MMGO

- Describe the steps that were followed in the intervention described in this chapter to affect improvement in the health domain

- List the strategies designed to promote improvement in the achievement domain in the intervention described in this chapter

- Identify the strategies used in this intervention that were designed to promote improvement in the social domain

- Describe the main strategies designed to develop interdisciplinary skills in the intervention described in this chapter

- Provide examples of goals for personal improvement across different human action domains and life contexts

The study presented here was part of the doctoral dissertation of D. Milosis under the supervision of A. Papaioannou. The thesis was conducted at the Democritus University of Thrace.

In the last decade we witnessed an increased interest in positive **motivational climate** in physical education. This is exemplified by the chapters in this book devoted to this topic, important reviews of research in this area (e.g., Biddle, 2001; Duda, 1996) and articles providing instructions for creating a positive motivational climate in physical education (e.g., Papaioannou & Goudas, 1999; Treasure & Roberts, 1995).

This line of research was based on Nicholls' (1989) theory of achievement goals and Ames' (1992) pioneering work on motivational climate in school. According to this tradition, positive motivational climate occurs when teachers emphasise task involvement, competence development and optimum challenge for all students. At the same time, teachers are encouraged to avoid normative comparisons in order to decrease students' ego involvement. To these teaching instructions that directly stem from achievement goals theory, Ames (1992) added suggestions stemming from self-determination theory (Deci & Ryan, 1985), such as the promotion of students' autonomy and the reduction of teachers' controlling behaviours in order to enhance students' **intrinsic motivation.**

Following all these suggestions, we conducted one-year **intervention** studies aiming to increase positive motivational climate in physical education classes (e.g., Christodoulidis, Papaioannou & Digelidis, 2001; Digelidis, Papaioannou, Laparidis & Christodoulidis, 2003). Our endeavours had positive results, but we were not fully satisfied with the final outcome. The positive effects were significant but not impressive. We had either small or medium effect sizes, not large ones as we had wished. During these intervention studies, feedback from teachers and students revealed that many students resisted following the suggested activities. This resistance can be epitomised in the following question of a student: 'Learning new skills in physical education is a nice thing, but why should we work hard to do it? We are bombarded by challenges all day; don't you think that we need some time to relax?' Although we disliked what we heard, we confessed that adolescents face many challenges in their lives. On the other hand, we knew that most of the low-task-oriented students in physical education are probably low-task oriented in other school subjects too (Duda & Nicholls, 1992). Taking into consideration that school physical education constitutes only a small part of student life, it would be rather naive to believe that we can substantially increase students' task involvement in physical education without taking notice of whether they are task involved in other contexts as well.

In our effort to study multiple goals concurrently, we faced an important theoretical obstacle. Existing achievement goals theories and corresponding teaching instructions adopt a one-dimensional focus. Researchers and practitioners usually focus on youngsters' achievement goals in one context, such as school or sport, without considering how these goals are linked with achievement goals in other life contexts. Likewise, we have limited knowledge about the connection of students' achievement motivation with non-achieving behaviours such as social behaviour and related cognitions and emotions. Nevertheless, people organise their ideas about the self into coherent and consistent personal theories (Kelly, 1955; Rogers, 1950). Taking into consideration that adolescents adopt an integrated theory of self, we can hardly fully understand the antecedents and consequences of their achievement goals with one-dimensional theoretical perspectives.

Multidimensional Model of Goal Orientations

To circumvent the aforementioned theoretical barrier, Papaioannou (1999) introduced the **multidimensional model of goal orientations (MMGO).** Based on established theories of motivation and goals (Carver & Sheier, 1998; Vallacher & Wegner, 1987) suggesting that goals vary in their levels of abstraction, he proposed that goal orientations should be examined at different levels of abstraction. General life goal orientations occur at a high level of abstraction, goal orientations across varying life contexts are at an intermediate level of abstraction and present-moment goal orientations are at a lower level of abstraction (see figure 10.1). Vallerand (1997) proposed these three levels to define intrinsic-extrinsic motivation at the global, contextual and situational levels of generality, respectively. Papaioannou (1999) also suggested that goal orientations have implications to nonachieving behaviours, such as responsibility, morality, risk and health-related behaviours. According to his model, people construe goal orientations at four levels of abstraction, which are probably classified in a hierarchical order such as that shown in figure 10.1.

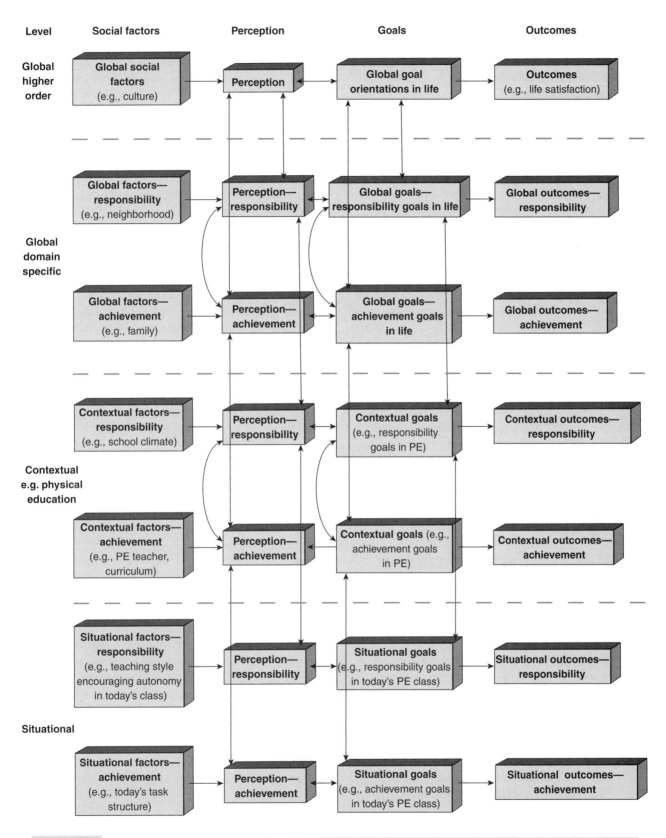

Figure 10.1 Example of determinants and consequences of goal orientations at four levels of abstraction.

At the higher level of abstraction, goals can be defined as follows. A *personal improvement goal* in life aims at improving one's qualities across a variety of human actions and life contexts. An *ego-strengthening goal* implies the pursuit of positive evaluation from others. On the other hand, an *ego-protection goal* connotes attempts to avoid negative judgments from others. Finally, people might pursue *social approval goals* through the adoption of various actions across different life settings.

At every level of abstraction, goal orientations have important antecedents and consequences. Teachers, coaches, parents, friends, idols, the media and maybe other social factors affect students' goal orientations at varying levels of abstraction. Then, depending on goal adoption, specific emotions, cognitions and behaviours arise. For example, personal improvement goals facilitate the adoption of efficient self-regulation cognitive strategies, such as self-monitoring, information management and planning, but ego-oriented goals facilitate strategies such as superficial thinking and impression management (Ommundsen, 2003; Theodosiou, 2004). In return, these outcomes are likely to reinforce the goals that triggered them. For example, in a recent longitudinal study we found that participation in sport and exercise had a positive impact on the development of personal improvement goals (Papaioannou, Bebetsos, Theodorakis, Christodoulidis & Kouli, 2006).

MMGO and the Development of Interdisciplinary Skills

The MMGO is useful in interdisciplinary teaching. In 2003 the Greek Institute of Education (GIE) took an initiative to promote an integrated thematic curriculum in Greek elementary and secondary education. According to the GIE, 'The integrated thematic approach is broader than the interdisciplinary approach and offers the potential to students to form an integrated whole of knowledge and skills, a holistic notion of knowledge, that allows them to shape a personal view for themes of sciences that are related between each other as with issues of everyday life.' (Greek Ministry of Education, 2003). At the core of the integrated thematic curriculum are the fundamental concepts and the interdisciplinary skills that are found in different sciences and school subjects. For example, *system* and *interaction* are funda-

mental concepts that are found in physics, in human sciences and in sport, and *communication* and *problem-solving skills* are interdisciplinary skills that are important in all school subjects. The fundamental concepts and the interdisciplinary skills constitute the basic links for a horizontal connection of school subjects.

We believe that the MMGO is useful in teaching some important interdisciplinary skills. For example, problem-solving skills require planning and **goal setting,** monitoring, evaluation and corrective intervention strategies. We know that these cognitive strategies are triggered by task or personal improvement goals both in academic subjects (Ames & Archer, 1988; Nolen, 1988; Vermetten, Lodewijks & Vermunt, 2001) and in physical education (Ommundsen, 2003; Solmon & Lee, 1997; Theodosiou & Papaioannou, 2006). This and other research also imply that personal improvement goals facilitate the development of other important interdisciplinary skills, such as critical elaboration of information and values, creative invention and cooperation, in both school and sport (Duda, Fox, Biddle & Armstrong, 1992; Nicholls, 1989; Nicholls, Cobb, Wood, Yackel & Patashnick, 1990; Nolen & Haladyna, 1990; Papaioannou & Macdonald, 1993).

The MMGO allows a teacher to reinforce the importance of personal improvement goals at a higher level of abstraction. For example, the motto that we adopted in the intervention described in this chapter was 'by improving myself everywhere, I will live better'. This motto provides a reason for high effort across a variety of learning tasks, school subjects and life settings. In other words, it strengthens the meaningfulness of pursuing personal improvement goals in concrete tasks embedded in divergent achievement and social domains. Importantly, this abstract motto is helpful across a variety of situations in which the benefits of personal improvement and high effort are not immediately visible. Students adopting this motto are more likely to try hard to develop knowledge and skills whose importance is not easily comprehensible.

How can we persuade students to adopt this motto? Social learning theory suggests that verbal persuasion is a potential vehicle, but enactive learning is most effective (Bandura, 1986). Hence, teachers might do well to use persuasive arguments to strengthen the importance of this motto, but students are more likely to adopt it if they learn from experience. Accordingly, in our intervention we first provided a wealth of task-involving experiences in physical education, and then we asked students to transfer what they learned to other life contexts. We particularly focused on two academic subjects (math and Greek language) and on a nonschool setting (the home environment). Apart from achievement, we set personal improvement goals in the responsibility domain.

Overall, our strategy was as follows: For the main part of the physical education lesson we particularly tried to use task-involving activities, personal goal setting and cognitive strategies that facilitate task involvement. In the last minutes of the physical education lesson, we discussed how students could use the goals and strategies from their physical education lesson in math and Greek language classes and at home. Then we asked students to set goals and employ strategies for personal improvement in these contexts. A few days or weeks after the practice of personal improvement goals and strategies in other life settings, we reviewed with students their experiences, the pros and cons of applying personal improvement goals and strategies in these life settings, the barriers and weaknesses or mistakes that emerged and the coping skills they used to overcome obstacles and mistakes. We then asked students to revise their goals and strategies and apply them again. Throughout this process we implicitly and sometimes explicitly reinforced the importance of the motto 'by improving myself everywhere, I will live better'.

MMGO and the Multidimensional Self-Concept

'Self-esteem is the panacea of modern life. It is seen as the key to financial success, health, and personal fulfillment, and it is regarded as the antidote to underachievement, crime, and drug abuse' (Brown, 1998, p. 190). The development of self-esteem has been the primary goal of developmental curriculum models in education and physical education (Jewett, Bain & Ennis, 1995). Contemporary leaders in the field of physical education even argued that helping children develop positive self-esteem is more important than helping them develop competence (Corbin, 2002, p.136). Undoubtedly, the development of self-esteem is considered a major goal in modern physical education.

The term *self-esteem* is used in three different ways. Most often it is used to describe the way people generally feel about themselves. It is also used to refer to the way people evaluate their various abilities and attributes. Finally, it is used to refer to temporary emotional states, particularly those that arise from a positive or negative outcome. It is interesting to note that these three approaches correspond to the different levels of abstraction of the MMGO.

In our intervention we adopted the multidimensional **self-concept** construct (Shavelson, Hubner & Stanton, 1976). This defined self-concept as a person's perception of self, both descriptive and evaluative, that is formed through experiences with the environment, interactions with significant others and attributions of the person's behaviour. The organisation of self is multifaceted and hierarchical, with perceptions about the self moving from subareas (e.g., sport) to broader areas (e.g., academic and nonacademic self-concept). Based on this model Marsh, Parker and Barnes (1985) developed the *Self-Description Questionnaire II* for middle and high school adolescents. This 11-scale measure captures self-perceptions concerned with general school, mathematics, verbal and physical abilities, physical appearance, relations with same sex and opposite sex peers, relations with parents, honesty and emotional stability. Moreover, one of its scales captures general self-esteem.

We expected that our intervention would have a positive impact on all subcomponents of self-concept. Take the example of physical education. The adoption of personal improvement goals would allow students to feel better about themselves in physical education. When personal standards of evaluation are adopted, success is judged according to one's own personal progress. All students of a class can describe themselves as good sport performers, as long as they have improved their sport abilities. Taking into consideration that our intervention aimed at strengthening personal improvement goals across different life contexts and human action domains and at different levels of abstraction, we expected that the intervention would affect all subcomponents of self-concept.

Participants

A total of 292 students (162 male, 130 female) from the first grade in junior high school (aged 12.38±0.68) from six different schools and from different areas of Thessaloniki, a Greek city with about 1.5 million people, participated in our study. The experimental group consisted of 99 students from four classes. These were taught by a specially trained PE teacher for a six-month period (each student had three school classes per week). The teacher had a master's degree in motivation in PE, and the present research was a part of his doctoral dissertation. The control group consisted of 193 students from eight classes who were taught the typical PE subject by three male and four female teachers. All the participants in this research (teachers and students) were informed about the study, and their participation was voluntary and willing. Furthermore, the necessary licence from the Greek Institute of Education was obtained as well as a licence from the schools' headmasters to carry out the research at their schools.

Measures

A researcher (not the PE teacher who applied the intervention programme) visited the schools the first week of the academic year and one week after the completion of the intervention and collected the questionnaires. All students were told that the purpose of the questionnaire was to examine the validity of measures assessing their attitudes and self-concept in different school subjects. The participants completed questionnaires that assessed (1) four achievement goals (personal improvement, ego strengthening, ego protection and social approval) in three different contexts (PE, mathematics and Greek language) (Papaioannou, Milosis, Kosmidou & Tsigilis, 2002); (2) multidimensional self-concept (general self, general school, physical abilities, mathematics, verbal, physical appearance, relations with parents, honesty-trustworthiness and emotional stability) (Marsh et al., 1985); (3) satisfaction in PE, math and Greek language (the questions were formed on the basis of the questionnaire estimating satisfaction in PE; Duda & Nicholls, 1992); and (4) students' intrinsic-extrinsic motivation and amotivation in PE (the *Sport Motivational Scale, or SMS,* adapted for PE; Pelletier et al., 1995).

Students responded to items in a five-point scale (*I absolutely agree* = 5; *I absolutely disagree* = 1) for goal orientations, satisfaction and motivation, and in a six-point scale (*false* = 1, *true* =

6) for self-concept. Finally, students' academic achievement was evaluated through their marks (on a 20-point scale) in math and Greek language in the last semester of the first grade in junior high school. Students' marks in math and Greek language in the previous year were used as control variables. After the first completion of the questionnaires, the students in the experimental group were informed about the programme that was going to be taught this year, the purpose and the aim of it, its main characteristics and its importance.

Procedure

The intervention targeted all elements of the MMGO, both goals and their outcomes at different levels of abstraction (see figure 10.2).

The intervention on personal improvement goals and outcomes was made in three domains of human action: (1) the health domain, (2) the achievement domain (in the contexts of PE, math and Greek language) and (3) the social domain. To enhance personal improvement goals in the health and achievement domains in physical education, guidelines from the TARGET model were followed (task, authority, rewards, grouping, evaluation, timing) (Epstein, 1989; Treasure, & Roberts, 1995). As for the social domain, the formation of a positive climate and responsibility were emphasised (Hellison, 1995; Lickona, 1991; Nelsen, Lott & Glenn, 1997; Siedentop, 1994). Moreover, in line with the tradition in motivational climate research, an important scope of the intervention was the enhancement of students' autonomy and intrinsic motivation. Furthermore, through positive feedback and inclusion (Mosston & Ashworth, 1994), the teacher tried to create successful experiences for all students and enhance their self-concept.

The aim of **interdisciplinary teaching** was to intervene on goals, self-concept and outcomes across different school disciplines and life contexts and to strengthen their horizontal connection. Tasks aiming at the development of self-regulation skills in sport, school and life were incorporated (Boekaerts, 1997; Pintrich, 2000; Zimmerman, 2000; Zimmerman, Bonner & Kovach, 1996; Zimmerman & Kitsantas, 1996), and projects connecting themes across sport and academic disciplines were assigned. Finally,

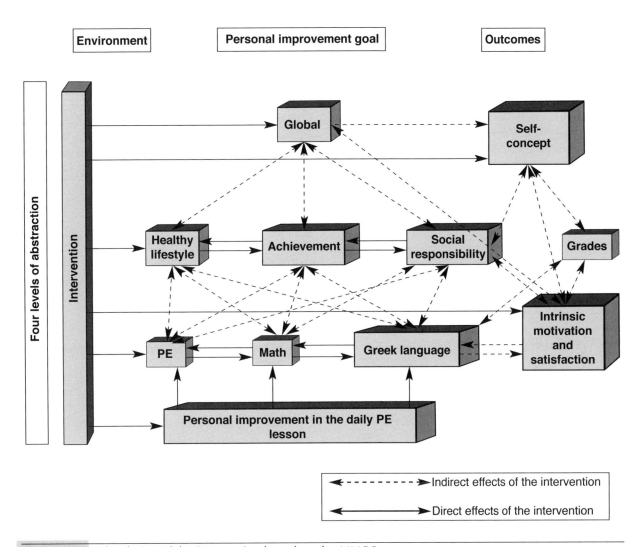

Figure 10.2 The design of the intervention based on the MMGO.

alternative patterns of evaluation were used, such as self-assessment, peer evaluation, systematic observation and portfolios.

Emphasis on Improvement in the Health Domain

Our major focus in the health domain was to bolster personal improvement goals and behaviours in the exercise domain. Accordingly, we implemented a goal-setting programme and encouraged students' participation in exercise activities in the afternoons.

Intervention on Goals: Goal-Setting Programme to Improve Health Indexes

A personal goal-setting programme was used to improve students' flexibility, strength, endurance

and body composition. The flexibility, sit-up, shuttle run of speed tests (EUROFIT; Council of Europe, 1992) and body mass index (Wilcox, 1994) were choosen. Students' scores in these indexes were assessed. These tests were called health indexes to eliminate perceptions of performance evaluation. Before the start of the testing procedure, the following benefits of regular assessment of health indexes were pointed out:

- They show us how good our health is.
- They are a starting point for future improvement (first measuring).
- They help us define goals to improve our health.
- They help us draw up specific personal training programmes.
- They help us check our progress.

- They help us increase our self-confidence, our self-concept and our motivation for continual training.

- They give more meaning to the PE lesson and leisure-time physical activities.

It was also stressed to the students that their performance on the tests should not be a point of comparison with their classmates and that the tests would not be used for grading.

Students kept their scores in a PE notebook. After the completion of the tests in the beginning of September, and after a brief reference to the goal-setting procedure, students were asked to set a goal for personal improvement of 10 to 30 percent by the end of the term. The assessment of the health indexes was repeated again three months later (in December).

Intervention on Outcomes: Promotion of Exercise

Students were encouraged to come voluntarily to school in the afternoons to participate in physical activities. They were encouraged to choose activities, space, equipment and teams and to exercise. They were reminded of the goal for personal improvement everywhere, when necessary, and the PE teacher helped them perform the skills being taught in the lesson (e.g., physical condition, cooperation, goal setting, self-talk). The PE teacher was present two afternoons per week from 4:00 p.m. to 7:00 p.m. and on Saturdays from 10:00 a.m. to 1:00 p.m.

In agreement with the school director and in cooperation with the PE teachers of other classes, students were encouraged to get involved in sport activities during breaks between academic subjects. They were given the necessary sport material (e.g., balls for different sports, badminton rackets, ropes, long ropes for 'team hopscotch'). At the same time, students' responsibility was reinforced by asking them to obey rules set in common (e.g., play safely, play together, return sport material to their proper places).

Emphasis on Improvement in the Achievement Domain

The aim of this part of the intervention was students' improvement in three achievement domains: PE, math and Greek language. Accordingly, the intervention on students' goals focused on the importance of personal improvement, on the reduction of competitive activities and on inclusion. As with the intervention on motivational outcomes, we emphasised increasing academic learning time and using a reciprocal teaching style.

Intervention on Goals: Orientation Toward Personal Improvement

Emphasis was on students' orientation toward personal improvement in achievement domains such as PE, math, Greek language and other academic subjects. This was initially pursued through discussions and the goal-setting programme described later, first in the physical context and then in the academic context.

Intervention on Goals: Reduction of Competitive Activities

Few competitive activities, but a large number of cooperative activities, were used. Activities were chosen that would expose students to the negative effects of an ego orientation and the positive effects of a personal improvement orientation. The following activity is an example: Students in groups of four competed in 30-metre (33-yard) speed running. They ran four times with the goal of being the first in their group. Before every try, in a specially formed task sheet, after the statement 'your goal is to come in first in your group', they evaluated their self-efficacy by answering the question, 'How certain are you that you can be first in your group?' After each trial, the PE teacher told them their place in the class and approximately the time they had done. They wrote down their place in the class and reevaluated their self-efficacy. After four attempts, students summarised how they had felt during the activity. Most students realised that they could not take first place and that their sense of self-efficacy was decreasing as a result.

The students then changed from competitive goals to personal improvement goals. They ran four times again with the goal of improving their performance. Before every trial, after the statement 'your goal is to run 30 metres in _____ seconds' on the task sheet, they evaluated their self-efficacy by answering the question, 'How certain are you that you can run 30 metres in _____ seconds?' After each trial, the PE teacher told them the time they had done and they checked whether they had accomplished their goal. Students then reevaluated their self-efficacy. After the end of the four trials, students summarised how they had felt. At the end of the lesson, students discussed their experiences and their feelings about the two different approaches. The PE teacher summarised the importance of goal setting for personal improvement, explaining that their achievement depends on factors they control themselves. When they try to overcome others, their achievement depends on external factors that they cannot control.

Cooperation was emphasised in all kinds of activities, even the competitive ones. For example, in a game of ball possession in basketball, the point went to the team in which every player managed to get a pass; in a game of volleyball, the point went to the team that managed to send the ball to the opposite court after having swapped three passes first. Furthermore, the students were frequently reminded to avoid (1) comparing each other, (2) criticising their schoolmates and (3) negative comments that might hurt others' feelings.

Intervention on Goals: Inclusion

Inclusion was emphasised so that all students had the opportunity to participate actively in the lesson. This philosophy of giving equal opportunities for success to all students predominated in every lesson, even when students practised team games. For example, in basketball, every player on the team got a chance to pass before the team tried to score; in football involving boys and girls together, a goal from a girl counted double points; in volleyball, players could choose the distance to serve the ball. These rules were created in discussions with the students. When students practised to improve performance or technique, they were given the authority to choose their own training conditions so they would succeed. For example, they could adapt the distance, the number of trials or the weight according to their personal needs.

Intervention on Outcomes: Increased Academic Learning Time

The efficient organisation of the available time and equipment was emphasised to maximise students' academic learning time and achievement (e.g., to avoid long queues and wasted time, students exercised in groups of four to six, using task cards).

Intervention on Outcomes: Reciprocal Teaching Style

The reciprocal teaching style was implemented approximately 10 percent of the total teaching time (Mosston & Ashworth, 1994) to increase communication, responsibility and cooperation. Peers who acted as teachers or observers of their classmates' performances were particularly reminded to use positive feedback and avoid negative comments.

Emphasis on Improvement in the Social Domain

To facilitate improvement in the social domain, we adopted the model of Hellison (1995), which encourages responsible behaviour, moral thinking and student empowerment.

Intervention on Goals: The Responsibility Domain

In addition to the goal-setting programme for the improvement of responsibility that is described later, students were taught the levels of responsibility suggested by Hellison (1995): (0) irresponsibility, (1) respect, (2) participation, (3) self-direction, (4) caring and (5) responsibility outside the gym. Then they were encouraged to move from lower-order levels to higher-order levels of responsibility.

Intervention on Outcomes: Promotion of Responsible Behaviour

A constructive discipline atmosphere was created through the following content:

- Students were involved in setting rules and taking personal and social responsibility for keeping them.
- Reasonable and fair consequences for rule breaking were set (for some rules, in cooperation with students).
- Consequences were imposed depending on the case.
- Acceptable behaviour was rewarded and reinforced.
- Self-monitoring was reinforced to encourage self-discipline.
- Students were involved in the solution of discipline problems by being given the

chance to listen, express their opinions and make comments.

- Every effort was made to create an atmosphere in which all students would feel accepted (e.g., giving all students chances for success, emphasising cooperation, avoiding comparisons with each other, avoiding negative comments and criticism from the PE teacher and schoolmates).

- In some classes, life skills and psychological strategies were taught as described later.

- The teacher tried to act as a model by treating students fairly and objectively, treating students with respect and avoiding insulting behaviour.

Intervention on Outcomes: Moral Thinking

Students were involved in activities based on the programme 'Fair Play for Children' (Commission for Fair Play, 1990; Gibbons, & Ebbeck, 1997). In this playing situation, students were faced with moral dilemmas and were asked to solve moral disputes by playing different roles each time (e.g., the player who violates a rule when the referee isn't looking, the referee who makes a bad decision, a player or team that is judged unfairly).

Intervention on Intrinsic Motivation: Promotion of Autonomy and Student Empowerment

Students were authorised to make decisions personally or in groups about the activities, games, area or equipment of their choice. They were also encouraged to participate in different roles in sports, such as scorekeeper, referee, coach or organiser (Hellison, 1995; Siedentop, 1994).

Students were encouraged to participate actively in the modification of game rules. This enabled everyone to participate actively in the class, to have chances for success and to have fun. Moreover, students were encouraged to cooperate to create new games (Almond, 1986; Bunker & Thorpe, 1982). As a group, they created two new games with specific restrictions in terms of place, number of players and equipment.

Teaching responsibility was gradually transferred to students, shifting part of the responsibility for students' learning to the students themselves in the following ways: (1) by asking them to use self-monitoring, (2) by helping them set goals and choose strategies based on the results of self-monitoring and (3) by using student-centred teaching styles, such as the reciprocal, inclusion, self-check, discovery and divergent styles (Mosston & Ashworth, 1994).

At the end of every lesson, class conferences were organised to summarise the aims of the lesson and what was achieved. Class conferences were also called, when necessary, to solve serious organisational or behaviour problems (Nelsen et al., 1997).

Emphasis on Teaching Interdisciplinary Skills

The interdisciplinary teaching used tasks aiming at the development of self-regulation skills in sport, school and life, and included projects connecting themes across sport and academic disciplines. Central to the intervention was a goal-setting programme facilitating the adoption of personal improvement goals across a variety of human action domains and life contexts. Furthermore, students were taught and urged to apply specific psychological strategies and **learning strategies** to accomplish their goals.

Intervention on Goals: Self-Assessment and Self-Monitoring

First, students were asked to assess their records in health index tests. Then, this technique was applied gradually to other contexts, such as other school subjects (math, language) and other domains of human action, such as responsibility. For example, in math they were asked to assess the time needed to study and to solve an unfamiliar exercise; in the responsibility domain they had to assess their level of respect for others using questionnaires (Glazer, 1997; Hay, Ashman & Kraayenoord, 1997; Nichols & Utesch, 1998).

Students were encouraged to monitor their progress in goal achievement and to write it on a goal-setting form. This procedure was not checked by the PE teacher; rather, it was a particularly useful procedure for tracking their progress and choosing techniques that would result in personal improvement.

Intervention on Goals: Goal Setting Across Different Life and Action Domains

The goal-setting strategy was taught in the first sessions of the year. After a brief description of the programme and how to apply it, students were urged to practise the procedure. First, they were asked to set long-term goals for their life after graduation. Then, they were asked to set yearly goals for school and sport. In every stage of goal setting, the strategies to accomplish their goals were discussed. Students were helped afterward to set more specific goals in PE, in other academic subjects (e.g., math, language) or in school generally and in responsible behaviour. After they had assessed their previous level on specific goals suggested by the PE teacher, students were asked to set a personal goal in each domain (achievement, social) and commit themselves to achieving it (see figure 10.3).

One class was devoted to helping students understand how to set challenging goals. The tasks shown in figure 10.4 were used. Then

My goals for the first three-month period are . . .
In every column, circle the goals that you want to achieve.

In physical education	In math (from the exercise the teacher asks us to do at home, to always solve . . .)	In Greek language (from the tasks that the teacher asks us to do at home, to always prepare . . .)	Generally in school	In responsible behaviour
To exercise vigorously at least three times per week	More than those we are asked to solve	All the tasks and read a little more than that	To read two hours more every day than I used to do last year	Every day . . . • to help with chores • to help my sister or brother or a friend in reading
To exercise vigorously at least two times per week	All the exercises	All the tasks	To read one hour more every day than I used to do last year	At least four or five days per week . . . • to help with chores • to help my sister or brother or a friend in reading
To exercise vigorously at least one time per week	About half of them	About half of them	To ready everyday half an hour more than I used to do last year	At least two or three days per week . . . • to help with chores • to help my sister or brother or a friend in reading

I can achieve my goals with a lot of effort!
I am pledged to my goals.
By improving myself everywhere, I will live better.
Signature: _____

Figure 10.3 Sample goal-setting form.

students were encouraged to set challenging goals in every PE class until the end of the year. The next step was to help students set weekly goals and to monitor their behaviour using a form such as that in figure 10.5. Initially, the aim of this goal-setting programme was to improve motor and psychological skills. Throughout the goal-setting process, students were told that it was important to set personal goals of improvement, goals that suited them, and not to get carried away by others' goals. The procedure of goal setting was boosted in each instructive unit, including at least one activity during which students practised goal setting for improvement using either outcome goals (e.g., 5 out of 10 serves to the other side of the court—'In the next set I will try to hit 6') or process goals (e.g., 'to stress my knees' and 'to do the follow-through in the next 10 free throws I perform')

Student's name: _____

Your goal is to throw the sachet inside the box, from the **first** line (**2 points** for every success).

Check how many times you believe you can achieve the goal if you throw the sachet six times.

Throw the sachet six times. | 1 | | 2 | | 3 | | 4 | | 5 | | 6 |

Write how many times you achieved the goal: _____

Write how many points you collected: _____

Your goal is to throw the sachet inside the box, from the **second** line (**4 points** for every success).

Check how many times you believe you can achieve the goal if you throw the sachet six times.

Throw the sachet six times. | 1 | | 2 | | 3 | | 4 | | 5 | | 6 |

Write how many times you achieved the goal: _____

Write how many points you collected: _____

Your goal is to throw the sachet inside the box, from the **third** line (**6 points** for every success).

Check how many times you believe you can achieve the goal if you throw the sachet six times.

Throw the sachet six times. | 1 | | 2 | | 3 | | 4 | | 5 | | 6 |

Write how many times you achieved the goal: _____

Write how many points you collected: _____

From which line do you like to throw the sachet the most? _____

Why? _____

From which line do you like to throw the sachet the least? _____

Why? _____

From which line did you collect the most points? _____

From which line did you collect the least points? _____

Finally, which line do you believe is best for you? _____

Why? _____

Figure 10.4 Sample tasks in goal setting.

My goals for next week (dates): _____

Name: _____

Context	Monday	Tuesday	Wednesday	Thursday	Friday	Saturday	Sunday
Physical education	Go to school in the afternoon to exercise YES–NO	Do 15 sit-ups and 15 back extensions YES–NO	Go to school in the afternoon to exercise YES–NO	Say five times to myself: 'I am becoming better and better everywhere' YES–NO	Go to school in the afternoon to exercise YES–NO	Say five times to myself : 'Today I feel wonderful' YES–NO	Do whatever I did not do last week YES–NO
	Do relaxation techniques YES–NO	Say five times to myself: 'I have confidence in myself' YES–NO	Do relaxation techniques YES–NO	Do a handstand against the wall five times YES–NO	At home: Imagine five successful basketball shots YES–NO	Do 10 push-ups and 15 vertical jumps YES–NO	Do relaxation techniques YES–NO

I commit myself to achieve my goals.

Signature: _____

Figure 10.5 Sample weekly goals.

(Zimmerman & Kitsantas, 1996). In the practice of goals in each session, at home and in free time activities, exercises were included that aimed at improving students' health indexes. Furthermore, during the PE session and in the various tasks that were given, students were reminded frequently to use positive thinking such as 'I want to, and I can, improve in whatever I do', or, 'By improving myself, I will live better'.

Gradually, this goal-setting programme was expanded to the responsibility domain (e.g., 'make my bed every day', 'help my brother or sister or a friend study', 'help my parents on a task without being asked'), to core academic subjects (e.g., math, language) and to school in general. In academic subjects and in school in general, students recorded for a week the time they had spent preparing for each lesson and the strategies they had followed (e.g., exercises they solved, the way they studied a text). On this basis, students were encouraged to set personal goals for improvement (e.g., 'spend 10 more minutes studying each subject', 'solve one more math problem the teacher gives us', 'study grammatical rules for 30 minutes', 'write a summary of the text I read').

Gradually, the responsibility of goal setting was transferred to students. Specifically, in addition to the goals set by the PE teacher on a form such as that in figure 10.5, students were encouraged to select some goals on their own with the prompt 'write by yourself' until they were gradually able to set their own goals. In the second term, a programme of student self-regulation was implemented. Students, first with the help of the PE teacher and then alone, chose specific skills from the health, achievement and social domains in which they would evaluate their performance; they would then set monthly goals for their personal improvement. Examples of monthly goals are shown in figure 10.6. Students had the opportunity to choose one or two tasks from each sport, academic subject and action domain (responsibility, health) and set their goals for improvement.

Intervention on Outcomes: Psychological Strategies

A number of **psychological strategies** that are widely used in sport to control emotion, cognition and behaviour, such as positive self-talk and relaxation techniques, were incorporated in the

syllabus. After a short discussion about these strategies, students were encouraged to use them in the lesson and in out-of-school activities. Examples are as follows:

Students were asked to start the session with positive brainstorming or to respond to a negative stimulus from the PE teacher or classmates using positive thoughts. Also, during motor skills students were encouraged to use positive phrases such as 'I see the target', 'I can', 'I will do better than before' and 'I am sure about myself'. Furthermore, students were motivated to perform some skills mentally before doing them in reality and to use some relaxation techniques.

Students were involved in situations that usually cause negative self-talk and were told to voice all the negative thoughts they could think of. Then in small group discussions they tried to change them to positive thoughts. For example, at the beginning of one lesson students were informed that the schedule had been changed and they would not have PE but math. Suddenly, the math teacher appeared and announced that they were going to have a test. A few minutes later, the PE teacher appeared and asked the students to apply a relaxation technique. A discussion with the students followed concerning their feelings and their thoughts after the unacceptable and unpleasant situation they had experienced. Students were encouraged to replace negative thoughts such as 'I am not prepared' and 'I will fail' with positive ones such as 'I will concentrate and I will do my best', 'I will not give up' and 'I am sure about myself'.

Through role-playing, students experienced situations that created various negative feelings such as nervousness, anger and fear (e.g., two classmates play a game and one of them deliberately cheats or breaks the rules all the time). Students were encouraged to try to identify such feelings early and control them with self-talk and the relaxation techniques they had been taught.

Students were exhorted through the goal-setting programme to use these strategies outside of school. For instance, goals for home were (1) to repeat a particular positive thought (e.g., 'I can, and I want to, improve in whatever I am doing') and (2) immediately after the completion of their homework to imagine being in a difficult or stressful situation (e.g., during a writing test or an oral examination in class) and to cope with this as they were taught.

Name: _____

Complete this form and keep it to evaluate your progress.

Guidelines: Choose at least one exercise from three different activities or sports. Do it. Evaluate your performance and fill in the cell "Present performance" (if you need help, ask a peer or your teacher). Set a goal for improvement for the next month (e.g., in the cell "January goal"). At the end of the month reevaluate your performance and fill in the next cell (e.g., in the cell "January assessment") and set a new goal for the next month.

Remember: Your goal should reflect your personal improvement based on your current performance. Don't lose your focus because of what others say or do. Set your own goals for development.

Physical fitness	Present performance	January goal	January assessment	February goal	February assessment	March goal	March assessment
Number of continuous push-ups							
Number of sit-ups I can do in 30 minutes							
Number of continuous jumps I can do with the rope							

Basketball	Present performance	January goal	January assessment	February goal	February assessment	March goal	March assessment
Number of times out of 10 I can sink a basket from the front half-circle of the court							
From 2.5 metres (8 feet) I pass continuously on the wall. How many I did in 30 seconds							

Volleyball	Present performance	January goal	January assessment	February goal	February assessment	March goal	March assessment
Number of successful serves I make out of 10							

IN MATH						January goal	January assessment	February goal	February assessment	March goal	March assessment
The last month . . .		Assessment									
From the exercises that I had to do in home, I solved …	More	All	About half	Fewer than half	None						
Amount of time I spend on math homework	30-40 minutes	20-30 minutes	10-20 minutes	5-10 minutes	0-5 minutes						
I actively participated in the class …	All the time	About 30 minutes	About 20 minutes	About 15 minutes	Less than 5 minutes						
In the math quiz my score was	Over 19	16-18	13-15	10-12	Below 10						

IN GREEK LANGUAGE						January goal	January assessment	February goal	February assessment	March goal	March assessment
The last month . . .		Assessment									
My preparation was . . .	Perfect	Very good	Average	Poor	Absolutely nonexistent						

I can, and I want to, always improve in whatever I do!
I commit myself to achieve my goals.

Signature: _____

Figure 10.6 Sample self-evaluation form.

Intervention on Outcomes: Learning Strategies

Students were taught and urged to apply cognitive, metacognitive and resource management strategies (Lapan, Kardash & Turner, 2002; Pintrich, 1999; Weinstein & Mayer, 1986). After a brief talk (at first five to eight minutes) about the **learning strategies** and their usefulness for the improvement of academic achievement, the students were given as homework a short reading (150 to 250 words) that referred to the following concepts: goal orientation, goal setting, intrinsic-extrinsic motivation, self-talk, mental imagery and physiology principles. In all cases examples from sport and exercise as well as school were used. Students were encouraged to apply the following learning strategies: (1) Read the text aloud; (2) write a heading for each paragraph; (3) write a summary of the text; (4) ask themselves why the arguments and the implications presented in the text were correct; (5) find and underline the key words; (6) relate what they had read to what they already knew; (7) discuss the text with their parents, a sibling or a friend; (8) check the time they spent putting the strategies into practice and (9) check their self-efficacy related to learning the text, on the basis of the strategies they had followed. In the next meeting with the same students, five minutes were dedicated to discussing the subject of the reading, the effectiveness of learning strategies in comprehending the reading or the problems in applying these strategies. They were encouraged to use these learning strategies in other lessons and during leisure time (see figure 10.7).

Organisation

The PE teacher of the intervention classes assigned homework in various subjects and asked students to bring a portfolio up to date, to implement learning strategies in different subjects and to participate in a project. Finally, alternative patterns of evaluation were used to assess students, such as portfolios, self-assessment, peer evaluation and systematic observation.

Instructions to students: Read the text concerning task and ego orientation in sport and school that was given by the teacher, then answer the following question by circling the appropriate number:

A. How confident are you that you can respond to five questions concerning the text and get full marks for all of them?

Not confident at all				So-so				Absolutely confident	
1	2	3	4	5	6	7	8	9	10

B. How much time did you need to finish the task?

Read the text again carefully.

1. Write a headline that describes the text.
2. Write three or four key words for every paragraph of the text.
3. For every paragraph, ask yourself, "Why are the arguments and the implications presented here correct?"
4. Write a brief abstract (five or six lines) from the text.
5. Explain to your parents the theme of the text.

Now respond again to question A.

Signature of parent: _____

Learn to follow these strategies in other subjects when you have to understand a text. They will help you improve your comprehension.

Figure 10.7   Sample learning strategies form for reading comprehension.

Assignments

Students were asked to keep a portfolio in which they collected all printed material that was given in PE sessions. Small groups of two to four students were asked to choose a subject (e.g., violence and aggression, healthy diet) and to gather material from magazines, books, the media and so on. After two months, each group would present in class the subject it had chosen.

Students were also asked to complete homework on various topics—for example, to develop a physical conditioning programme for a month or to turn negative thoughts into positive ones.

Students were taught learning strategies and encouraged to put them into practice to understand texts given for homework, as well as to apply these strategies to other subjects (e.g., 'write a summary of 150 words for the text you read in language class'). Also, homework was assigned so that students would express their opinions across a variety of topics (e.g., 'why I try to be a good student', 'how I feel about myself and my teacher when I get a bad mark on a test' and 'what I think my parents and my friends will say'). When students completed their homework, the topic was briefly discussed in the class.

Students were assigned homework that included math problems—for example, how a person can lose weight in combination with exercise and diet. The subject was discussed in class, or students were asked to discuss it with their parents. Assignments included taking their pulse in a state of relaxation every day for a week, finding their average pulse, estimating the total number of heartbeats of two different people—a trained one and an untrained one—and estimating the number of calories they take in every day for a week.

At the end of the second term, students were involved in a research project in which they had to administer questionnaires assessing the attitudes toward healthy behaviours (physical activity, nutrition, smoking) of their parents or two other adults. The PE teacher analysed the data and discussed with the students the purpose of the study, the research method, the statistical analysis, the graphical representation of the results and the implications of the findings. Then, students were encouraged to apply a programme to try to change their parents' attitudes toward specific behaviours (distributing leaflets, targeting discussions, encouraging their parents to participate in physical exercise). Three months later, they reassessed their parents' attitudes. The primary aim of this project was not to change the attitudes of parents, but to increase students' sense of responsibility and consciousness concerning healthy behaviours and to help them understand the importance of math in the sport and health domains.

Assessment

The main purpose of assessment was to keep track of students' progress and to provide appropriate feedback. Students' progress was judged based on their former level of attainment in the cognitive, emotional and motor domains. On this basis the teacher assigned the marks at the end of the term for the PE lesson.

Self-Assessment

Self-assessment was achieved through the goal-setting process that was previously described. Students assessed their performance in relation to their initial levels in the motor, cognitive and emotional domains. Through this process students checked the appropriateness of their goals and strategies so that they could make the necessary corrections, if necessary.

Assessment From Schoolmates

Assessment from schoolmates was done through cooperative learning procedures (e.g., reciprocal teaching), and its main purpose was to develop students' sense of responsibility, communication, cooperation and critical thinking.

Assessment From the Teacher

Once a month, the teacher assessed students' portfolios, PE notebooks and goal-setting forms. Based on this assessment, the teacher provided feedback and additional information about resources. Furthermore, every week students' goal-setting forms were assessed to examine whether students set goals by themselves and how closely they attended to their progress.

Assessment of Students' Cognitive and Motor Development

Once in a term multiple-choice tests and open-ended questions were used to assess students' knowledge development in the cognitive domain.

Every day the teacher assessed whether students achieved their personal goals, either outcome or process. At the end of the term the teacher also assessed students' improvement in flexibility, sit-ups and a shuttle run test for speed. Finally, the teacher assessed whether students' improvements were in line with their monthly goals (see figure 10.6).

Systematic Observation

According to the goals of the daily lesson, students' behaviour was recorded. Checklists and video analyses were used to assess the effectiveness of the programme, the level of students' task involvement and student behaviour. Behaviours that were assessed included active participation, intensity of effort, goal commitment, disruptive behaviour, self-control, respecting and helping others and conflict resolution. The major purpose of this assessment was to give teachers feedback to help them make the appropriate adjustments to their programmes.

Results

Confirmatory factor analyses established the structural validity of the goal orientations, satisfaction and self-concept questionnaires. For reasons of simplicity, these results are not reported here. Reliability analyses supported the internal consistency of all scales (see table 10.1).

To evaluate the differences between the two groups (experimental and control) in the final measures after the adjustment of initial differences between them, multivariate analyses of covariance (MANCOVAs) were computed. In each analysis the initial measures were used as covariates, the final measures were used as dependent variables, and the type of treatment (experimental group vs. control group) was used as an independent variable. In all cases there were significant main effects. As shown in table 10.1, after adjusting for differences in the initial measurements, students in the experimental group—compared with those in the control group—displayed the following statistically significant effects:

Table 10.1 Scale Reliabilities and Results of the Final Measurements After Covariance Analyses Controlling for the Initial Measurements

		Experiment		Control				
Goals	Contexts	M_{adj}	SE	M_{adj}	SE	F	Eta squared	Alpha
Personal development	PE	4.55	.074	4.01	.055	19.25***	.11	.82
	Math	4.55	.071	4.24	.053	18.30***	.11	.86
	Language	4.56	.070	4.16	.052	15.07***	.09	.86
Ego strengthening	PE	2.44	.097	3.18	.072	19.72***	.12	.87
	Math	2.85	.090	3.58	.067	20.25***	.12	.90
	Language	2.68	.103	3.63	.079	31.82***	.17	.89
Ego protection	PE	2.11	.104	2.90	.077	21.46***	.13	.90
	Math	1.75	.105	2.79	.078	40.48***	.21	.91
	Language	1.80	.097	2.83	.063	41.45***	.21	.89
Social approval	PE	4.11	.096	3.87	.071	3.56*	.02	.89
	Math	4.20	.093	4.06	.078	2.49	.01	.93
	Language	4.21	.084	4.09	.063	5.76	.01	.92

Self-concept	Experiment		Control				
	M_{adj}	SE	M_{adj}	SE	F	Eta squared	Alpha
General self	4.85	.066	4.45	.051	13.65***	.08	.75
General school	5.07	.082	4.45	.064	19.98***	.11	.82
Mathematics	4.54	.097	4.07	.075	17.01***	.10	.86
Greek language	4.69	.083	4.24	.064	13.39***	.08	.82
Physical abilities	5.09	.091	4.60	.071	10.49***	.06	.72
Physical appearance	4.58	.081	4.29	.063	5.97**	.04	.83
Parents	5.34	.078	4.79	.060	15.87***	.09	.79
Emotional stability	4.04	.098	3.56	.075	7.54***	.05	.81
Honesty and trustworthiness	3.95	.089	3.74	.069	7.75***	.05	.79

Satisfaction	Experiment		Control				
	M_{adj}	SE	M_{adj}	SE	F	Eta squared	Alpha
PE	4.45	.084	4.05	.065	8.01***	.06	.84
Math	4.22	.108	4.07	.083	1.63	.007	.86
Language	4.14	.107	3.81	.082	4.43*	.02	.88

Motivation	Experiment		Control				
	M_{adj}	SE	M_{adj}	SE	F	Eta squared	Alpha
Intrinsic	4.07	.072	3.90	.055	2.73*	.02	.87
Extrinsic	3.26	.065	3.54	.058	9.99***	.07	.72
Amotivation	1.96	.091	2.60	.070	17.83**	.11	.71

Grades	Experiment		Control			
	M_{adj}	SE	M_{adj}	SE	F	Eta squared
Math	14.94	.366	15.60	.276	2.11	.01
Language	14.89	.297	14.08	.224	3.27*	.03

M = estimated marginal means, controlling for initial differences before the intervention.

SE = standard error of the mean.

Eta squared = magnitude of difference between the two means. The magnitude of difference is taken into consideration when it has been already established that the two means differ between each other at an appropriate level of confidence (e.g., $p < .05$). When eta squared is higher than .15, the difference is considered large; when it is between .06 and .14, the difference is considered moderate; when it is less than .06, the difference is considered small.

Alpha = Cronbach's alpha reliability; when it is higher than .70, the scale is considered reliable.

The academic achievement of Greek students in junior high school is evaluated on a 20-point scale.

*$p < .05$, **$p < .01$, ***$p < .001$

- higher scores on personal improvement goals in PE, math and Greek language;
- lower scores in ego-strengthening and ego-protection goals in PE, math and Greek language;
- higher scores in social approval goal in PE;
- higher scores in all dimensions of self-concept;
- higher scores in satisfaction in PE and Greek language lessons;
- higher scores in intrinsic motivation in PE;
- lower scores in extrinsic motivation and amotivation in PE; and
- higher grades in Greek language lessons.

Taking into account Cohen's (1988) recommendation for η^2 effect size (small = .01, medium = .06, large = .15), the magnitude for most of these differences should be considered either medium or large.

Discussion

The results of this intervention were very satisfying. The effects on goals and self-concept were in line with our expectations. Students in intervention classes had substantially stronger personal improvement goals and were much less ego oriented than students in control classes were. In addition to physical education, these effects were extended to academic subjects such as math and Greek language. Moreover, students in intervention groups had substantially higher self-concepts across all aspects of their lives than control group students had. The stronger intervention effects were on general self-concept and general academic self-concept. Importantly, the magnitude of the effect on goals and self-concept was considerable.

Based on these findings we want to make two final comments. First, the outcome of this research has an important practical implication that we did not use in our intervention for methodological reasons. The investigation established that the motto 'by pursuing personal improvement goals, we will feel better about ourselves' is not an artifact but a reality that should be transmitted to students. The promotion of personal improvement goals has a considerable positive impact on students' self-concept. Students, teachers and parents should be aware of this.

Second, the multidimensional model of goal orientations is a theoretical framework with impor-

tant implications for practice. It provides specific recommendations with regard to where and how to intervene to strengthen personal improvement goals across all aspects of students' lives. When this happens, the positive effects on students' motivation and self-esteem are considerable. For some physical educators, the increase in self-esteem is more important than achievement per se (Corbin, 2002). In line with former developmental curriculum models in physical education (Hellison & Templin, 1991; Zakrajsek & Carnes, 1986), the multidimensional model of goal orientations emphasises the holistic, personal and emotional growth of the individual and the development of a sense of self and social responsibility. We hope that this model and the examples of practice provided in this chapter will be helpful to teachers adopting a similar approach in physical education.

Summary

The present chapter describes a six-month intervention in physical education (PE) that was based on the multidimensional model of goal orientations (MMGO; Papaioannou, 1999), which aimed at influencing students' goals and self-esteem not just in PE but also in math, language classes and life in general. The main focus was the strengthening of students' personal improvement goals in three domains of human action: (1) health, (2) achievement (in the contexts of PE, math and Greek language) and (3) social. In addition to the specific teaching strategies that were adopted for each of these domains, the intervention focused on the development of students' interdisciplinary skills, such as self-monitoring, self-assessment, planning and goal setting, self-talk and learning strategies across a variety of school subjects and life settings. The chapter provides a detailed description of the intervention and examples of the material that was distributed to the students. The intervention had a strong positive effect on students' multidimensional self-esteem and personal improvement goals in PE, math and language classes. On the other hand, the intervention had a strong negative effect on students' ego orientation in PE, math and language classes. These findings imply that the MMGO is a useful framework for teaching interdisciplinary skills such as planning, goal setting and self-monitoring and for the enhancement of students' multidimensional self-esteem and motivation in PE, school and other important settings in their lives.

Review Questions

1. Why should students adopt an orientation for personal improvement in whatever they do?

2. Why is the development of self-concept a main goal in contemporary analytical PE programmes?

3. Why must goal orientations be examined at different levels of abstraction according to the MMGO, and how are the four goal orientations examined at different levels of abstraction?

4. Describe the concept of multidimensional self-concept.

5. Describe three or four strategies for creating a positive climate of discipline.

6. Mention an example of goal setting to facilitate personal improvement in physical education, math, Greek language and responsibility at home.

7. Describe three ways to assess students in physical education.

8. What are the results of the present intervention on the emotional and cognitive domains of students?

Critical Thinking Questions

1. You want to design, apply and evaluate an intervention in physical education based on the MMGO. What steps will you follow?

2. What are the strengths and limitations of an intervention based on the MMGO?

Key Terms

goal setting—The process of elucidating expected outcomes in order to increase motivation and achieve a result. This process involves committing oneself to specific, proximal and challenging outcomes.

interdisciplinary teaching—A form of teaching that consciously applies methodology and language from more than one discipline to examine a central theme, issue, problem, topic or experience.

intervention—An influencing force or act intended to modify a given state of affairs. In the context of behavioural health, an intervention may be any outside process that has the effect of modifying a person's behaviour, cognition or emotional state.

intrinsic motivation—When people engage in an activity for its own sake and for the pleasure and satisfaction derived from participation without some obvious external incentive present.

learning strategies—Any activities, techniques or procedures used by learners to enhance their understanding of, or to improve their performance on, learning tasks.

motivational climate—A situation-induced environment that directs the goals of an action in achievement situations.

multidimensional model of goal orientations (MMGO)—A model that suggests that goal orientations occur in all human actions and life settings and that they differ in their levels of abstraction.

psychological strategies—Cognitive and behavioural skills used to maintain self-motivation and achieve personal goals.

self-concept—Self-perceptions that include one's attitudes, knowledge and feelings regarding one's abilities, appearance and social relationships. Self-concepts are formed through experience and one's interpretations of one's environment.

References

Almond, L. (1986). Games making. In R. Thorpe, D. Bunker & L. Almond (Eds.), *Rethinking games teaching* (pp. 67-70). Loughborough, UK: Department of Physical Education and Sport Science.

Ames, C. (1992). Achievement goals and the classroom motivational climate. In D.H. Schunk & J.L. Meece (Eds.), *Student perceptions in the classroom* (pp. 327-348). Hillsdale, NJ: Erlbaum.

Ames, C. & Archer, J. (1988). Achievement goals in the classroom: Students' learning strategies and motivation processes. *Journal of Educational Psychology, 80,* 260-267.

Bandura, A. (1986). *Social foundations of thought and action: A social-cognitive theory.* Englewood Cliffs, NJ: Prentice Hall.

Biddle, S.J.H. (2001). Enhancing motivation in physical education. In G.C. Roberts (Ed.), *Advances in motivation in sport and exercise* (pp. 101-128). Champaign, IL: Human Kinetics.

Boekaerts, M. (1997). Self-regulated learning: A new concept embraced by researchers, policy makers, educators, teachers, and students. *Learning and Instruction, 7*(2), 161-168.

Bunker, D. & Thorpe, R. (1982). A model for the teaching of games in the secondary school. *Bulletin of Physical Education, 10,* 9-16.

Brown, J.D. (1998). *The self.* Boston: McGraw-Hill.

Carver, C.S. & Scheier, M.F. (1998). *On the self-regulation of behavior.* Cambridge, UK: Cambridge University Press.

Christodoulidis, T., Papaioannou, A. & Digelidis, N. (2001). Motivational climate and attitudes towards exercise in Greek senior high school: A year-long intervention. *European Journal of Sport Science, 1*(4), 1-12.

Cohen, J. (1988). *Statistical analysis for the behavioral sciences* (2nd ed.). Hillsdale, NJ: Erlbaum.

Commission for Fair Play. (1990). *Fair play for kids.* Gloucester, ON: Commission for Fair Play.

Corbin, C.B. (2002). Physical activity for everyone: What every physical educator should know about promoting lifelong physical activity. *Journal of Teaching in Physical Education, 21,* 128-144.

Council of Europe. (1992). *EUROFIT: Eurotest for the assessment of physical fitness.* Strasbourg, France: Council of Europe.

Deci, E.L. & Ryan, R.M. (1985). *Intrinsic motivation and self-determination in human behavior.* New York: Plenum.

Digelidis, N., Papaioannou, A., Laparidis, K. & Christodoulidis, T. (2003). A one-year intervention in 7th grade physical education classes aiming to change motivational climate and attitudes towards exercise. *Psychology of Sport and Exercise, 4,* 195-210.

Duda, J.L. (1996). Maximizing motivation in sport and physical education among children and adolescents: The case for greater task involvement. *Quest, 48,* 290-302.

Duda, J.L., Fox, K.R., Biddle, S. & Armstrong, N. (1992). Children's achievement goals and beliefs about success in sport. *British Journal of Educational Psychology, 62,* 313-323.

Duda, J.L. & Nicholls, J.G. (1992). Dimensions of achievement motivation in schoolwork and sport. *Journal of Educational Psychology, 84,* 290-299.

Epstein, J. (1989). Family structures and student motivation a developmental perspective. In C. Ames & R. Ames (Eds.), *Research on motivation in education* (pp. 259–295). New York: Academic Press.

Gibbons, S. & Ebbeck, V. (1997). The effect of different teaching strategies on the moral development of physical education students. *Journal of Teaching in Physical Education, 17,* 85-98.

Glazer, S.M. (1997). To build self-esteem, know the self. *Teaching PreK-8, 27,* 102-103.

Greek Ministry of Education. (2003). *The official gazette, 303/13-03–2003.* Athens, Greece: Author.

Hay, I., Ashman, A. & Kraayenoord, C.E. (1997). Investigating the influence of achievement on self-concept using an intra-class design and a comparison of the PASS and SDQ I self-concept test. *British Journal of Educational Psychology, 67,* 311-321.

Hellison, D. (1995). *Teaching responsibility through physical activity.* Champaign, IL: Human Kinetics.

Hellison, D.R. & Templin, T.J. (1991). *A reflective approach to teaching physical education.* Champaign, IL: Human Kinetics.

Jewett, A.E., Bain, L.L. & Ennis, C.D. (1995). *The curriculum process in physical education.* Dubuque, IA: Brown & Benchmark.

Kelly, G.A. (1955). *The psychology of personal constructs.* New York: Norton.

Lapan, R.T., Kardash, C.M. & Turner, S. (2002). Empowering students to become self-regulated learners. *Professional School Counselling, 5*(4), 257-265.

Lickona, T. (1991). *Educating for character: How our schools can teach respect and responsibility.* New York: Bantam.

Marsh, H.W., Parker, J. & Barnes, J. (1985). Multidimensional adolescent self-concepts: Their relationship to age, sex, and academic measures. *American Educational Research Journal, 22,* 422-444.

Mosston, M. & Ashworth, S. (1994). *Teaching physical education.* New York: Macmillan.

Nelsen, J., Lott, L. & Glenn, H.S. (1997). *Positive discipline in the classroom.* Rocklin, CA: Prima Publishing.

Nicholls, J.G. (1989). *The competitive ethos and democratic education.* Cambridge, MA: Harvard University Press.

Nicholls, J.G., Cobb, P., Wood, T., Yackel, E. & Patashnick, M. (1990). Assessing students' theories of success in mathematics: Individual and classroom differences. *Journal for Research in Mathematics Education, 21,* 109-122.

Nichols, J.D. & Utesch, W.E. (1998). An alternative learning program: Effects on student motivation and self-esteem. *The Journal of Educational Research, 91,* 272-278.

Nolen, S.B. (1988). Reasons for studying: Motivational orientations and study strategies. *Cognition and Instruction, 5,* 269-287.

Nolen, S.B. & Haladyna, T.M. (1990). Motivation and studying in high school science. *Journal of Research in Science Teaching, 27,* 115-126.

Ommundsen, Y. (2003). Implicit theories of ability and self-regulation strategies in physical education classes. *Educational Psychology, 23*(2), 141-157.

Papaioannou, A. (1999). *Towards multidimensional hierarchical models of motivation in sport* (pp. 45-52). Proceedings of the 10th European Congress of Sport Psychology-FEPSAC. Prague: Charles University.

Papaioannou, A., Bebetsos, E., Theodorakis, Y., Christodoulidis, T. & Kouli, O. (2006). Causal relationships of sport and exercise involvement with goal orientations, perceived competence and intrinsic motivation in physical education: A longitudinal study. *Journal of Sport Sciences, 24,* 367-382.

Papaioannou, A. & Goudas, M. (1999). Motivational climate in physical education. In Y. Vanden Auweele, F. Bakker, S. Biddle, M. Durand & R. Seiler (Eds.), *Psychology for physical educators* (pp. 51-68). Champaign, IL: Human Kinetics.

Papaioannou, A. & Macdonald, A.I. (1993). Goal perspectives and purposes of physical education as perceived by Greek adolescents. *Physical Education Review, 16*(1), 41-48.

Papaioannou, A., Milosis, D., Kosmidou, E. & Tsigilis, N. (2002). Multidimensional structure of goal orientations: The importance of adopting a personal development goal in physical education. Ψυχολογια *[The Hellenic Journal of Psychology], 9*(4), 494-513.

Pelletier, L.G., Fortier, M.S., Vallerand, R.J., Tuson, K.M., Brière, N.M. & Blais, M.R. (1995). Toward a new measure of intrinsic motivation, extrinsic motivation, and amotivation in sports: The sport motivation scale (SMS). *Journal of Sport & Exercise Psychology, 17,* 35-53.

Pintrich, P.R. (1999). The role of motivation in promoting and sustaining self-regulated learning. *International Journal of Educational Research, 31,* 459-470.

Pintrich, P.R. (2000). The role of goal orientation in self-regulated learning. In M. Boekaerts, P.R. Pintrich & M. Zeidner (Eds.), *Handbook of self-regulation* (pp. 452-502). New York: Academic.

Rogers, C.R. (1950). The significance of the self-regarding attitudes and perceptions. In M.L. Reymert (Eds.), *Feelings and emotions: The Mosehart Symposium* (pp. 374-382). New York: McGraw-Hill.

Shavelson, R.J., Hubner, J.J. & Stanton, G.C. (1976). Self-concept: Validation of construct interpretations. *Review of Educational Research, 46,* 407-441.

Siedentop, D. (1994). *Sport education: Quality PE through positive sport experiences.* Champaign, IL: Human Kinetics.

Solmon, M.A. & Lee, A.M. (1997). Development of an instrument to assess cognitive processes in physical education classes. *Research Quarterly for Exercise and Sport, 68*(2), 152-160.

Theodosiou, A. (2004). *Metacognitive strategies and motivational climate in physical education.* Unpublished doctoral dissertation, Democritus University of Thrace, Greece.

Theodosiou, A. & Papaioannou, A. (2006). Motivational climate, achievement goals and metacognitive activity in physical education and exercise involvement in out-of-school settings. *Psychology of Sport & Exercise, 7,* 361-380.

Treasure, D.C. & Roberts, G.C. (1995). Applications of achievement goal theory to physical education: Implications for enhancing motivation. *Quest, 47,* 1-14.

Vallacher, R.R. & Wegner, D.M. (1987). What do people think they're doing? Action identification and human behavior. *Psychological Review, 94,* 3-15.

Vallerand, R.J. (1997). Toward a hierarchical model of intrinsic and extrinsic motivation. In M.P. Zanna (Ed.), *Advances in Experimental Social Psychology* (pp. 271-360). New York: Academic Press.

Vermetten, Y.J., Lodewijks, H.G. & Vermunt, J.D. (2001). The role of personality traits and goal orientations in strategy use. *Contemporary Educational Psychology, 26,* 149-170.

Weinstein, C.E. & Mayer, R.E. (1986). The teaching of learning strategies. In M. Wittrock (Ed.), *Handbook of research on teaching* (pp.315-327). New York: Macmillan.

Wilcox, K.L. (1994). *BMI: Improving its ability to predict body fat.* Unpublished master's thesis, Brigham Young University, United Kingdom.

Zakrajsek, D. & Carnes, L.A. (1986). *Individualizing physical education.* Champaign, IL: Human Kinetics.

Zimmerman, B.J. (2000). Attainment of self-regulation: A social cognitive perspective. In M. Boekaerts, P.R. Pintrich & M. Zeidner (Eds.), *Handbook of self-regulation* (pp. 13-39). San Diego, CA: Academic Press.

Zimmerman, B.J., Bonner, S. & Kovach, R. (1996). *Developing self-regulated learners: Beyond achievement to self-efficacy.* Washington, DC: American Psychological Association.

Zimmerman, B.J. & Kitsantas, A. (1996). Self-regulated learning of a motoric skill: The role of goal-setting and self-monitoring. *Journal of Applied Sport Psychology, 8,* 60-75.

part four

Promotion of Motor Skills for Life

Beatrix Vereijken

Physical education is a multifaceted subject that presents teachers with challenges at many levels. Some of these challenges focus on the characteristics of individuals—such as self-esteem and cognitive skills—whereas others focus on group dynamics and abilities extending beyond the individual—such as social interaction and communication. Underlying all these challenges is the focus on the physical activity itself.

Teaching motor skills remains a central task for physical educators. This comprises teaching not just traditional sport skills but also basic motor skills for life, such as general body control and coordination, balance, flexibility and adaptability. Furthermore, teaching motor skills can stretch across the entire life span, including teaching children, adolescents, adults and the elderly.

Both the skills we teach and the approach we take differ depending on who our students are. Physical education for children will often focus on teaching basic motor skills to stimulate and facilitate their physical and functional development. With adolescents, the focus might be on making physical activity fun and inspiring in the hope of motivating them to remain active later in life. With the elderly, the focus might be on maintaining movement abilities to promote activities of daily life and an independent lifestyle. The underlying assumption in all these age groups is that physical activity and health are closely related and that health can be promoted by an active lifestyle.

In part IV we look at different concepts and issues that are central to the promotion of motor skills across the life span. Some of the chapters focus on specific age groups, whereas others focus on specific ways of teaching or specific elements guiding the learning process. The chapters draw on expertise from the United Kingdom, Finland, the Netherlands and Norway. A variety of different yet closely related theoretical dispositions are addressed across the chapters. The main goal in all chapters, however, is to provide physical educators with practical tools for promoting motor skills in different settings and with students of different ages. Furthermore, the different theoretical perspectives, though distinct in their respective foci and central concepts, all reflect modern views on the teaching process. For example, all chapters point out the need to rethink traditional ways of teaching and move away from telling-showing-instructing and toward embedding these traditional tools in a much wider perspective on the teaching process. Another goal of this part is to make physical educators more reflective and aware of how modern approaches can help them restructure and reorganise their teaching of motor skills.

In chapter 11, Ingunn Fjørtoft and Kari Aasen Gundersen focus on promoting motor skills in preschool children. Preschool children present special challenges to the physical educator. On the one hand, they have quickly changing bodily characteristics and abilities, and their rapid development calls for a different approach than with adults or adolescents. At the same time, they have an enormous capacity for acquiring new skills. This places more demands and more responsibilities in the hands of physical educators. The main focus in this chapter is on the organisation and adaptation of the teaching process so that children can learn motor skills in a natural way rather than through traditional instructional teaching. The theoretical framework for this chapter is derived from dynamic systems approaches to the development of motor behaviour.

A more comprehensive description of dynamic systems approaches and their application to learning is provided in chapter 12, in which Øyvind Bjerke and Beatrix Vereijken focus on promoting motor skills in school children and adolescents. The main focus is on the interactive nature of learning and the importance of exploring a wide range of techniques to facilitate the learning process. The chapter explains that multiple interactions among students' unique characteristics, their environment, the task and their own personal histories shape both the process of learning and its eventual outcome. The chapter discourages teachers from focusing exclusively on imitating or reproducing the final outcome when teaching motor skills; rather, they should stress successive changes in movement coordination that may gradually drive the system toward the final outcome. Furthermore, the authors explain that training should not be limited to repeating skills to enhance performance but rather should provide a variety of situations that will induce changes in coordination. This gives students a new set of experiences that will lead to their discovery of the final outcome.

Regardless of the age of the learner, the acquisition of motor skills is heavily influenced by information from the environment. In chapter 13, Geert Savelsbergh, John van der Kamp, Martine Verheul and Dilwyn Marple-Horvat focus on visuomotor control of movement acquisition, specifically on how to help learners tune their actions to changing circumstances in the environment. Following the theoretical framework of ecological psychology, the chapter illustrates that perceptual information guides action and that action generates perceptual information. The authors present a model of stages in the process of information–movement coupling and discuss the implications of the model for teachers and coaches regarding their practice and learning sessions. In line with the previous chapters, this involves moving away from instructing and correcting and toward designing classes in which tasks guide students to discover specific information sources.

In the last chapter in part IV, Veikko Eloranta and Timo Jaakkola focus on how teaching contributes to learning. The main focus is on students' own actions and individual motor backgrounds. Again, we see a move away from the traditional teacher role in physical education as the major antecedent to effective learning toward an explicit recognition that students' own actions determine to a large extent the quality of learning. The core-based model of motor teaching emphasises that students' backgrounds and histories are the antecedents to learning and determine how the teaching–learning process is organised. This model also takes into account individual differences among students regarding their behaviours, skills and attitudes.

Taken together, the chapters in this part underscore that the promotion of motor skills is an endeavour that continues across the life span. From the early development of motor skills in infants and children to the maintenance of a physically active lifestyle throughout adolescence, adulthood and old age, the examples throughout the chapters illustrate how physical education can and should be structured to enhance physical performance. Drawing from several modern perspectives on development, learning and teaching, this part helps physical educators reflect on their roles and provides a valuable toolbox for promoting motor skills for life.

chapter eleven

Promoting Motor Learning in Young Children Through Landscapes

Ingunn Fjørtoft
Telemark University College, Norway
Kari Aasen Gundersen
Agder University College, Norway

After reading this chapter, you will be able to do the following:

- Discuss the importance of learning environments to young children

- Explain and contrast the qualities of indoor and outdoor environments

- Discuss how learning environments afford physical activity and promote motor development

- Understand the concept of affordances: Perceiving environmental objects is to perceive what they afford

- Understand that motor abilities are task specific and that they need to be trained in the context of the environment

- Organise and facilitate activities in outdoor and indoor landscapes to promote motor learning in young children

Young children, 3 to 12 years of age, comprise a special group within physical education. Because they have rapidly changing body characteristics, they are still in the process of establishing the full repertoire of **fundamental motor skills.** For this reason they need to be approached in a different way than adults or adolescents. At the same time, children have an enormous potential to acquire new skills. This places both more demands and more responsibilities in the hands of physical educators.

In this chapter we will focus on how to organise and adapt the teaching process so that children can learn motor skills in a natural way, rather than through traditional instructional teaching. The learning process takes place in the context of a certain environment. Because the environment has significance for learning, physical educators should consider the **physical environment** as a learning arena in which to promote motor skill development in children. The physical environment refers to objects and structures that constitute landscapes as learning arenas, outdoors and indoors. The physical environment should be stimulating, challenging, explorative and diverse and focus on open-ended and problem-solving tasks. In this chapter we focus on outdoor and indoor **landscapes** that promote motor learning in young children.

Importance of Motor Learning in Young Children

Motor learning is considered to be the most fundamental of all learning in children. Children learn movements and gain bodily experiences by exploring different environments. Through bodily experiments, children explore the details and quality of movements such as speed, agility, force and weight (Sheet-Johnstone, 1999). Motor learning is not only a result of maturation, but also a process of learning through experiences and activities. Several studies indicate that motor learning is also of profound importance to other areas of development such as cognition, socialisation and emotional and psychological competence (Hopkins & Butterworth, 1997; Sheet-Johnstone, 1999; Thelen & Smith, 1994).

Most definitions of learning are based on the process of behaviour; that is, learning manifests through adaptive changes in behaviour as a result of experience and the development of responses to the environment. Dudai (1995, pp. 6-7) redefined the notion on learning as follows:

Learning is here defined as an experience-dependent generation of enduring internal representations, and/or experience-dependent lasting modifications in such representations. "Ending" and "lasting" mean at least a few seconds, but in most cases much longer, and in some cases up to a lifetime. Retrieval is use of memory in neural and behavioural operations. . . . The neurobiology of learning investigates the neuronal substrates that are expected to subserve internal representations, and specifically experience-dependent modifications in these substrates.

Figure 11.1 illustrates that development manifests as changes in motor behaviour as well as in neuronal structures in the central nervous system. Learning leads to development, and the development of behaviour and internal representations are the results of learning (Dudai, 1995). Learning and development are thus processes that are dependent on experience.

The dynamic systems approach to the development of motor behaviour (Haywood & Getchell, 2001; Thelen & Smith, 1994; Vereijken & Bongaardt, 1999) places the responsibility of developing motor abilities on the child. Children develop by using their biological abilities, the tasks presented to them and the environment (Newell, 1986). The road to skilled movement acquisition is a proficient balance between too many and too few degrees of freedom, as explained by Bernstein (1967) and Vereijken and Bongaardt (1999). Children adapt to any learning situation to obtain control. Through the stages of elimination, exploration and exploitation of degrees of freedom, children adapt to the skill being controlled and to the context in which the skill is performed. A complex learning environment may provide young children a diversity of tasks, which will challenge the selection, the coupling and the exploitation of degrees of freedom that will promote the development of motor skills. The physical environment as an important determinant for the promotion of fundamental motor skills in young children will be exemplified throughout this chapter.

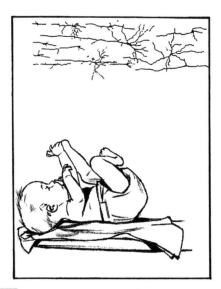

Figure 11.1 The child develops through movements: Development in behaviour and internal representations such as synaptic formation are the results of learning.

© Norges Idrettsforbund. Illustrator Asbjørn Tønnesen.

Motor Abilities in Young Children

Physical fitness is multifaceted, made up of several factors or components such as endurance and strength (Haywood & Getchell, 2001). It is generally accepted that training influences these components. Physical fitness in children is usually related to their health. The health-related components of fitness are generally referred to as muscular strength, muscular endurance, aerobic endurance and flexibility (Gallahue, 1987). The performance-related components of fitness, however, are generally referred to as motor fitness, or simply motor abilities. **Motor abilities** are related to the qualities of a person's movement performance. For example, children who display skills in climbing, throwing and skiing possess good motor abilities. Motor abilities may be specified as coordination, speed, agility, power and balance (Gallahue, 1987, Gallahue & Ozmun, 2002). Movements are controlled by balance and coordination coupled with the force-production factors of speed, agility and power.

These abilities, however, cannot be trained in isolation because they are always parts of different movements. Different abilities do not correlate strongly with each other, not even similar balance tasks (Drowatzky & Zuccato, 1967; Fjørtoft, 2000b). Bernstein (1967) also demonstrated that the same tasks were never performed exactly alike when repeated. This means that the motor abilities are always put into function in slightly different ways as a result of the character of the task and the options of the environment.

Motor abilities such as coordination and balance constitute parts of different movements and motor skills. Because they are always integrated in a motor skill, it is difficult to judge how much the specific ability contributes to the totality of the skill. In different movements, motor abilities also contribute differently because they are task specific. Motor abilities are trained by practising motor skills in context with the environment, where different environmental structures challenge the movements. A simple example is a child walking on different surfaces. An advanced walker on a flat floor must practise to achieve the same controlled walking pattern on a rough woodland floor. Balancing on a beam is different from balancing on a log across a stream.

Children develop perceptual-motor skills through natural, spontaneous interaction with the environment. They seek stimulation and physically explore, discover and evaluate the environment in relation to themselves (Jambor, 1990). Such skills, generally called basic motor skills or basic movements, comprise rolling, crawling, climbing, jumping, hurdling, hopping, running, walking, pulling, pushing and throwing. The context in which these skills are performed will require movement qualities such as coordination and balance, the perception of the body in space, rhythm and temporal awareness, rebound and airborne movements and the projection and reception of movement. The perceptual and motor information the child takes in by performing such skills in complex environments enables the child to adapt to challenging movement situations (Fjørtoft, 2000a, 2004; Gallahue & Ozmun, 2002; Jambor, 1990). Figure 11.2 illustrates some basic movements of rocking and jumping, in which the child perceives the function of objects such as a hula hoop and a jump rope.

Spatial relations are an important part of motor development. Spatial experiences promote the quality of room orientation: the perception of self in a context. Exploring space both indoors and outdoors develops skills in orientation, finding directions and spots in the environment. Lines, open spaces and landmarks are structural determinants that children can follow easily (Fjørtoft & Sageie, 2000). The outdoors is the perfect place to experience a variety of spatial contexts, and children should explore different environments to train their spatial competence. Neighbour-

hood wilderness, forests, meadows, beaches and gardens are landscapes where children can train their spatial awareness. Examples of spatial training are given later in the chapter.

Learning Through Landscapes

The didactic approach to basic movement skills acquisition that we recommend is 'learning through landscapes'. In this approach the terrain is the facilitator of diverse movements that challenge motor behaviour, and tasks are adapted to individual circumstances. Landscapes can be both outdoors and indoors. Figure 11.3 shows the connections between learning environments, physical activity and motor development. Learning environments afford physical activity, which in turn promotes motor development. Landscapes both indoors and outdoors stimulate physical activity. Through physical activity in stimulating environments, children experience a variety of movements, which promotes motor development and the learning of motor skills.

To promote motor development and enhance motor skills, learning environments and physical activity must be adequate for the given purposes. **Outdoor environments** consist of topography and vegetation. The topography may be flat, sloping, hilly, steep or rocky. The physiognomy of the vegetation represents the structure of different plants—for example, the branching of a tree and the density of shrubs. Loose materials include sticks, branches, logs, leaves, cones and stones. The outdoor environment changes over time and with the seasons. The winter season may afford a lot of challenging activities on snow and ice. These environments may certainly promote experienced-based motor development in children. For practical reasons, the landscape described here will be based on the summer season outdoors.

Indoor environments for physical activity are traditionally gyms, but they may also include playrooms in kindergartens and in homes. Typical landscape structures in a gym are the fixed materials and large apparatus. Loose materials are the balls, bean bags, rocking wheels, mats, soft mats and so forth. These landscape structures promote activities that develop basic movements such as walking, running, jumping, crawling, climbing and throwing.

Figure 11.2 The child perceives the functions of rocking and jumping.

© Norges Idrettsforbund. Illustrator Asbjørn Tønnesen.

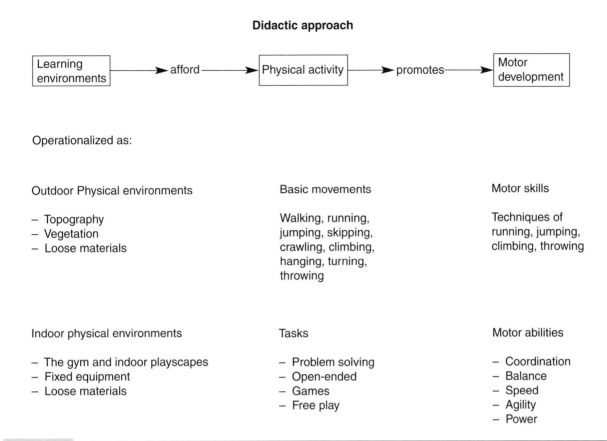

Figure 11.3 Learning through landscapes: A didactic approach to motor learning.

Adapted from I. Fjørtoft, 2004, "Landscape as playscape. The effect of natural environments on children's play and motor development," *Children Youth Environments* 14(2): 21-46.

Indoor landscapes also include swimming pools and bowling halls. For practical reasons, however, we will focus on the indoor landscapes most often used daily by children.

Through the specific landscape elements both indoors and outdoors, children's basic movements are challenged through task-oriented activities such as games and free play, including problem-solving and open-ended tasks. Practising basic skills in many different ways and settings will promote the development of motor skills in children.

Diverse natural environments support richer play behaviour and motor development in young children. A Norwegian study of natural playgrounds (Fjørtoft, 2000a, 2001) described natural environments as diverse and challenging play habitats for children. Natural landscapes afforded more diverse play forms and promoted more physical play behaviour in the children. A quasi-experimental study was conducted on five-, six- and seven-year-old children in two playgrounds. The experimental group (*n* = 46) played in a natural

environment one to two hours every day when they attended kindergarten. The natural environment was a forest close to the kindergarten, where the landscape, the topography and the vegetation constituted the arena for all-around physical play. The reference group (*n* = 29), equal to the experimental group in age, sex and socioeconomic conditions, participated in normal playground activities. Both groups were tested using the EUROFIT Motor Fitness Test before and after the intervention period of nine months. The experimental group showed significant improvement (*p* < .05) in all of the test items compared to the reference group. The intervention effect was typically more prominent in balance and coordinative skills. The full-time kindergarten experimental groups, who played in the forest every day, clearly achieved better results than children who attended kindergarten only two or three times a week. The study indicated that, for young children, the natural environment is a stimulating arena for mastering and learning motor skills.

Motor development and mastering motor skills are of great benefit to small children. Therefore, the objectives of a physical education programme should be to facilitate a diverse environment for learning motor skills through challenging and explorative physical activities. Young children would benefit greatly from the following:

- Performing basic skills such as walking, running, hopping, jumping, climbing, sliding, swaying, rolling and throwing with competence
- Performing basic skills with competence in different environments
- Performing basic skills in challenging tasks
- Applying basic skills in complex environments

Learning Environments

Learning environments can be either outdoors or indoors. In this section we will describe these learning environments in more detail. Frost (1992) described children's **playscapes** as any landscape where children play. Landscapes afford challenges to children in different ways; and the more diverse they are, the more challenging they are. The theory of affordances (Gibson, 1979) described the **affordances** of landscapes as the options and functions they provide according to what the person perceives. Children perceive and interpret what landscapes offer as functions to play, and they operationalise the affordances into action. For example, a properly branched tree will be perceived by the child as 'climbable'; it affords climbing on, and the child will intuitively climb it. A shrub vegetation may be perceived as a site for constructing a den or suitable for role-playing, such as playing house. Perceiving environmental objects is to perceive what they afford. If a stone fits the hand, it is throwable; if a rock is fit for climbing, it is climbable. Children perceive landscape elements as functions and use them in functional ways: trees for climbing, logs for balancing, cones for throwing and so on. Learning landscapes constitute the functions they afford the child.

Fjørtoft and Sageie (2000) explained that natural landscape characteristics and qualities correspond to children's uses of landscape features. Children's play in a complex natural environment showed significant effects on their motor development and fitness acquisition (Fjørtoft, 2000a).

Indoor environments such as gyms and playrooms in kindergartens or homes also constitute playscapes for children. Children's play may be facilitated in a gym using fixed and loose apparatus traditionally installed in the gym (Gundersen, 1993; Gundersen & Mjaavatn, 2003). In terms of learning landscapes, the indoors has great potential for becoming a challenging playscape for children. Early childhood educators and physical education teachers should pay more attention to the affordances of outdoor landscapes as well as indoor landscapes and interpret them through the mind of a child. In the following sections we present examples of landscapes that promote motor skills in young children.

Promoting Motor Skills Through Outdoor Environments

Outdoor environments are the most important determinants of children's physical play. Playgrounds, backyards, woodland areas and other natural sites are the most inviting landscapes because they encourage many different play forms. Functional games such as tag or hide-and-seek may challenge basic motor skills in children. Likewise, activities such as climbing trees and rocks, tumbling down slopes and throwing cones and sticks at targets or at each other are activities that typically promote motor development in children (Fjørtoft, 2000a). Also, other play forms such as role-playing and fantasy play involve a variety of movement behaviours such as moving to and from imaginary locations and pretending to be family members, animals, monsters or pirates. Construction play demands a variety of physical activities, such as carrying logs and branches and other materials for building dens and other structures.

Through different play forms children train their motor skills in a natural way using a variety of basic movements. The playscape illustrated in figure 11.4 shows a diversity of landscape elements that challenge basic motor skills, such as climbing, beam walking, running, jumping and throwing. The landscape affords rough and uneven surfaces and obstacles that encourage the use of a variety of bodily skills as well as open-ended and problem-solving tasks.

Figure 11.4 Landscape as playscape: A diversity of landscape elements affords physical activity that challenges motor skills.

© Norges Idrettsforbund. Illustrator Asbjørn Tønnesen.

Natural environments typically offer a variety of play forms that challenge motor skills in children. Meadows and open spaces invite running, skipping and tumbling. These areas are also great areas for skiing and playing in the snow during the wintertime. Woodland areas with diverse vegetation (trees and shrubs) and loose materials are more likely to invite children to climb trees, build structures and engage in fantasy play. Landscapes with steep slopes and rocky hills typically invite a variety of climbing and sliding activities. Table 11.1 shows how different landscape elements offer a variety of play opportunities that promote motor development in children.

Practical Examples for Promoting Motor Skills Outdoors

Natural environments offer children many opportunities for free play and physical activity.

Table 11.1 Play Activities Related to Landscape Characteristics

Vegetation		
Trees	Deciduous, conifer	Climbing, construction play, building dens
Shrubs	Open, scattered, dense	Running, playing tag, catch-and-seek, construction play, fantasy and role play, hiding, hide-and-seek
Meadows	Open, flat, even	Running, playing tag, catch-and-seek, acrobatics, skiing, building, playing with snow
Topography		
Slope	Less than 30 degrees	Rolling, crawling, sliding, downhill skiing, ski jump
Roughness	Rocks, cliffs, boulders	Climbing and bouldering

Children interpret the landscape structures as functions: the function to climb, to slide, to hide, to run and to throw. For example, trees and rocks are to be climbed according to their structural constitution of branches, slope and projections. Such structural determinants constitute functional affordances because they challenge activities that develop children's climbing skills.

Climbing trees requires different climbing skills than climbing rocks or bouldering. Climbing trees requires keeping the body close to the trunk and keeping the legs crossed around the trunk, while the arms are helping to elevate the body (figure 11.5). The tree affords climbing, but at the same time it also challenges a specific technique of climbing. Rocks afford other climbing techniques, such as bouldering, using hands and feet in a four-point vertical or horizontal movement, like a spider (figure 11.6). Both trees and rocks afford climbing, but each object demands a specific climbing technique due to the character of the nature object. These are examples of how different environmental structures afford climbing skills to children.

Shrubs afford hiding places and encourage children to build dens, role-play and engage in fantasy play. A juniper bush, for example, may invite a whole group of children into its branches for fantasy play.

Typically, boys are more vigorous in their outdoor play than girls are, and, given the opportunity, they seek extreme challenges. The boys in figure 11.7 are playing with the laws of Newton: gravity and centrifugal force.

Unstructured outdoor environments naturally afford unlimited challenges to children's play. Learning landscapes should allow the learner to

Figure 11.5 Climbing trees demands a specific technique.

Photo courtesy of Per Åge Eriksen.

explore and eventually exploit objects and structures of the environment. The physical environment encourages children to explore the environment by climbing swinging vines and boulders. The environment affords a diversity of movement solutions that the children may achieve through exploring different habitats for play.

Figure 11.6 Climbing rocks is 'the art of bouldering'.
Photo courtesy of Per Åge Eriksen.

Figure 11.7 Exploring environmental challenges.
Photo courtesy of Per Åge Eriksen.

Other natural environments afford activities due to their forms and structures: Meadows invite more vigorous activities, such as running, jumping, tumbling and other acrobatics. Logs, stumps and stones constitute obstacles that challenge motor control in many ways, whereas loose materials can become construction materials and objects to throw (see table 11.1).

Simple Outdoor Constructions to Promote Basic Skills

In landscapes that lack affordances for basic skill acquisition, teachers can construct simple equipment from ropes, ladders, logs and other materials.

Simple rope arrangements, such as parallel ropes and swings, invite children to balance, hang and swing. A *spider web* invites children to climb, move through and creep over and under. *Ladders* encourage climbing when fixed vertically and as 'suspension bridges'; they encourage balancing, walking and crawling when fixed horizontally. *One simple rope* hanging from a tree makes a wonderful swing that 'makes your belly go round'.

Figure 11.8 Simple ropes hanging from a tree make wonderful swings.
Photo courtesy of Per Åge Eriksen.

Figures 11.8 and 11.9 show how to use simple materials to build equipment that invites climbing, hanging, balancing and swinging.

Figure 11.9 Ladders and spider webs afford basic skills in climbing and crawling.

Photo courtesy of Per Åge Eriksen.

Outdoor Activities

Where natural environments are available, the physical educator should adopt a neighbourhood wilderness area, such as a forest, meadow, beach or gardens, and use the available landscape elements of hills, slopes, plains, rocks, trees, shrubs, stumps and stones for a variety of physical activities.

Following are some practical ideas for how to make use of natural environments for physical activity:

Steeplechase with hurdles, which includes available landscape elements: Make sure that the obstacles are as diverse as possible and ensure the children various options (moving over, under and around, hanging, rolling and tumbling). Use trees, shrubs, stumps, rocks, branches and other objects as obstacles in the steeplechase.

Trail: Make a marked route for the children to follow. Place the marks so that the children must be alert to find the way. Use natural materials such as cones, sticks and leaves.

Pathfinder: Mark some distinct landscape elements. Gather the children at a meeting point, show them pictures or a map of the landscape, and explain which landscape elements they are going to find. Explain in which direction they should go. For each landscape element that the children discover, they must return to the meeting point for new tasks. The whole setting should be within a reasonable distance. Give a badge award for spatial knowledge.

Problem-solving tasks: Use stationary elements in the landscape for special tasks: climbing up a slope and sliding down again, crawling under or jumping over sticks or branches, going around tree trunks, climbing a rock or boulder or using cones or sticks for throwing at targets such as stumps or trees.

Foxhunt: Two or more children are hunters, and the others are foxes. The foxes run away in different directions, leaving visible marks behind: pieces of paper, sticks or cones, for example. When all the marks are arranged, the foxes hide close by their last marks. At a signal the hunters start tracking the foxes. When all foxes have been found, the game is over. New foxes and hunters are chosen, and the game may go on.

CONCEPTS EXPERIENCED BY BODILY AWARENESS IN OUTDOOR ENVIRONMENTS

Topography: Hill, slope, plain, steep, flat, rough, even, uneven, soft, hard

Geometry: Directions, distance (far/near), configurations (open/close, over/under, in front/behind, around, up/down)

Kinetics/physics: Force, speed, agility, gravity, centrifugal and centripetal forces

Promoting Motor Skills Through Indoor Environments

Just like the outdoor environment, the indoor environment can stimulate children to explore their movement capacity. As soon they are on their feet, children move around to explore the environment. They walk, run, climb stairs and climb onto and jump down from any object they can manage. Children learn to solve problems by mastering their bodies in the context of their environment.

Children are exposed to different indoor environments at home and in school. These indoor playscapes afford diverse opportunities to develop their motor skills.

Traditional gyms and playrooms can be changed into landscapes for motor learning. Different fixed apparatus can be combined with loose materials in a number of ways to motivate children to practise basic skills, such as walking, running, jumping, hopping, rolling and climbing. Through basic movements, various fundamental abilities (locomotor, manipulative and stability) are developed. As the child begins to master movement patterns and motor skills, the learning environment should be changed to ensure that it continues to provide a challenge (see figure 11.10).

Exploring and Adventure

In play settings the environment is often a scene for the action, and the equipment in the playroom should be arranged to fit the situation. The equipment can invite children to move freely around or can be arranged for particular problem-solving or adventurous purposes. The basic apparatus traditionally found in the gym or playroom will suffice:

Figure 11.10 Promoting motor skills through indoor environments.

© Norges Idrettsforbund. Illustrator Asbjørn Tønnesen.

Fixed equipment: Wall bars, ropes from the ceiling, ladders, rings, basketball goals

Standard equipment: Balance beam, gym bench, mats, trampoline

Loose materials: Ropes (double rope, magic cord, jump rope), jumping stand hoop, balls, bean bags, ribbons, rhythm instruments

How apparatus are combined in the playscape or gym also depends on the learning situation. If the objective is to create a playground, for example, the environment should be challenging, explorative, diverse and focused on problem-solving and open-ended tasks. A teacher who wants to emphasise special fundamental skills should adjust the apparatus to the children's level of motor skills. Observational assessment of the child's movement abilities will enable the teacher to plan experiences and strategies that will help the child establish mature patterns of movements.

Teachers should create a positive and safe atmosphere so that children feel free to explore, try and fail. In addition to promoting motor development in young children, teachers also encourage them to be adventurous. Teachers can easily transform the gym into a circus arena with an atmosphere of exploration and adventure.

Indoor Constructions for Promoting Basic Skills

An indoor playscape can provide a variety of play opportunities that promote motor development. As described earlier, the natural landscape offers endless possibilities for children to explore and refine their motor skills. Teachers can construct indoor landscapes that are similar to the outdoors by using fixed and loose equipment, as seen in figure 11.10. Wall bars may substitute for trees; crash mat and mats, for a lawn or forest floor and benches, for logs. Such an environment stimulates children to climb, roll, slide, balance, hang, run and jump.

Another approach is to create a 'jungle' using the large equipment in the gym. A variety of combinations can encourage activities such as climbing, hanging and swinging, landing on a crash mat, mounting the rigging of a vertical wall bar, balancing on a gangway (double beam), tightrope walking, stepping stones (medicine balls) and target throwing (bean bags and a rocker wheel). Tasks should be open ended and offer a variety of

solutions. Children will use many motor skills as they explore being Tarzan or Jane.

Teachers may want to vary the arrangement of equipment to encourage different movements. By changing the elevation above the floor or the distance to walk, climb, jump or throw, teachers can challenge the motor abilities of children at different stages of skill acquisition. Such variations should offer children problem-solving tasks that require open-ended solutions, as shown in figure 11.11.

Examples of Open-Ended Indoor Arrangements

Equipment such as a crash mat, racks and a magic cord create affordances for the high jump. Figure 11.12 shows a little boy who is afraid of high jumping. He is unsure—but he really wants to jump. Will he jump? Yes, he will, but first he imagines himself as a dog. He stands on all fours, waits, adjusts the height and jumps like a dog. After using role-playing for a while, he becomes a high jumper.

Ropes hanging from the ceiling invite children to climb, hang and swing (see figure 11.13). In this situation the child may imagine herself as a circus artist, which helps her explore the affordances of the ropes.

Figure 11.11 Problem solving affords learning.

Figure 11.12 High jump using the imaginary technique of a dog.

© Norges Idrettsforbund. Illustrator Asbjørn Tønnesen.

Tumbling and rolling, turning cartwheels and doing somersaults 'make the belly go round'. Exploring gravity and centrifugal forces is exciting to children. With the proper equipment, even small children can do acrobatics. Following are some examples of simple acrobatics for children:

■ *Tumbling and rolling:* Start with a crash mat and let the children tumble around. Add some soft pillows and let the children roll over them. Also let the children roll into the crash mat from a standing position.

■ *Somersault:* Standing on a platform that is higher than the crash mat, children can easily perform rolls that gradually turn into somersault movements. Making the platform even higher and adding an extra somersault pillow will invite the children to explore the joy of a somersault.

■ *Handstands and cartwheels:* Let the children try handstands into the crash mat. They can

Figure 11.13 Rope climbing like circus artists.

© Photo courtesy of Per Åge Eriksen.

perform small cartwheels across a small somersault pillow. When they can manage this safely, they should move to a gym mat and continue the exercise. Allowing children to do cartwheels across the top of a bench will help them improve their cartwheels.

■ *Jumping:* Children love to jump down from high objects, on trampolines, on a crash mat or from a trampoline onto a crash mat. Arrange gym benches, mats and trampoline in various combinations to challenge more advanced jumping skills.

Children love to throw and kick balls. A variety of arrangements may help children use different

CONCEPTS EXPERIENCED BY BODILY AWARENESS IN INDOOR ENVIRONMENTS

Topography: Apparatus; plain, steep, flat, rough, even, uneven, soft, hard

Geometry: Directions, distance (far/near), configurations (open/close, over/under, in front/behind, around, up/down)

Kinetics/physics: Balance, speed, agility, gravity, centrifugal and centripetal forces manipulative skills, such as throwing, putting or kicking.

- *Throwing:* Arranging targets at different heights on a wall bar will encourage children to use different throwing techniques. The children who choose high targets will naturally practise the overarm throw. Those who throw at lower targets will practise the underarm throw.

- *Throwing and kicking long distances:* Mark off a section of the gym for throwing and kicking balls at different distances. Let the children try different balls such as softballs, gymnastic balls, basketballs, medicine balls and tennis balls. The children can throw and kick different balls and experience the weight and quality of the balls as well as different throwing and kicking techniques. By using targets, children naturally develop techniques for throwing and kicking.

Comparing Outdoor and Indoor Learning Environments

The natural way for young children to learn motor skills is through free play in an environmental context. The physical environment constitutes a learning arena, a landscape as a playscape. A diverse and challenging learning environment is crucial to ensure beneficial movement experience and motor learning.

Outdoor environments are dynamic systems that change over time and thus afford changing landscapes. Outdoor landscapes may differ throughout the seasons; in some places they offer activities on snow and ice in the winter. The outdoors has more rough and hilly topography, trees and rocks to climb, shrubs and woodlands to explore. Being outdoors is the strongest correlate of physical activity in children, and outdoor environments afford various options for activities, free play and games.

Outdoor environments promote motor learning through the affordances of the landscapes and through the structural determinants of topography and vegetation that challenge physical activity and motor learning. The outdoors facilitates learning by encouraging children to explore the structures and objects that the environment affords.

Indoor environments offer more controlled arenas for physical activity than outdoor environments do. They are more static, with fixed equipment and a constant climate. By encouraging a little fantasy and creativity, teachers can make the indoors into a dynamic learning environment. Indoor landscapes include gyms, playrooms in kindergartens and at home, swimming pools and other activity areas where children can practise free play. Through intentional planning, physical educators can encourage motor learning in indoor landscapes by varying the arrangement of equipment and offering problem-solving tasks.

Reflections

Being outdoors is the strongest correlate of physical activity in preschool children (Baranowski et al., 2000; Faber Taylor, Kuo & Sullivan, 2001; Fjørtoft, 2000a, 2004). Given the opportunity, children have a natural drive to be active and play freely. Because most of children's free play includes a lot of physical activity, children in free play will be moving. Physical activity is the number one remedy for a healthy lifestyle throughout the life span, and giving children healthy habits in the early years certainly will pay off in adulthood.

Several studies of children's health revealed a strong tendency for children to become sedate, overweight and increasingly exposed to lifestyle diseases such as diabetes II, coronary diseases, cancer and osteoporosis. Risk of overweight (Ogden, Flegal & Johnson, 2002) and sedentary behaviour (Reilly et al., 2004) are increasingly evident in young children, which has implications for subsequent ages. Physical activity has proven to be associated with healthy lifestyles and preventing lifestyle diseases (Baranowski et al., 2000; Frost-Andersen et al., 2005; Fulton et al., 2001; Moore et al., 2003; Narayabn, 2003; Strong et al., 2005). Such benefits have also been explored in a Norwegian study focusing on the importance of physical activity in childhood (Mjaavatn, Aasen Gundersen, Segberg & Bjørkelund, 2003; Mjaavatn & Gundersen, 2005). In all, 80 Norwegian children representing three different schools were followed closely from grade 1 (six years old) to grade 4 (nine years old). The results showed that a high level of physical activity is associated with higher scores on physical fitness tests, higher scores on gross motor tests, lower BMI (body mass index) scores and less time spent viewing television.

The study has shown that the development of gross motor skills in children was associated with the level of their parents' education (especially mothers), the age of their mothers, the existence of older siblings and family leisure-time activities. Above-average gross motor skills were associated with high sociometric status and high social self-esteem. Physical activities in childhood seem to have a positive effect on children's physical development and social lives. The study also showed that children with high scores on motor tests KTK—Körper Koordinationstest für Kinder ('Coordination Test for Children') and AST—Allgemeiner Sportmotorisher Test für Kinder, ('Sportsmotor Test for Children') were the most popular playmates. These results indicate the importance of developing basic movement patterns during the preschool years, which are the foundation for a wide range of physical activities at later ages.

Summary

After reading this chapter, you should have a better understanding of how learning environments afford physical activity and promote motor development in young children. Variability and diversity in learning environments offer children ample opportunities for a variation of practice situations and task solutions to fit their needs and capabilities. Young children learn motor skills through physical activity. Because motor abilities are task specific, they need to be trained in the context of the environment. Using basic concepts and principles from dynamic systems theory, we have illustrated how tasks and environments can manipulate constraints that stimulate learning motor skills. Having studied how to facilitate outdoor and indoor landscapes for motor learning, you should be able to help young children develop basic motor skills.

Review Questions

1. Why are outdoor environments important to motor learning?
2. How do outdoor environments afford physical activity?
3. How do different environments promote motor learning?
4. What are the determinants in a landscape that promote activity?
5. How would you arrange activities in outdoor landscapes to promote basic movement skills?
6. What is the didactic approach to 'learning through landscapes'?
7. What kinds of indoor landscapes are likely to promote motor development in children?
8. What are the advantages and disadvantages of indoor environments as learning landscapes for young children?
9. What kinds of facilities are needed to create an indoor playscape?
10. Explain the concept of affordances.

Critical Thinking Questions

1. Discuss the importance of learning environments to young children.
2. Compare indoor and outdoor landscapes as learning environments for promoting motor skills in children.
3. In what way do learning environments afford physical activity and promote motor development?
4. Discuss the fact that motor abilities are task specific and that they need to be trained in the context of the environment.
5. How can you organise and facilitate outdoor and indoor landscapes for motor learning in young children?
6. You are a preschool teacher. Based on what you have learned in this chapter, what would you consider to be the most important factors for creating an indoor playscape for five-year-old children?

7. Design an apparatus combination. Which fundamental skills do you expect the children to learn? What kinds of tasks do you want to introduce to help the children obtain adequate skills?

8. In what way is 'learning through landscapes' a didactic approach to motor learning?

9. Given the opportunity to create an outdoor playscape for young children, what would you emphasise in planning and arranging for activities that promote motor development in the children?

10. At a school meeting with parents, you plan to present a curriculum for outdoor activities. Explain how you would convince the parents that the outdoors is beneficial to the children's health.

Key Terms

affordances—The options and functions that landscapes provide according to what the person perceives (for example, climbing trees, rocks or wall bars).

fundamental motor skills—Basic movements, such as crawling, walking, running, jumping, climbing and throwing.

indoor environments—Environments inside buildings, such as gyms, playrooms and homes; they include both fixed and loose materials.

landscapes—Outdoor and indoor learning arenas.

motor abilities—Qualities related to a person's movement performance, such as coordination, speed, agility, strength, power and balance.

motor learning—A change in motor behaviour as a result of practice and previous experience.

outdoor environments—Natural environments, local environments and outdoor playgrounds.

physical environment—The structures and objects that constitute a landscape.

playscapes—Outdoor and indoor landscapes where children play.

References

Baranowski, T., Mendlein, J., Resnicow, K., Frank, E., Cullen, K.W. & Baranowski, J. (2000). Physical activity and nutrition in children and youth: An overview of obesity prevention. *Preventive Medicine, 31,* S1-S10.

Bernstein, N. (1967). *The co-ordination and regulation of movement.* London: Pergamon Press.

Drowatzky, J.N. & Zuccato, F.C. (1967). Interrelationships between selected measures of static and dynamic balance. *Research Quarterly, 38,* 509-510.

Dudai, Y. (1995). *The neurobiology of memory: Concepts, findings, trends.* Oxford, UK: University Press.

Ege, M.J. & von Kries, R. (2004). Epidemiology of obesity in childhood and adolescence. In Kiess, W., Marcus, C. and Wabitsch, M. (Eds.). *Obesity in childhood and adolescence.* Basel, Switzerland: Karger Press.

Faber Taylor, A.F., Kuo, F. & Sullivan, W. (2001). Coping with ADD: Surprising connection to green play settings. *Environment and Behavior, 33*(1), 54.

Fjørtoft, I. (2000a). *Landscape as playscape: Learning effects from playing in a natural environment on motor development in children.* Doctoral dissertation. Norwegian University of Sport and Physical Education, Oslo.

Fjørtoft, I. (2000b). Motor fitness in pre-primary school children: The EUROFIT motor fitness test explored in 5- to 7-year-old children. *Pediatric Exercise Science, 12,* 424-436.

Fjørtoft, I. (2001). The natural environment as a playground for children: The impact of outdoor play activities in pre-primary school children. *Early Childhood Education Journal, 29*(2), 111-117.

Fjørtoft, I. (2004). Landscape as playscape. The effect of natural environments on children's play and motor development. *Children, Youth and Environments, 14*(2), 21-44.

Fjørtoft, I. & Sageie, J. (2000). The natural environment as a playground for children: Landscape description and analyses of a natural playscape. *Landscape and Urban Planning, 48,* 83-97.

Frost, J.L. (1992). *Play and playscapes.* New York: Delmar.

Frost-Andersen, L., Lillegaard, I.T.L., Overby, N. et al. (2005). Overweight and obesity among Norwegian schoolchildren: Changes from 1993 to 2000. *Scandinavian Journal of Public Health, 33*(2), 99-106.

Fulton, J.E., Burgeson, C.R., Perry, G.R., Sherry, B., Galuska, D.A., Alexander, M.P., Wechsler, H. & Caspersen, C.J. (2001). Assessment of physical activity and sedentary behavior in preschool-age children: Priorities of research. *Pediatric Exercise Science, 13,* 113-126.

Gallahue, D.L. (1987). *Developmental physical education for today's elementary school children.* New York: Macmillan.

Gallahue, D.L. & Ozmun, J.C. (2002). *Understanding motor development.* New York: McGraw-Hill.

Gibson, J. (1979). *The ecological approach to visual perception.* Boston: Houghton Mifflin.

Gundersen, K.A. (1993). *Barn og idrett [Children and Sport].* Oslo: Universitetsforlaget.

Gundersen, K.A. & Mjaavatn, P.E. (2003). Barn bevegelse og oppvekst: En modell for en aktiv skolehverdag [Child-Movement-Childhood: A model for an active school day, grades 1-4]. *Kroppsøving, 6,* 22-27.

Haywood, K.M. & Getchell, N. (2001). *Life span motor development* (3rd ed.). Champaign, IL: Human Kinetics.

Hopkins, B. & Butterworth, G. (1997). Dynamical systems approaches to the development of action. In G. Bremner, A. Slater & G. Butterworth (Eds.), *Infant development: Recent advances* (pp. 75-100). Hove, East Sussex, UK: Psychology Press.

Jambor, T. (1990). Promoting perceptual-motor development in young children's play. In S.C. Wortham & J.L Frost (Eds.), *Playgrounds for young children: National survey and perspectives.* Reston, VA: The Committee on Play, American Association for Leisure and Recreation, American Alliance for Health, Physical Education, Recreation and Dance.

Mjaavatn, P.E., Aasen Gundersen, K., Segberg, U. & Bjørkelund, L.A. (2003). Physical activity, health and social skills in 6-9 year old Norwegian children. *Medicine & Science in Sports & Exercise, 35*(5), 63.

Mjaavatn, P.E. & Gundersen, K.A. (2005). *Barn, bevegelse, oppvekst [Child-Movement-Childhood. The importance of activity in childhood].* Oslo: Akilles.

Moore, L.L., Gao, D., Bradlee, M.L., Cupples, L.A., Sundarajan-Ramamurti, A., Proctor, M.H., Hood, M.Y., Singer, M.R. & Ellison, C. (2003). Does early physical activity predict body fat change throughout childhood? *Preventive Medicine, 37,* 10-17.

Narayabn, K.M., Boyl, J.P., Thompson, T.J. et al. (2003). Lifetime risk for diabetes mellitus in the United States. *Journal of the American Medical Association, 14,* 1884-1890.

Newell, K.M. (1986). Constraints on the development of coordination. In M.G. Wade & H.T.A. Whiting (Eds.), *Motor development in children: Aspects of coordination and control* (pp. 341-360). Martinus Nijhof, the Netherlands: Dordrecht.

Ogden, C.L., Flegal, K.M. & Johnson, C.L. (2002). Prevalence and trends in overweight among US children and adolescents, 1999-2000. *Journal of the American Medical Association, 288,* 1728-1732.

Reilly, J.J., Jackson, D.M., Montgomery, C., Kelly, L.A. et al. (2004). Total energy expenditure and physical activity in young Scottish children: Mixed longitudinal study. *Lancet, 363,* 211-212.

Sheet-Johnstone, M. (1999). *The primacy of movement.* Amsterdam: John Benjamins.

Strong, W.B., Malina, R.M., Cameron, J.R., Blimkie, C.J.R., Daniels, S.R., Dishman, R.K., Gutin, B., Hergenroede, A.C., Must, A., Nixon, P.A., Pivarnik, J.M., Rowlan, T., Trost, S. & Trudeau, F. (2005). Evidence-based physical activity for school-age youth. *Journal of Pediatrics, 146*(6), 732-737.

Thelen, E. & Smith, L.B. (1994). *A dynamic systems approach to the development of condition and action.* Cambridge, MA: MIT Press.

Vereijken, B. & Bongaardt, R. (1999). Complex motor skill acquisition. In Y. Vanden Auweele, F. Bakker, S. Biddle, M. Durand & R. Seiler (Eds.), *Psychology for physical educators.* Champaign, IL: Human Kinetics.

chapter twelve

Promoting Motor Skills in School Children and Adolescents

Øyvind Bjerke
Beatrix Vereijken
Norwegian University of Science and Technology

After reading this chapter, you will be able to do the following:

- Identify the main concepts of a dynamic systems perspective

- Understand how these concepts can be applied to physical education

- Describe three phases of skill learning in terms of changing degrees of freedom

- Develop your own physical education programme from a dynamic systems perspective

- Understand what exercises are suitable to promote motor skills from a dynamic systems perspective

John is a physical education teacher in the fifth grade with 25 pupils running around in the gym. Because he has heard that variability in movements and exercises stimulates children's movement behaviour, he has distributed many different pieces of equipment throughout the gym for the children to play on. John notices that some of the children are very eager and do the most spectacular movements, such as somersaults and high jumps. A few children, however, do not participate unless they are asked to do so. He also notices that many of the children who do not participate have revealed problems in performing coordinated movements in other tasks and situations. John wonders why some children have better motor skills than others and how he can promote coordinated movements. John wonders what kind of activity he should organise to include both the children with good motor skills and those who are having difficulty.

Physical activity has been part and parcel of human existence in many different guises throughout human history: hunting, labor, games and common activities of daily life. In recent times, however, there is an increasing public and political concern that children in Western societies are less active than children of past generations, spending hours watching television or playing video games (e.g., Hoos, Gerver, Kester & Westerterp, 2003). This in turn has raised questions about possible negative consequences for development in general and health in particular (e.g., Grund et al., 2000; Hands & Larkin, 2002). Researchers studying children's motor skills are likewise concerned because many studies report an increasing percentage of children having severe motor problems (Henderson & Hall, 1982; Mæland, 1992; Sigmundsson, Whiting & Ingvaldsen, 1999). Furthermore, in recent literature, these problems in motor skills have been linked to difficulties some children have with reading and writing (Estil, Whiting, Sigmundsson & Ingvaldsen, 2003). These concerns have resulted in an increased focus on the importance of physical activity during school hours. Because children spend a significant amount of their time in school, this is a natural arena in which to get physical stimulation and exercise. Although the terms *sport* and *training* typically refer to planned, organised physical activity, the term *physical activity* itself refers more generally to any form of muscular activity above resting energy expenditure (Bouchard,

Shepard & Stephens, 1994). As fewer children seem to attend organised training in their leisure time, it becomes more essential that the physical stimulation they receive in school be as valuable as possible and that they have positive experiences with physical activities in school.

In this chapter we will look closely at how to structure physical education classes for children and adolescents. Our theoretical departure point and source of inspiration is dynamic systems theory, a theory originally developed in physics and mathematics but increasingly applied to social sciences in recent years. Its explicit focus is on pattern formation and change in complex systems comprising many interacting components. In each of the following three sections, we will first explain some of the main concepts and principles of dynamic systems theory, subsequently translate them to a physical education setting and then illustrate with practical examples how to apply these concepts and principles in physical education classes.

The first question to address is what kinds of motor skills are important for school children to develop. According to Magill (1998), the concept of motor skills refers to any action or task that has a goal and that requires voluntary body or limb movement to achieve the goal. This definition includes a broad range of activities. Many physical education teachers have personal beliefs about what kinds of physical activity are important. Although most teachers have to adhere to national principles for education, these directives are usually formulated rather vaguely. For example, in the previous Norwegian principles for education, one of the objectives in the fourth grade is that the children should learn basic movements for running, jumping and throwing (Directorate for Primary and Secondary Education, 1997). The principles do not specify, however, what kinds of movements are basic for throwing or jumping. In other words, it is up to the individual teacher to decide what is essential. It is not our intention here to describe or discuss the national principles. Rather, our intention is to describe *why* physical activity is important for developing motor skills, *how* this development can be brought about and *what kinds* of activities should be included.

Why do we focus on children and adolescents in this chapter? The importance of physical activity for the development of children is generally recognised (Blair, Kohl, Gordon & Paffenberger,

1992; Marshall & Bouffard, 1997). However, physical education remains important during adolescence because major physical and psychological changes occur at this age. Hormonal levels change and bone lengths increase without necessarily a matching increase in muscular strength. These bodily changes and their effects on coordination can be frustrating for adolescents and possibly result in clumsy motor performance and behaviour in general.

Despite the importance of continued physical education, several surveys report that many children and adolescents are ceasing their participation in sports and exercise (cf. Biddle, 1995). Children choose not to participate for various reasons, including perceptions of competence, external **constraints** (such as money and friends), degree of support from significant others and past experience, including physical education in school. This is supported by Saarinen (1987), who found that those who have negative experiences in physical education also expressed a negative attitude toward physical activity outside school. Continued focus on the physical activity and the development of motor skills is thus important also for this particular age group. With adolescents in particular, it is important to offer a variety of activities, both to enhance motor development and to prevent an aversion to physical activity. In this chapter we outline important concepts about development and dynamic systems theory and how they may help us understand how to organise and structure physical education classes for children and adolescents.

Balancing Stability and Flexibility

Imagine a basketball player approaching the basket in the middle of an attack. To score, he needs to steer clear of opponent players in different positions performing a variety of blocking moves. When an opportunity to score arises, he needs to place the ball reliably in the basket despite variations in approach angle and jumping height and ongoing perturbations from other players. In other words, a proficient basketball player needs **flexibility** in his movements while at the same time securing **stability** of outcome. These characteristics are not limited to basketball. For any physical performance to be reliable,

motor skills need to be stabilised against ongoing internal and external changes and against possible perturbations from the environment. At the same time, motor skills also need to be flexible to adjust to ongoing changes and to adopt new movement patterns when circumstances require. This means that motor skills have to be balanced between the seemingly opposing characteristics of stability and flexibility. How is this achieved?

From a dynamic systems perspective, the characteristics of stability and flexibility are not independent but form two sides of the same coin. Stability of performance can be achieved by forming so-called **coordinative structures** across muscles and joints that operate as a functional unit. Within this functional unit, changes occurring in one part are counterbalanced by changes in other parts. This way, the overall integrity of the performance is preserved. This was demonstrated in a study of expert marksmen by Arutyunyan and his colleagues (Arutyunyan, Gurfinkel & Mirskii, 1968, 1969). They demonstrated that in achieving their shooting precision, expert marksmen distinguished themselves from less expert shooters and novices in two important ways. First, they were able to maintain a steadier posture with less body sway, thereby securing a more stable base for arm and gun movements. More important, though, small movements in the shoulder joint were counterbalanced by opposite movements in the wrist joint, thereby keeping the gun aimed at the target. In less expert shooters and novices, movements in shoulder and wrist joints were not coupled, thereby adding to imprecision and increasing shooting error. The same principle of cooperation between body parts to preserve performance was shown with respect to the timing of movements in table tennis by Bootsma and van Wieringen (1990). Their analyses demonstrated that expert players speeded up their forward arm movements when a stroke was initiated late, and slowed them down when the stroke was initiated early. These adjustments ensured that the ball was hit at just the right time in a stable fashion.

Stability is thus a necessary characteristic of motor skills that ensures reliable performance and enhances the efficiency of performance. Stability of performance across a broad range of situations can be promoted by letting a child or adolescent experience a wide array of initial conditions, postures or environmental characteristics. Practising under different conditions will strengthen the performance and increase its flexibility. A good example of this can be found in a training situation for soccer players in which the teams are playing volleyball with a soccer ball, using head, knees and feet instead of hands and arms. The players are using familiar skills in a context that has different rules, thus promoting skill flexibility. Another example is using balls of different sizes and weights in learning to pass and receive a basketball or handball (cf. Corbetta & Vereijken, 1999).

To be able to adjust their performance to ongoing changes in the task and the environment, or to adopt new movement patterns when wanted or needed, players must balance stability of motor skills with flexibility. Without flexibility in motor skills, stability becomes rigid and prevents adjustment, attunement and changes in performance. When performance is rigidly stable, change to other coordination patterns, or development toward newer and more advanced motor skills, is hampered. This tendency to persevere with an established coordination pattern is often seen when tennis players switch to a game of squash. They maintain their former habit of locking the wrist joint instead of using flexion in the wrist joint to give extra effect to the ball. For a change to occur, the stability of the established movement organisation (e.g., a locked wrist joint in tennis) needs to be broken down so that a transition can be made to a different organisation (i.e., use of the wrist joint in squash). To this end, prior stability needs to give way to **instability** so that the system can search for, find and implement a new movement organisation. This instability of performance can be observed both between two existing stable states and prior to an infant's transition to a more advanced movement organisation or motor skill in learning and development. Examples of the former can be seen in horses making transitions between different locomotion patterns, such as walking, trotting and galloping (Hoyt & Taylor, 1981) or in table tennis players switching between forehand and backhand strokes (Sørensen, Ingvaldsen & Whiting, 2001). Examples of the latter can be seen in a decline in sitting stability when infants start to reach (Spencer, Vereijken, Diedrich & Thelen, 2000), and their return to a less advanced two-handed reach when they are learning to walk (Corbetta & Bojczyk, 2002).

Balancing Stability and Flexibility in Physical Education

We have explained the importance of stability and flexibility in a dynamic systems perspective. In the context of physical education, the system in question is the child's body and its movements. During learning, children undergo a gradual change from unstable to more stable performance. Mastery of a particular skill is indicated by a reliable, stable performance. This can be observed in kicking a ball in soccer, for instance. At first the player cannot hit the target. After practice, the player manages to put the ball at the intended spot, not only once by coincidence, but several times in a row. A detailed analysis of the movements reveals an increase in functional couplings between body parts and a decrease in the standard deviation of the outcome. A stable performance is typically also more efficient in that less energy is spent correcting for deviations and unwanted reactive forces.

Achieving stability in task performance is thus an important goal in many situations, but children also need to ensure flexibility simultaneously to be able to meet new demands and situations. A good soccer player needs to perform a precise kick under different conditions and during changing circumstances. Whether she is playing indoors or outdoors, on gravel or on grass, she needs to execute and direct the kick precisely. The ball must reach the intended place despite changes in initial conditions and circumstances. This demands flexibility in performance. During development and learning, flexibility in the organisation of the body parts is essential to allow new and more skilled movements to arise. It is the flexibility of the system that allows transitions from one stable coordination pattern to another. Only when existing coordination patterns are sufficiently destabilised can other patterns become possible.

The concepts of stability and flexibility can give physical education (PE) teachers an understanding of development and learning and hence help them select appropriate teaching strategies. Learning is defined as a change in the capabilities of a person—in other words, a relatively permanent improvement in performance as a result of practice or experience (Magill, 1998). Because physical educators must know how children learn practical skills, the principles of stability, flexibility and transitions should play an important role in their teaching.

Children's flexibility is reflected in the way they deal with new challenges. A child who has been performing a variety of movements in different ball games in many different situations is often more flexible with respect to ball handling than a child who has been performing the same kinds of movements across different situations and ball games. During the learning process, children need time to practise particular skills to stabilise their coordination patterns. At the same time, the teacher must vary the tasks to ensure the development of flexibility.

Children's explorations of alternative movement strategies in different situations can decrease the stability of established movement solutions, thereby promoting the development of, or transition to, new coordination patterns. For example, a soccer kick is executed from a standing position at first, but players should later be able to kick the ball after a run-up or a sudden turn or while running. Destabilising existing coordination patterns could be done by introducing new and unfamiliar situations in the PE class, thereby promoting flexibility in established coordination patterns. For example, introducing a run-up before kicking the ball destabilises the earlier movement pattern of kicking from a standing position, promoting increased flexibility in the skill of ball kicking in general. With this in mind, physical educators must design many different experiences to provide pupils with transitions from one coordination pattern to another.

Changing the conditions of a given task (such as altering the pace, changing the playing rules or adding extra constraints) can also break rigid stability and create positive conditions of instability. Instability in a learning process can result in a period of disorder and frustration for the learner, but it is a necessary step toward developing a new, stable coordination pattern. After a temporary period of instability, the performer can make a transition to a more advanced coordination pattern that then enters a more stable phase, with an improvement in skill as a consequence. Training this way, a skilled soccer player manages to pass the ball precisely during a free kick as well as during an interactive situation. Because learning requires frequent switching between stable and unstable periods several times over an extended period, it has often been described as occurring in stages (Adams, 1987; Bernstein, 1967; see also the next section). Varying the conditions and

the constraints in a task can also individualise the teaching, which allows children to develop skills at their own pace. This is considered an essential teaching strategy (cf. Powers & Howley, 2004). The important question is how the teacher can stimulate variation to destabilise established coordination patterns. Often it is not enough to merely tell or show the children alternative ways to deal with a movement problem. Using a series of exercises and environmental situations can be one way to lead the children into the desired movement pattern. The manipulation of different constraints is another (see the next section).

Variations in conditions can be achieved using outdoor activities. Outdoor activities have several advantages over artificial indoor facilities, such as access to a larger area with typically a higher degree of variation. Forest terrain, for example, offers a variety of stimulation for children that is unparalleled in most indoor facilities. Changes in both the terrain and the weather encourage different play behaviours in children (see also chapter 11). For example, running in the forest requires that the children move on bulky surfaces, negotiate obstacles and navigate on uneven terrain. This destabilises a rigid running pattern and promotes a flexible one. To avoid stumbling over roots, trees and small rocks, children must make continuous adjustments in their coordination patterns. All the senses are stimulated, which promotes the coupling between what is perceived and what can or needs to be done (see chapter 13). Outdoors, the sky is the limit, the major constraint being PE teachers' and children's creativity in inventing new exercises and games.

Whereas outdoor activities can make use of a large area that is naturally diverse, indoor activities are often constrained by available space and equipment. However, the indoor space can be exploited by using the walls of the gym and the available equipment to create interesting environments. Depending on the aim of the lesson, an artificial terrain in the gymnasium can be made complex and diverse so that it stimulates the coupling between perception and action. If the aim is to teach the children a basic skill in gymnastics, such as balance, different exercises with variations in the environment are essential. To this end, the terrain, whether natural or artificial, should consist of stable and unstable obstacles. In a forest, for example, walking on fallen trees, balancing on rocks or climbing in

Natural environments offer unlimited opportunities for creative play.

Photo courtesy of Geir Oterhals.

trees are examples of activities that stimulate a variety of coordination patterns while balancing. Indoor balancing activities can be performed on foam rubber, wide and narrow beams or medicine balls. The intentions of these exercises are to create, and expose the children to, a variable environment so that their established movement patterns are challenged and perturbed and they can discover new patterns.

Examples of Challenging Existing Coordination Patterns

A concrete example of an exercise that perturbs and challenges established coordination patterns is a game called 'dogs and rabbits'. This is a tagging game in which children move rapidly and in specific ways across a variety of pieces of gym equipment. The children are not allowed to touch the floor, just the different obstacles and pieces of equipment such as ropes, benches, mats and so on. One or two children are the dogs; the other

children are the rabbits. The dogs chase the rabbits across the pieces of equipment. If a dog manages to catch a rabbit, the rabbit has to leave the game for a certain period of time, do a number of sit-ups or perform another type of penalty. If a rabbit touches the floor, he is regarded as being caught. If a dog touches the floor, she has to do sit-ups or another form of penalty as well. The teacher is the referee. After about three minutes, new dogs should be selected to avoid boredom. The duration of this game can be around 15 to 20 minutes.

Another example of challenging an established coordination pattern can be found in ice skating. Skating involves a particular technique that has to be learned. After a few sessions, the basic skating technique is learned and becomes an increasingly stable coordination pattern. To challenge this coordination pattern and increase flexibility, a new exercise can be added to the existing one. For example, a stick and a puck can be given to each child to turn free skating into ice hockey. This requires several adjustments in the skating technique. In addition to controlling their skating, the children now have to control the hockey stick and the puck as well. At yet a later stage, teams can be formed so that the children have to coordinate their own movements with those of other team members and their opponents. This again will increase the **complexity** of the exercise, introducing the need for sudden turns and skating backward, and dividing the focus among skating, the puck, the stick and other players. In short, by adding exercises to the current ones, children's established coordination patterns are challenged, and they must explore new patterns, which will increase their flexibility and skill.

INCREASING CHILDREN'S CONFIDENCE WITH PIECES OF GYM EQUIPMENT

One challenge for physical educators is to teach children to be confident with the different pieces of gym equipment and not to be afraid of using them. One way to instill confidence in children is to play music and let the children move around in the gym. When the teacher stops the music, the children have to perform a specific activity on the piece of equipment closest to them—for example, 'everybody should lie on their backs on a piece of equipment', or 'everybody should have their body weight on their hands'. In this way, children become familiar with the different pieces of equipment in a playful and enjoyable manner so they are not intimidated by them in a game situation later.

New coordination patterns are needed to move around on ice.

Photo courtesy of Christophe Pelabon.

Handling Complexity

Everyday motor skills as well as sport skills are characterised by high complexity. Many, if not all, body parts are involved in the execution of physical performances. This is beautifully demonstrated in the golf swing of Tiger Woods. Even though his arms and hands seem to produce the swing, his movements are not restricted to his upper extremities. On the contrary, his entire body enters the performance with the hip and the trunk twisting and the body following the swing with a smooth and floating movement. The same is true, although perhaps at times less obvious, for a handball player throwing a ball, a soccer player taking a penalty kick and a child balancing on a beam.

In human movement science, the different body parts and their endless possible organisations are referred to as **degrees of freedom.** Depending on one's perspective, the number of degrees of freedom varies from about 10^2 joints, to about 10^3 muscles, up to 10^{14} cellular units in 10^3 varieties. Counting their number is not the crucial issue here, but their control is. How do we organise and control so many body parts and movement possibilities in everything we do? The two key concepts here are constraints and, again, the aforementioned coordinative structures. Constraints reduce the number of movement possibilities by excluding certain movements or organisations, or by making them less efficient or less likely to occur. The remaining degrees of freedom are taken care of by organising them in functional units, the so-called coordinative structures.

Constraints come in many guises that can act in different ways. One of the earliest and most useful ways of organising them stems from Newell (1986). He divided constraints according to their origin, which can be situated in the organism itself, the task in particular or the ambient environment in general. Organismic constraints reside in the individual and can be, for example, anatomical, physiological or psychological characteristics that reduce the number of movement possibilities and movement organisations. Prior experience, motivation and ambition can also act as organismic constraints by influencing performance. Task constraints are external factors related to the specific task that influence the number of movement possibilities—for example, the rules of a game or the characteristics of sports equipment. Finally, environmental constraints are general external factors and come in the form of gravity and other external forces, information, lighting conditions and so on. Manipulating constraints is a powerful tool in coaching and physical education; we will give several examples later.

In the acquisition of a new skill, the body's degrees of freedom need to be reorganised to accommodate the new task requirements. This can be quite an overwhelming task, particularly because uncontrolled degrees of freedom can generate unwanted reactive forces, which in turn need to be counteracted by active muscle forces. A common strategy is therefore to reduce the number of degrees of freedom included in the coordinative structure, either by freezing individual body parts in a rigid position or by coupling several body parts together so that they move in unison (cf. Bernstein, 1967). Although this is a useful strategy at the start of coping with an otherwise overwhelming movement problem, it has the obvious disadvantage of reducing flexibility. With fewer degrees of freedom entering the task solution, fewer possibilities for organising them are available, thereby reducing flexibility. As practice continues, therefore, one often sees the gradual incorporation of additional degrees of freedom in the coordinative structure, thereby improving both the movement and its flexibility. In a final stage, the coordinative structure increasingly exploits existing reactive forces, instead of trying to fight them or neutralise them, making the performance more efficient.

Evidence of the differential use of degrees of freedom in different **learning stages** was provided in earlier studies on a so-called ski apparatus (see figure 12.1). Vereijken and her colleagues (Vereijken, van Emmerik, Whiting & Newell, 1992) showed that novices, in their first encounter with the apparatus, kept their hip, knee and ankle joints at fairly rigid angles. This allowed for little movement in those joints, serving to keep the number of controlled degrees of freedom and the generation of reactive forces to a minimum. Simultaneously, however, it also allowed for little contribution of these joints to the performance. Furthermore, cross-correlations between these body angles were moderate to high, indicating tight couplings between joint movements. This limited the number of controlled degrees of freedom, but it also limited the range of possible movements while learning how to perform on the apparatus.

Figure 12.1   The ski task.

With increased practice, movements in the joints increased and couplings between them decreased in strength, indicating an increase in their contribution to the movement solution. Evidence for the last stage, increased used of reactive forces, can be found in several studies showing decreases in oxygen uptake despite increases in performance (e.g., Paavolainen, Häkkinen, Hämäläinen, Nummela & Rusko, 1999), indicating that performance was becoming more economical and efficient.

Handling Complexity in Physical Education

From a dynamic systems perspective, the concept of complexity is an important one. Even a simple movement often turns out to be complex when it is analysed in detail. A good example is throwing a ball. Although this is a relatively easy task, many factors have to be controlled for the throw to be proficient. The grip of the hand has to be firm enough to hold the ball, but no firmer than

that. The trajectory of the arm movement has to be as long as possible to create optimal force and power. The opening of the fingers has to occur at a specific instant so that the ball can hit its target with the desired effect. An optimal throw also involves correct movements of the legs and feet, optimal balance of the body and adjustments to the rhythm and flow of the entire movement. How can physical educators help their pupils handle the complexity of such a movement task?

The task of a physical educator is to organise activities in such a way that children have the opportunity to experience the complexity of a movement in a controllable way. As indicated in the previous section, three kinds of constraints can be manipulated to reduce or increase the complexity of an activity: the environment, the task or the organism (Newell, 1986). By structuring the environment, the physical educator can help children explore the task in gradually increasing degrees of complexity. This is achieved by organising the activity so that the children are led through specific movement patterns, such as a designed course with obstacles and hindrances, or playing soccer on gravel instead of on grass. Another way to change the environmental factors of an exercise could be by making the field bigger or smaller. This could be an effective way to manipulate the available space in soccer, for example. At a novel phase in soccer, the children need extended time to achieve control over the ball. At that stage, a large field with few players may be suitable, giving the children more space and time to handle the ball. When the children become better at receiving the ball, a reduction in the size of the playing field forces them to achieve control over the ball more quickly. Increasing the number of players will have the same effect. Another way of manipulating environmental factors would be to make use of different weather conditions (e.g., letting the children play in mud or on wet grass).

Manipulating task constraints is another way of helping children in the learning process. Making new rules and directories in the game can demonstrate this. Allowing two or three touches in basketball before the player has to pass the ball is one example of manipulating task constraints. Another is requiring that all players touch the ball before the team can score. The latter promotes within-team cooperation and interaction. By using new rules and constraints, the teacher can influence the learning of new behaviour.

Finally, the PE teacher can manipulate organismic constraints as well—for example, by altering the child's weight. Weight is an important variable in many sports, especially those that are related to power. By changing the weight of the players (e.g., having them wear weight belts or play games in a swimming pool), this organismic constraint is changed. After some training sessions with the weight belt, the belt can be removed, and the effect will be increased power in the legs. When playing handball in a swimming pool, for example, the upward lift of the body (because of its buoyancy in water) changes the way one can move around. At the same time, the water creates more resistance to the body, slowing the movements down. These effects can be exploited in a variety of games with a variety of intentions.

Playing soccer offers several opportunities for manipulating constraints.
Photo courtesy of Christophe Pelabon.

USING PLAY TO MOTIVATE PARTICIPATION IN PHYSICAL ACTIVITY

At times, school children and adolescents dismiss participation in physical exercises as too strenuous, exhausting or boring. Using play themes or play settings can prevent these experiences. Play can help stimulate children in a fun and exciting way and is often self-regulating with respect to individual skill levels. A play theme that can easily put the fantasy of youngsters into action is 'the jungle', particularly if used together with 'jungle music'. Pieces of gym equipment should be used that allow the children to climb, walk, jump, run, toss and balance. These are distributed over the gym to create a jungle. Ropes can represent vines, beams and benches can be fallen trees or bridges over water and ravines, wall bars can represent rocky hill sides and so on. (An example of an outdoor jungle is shown on page 232.) The PE teacher can tell the children that they have to toss themselves over a river full of crocodiles or that they have to balance over an unstable bridge or act like Tarzan swinging on a vine. This play stimulates all the senses together with the fundamental motor skills, such as balancing, eye–hand and eye–foot coordination, rhythm, space perception, agility and so forth.

Examples of Manipulating Constraints

As argued in the previous section, an important task for physical educators is to aid the learning process by manipulating the constraints that act on children and adolescents. A practical example of how different types of constraints can be manipulated in a single task is using a series of increasingly complex exercises on equipment to increase balance. Most gyms have benches differing in width or benches that are wide on the side one sits on but more narrow when turned upside down. For small children, it can be challenging enough to walk and balance on a broader bench. After practice the benches can be turned upside down, or narrower benches can be used, so the children can learn to balance on the narrow part. Walking first forward and then backward makes the task even more difficult. To further increase the number of degrees of freedom the children need to control, teachers could add several tasks for the children to perform while standing or walking on the bench. For example, using a jumping rope or juggling while balancing would increase the complexity and challenge of the balancing task. Using a balance rod makes the task easier, whereas removing it makes it more difficult again. Balancing with the hands held behind the back or the eyes closed also makes the task more difficult. PE teachers can also invite the children to add or remove additional aids.

Ice skating is another practical example that allows for manipulation of different types of constraints. Children skating for the very first time have problems just standing upright on the ice. With their skates on, they flap their arms to maintain their balance. When they try to move forward, their performance is characterised by large, stiff movements of their arms and legs, with only small movements in their knee joints. This is a typical strategy early in the learning process for controlling degrees of freedom and reactive forces. Typically, the children are particularly unsteady in their ankles. This problem can be solved using hockey skates or figure skates, which are more supportive of the ankles than speed skates are. Another way of supporting the ankles and thereby helping to maintain balance is to tape the ankles or tighten the laces firmly. After some practice, when the children have more control over their skating movements, the tape or the laces can be loosened a little to increase the degrees of freedom of the ankles. Finally, the tape can be removed entirely, and the children can learn to be in full control of their ankles.

The environmental constraints can be manipulated by creating a track on the ice for the children to follow. The track should be created in such a way that the children have to make turns between cones, jump over one or several obstacles or skate backward or in circles. Other manipulations that can be helpful in teaching the children to skate on ice can be directed to the task itself or to the body. For example, by pairing the children, one child can be pulled forward by another child. This is an effective way of helping the children discover how to create velocity on ice. The child who pulls the other child is forced to use his legs to create speed. Pairing the children face to face creates a situation in which one child can help the other child to skate backward.

Exploration Versus Prescription

Traditionally, instructions play an important role in physical education. Instructions inform about the rules of the game, give important feedback about performance, help to direct attention and so on. Yet for all the useful and sometimes crucial information instructions can provide, prescribing what pupils need to do should only complement self-practice, not replace it. To get a feel for the ball, children need to handle it. To learn to balance, children need to engage in a multitude of balancing tasks. And to learn to ride a bicycle, children need to mount one and try it. This necessity of active self-experience is nowhere seen as clearly as in a newborn child. An infant this young cannot be instructed what to do, how to do it or when to do it. As Sheets-Johnstone (1999) phrased it so aptly, we were all, as infants, 'apprentices of our own bodies' (p. 225). When an infant is born, she needs to figure out by herself that she has a body, how to move the different body parts and how to gain control over self-generated reactive forces and other movement consequences. Even after childhood, there is ample evidence that explicit learning methods—based on explicit knowledge about rules and instructions—can be more disturbing than helpful, and that learning a skill with implicit methods can be more effective (cf. Masters, 1992). The key concepts here are **exploration,** variation, trial and error, discovery learning, and learning by doing. Together, these processes create a task solution that is based on **self-organisation,** which stands in stark contrast to a solution based in instructions.

Let us start with the dynamic systems' concept of self-organisation. When many components in a complex system interact, an organisation arises that need not be directed or instructed by any of the contributing components. Easy-to-understand examples can be found all around us in nature, such as the formation of clouds and storms, fish schooling together, termites building and defending impressive anthills or the movements of planets around a star. We readily assume that these patterns do not arise from a blueprint hidden somewhere in the system, but that interactions among many factors and forces generate the patterns that we call the weather, a school of fish, a termite colony or a solar system. In the 1980s a group of movement scientists began to study the development and generation of human movement patterns using the same line of thought; namely, that organised movement patterns can arise from interacting components without an a priori need for instructions or prescriptions (e.g., Kelso, Holt, Kugler & Turvey, 1980; Kugler, 1986; Kugler, Kelso & Turvey, 1980). In subsequent decades, many examples have been provided of self-organising processes in the formation of behavioural patterns, the process of development and the learning of new motor skills (e.g., Kelso, 1995; Thelen & Smith, 1994; Vereijken, 1991).

As indicated earlier, many interacting factors contribute to a process of self-organisation. This is also the case in the formation of movement patterns in humans. Relevant factors include the anatomical and physiological characteristics of the moving person, specific aspects of the task and current environmental conditions, but also the prior history of the moving person, his motivation, skill level and intentions. Here lies the key to within- and between-subject **variability.** Because the formation of movement patterns is influenced by many individual and environmental characteristics that differ among persons and from situation to situation, these intrinsic and extrinsic characteristics contribute to variability between individuals and variability between repeated attempts within an individual. Whereas traditional psychological views have tended to regard within- and between-individual variability as noise to be filtered away in order to find the essential characteristics of performance, the dynamic systems view regards variability as an important source of information about specific intrinsic and extrinsic dynamics that contribute to the performance.

Performance can thus be considered an individual act of problem solving, different from moment to moment and from person to person. When the performance is heavily influenced by constraints, within- and between-**individual variability** will consequently be smaller. When it is less severely influenced by constraints, there will be more room for inter- and intra-individual variability (e.g., Vereijken & Adolph, 1999). To facilitate this individual act of problem solving, it is crucially important to explore a variety of possible solutions and vary the initial conditions when repeating the process. From this perspective, merely repeating the solutions can be ineffective or even counterproductive. Instead, the performer, learner or developing child should be given room to explore possibilities, select a possible solution and experience the outcome. In this way, something more can develop from something less.

Exploration Versus Prescription in Physical Education

Until the 1950s physical education consisted mainly of line gymnastics that had their origin in military exercises and the system of gymnastics developed by Per Henrik Ling, also known as the Swedish system (cf. Thulin, 1931, in Mechikoff & Estes, 2002). Line gymnastics adhered to strict movements executed in a strict order, often with an aesthetic purpose. Many of these activities allowed for little freedom when it came to how each movement should be performed. In line gymnastics, the use of instructive (or so-called deductive) learning methods dominated heavily. School children were instructed very strictly about how they should behave and how they should move. Little, if anything, was up to the children themselves, and minimal creativity was involved in the learning process. In short, deductive, or instructive, learning methods do not stimulate children's own contributions about how to carry out a movement task to the same extent as inductive learning methods, such as discovery learning, do.

As explained previously, a dynamic systems perspective does not emphasize any single causal factor, such as instructions, but takes the possible contribution of many factors into consideration. Learning new movement patterns depends on the task, the environment and the children's own characteristics, their so-called intrinsic dynamics. In each new learning situation, the environment provides new sources of information and other stimuli to the individual. In this respect, just as

one cannot step into the same river twice, every task has to be solved anew in its own unique way. The more varied the situations that a person has experienced, the better equipped the person becomes to adjust her movements to the environment and the task at hand. Because personal experiences are unique and influence subsequent strategies and performances, everyone's movements are also a result of the confluence of his or her own constraints on action. An instructive, or prescriptive, teaching method cannot and does not elaborate on the uniqueness of each individual movement pattern to the same extent.

Because of the importance of exploration and individual experiences, a stimulating environment is of great importance. The PE teacher's task is to guide the children through different terrains and situations so they can detect the dynamics and possibilities of the environment. When they are given settings that offer opportunities to explore how to move and how to solve movement challenges, children can adjust their techniques to every new situation. According to a dynamic systems perspective, each person can have his own strategy for solving a particular movement task, depending on, for example, the length of different body segments, the strength of his muscles, his prior experiences and so forth. By arranging activities in a diverse environment in which numerous stimuli exist, physical educators give children an opportunity to detect their intrinsic dynamics and to exploit task dynamics and task solutions according to their own body characteristics.

For school children and adolescents, the natural environment will meet most demands for a suitable area for PE classes. The natural landscape, with its many objects, obstacles and challenges, provides a stimulating playing area. Research has demonstrated the relations between the landscape's ecology and where and how children play (e.g., Fjørtoft, 2000, 2004). An uneven terrain, for example, forces the children to adjust the positioning of their feet to stay balanced. Jumping from rock to rock or balancing on fallen trees stimulates many senses at the same time. In addition, children have to adjust the forces they exert according to each situation. This will also differ from child to child, depending on the child's body composition and earlier experiences in similar situations. The physical educator's primary task is to help the children detect the dynamics

A challenging artificial outdoor environment.

Photograph by Geir Oterhals.

of the situation and the environment. If there is a lack of natural terrain and landscapes in the direct vicinity of the school, a stimulating outdoor area can be created by using different artificial equipment such as old tires and ropes. Guiding the children into different situations provides them with the opportunity to detect and exploit their own constraints in each specific situation.

An indoor arena can also satisfy the need for an open and challenging environment. However, this requires obstacles such as benches, foam rubber and so on. By way of example, teaching how to throw a ball can be done in several ways. From a dynamic systems perspective, using balls or objects of different sizes can help children detect the secrets of a successful throw. Throwing a light ball requires a different movement pattern than throwing a heavy ball does.

To detect their own intrinsic dynamics and how to work with them in actual tasks, children should be exposed to a variety of challenges, as described earlier. This variety should be brought into the PE class in a playful way, preferably with the degree of difficulty adjusted to each child's needs and capacities. One way of doing this is to use games as inspiration and as an entry into learning. The purpose is thus not necessarily to play the game itself. Rather, the game is used as a means to an end—in this case, advancing motor skills.

Play theories were debated as early as the 19th century (cf. Mechikoff & Estes, 2002). At the time, physical educators believed that play should have only a secondary role within physical education; it was seen as a tool for improving posture and building character. It was not regarded as the primary instrument for physical education (Mechikoff & Estes, 2002). Even today, the most typical use of games in PE classes is to warm up before the main part of the class or as a fun way to end the class. Games, however, can also help children learn a technique or part of a technique. For example, to learn how to jump, children must acquire several elements. They need to know how to adjust their speed, how to perform the run-up and push-off phases, which foot to jump from and so on. Instructing the children verbally in all these mechanisms can quickly become too boring and abstract. Games can help the children discover the same mechanisms of jumping in a less formal, more playful way than instructions can. The children are then learning through discovery rather than through instructions. Instructions often leave too few opportunities for the child to solve a motor task in a way suited to that particular child. If the games force or inspire the children to jump, this would be a method where the children are exploiting and experiencing their degrees of freedom and making the movement efficient according to their constraints. The responsibility of the PE teacher is therefore to create terrains and games with specific purposes. In this sense, the physical educator does not function as an instructor, but as a guide. Similarly, the children are not passive receivers of knowledge and instructions. Rather, they actively create their own understanding of a specific task and a solution suited to their present needs and capabilities.

Examples of Exploration in Skill Learning

Teaching children how to perform a skill, such as a basic throw, is not simple. The technical instructions are often extensive and may be difficult for the children to understand and implement. The challenge for the PE teacher is to use teaching and learning methods that encourage the children to find solutions for the outcomes best suited for them; these are called inductive learning methods. One exercise that can be used in learning to throw involves dividing the class into two groups, A and B (see figure 12.2). A large ball (e.g., a medicine ball or basketball) is placed between the two groups with an approximate distance of 5 metres (5 yards) from each group to the ball. Each group is supplied with many balls of different sizes (no smaller than a tennis ball and no larger than a soccer ball). Both groups have to stand behind a specified line when they are throwing the smaller balls at the medicine or basketball. The aim of the game is for everyone in each group to throw

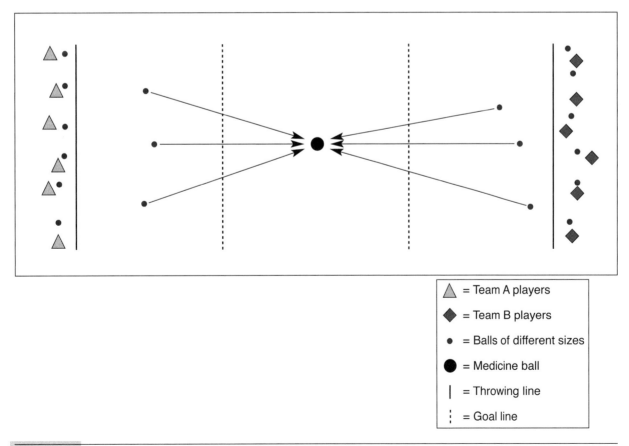

△	= Team A players
◆	= Team B players
•	= Balls of different sizes
⬤	= Medicine ball
│	= Throwing line
⋮	= Goal line

Figure 12.2 Schematic drawing of the ball-throwing game.

the small balls at the large ball to start it rolling. If the large ball rolls over a prespecified line, one point is given to the group that managed to roll the ball over the line. The number of points each group has to collect to win can vary, but three points can be an adequate starting point. Collecting balls in the centre area is allowed, but the throwing itself always has to be done from behind the line. This exercise is suitable because the children get many repetitions, they observe the results of their throws immediately and they can try different ball sizes—and because it is a fun and exciting exercise.

A second example of using exploration to facilitate learning involves learning to place a ball by kicking in soccer. The teacher makes a target on a wall and has the children stand in front of the wall and try to kick the ball at the target. The target could be a line, with the purpose to hit the ball above the line, or a specific point on the wall. The children get immediate visual feedback about whether they hit the target. In addition, if they kick the ball straight at the wall, the ball will return directly to them, making the exercise quick and efficient. This also gives immediate feedback about their performance without necessary instructions from the teacher. Furthermore, with this strategy, the children will increase the number of repetitions of kicking the ball, giving them more practice. In the beginning, the children could stand in front of the wall at a distance of approximately 5 metres (5 yards). Gradually increasing the distance to the wall, or making the target point smaller, will increase the degree of difficulty. The PE teacher should encourage the children to try different methods of kicking the ball. Using this exercise, the children also learn how to receive and stop the ball in addition to learning how to kick it.

A third exercise involves children learning how to bounce a ball. By receiving instructions such as 'try to make as much noise as possible when bouncing the ball', or 'bounce the ball as gently as you can', the children are encouraged to explore and discover how to solve the task. To give the children an extra challenge of bouncing a ball in different ways and situations, the teacher could make an obstacle course, in which the children have to bounce the ball below a hindrance, bounce the ball while walking on a beam, bounce the ball while lying on their bellies, bounce the ball while moving between cones and so on. In this way, the children are more engaged with their own tasks and are not looking at each other. At the same time, they can explore the qualities of the bounce of the ball and how they can perform in different circumstances.

Summary

Remember John, the physical education teacher from the introduction? After reading this chapter, you should have a better understanding of how variability in movements and exercises can stimulate the acquisition and improvement of motor skills. Variability in games and exercises allows for more variation in the problem-solving process, thereby giving children and adolescents ample opportunities for variation of practice and selection of task solutions that fit their needs and capabilities. You should also have a renewed appreciation for the unique set of personal characteristics that each child and adolescent brings to the PE class, which contribute to individual differences in motor skill, motivation and development. Using basic concepts and principles from dynamic systems theory—stability, instability, flexibility, self-organisation, degrees of freedom, constraints, exploration and variability—we have illustrated how these concepts and principles translate to the field of physical education. We have also given practical examples for how to apply them in PE classes so that you as a teacher can challenge established coordination patterns, change and gradually improve movement patterns by manipulating constraints and stimulate the exploration of possible task solutions.

Review Questions

1. What are the main concepts of a dynamic systems perspective?
2. What are the characteristics of stable performance?
3. Why is flexibility of movement patterns necessary to play team sports?

4. Why is destabilisation of established coordination patterns important to manage a new coordination pattern?
5. What are constraints?
6. What are the three phases in skill learning?

Critical Thinking Questions

1. What are different ways to challenge an existing coordination pattern?
2. How can you manipulate the different constraints in physical education?
3. What kinds of exercises are suitable to promote motor skills as seen from a dynamic systems perspective?
4. How can you incorporate the phenomena of stability and instability into the concept of learning strategies?
5. How can you promote variability in an outdoor environment to challenge the coordination patterns of the pupils in your physical education class?

Key Terms

complexity—A quality that is the opposite of simplicity; this can refer to structures, information content or behaviours that are high dimensional and nonlinear. For example, a system can be said to be complex when it consists of many parts that interact with each other.

constraints—Conditions that restrict the degrees of freedom of a system by eliminating or restraining certain configurations or movement patterns while enabling or permitting others.

coordinative structure—A functional, task-specific grouping of muscles spanning one or several joints to achieve a certain goal. Bernstein (1967) introduced coordinative structures as a solution to the degrees-of-freedom problem, because muscles need not be controlled as separate units.

degrees of freedom—The number of independent coordinates needed to uniquely describe the state of a system, or the number of ways in which the spatial configuration of a system can change. The knee, for example, has one degree of freedom, flexion-extension; whereas the ankle has two, dorsiflexion-plantar flexion and eversion-inversion.

exploration—A series of movements and acts for the purpose of gathering information about the task, the environment and one's possibilities for action.

flexibility—The ability to adapt to different circumstances by virtue of having a range of possible solutions for a task at one's disposal.

individual variability—Interindividual, or between-individual, variability refers to differences between organisms in characteristics, traits, strategies and so on. Intra-individual, or within-individual, variability refers to differences within an individual across tasks or over time.

instability—The loss of stability, characterised by increased variability and reduced resistance against perturbations to the system, thereby enabling or facilitating change.

learning stages—Identifiable periods in an ongoing learning process that are qualitatively different from one another.

self-organisation—A process by which new structures or patterns emerge from collective interactions among the parts of a system. These structures or patterns are not prescribed or specified from the outside, but arise from internal processes.

stability—The ability of a system to withstand perturbations. Stability is a prerequisite for behaviour to be functional and observable.

variability—Variation, or differences, in exercises, movement patterns or environments. Variability can also refer to differences in scores or characteristics between different groups or between different people within a group.

References

Adams, J.A. (1987). Historical review and appraisal of research on the learning, retention, and transfer of human motor skills. *Psychological Bulletin, 101,* 41-74.

Arutyunyan, G.H., Gurfinkel, V.S. & Mirskii, M.L. (1968). Investigation of aiming at a target. *Biofizika, 13,* 536-538.

Arutyunyan, G.H., Gurfinkel, V.S. & Mirskii, M.L. (1969). Organization of movements on execution by man of an exact postural task. *Biofizika, 14,* 1162-1167.

Bernstein, N.A. (1967). *The coordination and regulation of movement.* London: Pergamon Press.

Biddle, S.J.H. (1995). Exercise motivation across the life span. In S.J.H. Biddle (Ed.), *European perspectives on exercise and sport psychology* (pp. 3-25). Champaign, IL: Human Kinetics.

Blair, S.N., Kohl, H.W., Gordon, N.F. & Paffenberger, R.S. Jr. (1992). How much physical activity is good for health? *Annual Review of Public Health, 13,* 99-126.

Bootsma, R.J. & van Wieringen, P.C.W. (1990). Timing an attacking forehand drive in table tennis. *Journal of Experimental Psychology: Human Perception and Performance, 16,* 21-29.

Bouchard, C., Shepard, R.J. & Stephens, T. (1994). *Physical activity, fitness and health.* Champaign, IL: Human Kinetics.

Corbetta, D. & Bojczyk, K.E. (2002). Infants return to two-handed reaching when they are learning to walk. *Journal of Motor Behavior, 34,* 83-95.

Corbetta, D. & Vereijken, B. (1999). Understanding development and learning of motor coordination in sport: The contribution of dynamic systems theory. *International Journal of Sport Psychology, 30,* 507-530.

Directorate for Primary and Secondary Education. (1997). *The curriculum for the 10-year compulsory school in Norway.* Oslo, Norway: Norwegian Directorate for Education and Training.

Estil, L.B., Whiting, H.T.A., Sigmundsson, H. & Ingvaldsen, R.P. (2003). Why might language and motor impairments occur together? *Infant and Child Development, 12,* 253-265.

Fjørtoft, I. (2000). *Landscape as playscape: Learning effects from playing in a natural environment on motor development in children.* Skien, Norway: Thure Trykk.

Fjørtoft, I. (2004). Landscape as playscape: The effect of natural environments on children's play and motor development. *Children, Youth and Environments, 14*(2), 21-44.

Grund, A., Dilba, B., Forberger, K., Krause, H., Siewers, M., Rieckert, H. et al. (2000). Relationship between physical activity, physical fitness, muscle strength and nutritional state in 5- to 11-year-old children. *European Journal of Applied Physiology, 82,* 425-438.

Hands, B. & Larkin, D. (2002). Physical fitness and developmental coordination disorder. In S.A. Cermak and D. Larkin (Eds.), *Developmental co-ordination disorder.* Albany, NY: Delmar Thomson Learning.

Henderson, S.E. & Hall, D. (1982). Concomitants of clumsiness in young schoolchildren. *Developmental Medicine and Child Neurology, 24,* 448-460.

Hoos, M.B., Gerver, W.J.M., Kester, A.D. & Westerterp, K.R. (2003). Physical activity levels in children and adolescents. *International Journal of Obesity, 27,* 605-609.

Hoyt, D.F. & Taylor, C.R. (1981). Gait and energetics of locomotion in horses. *Nature, 292,* 239-240.

Kelso, J.A.S. (1995). *Dynamic patterns: The self-organization of brain and behavior.* Cambridge, MA: MIT Press.

Kelso, J.A.S., Holt, K.G., Kugler, P.N. & Turvey, M.T. (1980). On the concept of coordinative structures as dissipative structures: II. Empirical lines of convergence. In G.E. Stelmach & J. Requin (Eds.), *Tutorials in motor behavior* (pp. 49-70). Amsterdam: North-Holland.

Kugler, P.N. (1986). A morphological perspective on the origin and evolution of movement patterns. In M.G. Whade & H.T.A. Whiting (Eds.), *Motor development in children: Aspects of coordination and control* (pp. 459-525). Dordrecht, the Netherlands: Martinus Nijhoff.

Kugler, P.N., Kelso, J.A.S. & Turvey, M.T. (1980). On the concept of coordinative structures as dissipative structures: I. Theoretical lines of convergence. In G.E. Stelmach & J. Requin (Eds.), *Tutorials in motor behavior* (pp. 3-47). Amsterdam: North-Holland.

Magill, R.A. (1998). *Motor learning: Concepts and application* (5th ed.). Boston: McGraw-Hill.

Mæland, A.F. (1992). Identification of children with motor co-ordination problems. *Adapted Physical Activity Quarterly, 9,* 330-342.

Marshall, J.D. & Bouffard, M. (1997). The effects of quality daily physical education on movement competency in obese versus nonobese children. *Adapted Physical Activity Quarterly, 14,* 222-237.

Masters, R.S.W. (1992). Knowledge, nerves and know-how: The role of explicit versus implicit knowledge in the breakdown of a complex motor skill under pressure. *British Journal of Psychology, 83,* 343-358.

Mechikoff, R. & Estes, S. (2002). *A history and philosophy of sport and physical education* (3rd ed.). New York: McGraw-Hill Higher Education.

Newell, K.M. (1986). Constraints on the development of coordination. In M. Wade & H.T.A. Whiting (Eds.), *Motor development in children: Aspects of coordination and control* (pp.341-360). Dordrecht, the Netherlands: Martinus Nijhoff.

Paavolainen, L., Häkkinen, K., Hämäläinen, I., Nummela, A. & Rusko, H. (1999). Explosive-strength training improves 5-km running time by improving running economy and muscle power. *Journal of Applied Physiology, 86,* 1527-1533.

Powers, S.K. & Howley, E.T. (2004). *Exercise physiology: Theory and application to fitness and performance.* New York: McGraw-Hill.

Saarinen, P. (1987). Not all students take an interest in sports. In *Proceedings of the 7th Congress of the European Federation of Sports Psychology* (pp. 563-566). Leipzig, Germany: Deutsche Hauptschule für Korperkultur.

Sheets-Johnstone, M. (1999). *The primacy of movement.* Amsterdam: John Benjamins.

Sigmundsson, H., Whiting, H.T.A. & Ingvaldsen, R.P. (1999). 'Putting your foot in it'! A window into clumsy behaviour. *Behavioural and Brain Research, 102,* 131-138.

Sørensen, V., Ingvaldsen, R.P. & Whiting, H.T.A. (2001). The application of co-ordination dynamics to the analysis of discrete movements using table-tennis as a paradigm skill. *Biological Cybernetics, 85,* 27-38.

Spencer, J.P., Vereijken, B., Diedrich, F.J. & Thelen, E. (2000). Posture and the emergence of manual skills. *Developmental Science, 3,* 216-233.

Thelen, E. & Smith, L.B. (1994). *A dynamic systems approach to the development of cognition and action.* Cambridge, MA: MIT Press.

Vereijken, B. (1991). *The dynamics of skill acquisition.* Meppel, the Netherlands: Krips Repro.

Vereijken, B. & Adolph, K.E. (1999). Transitions in the development of locomotion. In G.J.P. Savelsbergh, H.L.J. van der Maas & P.C.L. van Geert (Eds.), *Non-linear developmental processes* (pp. 137-149). Amsterdam: Elsevier.

Vereijken, B., van Emmerik, R.E.A., Whiting, H.T.A. & Newell, K.M. (1992). Free(z)ing degrees of freedom in skill acquisition. *Journal of Motor Behavior, 24,* 133-142.

chapter thirteen

Visuomotor Control of Movement Acquisition

Geert Savelsbergh
Vrije Universiteit, the Netherlands, and Manchester Metropolitan University, UK

Martine Verheul*
University of Edinburgh, UK

John van der Kamp
Vrije Universiteit, the Netherlands

Dilwyn Marple-Horvat
Manchester Metropolitan University, UK

After reading this chapter, you will be able to do the following:

- Understand why perception and movement should be coupled
- Understand the relationship between the stage of learning and perceptual degrees of freedom
- Understand what is meant by specificity of practice
- Understand the constraints-led perspective on perceptual-motor learning
- Apply the constraints-led perspective in practice and training sessions
- Apply and teach perceptual skills based on principles from the constraints-led approach

*The studies presented here were conducted while the second author was at Manchester Metropolitan University.

Rachel is a promising young tennis player. Her technique is excellent. Strength training combined with technique training has made her service almost unreturnable. However, she runs into problems when she has to return an opponent's serve in a competitive situation. She appears to be at the right location in time, but the timing of her stroke is awkward. Because Rachel is by far the best player in her club, her coach has purchased a ball machine that can project balls with and without spin in various directions at high speeds. Rachel has intensively practised with the machine at the fastest setting and is now able to return 95 percent of the balls fast and accurately. However, returning an opponent's serve, which is probably often of a lower speed, remains problematic. Rachel is starting to get frustrated because she does not understand how she can improve. Her coach concludes that it must be 'nerves'. Or can it be a perception–action problem?

Professional soccer players exhibit highly skilled action. Beckham's smooth passes, Henry's rushes through the defence, Van Nistelrooy's headings—we admire them all. To reach such superb levels of ball control has taken these athletes years of (daily) practice. An important characteristic of skilled performance is the precise tuning of the action to the continuously changing circumstances of the environment. Perception is indispensable in this respect. Successful movement coordination demands conformity to highly constrained spatial and timing requirements, whereas perception provides the necessary information about environmental events.

One skill that is crucially dependent on visual perception is catching. Catching skills are an essential part of many sports (e.g., baseball, soccer, rugby, basketball and team handball). To make a successful catch, the catcher has to orient and locate his hand at a precise location at a precise time. In addition, he needs to anticipate the exact moment the ball will hit his hand in order to close his fingers around the ball. Reaching such high levels of performance and flexibility often takes years of development, learning and practice (see the sidebar on page 241 for a description of the development of catching).

The goal of this chapter is to elaborate on the role of visual information in the acquisition of a motor skill such as ball catching. Ball catching is used, in addition to other sport skills, to illustrate the theoretical approach. Then, a model of stages in the acquisition and development of the coupling of visual information and movement behaviour is described. This model of Savelsbergh and van der Kamp (2000) can be used as a framework to understand how information and movement are coupled under certain sets of **constraints.** After that, the model is illustrated with examples from training in one-handed catching, stopping a penalty in soccer and the role of eye movement practice in walking. The chapter concludes with practical implications and applications of the model.

Theoretical Perspective

In this section we explain the basic ideas of the constraints-led approach and illustrate these with examples from early and late motor behaviour. Bernstein's (1967) stages of learning and the change in use of the degrees of freedom are discussed. With respect to the latter, we show how the use of degrees of freedom can change in young children's one-handed catching.

Returning an opponent's serve requires perceptual and motor skills.

DEVELOPMENT OF CATCHING

The skill of catching develops gradually throughout childhood. Perceptual-motor skills that underlie catching can already be seen in infancy, when a sitting child stops a ball that rolls toward her or chases and stops a bouncing ball. Wickstrom (1983) gave a particularly detailed description of the development of catching, from its early onset to the various applications in sporting situations. Catching, defined as the stopping and controlling of an aerial ball or object using the hand(s) or other parts of the body, develops from the age of three. Like many other skills, the development of catching follows a proximal–distal pattern. This means that the skill involves large trunk and arm movements in the early stage and more refined hand and finger movements at later stages.

Initially, catching involves 'trapping', meaning that the ball is stopped between the trunk and arms. This type of catching often coincides with a fear reaction in children; namely, that a child may turn his head to the side and bend his trunk slightly backward. Experience with various ball sizes, including smaller balls, encourages the child to increase the contribution of his hands and progress from a trapping style of catching to a more mature technique. As the child acquires more advanced catching skills, he starts to lower his arms, with his elbows flexed and pointing downward, and position his palms and fingers in anticipation of a two-handed catch. In a successful catch, the hands make contact with the ball simultaneously. The mature form of catching, observed in late childhood, is characterised by correctly positioning the hand(s) with regard to the trajectory of the object and by successfully grasping the object. The latter phase involves a reduction of impact force of the ball on the hand by giving way in the approach direction of the object, which also results in an increase in time to perform the actual grasping motion. Various sporting situations require specialised catching actions, but these basic characteristics remain observable in all of these situations. For a detailed account of catching in basketball, soccer and baseball, see Wickstrom (1983).

Constraints-Led Approach

The theoretical paradigm for this chapter is based on the work of Bernstein (1967); Gibson (1979); Kugler, Kelso and Turvey (1982); and Newell (1986). In this perspective, the development of movement coordination is brought about by changes in the constraints imposed on the organism–environment system. Constraints are all the factors that provide boundaries for the occurrence or shape of a coordination pattern. They do not prescribe a coordination pattern, but they guide the direction of development by making certain patterns impossible or improbable. The development of walking, for instance, is constrained by anatomical, physiological, psychological and sociocultural factors. For example, the human upper extremities are especially suited for supporting the manipulation of the hands in space, whereas the lower extremities are built for weight-bearing and stable support. This makes walking a preferred manner of locomotion for humans. In addition, walking is a more energetically efficient means of locomotion than, for instance, crawling (try it!). Moreover, the desire of infants to move around while observing their environment (especially other humans) and to take objects with them further favours walking on two legs over going on all fours. Cultures in which crawling is strongly discouraged speed up the process of exploration and the selection of the walking pattern. Thus, the process of learning a new motor skill is guided by interacting constraints of various kinds.

Newell (1986) proposed three categories of constraints: organismic (e.g., the central nervous system, body weight), task (e.g., grasping an object that is out of reach, scoring a goal without using the hands) and environmental (e.g., surface, size of a soccer pitch, sociocultural factors). These constraints do not operate in isolation but interact with each other, leading to a task-specific organisation of the coordination pattern. Particular constraints may act as rate-limiting factors in the emergence of new behaviours, the mastering of new actions or even the sustaining of highly skilled actions. For instance, the body proportions of an infant (a relatively large head and relatively short legs) mean that the centre of mass is located high in the body, causing the infant to be 'top-heavy' and thus unsuited for upright locomotion. It is not until body proportions start to change that the infant can become a confident walker. In contrast, rapid changes in the physiology of an adult can be quite disruptive for motor functioning. Van der Kamp, Vereijken and Savelsbergh (1996) reported that, shortly after winning the world title in gymnastics in 1987, Aurelia Dobre was plagued by growth spurts. As a result, she failed to maintain her high level of performance, and she abruptly disappeared from international competition. In this case, a change in an organismic constraint disrupted the acquired movement organisation.

Thelen and colleagues (e.g., Thelen, Fischer & Ridley-Johnson, 1984) provided another classic example of the influence of a rapidly changing body on the development of leg movements. These researchers found that in eight-week-old infants held upright, the stepping movements that had been observed at a younger age had disappeared. This finding had traditionally been explained by the maturation of the brain, inhibiting the primitive 'stepping reflex'. However, when the infants were lying supine, they performed kicking movements that were kinematically similar to those observed earlier (Thelen & Fisher, 1983). If the disappearance was due to cortical inhibition, as the traditional explanation would have it, why would the cortex inhibit movements in the upright posture but not in the supine posture?

Thelen and colleagues hypothesised that the disappearance of newborn stepping movements is a consequence of the disproportionate growth of leg muscles and fat tissues. Specifically, during this period of development infants acquire fat at a greater rate than muscle mass, which leads to relatively less muscle force. They tested this hypothesis by taking infants in which stepping had disappeared and holding them upright in water. The upward pressure of the water made it easier for the infants to lift their legs, and as a result the stepping pattern reemerged. Moreover, attaching a weight to the legs of infants who showed the stepping 'reflex' made the movements disappear (Thelen et al., 1984). Indeed, a relationship exists between the disappearance of the stepping movements and the rate of weight gain in these young infants (Thelen, Fisher, Ridley-Johnson & Griffin, 1982). Interestingly, infants who practise the stepping movements can retain the movement pattern

throughout the first year of life (Zelazo, Zelazo & Kolb, 1972). Thus, the occurrence of stepping movements (the coordination pattern) is a consequence of the interaction between organismic constraints (muscle-to-fat ratio) and environmental constraints (orientation to the gravity vector, upward pressure), and not uniquely determined by neuromaturational constraints. Savelsbergh and van der Kamp (1994) made similar observations with respect to infant reaching.

Constraints not only influence the emergence or disruption of a skill, but also shape the coordination pattern. The style of crawling that an infant adopts, for example, critically depends on the prevailing constraints, most importantly the type of surface on which the infant learns to crawl. An infant learning to crawl on a wooden floor will adopt a pattern that is particularly suited for slippery surfaces. One such movement pattern consists of putting the hands in front of the body in a prone position and propelling the body forward in a bouncing-sliding motion. Infants who learn to crawl on a surface with more friction, such as a carpet, are probably more likely to select a commando-style, or 'tiger', crawl. Similarly, young soccer players who learn the skills of their sport on a wet and windy pitch in England are likely to adopt a technique somewhat different from that of their Brazilian peers.

According to the constraints-led perspective, there is not one factor that causes a particular motor skill. Instead, skills emerge with practice under a set of constraints. Learning or developing a skill over time is caused by many interacting constraints. Constraints act (and interact) over time. This is clearly illustrated by a phenomenon called the birth date effect (Dudink, 1994; Wilson, 1999). Elite athletes typically were the oldest in their group of peers when they were in school. Their slight physical advantage probably caused them to be more successful at sports and, in turn, receive more encouragement and opportunities to develop their skills to a very high level. This example shows how biological and environmental effects are inextricably intertwined. Therefore, it is impossible to state how much of her skill a 16-year-old sport talent has inherited from her parents and how much has been the result of training. During development and learning, constraints continuously interact and shape the coordination pattern that a learner acquires. From a constraints-led perspective, learning and development are not fundamentally different. In this chapter we use the terms *learning* and *development* interchangeably, and we present examples from both fields.

A central aim of the constraints-led perspective is to develop accurate explanations for changes in an observed behaviour by identifying the environmental and organismic constraints and their relative contributions. In this manner, the constraints perspective moves well beyond the descriptive accounts. Once a coach or teacher has identified the constraints that act on the learning process, he can manipulate them to facilitate and guide the learning process in a particular direction.

A study of van der Kamp, Savelsbergh and Davis (1998) examined how children aged five, seven and nine years reach, grasp and lift cardboard cubes of different sizes (ranging from 2.2 to 16.2 centimetres [0.87 to 6.4 inches] in diameter). Recordings were analysed and scored for the percentage occurrence of one-handed grasps. The findings showed that the older the child was, the higher the occurrence of one-handed grasps was (37, 46 and 55 percent for the five-, seven-

and nine-year-olds, respectively). Moreover, the older the child was, the larger the cubes were that were predominantly taken with one hand. From a constraints-led approach, it is hypothesised that the detected differences in grasping between the age groups are due to the increase of hand size with age. Indeed, the shift from one-handed to two-handed grasping occurred at the same body-scale ratio between cube size and hand span for all three age groups. In other words, the ratio between object size (task constraint) and hand size (organismic constraint) determined when children shifted from a one-handed to a two-handed grasping pattern.

Practically, this research provided evidence for the use of *body scaling,* a common practice in working with children: The pitch size is smaller, and the goals and the balls are smaller for smaller children. Paradoxically, however, a soccer ball ('Futbol de Salao' [FDS]) recently introduced for children's soccer is heavier than the ball that is commonly used (Button, Bennett, Davids & Stephenson, 1999; Chapman, 2003). This may

Some children will find it easier to keep the ball close to their body and dribble than others will.

seem contradictory to what the constraints-led perspective shows, but it is not. Task analysis shows that ball control is very limited in young children playing soccer. A ball that is heavier is easier to control and can thus aid in the learning process. Children will find it easier to keep the ball close to their body, dribble with it and send it in a preferred direction. Once children obtain a particular level of skill, they can transfer to the commonly used size 4 or 5 ball. The FDS ball is an example of a manipulation of task constraints to facilitate skill acquisition.

To summarise, there is now clear empirical evidence that (the changing of) constraints can cause motor abilities to emerge or disappear. Constraints act as rate-limiting factors on the emergence of new motor abilities and shape the coordination pattern that a learner adopts. A rather small change in one of the constraints (e.g. fat-to-muscle ratio, object size) can lead to changes in the observed coordination pattern. Changing a constraint, such as holding infants upright in water (an environmental constraint), can result in the reemergence of a coordination pattern that had been lost.

Degrees of Freedom and Constraints

An important characteristic of successful performance is that the movements of all the components (e.g., muscles, tendons, joints) of the motor apparatus of the human body have to be controlled. Bernstein (1967) realised that the nonlinear nature of the interactions among these different components of the human body makes separate regulation impossible. Bernstein inferred that to be able to control all these components, or degrees of freedom, the movements in all components have to be coordinated. Coordination, therefore, is the process of mastering the redundant degrees of freedom into a controllable system (cf. Bernstein, 1967, p. 127).

Several researchers (e.g., Vereijken, van Emmerik, Whiting & Newell, 1992) have provided evidence for three learning stages with respect to Bernstein's degrees of freedom: namely, *freezing, freeing* and *exploiting* the degrees of freedom. If one considers the typical progression in learning to kick a ball (Davids, Lees & Burwitz, 2000; Gallahue & Ozmun, 1995), these stages are readily apparent. Novices tend to keep their bodies

relatively rigid ('frozen') and involve only their lower bodies in the kicking action. Movements of different joints, such as the hip and knee joint, tend to be coupled: When the hip starts to flex, the knee starts extending at the same time. Coupling the movements of joints makes the control problem somewhat easier to solve. Imagine having a different steering wheel for each wheel in your car! Improvement of the skill is only possible by carefully letting go of the rigid couplings bit by bit and exploring how their inclusion can lead to better results. This trial-and-error learning is only possible by unfreezing, or freeing, the degrees of freedom. Finally, the most efficient coordination pattern typically involves making optimal use of ('exploiting') passive or reactive forces (in contrast to forces caused directly by the activation of muscles). Such forces are an indirect result of the movement of parts of the body, often in interaction with the environment. In the example of the soccer kick, timing the extension or flexion of the hip, knee and ankle in a chainlike fashion causes the knee to benefit maximally from the velocity generated at the hip, resulting in maximal velocity of the foot (Anderson & Sidaway, 1994). Thus, a skilled player performs the movement with maximal result in the most energetically efficient manner.

Often, the exploitation phase involves passive or reactive forces from outside the body. Think of the elastic properties of a tennis racket, which can cause a ball to be propelled very efficiently with high speed, *if* used correctly. Novices typically transfer only a small part of their energy into the movement of the ball. Vereijken, Whiting and Beek (1992) provided a nice example of this concept in a study that examined learning to ski on a ski simulator. Skiing on a simulator involves standing on a platform attached to a spring and moving the platform from side to side in ski-like fashion. Vereijken and colleagues (1992) found that at the beginning of practice, novices tried to apply force to the platform at a biomechanically inefficient moment. By using this strategy, they did not benefit from the available elastic forces stored in the stretched springs of the apparatus. With experience, the subjects learned to exploit the characteristics of the apparatus, postponing their application of force until after the platform had passed the centre of the apparatus and started to slow down. With this strategy, subjects made use of the elastic forces that gave them a 'free ride' back to the centre of the apparatus and beyond, allowing them to reduce their active muscle forces. Heise and coworkers showed that the duration of muscle activity during the knee flexion phase of the movement indeed decreased with practice (Heise, Caillouet, Cornwell & Sidaway, 1996). As a result, movement cost is decreased (Durand, Geoffroi, Varray & Préfaut, 1994).

Research into the skill of catching by Strohmeyer, Williams and Schaub-George (1991) and Fischman, Moore and Steele (1992) indicates that as children become more skilful, they more freely experiment with their responses. This exploration can be described as a shift from freezing to freeing the degrees of freedom. Another example of this concept stems from a paper published in 1937, in which Wellman identified three levels of development in two-handed catching. At the age of three and a half years, children hold their arms stiff and straight at the elbows, in front of their bodies (freezing degrees of freedom). At four years of age, children open their hands to receive the object even though their arms remain stiff. By five years of age, children assume a more relaxed position, with arms bent at the elbow and hands ready to receive the ball (freeing degrees of freedom).

To examine the impact of postural constraints on catching, Davids and his colleagues (Davids, Bennett, Kingsbury, Jolley & Brain, 2000) had good and poor catchers (10-year-olds) perform a one-handed catching action in both a seated and standing position. In the standing position the act of raising the arm to align the hand with the flight path of the approaching ball is constrained by the upright posture, and it also influences the perception of spatio-temporal information about the coupling of the hand and ball (Davids et al., 2000). The findings showed that poor catchers performed better in the seated position than in the standing position. These results suggest that reducing the degrees of freedom available (freezing) to be exploited in the seated position is beneficial for poor catchers. Reducing the degrees of freedom improves their performance (see also, Savelsbergh, Bennett, Angelakopoulos & Davids, 2005).

Recently, Savelsbergh and van der Kamp (2000) elaborated on the role of informational constraints in the control and learning of one-handed catching. They defended the thesis that information and movement are tightly coupled and that, as a result, specificity of training is required to get meaningful learning effects. They proposed the existence of different phases in the learning of **information–movement coupling** to explain the sometimes contradictory experimental findings with respect to adults' catching performance. The next section discusses the relevance of this multiphase model for the development of catching.

Perceptual Degrees of Freedom and Learning

Savelsbergh and van der Kamp (2000) considered the learning (and development) of information–movement coupling to be analogous to the learning sequence of freezing, freeing and **exploiting the degrees of freedom** as proposed by Bernstein (1967). The basic idea is that depending on the specific constraints (e.g., the available visual information) multiple information sources are involved. That is to say, different types of visual information (at different times) may be used to perform the required job successfully. Bernstein's concept of degrees of freedom, defined with respect to the motor system, can therefore be extended to incorporate the visual system. We refer to this concept as **perceptual degrees of freedom**, suggesting that multiple sources of information are available for controlling the same task.

During learning and development, perceptual degrees of freedom show the same sequence of freezing, freeing and exploiting the movement degrees of freedom show. More specifically, the couplings of information and movement take place following this sequence. First, the learning process starts with the emergence and strengthening of a coupling between information and movement (freezing; see figure 13.1a). That is, within a certain set of constraints, a particular coupling between information and movement emerges that fits the task requirements. With repetition, the strength of this (successful) coupling increases. In other words, the movement gets tuned to the information. As such, this coupling is likely to recur under a similar set of constraints. This eventually results in a freezing out of other potential couplings and an increasing stability of the pattern. However, when, in this early phase of learning and development, the particular set or interaction of constraints changes, the coupling

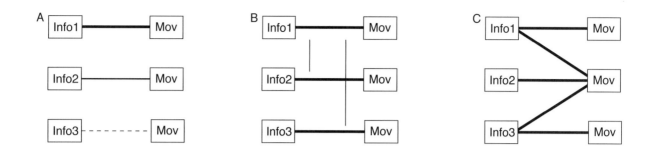

Figure 13.1 Stages of learning: (a) Strengthening: the coupling between information (info1) and movement (mov1) gets stronger during practice, but not for info2 and mov2; (b) Freeing: one can jump from one strong coupling to another; (c) Exploiting: information (info1) can be used for different actions (mov1 and mov2) and different perceptual information (info2 and info3) for the same movement (mov2).

From G.J.P. Savelsbergh and J. van der Kamp, 2001, "Training must be as specific as possible, but not always!" *Insight* 4: 48-49.

will be disturbed and the action will break down. An alternative coupling between information and movement may not be available or may be too weak to lead to successful performance. More practice will then be required to strengthen the alternative coupling between information and movement that is specific to the new set of constraints. This brings us to the next stage.

The second stage involves freeing different information–movement couplings (see figure 13.1b). Practice and experience under different sets of constraints will eventually lead to a whole repertoire of possible information–movement couplings for a certain task. Hence, if certain constraints change, the actor will be able to realise another available coupling, without the need to learn it from scratch. Moreover, in contrast to the early stage of learning, such a change of constraints will not lead to a complete breakdown of the action.

Skilled performance, from our perspective, can be characterised by the ability to exploit different information–movement couplings (see figure 13.1c). Because the learner now has a whole repertoire of information–movement couplings, she can now exploit the information that is available under a different set of constraints. That is to say, information (e.g., about time to contact) may be tuned to one movement (e.g., catching), but it may also be exploited for another movement (e.g., avoidance behaviour). Moreover, when the required information is absent, the learner may use different information (e.g., monocular or binocular information) for the same movement (e.g., punching a ball).

From this perspective, the learning process can be understood as a constraints-led approach in which the learner will go through the three stages (freezing, freeing, exploiting) every time a new coupling of information and movement emerges as a result of changing constraints.

Examples of the Freezing and Freeing of Perceptual Degrees of Freedom

In this section, the change in the use of the degrees of freedom is illustrated using the examples of one-handed catching, visual search strategies during goalkeeping, and eye movement practice that can lead to improvement in motor performance.

Training of One-Handed Catching: Freezing the Coupling

Savelsbergh and Whiting (1992) provided evidence of the freezing of information–movement couplings. In their experiment, relatively poor catchers (i.e., less than 20 percent successful catches) were trained under monocular and binocular viewing conditions to examine the effects of learning with binocular and monocular vision on putting the hand at the right place (that is, spatial prediction of the path of the ball). Earlier studies showed more spatial errors under the monocular condition than under the binocular condition.

This led Savelsbergh and Whiting (1992) to suggest that the superiority of performance in the binocular viewing condition might be attributed to the fact that participants simply have more experience with binocular viewing than they do with monocular viewing. In other words, the lack of experience and not the insufficiency of the monocular information was thought to have resulted in more spatial errors. To explore such a contention, it is necessary to allow subjects to spend enough time training under monocular viewing conditions to become attuned to the information available under these constraints (e.g., the rate of 'expansion' of the ball).

In the experiment, participants received training in a totally dark room with only the luminous ball visible. One group practised under the binocular condition and switched over to training under the monocular condition (binocular to monocular), whereas a second group followed the reverse path (monocular to binocular).

The findings showed a significant improvement in spatial prediction under the monocular condition up to the level reached under binocular conditions (see figure 13.2). The switch (see figure 13.3) indicates no significant improvement in spatial predictions when participants transferred from monocular to binocular training, whereas participants made more spatial errors when transferring from binocular to monocular training.

These findings demonstrate that under the monocular condition, catchers became attuned

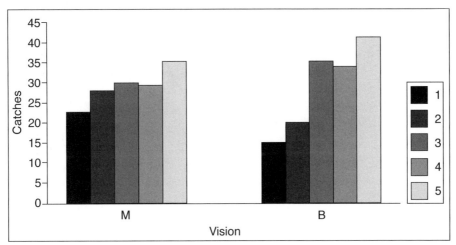

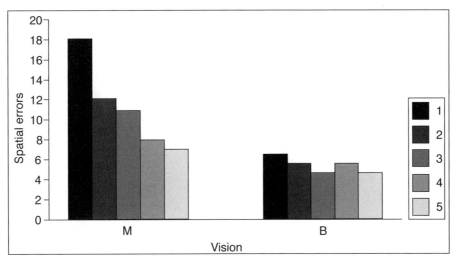

Figure 13.2 The results of the training for the monocular and binocular groups as a function of session with respect to successful catches (a) and spatial errors (b).

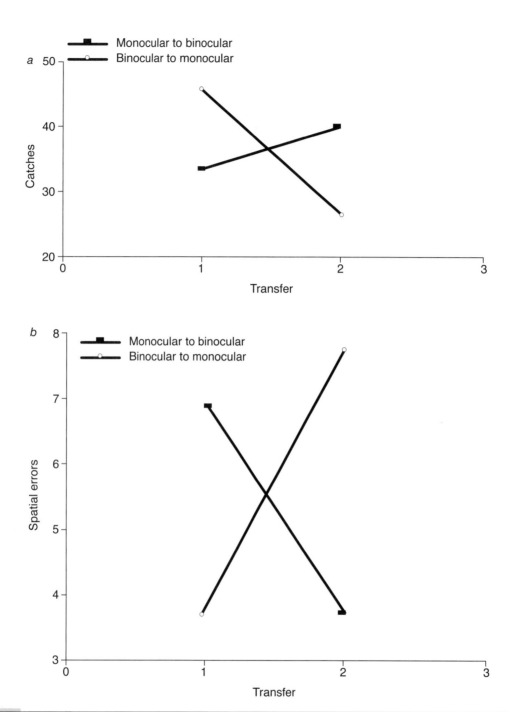

Figure 13.3 The transfer results from monocular to binocular, and the reverse, for successful catches (a) and spatial errors (b).

to the monocular information that was available and gained no added benefit from the additional binocular information (e.g., retinal disparity) when it became available. The performance increments in the monocular condition, attributed to a decrease in spatial errors, suggest that participants indeed used monocular information for their spatial predictions. In other words, the freezing between monocular

information and movement took place. The asymmetrical transfer effects are interesting, particularly because they show no adverse effects of training under monocular viewing when participants were subsequently required to perform and continue training under binocular viewing. In contrast, transfer from binocular to monocular viewing did produce adverse effects, apparently because a freezing of binocular information and movement had occurred, and, obviously, binocular information was no longer available under monocular conditions.

The findings suggest that subjects in the experimental monocular-to-binocular training group simply continued to make use of the monocular information that they had used during the first five sessions when they transferred from the monocular to binocular condition, or they transferred back to the use of binocular information because they had experienced this coupling previously. The latter would evidence freeing, or perhaps exploiting, the perceptual degrees of freedom (i.e., use whichever source is available and most optimal for the present situation). No new coupling was necessary. The catchers who practised under binocular viewing, however, showed a decrement in performance when they were required to perform under monocular viewing. This could be the result of (exclusively) making use of binocular spatial information (freezing of perceptual degrees of freedom) without being able to use monocular information for the catching movement.

Novices will make use of any source of information they happen to run into in the task and situation at hand, such as either monocular or binocular sources of information in the preceding catching example. This process by which information is selected is called 'attention' (Gibson, 1966). The process of coming to attend to the source of information that is *most useful* in the control of movement is commonly referred to as the 'education of attention'. Gibson described the process of education of attention as 'a greater noticing of the critical differences with less noticing of irrelevancies' and 'a progressive focusing or centering of the perceptual system' (Gibson, 1966, p. 52). In other words, the education of attention is the process by which one learns which sources of information to attend to in which situation and when to attend to these variables. As such, this process is inextricably linked to the proposal that perceptual learning should be considered a mastering of perceptual degrees of freedom. In the following section, we will describe another example that supports the idea that the education of attention can improve motor performance.

Differences in Attention Due to Differences in Expertise

In our laboratory we examined differences in the perceptual skills of goalkeepers during attempts to stop penalty kicks in soccer (Savelsbergh, Williams, van der Kamp & Ward, 2002; Savelsbergh, van der Kamp, Williams & Ward, 2005). Goalkeepers of different levels of expertise were required to move a joystick in response to penalty kick situations presented on a large screen. Participants had to anticipate the direction of each penalty kick quickly and accurately by moving the joystick as if to intercept the ball. If the joystick was positioned in the correct location at the right time (that is, before the ball crossed the goal line), the penalty was judged a successful save. It was found that the near-expert goalkeepers were generally more accurate in predicting the direction of the penalty kick, waited longer before initiating a response and made fewer corrective movements with the joystick as compared to novices.

We also assessed visual search behaviour using an eye movement registration system. Data presented in figures 13.4 and 13.5 are from the successful trials only—that is, those trials in which the penalties were stopped by the goalkeepers as indicated by the spatio-temporal pattern of the joystick movement.

Figure 13.4 shows that, with expertise, the number and duration of fixations change. There is change in visual search behaviour, indicated by a decrease in the number of fixations accompanied by longer fixation durations. This change in visual search may be interpreted as a freezing of the perceptual degrees of freedom, from being a complete novice to being a near-expert goalkeeper (or intermediate penalty stopper). In other words, the near-expert goalkeepers may attend longer to fewer sources of information, as would be found in the first phase of mastering the perceptual degrees of freedom. A similar interpretation comes to mind after inspection of figure 13.5.

Figure 13.5 depicts the regions of eye fixation on the opponent's body during the run-up to the ball (e.g., head, trunk, shoulder, kicking leg) as the percentage of time spent on each region for both the novices and the near-experts. On the one hand, the novices (see figure 13.5a) seem to 'visit' all possible regions of the opponent body; the percentages of time spent are quite evenly distributed over the regions (all between 5 and 12 percent, except the head area). The near-experts, however, show quite a different pattern (see figure 13.5b): They found the head, the kicking leg and the ball to be the most informative. A possible interpretation is that the novices' fixations still

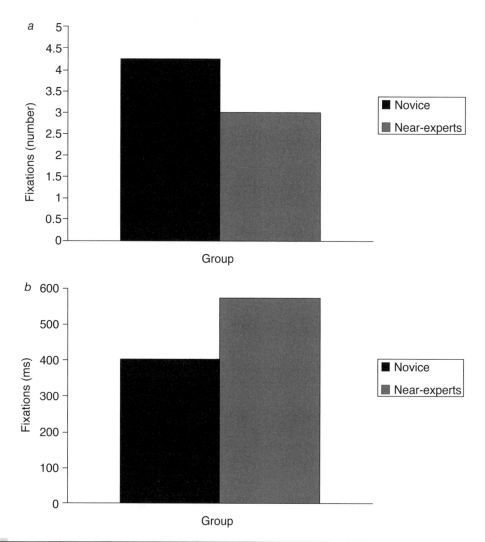

Figure 13.4 The number (a) and duration (b) of fixations as a function of level of expertise.

wander around without selectively attending to one of the possible sources of information. The near-expert goalkeepers have learned to attend to a few probably more informative regions. Nevertheless, these do not appear to be the most useful or indicative sources of information, given that even the near-experts goalkeepers stopped only about one third of the penalties. Again, this points to an initial freezing of the perceptual degrees of freedom.

Obviously, such an interpretation is quite speculative and needs careful scrutiny. It would predict, however, that because *expert* goalkeepers would have released or already exploited the degrees of freedom, they would visually search for more or more useful (i.e., specifying) regions of the opponent's body during the run-up to the ball (see, for example, Savelsbergh, van der Kamp, Williams & Ward, 2005).

In the next section, we illustrate the education of attention, the process by which one learns which sources of information to attend to in a locomotion task.

Direction of Attention Improves Movement Execution

Marple-Horvat and colleagues examined a test of functional mobility that demanded precise foot placement on a target at each step—that is, lights on the floor forming a walkway. The visually guided stepping was investigated by measuring the eye movements with a head-mounted eye-tracking system together with the footfall pattern. Healthy participants showed accurate stepping on the floor targets together with a clear pattern of saccadic eye movements. The eyes fixated on

a

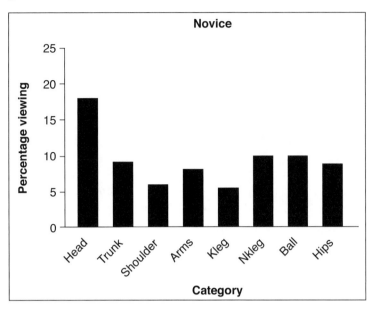

b

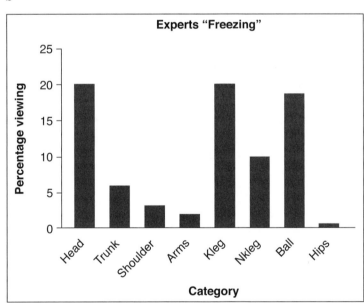

Figure 13.5 The percentage of eye fixation time spent on regions of the penalty taker's body during the run-up to the ball as a function of expert level: the novices (a) and the near-experts (b).

each target just before the foot was lifted. In other words, the gaze direction confirmed that these saccades serve to transfer the gaze between successive targets in the walkway sequence. Participants with cerebellar ataxia did not show these accurate anticipatory eye movements during walking (Crowdy, Hollands, Ferguson & Marple-Horvat, 2000; Marple-Horvat & Crowdy, 2005). Allowing these participants to practise their eye movements

by focusing on the targets without walking (that is, training their gaze to anticipate accurately) led to an improvement in their locomotion ability (Crowdy et al., 2002).

The key point here is that good eye movements, well coordinated with other actions, are key to performance. Bad eye movements result in bad performance; improving eye movements (by training or practice) improves performance.

Eye movements are key probably because looking at the right thing means that attention is on the right thing, but also because the brain seems to solve the problem of producing accurate visually guided behaviour by first moving the eyes and then moving the rest of the body, often in the same direction (Land & Hayhoe, 2001).

Implications for Application in Physical Education

The proposal that the road to perceptual expertise is characterised by a mastering of perceptual degrees of freedom has some important implications for the practice, or learning, process. Coaches, instructors and physical education teachers should consider the following points:

1. Visual information is lawfully related to events in the world. When a solid object (i.e., not changing in size) approaches a person, that object is optically expanding. If it is decreasing in size, then it must be moving away from the observer. Similarly, if you look ahead while walking, everything stationary in the environment optically expands. The centre of expansion corresponds to the direction in which you are heading. Thus, visual information, either produced by an object or by the observer himself, can 'tell' the observer how and when to move. However, in contrast to the lawful relationship between visual informa-

tion and occurrences in the world, the way the observer uses ('couples') the information to guide her movements has to be learned. In the case of a child heading a ball after a corner kick in soccer, for instance, the child must move at a precise time to successfully score a goal (Savelsbergh & van der Kamp, 2001). The information is available, but the child has to discover a successful information–movement coupling to score the goal. In most situations, an abundance of information is available; the challenge is to discover what best to use and how best to use it.

For example, to be successful in catching a fly ball in baseball, an outfielder must be at the right place at the right time (see the sidebar on this page for a description of how to catch a fly ball). Again, accurate perception is indispensable. Visual information about the ball flight trajectory 'tells' the child or the outfielder how and when to run. When a fielder tracks the ball, a moving image of the ball will form on the fielder's retina. Research has shown that the child should run until he cancels out the acceleration of the ball's image on the retina. If he manages this, he is sure to intercept the ball. Traditionally, psychologists would approach the problem of catching a fly ball as a computational problem. The catcher would need to work out how fast the ball is going, where it is, where it will be, how fast the catcher himself is running and where the interception point will be. However, the catcher is an active perceiver (i.e., is moving) and thereby actively altering the

CATCHING A FLY BALL

Chapman (1968) proposed that to intercept a baseball, the catcher has to run in such a way that he is zeroing out vertical optical acceleration. This hypothesis was empirically tested and supported by several researchers (e.g., Babler & Dannemiller, 1993; McBeath, Shaffer & Kaiser, 1995; McLeod & Dienes, 1993; Michaels & Oudejans, 1992). When a ball is travelling in the sagittal plane heading for the catcher's eye, the optical height of the ball on the image plane rises linearly during the ball's approach. Thus, when running for the ball, the catcher has only to keep the optical velocity constant. This strategy always brings the catcher to the interception point without the need to know the landing position in advance. Oudejans and colleagues had subjects running for balls and judging the catchability of approaching balls. They found that subjects used a strategy that is at least compatible with zeroing out optical vertical acceleration (also under monocular viewing), although conclusive statements with respect to the information regulating such a strategy could not be made. Results from an experiment in the dark with the approaching ball visible suggest that not only visual, but also extra-visual, information sources, such as the vestibular system and proprioception from ocular and neck muscles, might be involved (Oudejans, Michaels, Bakker & Davids, 1999).

visual information. All the catcher needs to do is advance when the ball is optically decelerating and retreat when the ball is optically accelerating. Few details of the ball's flight path need to be known. The catcher does not need to know how far to run or where exactly the ball will land. While running, the visual information will change and guide the catcher to the correct point. Hence, visual information specifies how to move, or, to put it differently, information and movement are tightly coupled. The catcher just needs to attune to this information.

2. The inseparability of perception and movement implies that *specificity of practice* is very important (Savelsbergh & van der Kamp, 2001). That is to say, what learners need to do during practice is couple information and movement. For instance, training should match the game situation as closely as possible. The visual information available during training should correspond with the information during the match. A gymnast who is used to performing in a relatively small sports hall with a low ceiling might have difficulty performing at the same level in a large sports hall with high ceilings because of the change in visual background information. In the case of teaching a child to head a ball, the training should involve running and jumping for the ball. Training involving just jumping from a standing position or tossing a ball to a stationary player is not likely to help the child get her head to the right place at the right time during the actual match. The key point here is that *the set of constraints* during training should be as similar as possible to those found in game situations. If they are not the same, then children may be forced to use different information to perform the task in the training and game situation and thus not be able to perform successfully during a game.

On the other hand, because information is redundant in most sporting situations, novices may develop strong suboptimal couplings with less useful information. To help learners discover the most optimal information–movement coupling(s) during practice sessions, a teacher or coach should carefully *design the practice environment* (a set of constraints) to create specific coupling of information and movement. In other words, a teacher has to create a training environment whereby the child is 'forced' to attune to a specific information–movement coupling. We call such an environment a *facilitative environment*

(see Buekers, 2000). In summary, the teacher or coach should make sure that the relevant information that is available during game situations is also available during practice, and vice versa. Furthermore, the teacher or coach can manipulate task constraints during practice to facilitate the discovery of preferred information–movement couplings (see also the case exercise at the end of this chapter).

3. Because information and movements are tightly coupled, changes in the available information will lead to changes in action and overall performance. Changes in action at the same time lead to perceptual changes. This means that a coach or teacher may be able to change movements by helping children attune to specific perceptual information.

4. It should be emphasised that the education of attention implied by our proposal concerning perceptual learning phases is not exclusively a matter of convergence to the most useful information sources. It also involves an accurate timing of attention to moments at which the most useful sources are available. Information is by definition dynamic rather than static; that is, it is defined by persistence under change (in time) (Gibson, 1979). As an example, research into gaze behaviour during dart throwing revealed that it is not just the duration of looking at the target but also the timing relative to the execution of the throwing movement (Vickers, Rodrigues & Edworthy, 2000) that resulted in successful performance. Oudejans, Van de Langenberg and Hutter (2002) recently corroborated this finding. They demonstrated that in the visual control of a basketball jump shot, the shooter must look at the target. This may occur early or late, depending on the style of shooting. In other words, not only the particular source of information, but also the moment at which it is available and thus detected, is a perceptual degree of freedom that may or may not be frozen, released or exploited.

5. The learning sequence is of great importance. From the present perspective, the processes of learning and development serve to establish and further refine information–movement couplings. We have argued that the learning process of coupling information to movement consists of a sequence of mutually overlapping phases—that is, freezing, freeing and exploiting perceptual information. Consider a youngster learning to contact and catch a ball. The approaching ball

provides a huge amount of visual information sources that can be used. This information 'tells' the catcher the amount of time until the ball reaches the hand, the speed and direction of the ball's approach, the distance between the ball and the hand and so on. The youngster faces the problem of finding out what information results in optimal performance—that is, positioning the hand correctly and absorbing the impact of the ball. Early in learning, the youngster selects one of multiple information sources that will do the job. At this stage the choice is unlikely to lead to optimal performance. For example, distance information can be used to position the hand more or less correctly. Practice under a similar set of circumstances will refine or increase the strength of the coupling between distance information and positioning the hand. However, for accurate ball control, distance information alone leads to errors. Under slightly different conditions (e.g., higher ball speeds), the coupling gets disrupted, leading to failure to control the ball (the hand is positioned late or the ball bounces from the hand).

After reaching a certain degree of stability in performance, the second learning phase starts, in which alternative information–movement couplings are explored (freeing). Practice will unavoidably take place under different circumstances at this phase. The child at this phase is forced to explore other sources of visual information as a means to control the ball; distance information alone appears insufficient. Eventually, this leads to a whole repertoire of information–movement couplings for the task of contacting and controlling a ball. As a result, the performance of the youngster becomes much more flexible. He learns to adapt to changing conditions (i.e., tunes in to different couplings) without having to start from scratch each time. The child is on his way to becoming a skilled performer.

Skilled performance is characterised by the ability not only to use different information couplings, but to exploit them as well. Because the youngster now has a whole repertoire available, she may use them for tasks other than controlling the ball. That is, information (e.g., about ball approach) may become coupled to the original movement (e.g., contacting and controlling a ball) but also to other movements in different conditions (e.g., hitting or heading). In short, the original information–movement coupling forms the foundation for new couplings to emerge.

In conclusion, particularly during the early phase of learning, specificity of practice is important because information is coupled only to movement under similar conditions. During later phases, however, practice should take place under more variable conditions so that the learner can form and further exploit a repertoire of couplings. What does this mean for the organisation of practice?

Summary

Remember the young tennis player, Rachel, from the introduction of this chapter? Her motor skill was clearly of a high level, and she was able to perform the required coordination patterns at a very high speed. However, you may have noted that she probably uses a limited number of perceptual degrees of freedom because she has practised intensively with balls being projected by a ball machine at a single, high velocity. As a consequence, she may have adapted a strategy for the timing of her movements relative to the movement of the ball that is effective only with balls of a constant velocity. She may time her stroke in relation to the location of the ball, initiating her downswing, for example, when the ball is at a particular distance. Alternatively, she might use the sound of the ball leaving the machine (a clearly audible 'thump' sound), starting her downswing when a specific amount of time has elapsed since the ball was ejected by the machine. For balls being delivered at varying velocities by a real opponent, a more useful source of information than elapsed time or distance information is velocity or time-to-contact information. To encourage Rachel to explore and discover these more effective sources of information, the coach should have her practise returning balls being projected at a wide range of velocities, or with balls being delivered by real opponents. Practising with real opponents has the additional benefit that Rachel might learn to pick up further predictive visual information from their behaviour, such as the direction of their gaze or the positioning of their feet. In summary, Rachel appears to have 'frozen out' potentially pertinent perceptual degrees of freedom and is relying on the use of a limited number of perceptual degrees of freedom. Her perceptual skills need to be developed so that she has a greater number of information–movement couplings at her disposal, thus enabling her to flexibly change between them when the situation changes.

With practise, motor coordination patterns emerge within organismic, environmental and task-related constraints. The same applies to perceptual-motor learning. Like the coupling between joint movements, the coupling between visual information and movement is not fixed. Similar to the motor domain, there is a redundancy of perceptual degrees of freedom. Multiple sources of (visual) information are available at any one time, and learners have to choose which sources to use and how to use them to guide their motor actions.

The perceptual-motor learning process typically involves the stages of *freezing, freeing* and *exploiting* perceptual degrees of freedom, meaning that a learner progresses from fully relying on being able to use only one source of information to being able to flexibly switch between information sources. The role of the teacher or coach is to design the learning environment in such a way that (1) information sources during practice resemble those in a game situation, but that (2) not all information sources are present at any one time, to encourage the learner to search for other sources of information that may be equally or more effective.

Review Questions

1. What are constraints? How do they influence the learning of a new motor skill?
2. What are the stages of perceptual learning? Name and describe each stage.
3. Why is it beneficial for an athlete to be able to exploit multiple perceptual degrees of freedom?
4. Could different athletes on the same team have different information–movement couplings?
5. What are the implications of the constraints-led perspective for the role of the coach or physical education teacher?

Critical Thinking Questions

Nine teaching or coaching situations (cases) follow these questions. Answer the questions for each case.

1. To improve the performance of the athlete, which desired outcome in terms of information–movement coupling or coordination pattern would you like the athlete to develop?
2. What are the relevant organismic, task and environmental (e.g., informational) constraints of this task?
3. How can the task constraints be altered or manipulated to encourage the athlete to pick up the required (visuo-)motor pattern? In other words, how would you design the learning environment? How would this change lead to the desired effect?

Case 1

Mark is an 18-year-old basketball player. He is tall and can jump like none of his teammates can. He has good tactical insight and is always at the right spot at the right time. Mark has one problem: His dribbling is clumsy and is not as smooth as you would like it to be. You have told him that he needs to use the tips of his fingers instead of the palms of his hands, but he is not taking your advice.

Case 2

You are faced with a team of eight-year-old soccer players. They are enthusiastic but have no clue about tactics. They all run after the ball from one end of the field to the other. They don't look around them to other players; they focus only on the ball. When a player takes possession of the ball, she runs with it across the field and tries to score the winning goal. You would like to increase the players' awareness of other players, improve their passing skills and ultimately improve their tactical insight.

Case 3

Your cricket team has a problem. When practising slip catching (i.e., catching the ball that is thrown by the bowler and subsequently bounces off the batsman's bat to the side), you see no problem; but when your team is in a real game situation, they don't seem to perform as well as they do under practice conditions. It is only since the team got promoted and started playing in front of big, cheering crowds that you have had this very specific problem. You have wondered whether it is 'nerves', but every other aspect of the game seems to be in order. Could it have anything to do with perception–action couplings?

Case 4

You have taught Sarah, a promising young soccer player, how to dribble with the ball. She has excellent control over the ball in practice drills, dribbling in a straight line or around cones. However, when she is in an actual game, she quickly loses the ball or gets into situations in which she is surrounded by opponents. Sarah and her teammates are quite frustrated about this and complain to you.

Case 5

Simon, a teammate of Mark's (case 1, basketball), is also not dribbling as well as he should be. You have noticed that he doesn't bend his legs enough. You have tried telling him so, but he believes he is bending his legs as far as he can. You of course know that that is not true and that he should bend them farther to really establish a good dribble technique. You know that this may feel strange and difficult at first, but that practising this will eventually pay off. You wonder how you can get through to him.

Case 6

You are coaching a soccer team of 15- to 16-year-old girls. They have learned to dribble in various drills during training and their technique is OK. However, they do not use dribbling in actual game situations. When they receive the ball, they quickly pass it on to a teammate (in this sense, they are quite the opposite of the team in case 2). You would like them to use their dribbling skills naturally in game situations.

Case 7

You are coaching a hockey team. You notice that the player with the biggest mouth is always getting the ball from the other players. Players decide too often to pass the ball to the person who is shouting for the ball. You believe the players should develop their visual skills. You want them to look around, see the other players' positions and pass to the person who is in the best tactical position.

Case 8

Your friend Tim, an accountant, has recently taken up golf in his spare time. He has difficulty with his technique, though. When you are out on the golf course with him one day, you notice that he is doing all the work with his arms. The rest of his body does not seem to be moving very much. You believe that he should turn his body in a synchronised manner with his arms. 'That's what I'm doing!' he tells you, laughing, after you have carefully tried telling him this. When he dries his hands with his towel to get a better grip on his club, an idea pops into your head: Could you possibly use the towel as a task constraint that would force Tim to adopt a better technique?

Case 9

Emilio is six years old. You are his physical education teacher. During a gymnastics session in which you practise the forward roll with him, you notice that he loses balance and falls sideways a lot. The cause is that he does not keep his legs together. With his feet pointing in different directions, quite asymmetrically, it is no wonder he loses balance halfway through the roll.

Key Terms

constraints—Boundaries that limit the number of coordination states available to a dynamical system at any instance of its search for an optimal state of organisation.

exploiting the degrees of freedom—The optimal use of the available degrees of freedom in the movement execution.

information–movement coupling—The inseparable relationship between the movement executed and the information used to execute that particular movement.

perceptual degrees of freedom—The number of possible visual information sources available.

References

Anderson, D.I. & Sidaway, B. (1994). Coordination changes associated with practice of a soccer kick. *Research Quarterly for Exercise and Sport, 65,* 93-99.

Babler, T.G. & Dannemiller, J.L. (1993). Role of image acceleration in judging landing location of free-falling projectiles. *Journal of Experimental Psychology: Human Perception and Performance, 19,* 15-31.

Bernstein, N.A. (1967). *The co-ordination and regulation of movements.* Oxford: Pergamon Press.

Buekers, M. (2000). Can we be so specific to claim that specificity is the solution for learning sport skills? *International Journal of Sport Psychology, 31,* 485-489.

Button, C., Bennett, S., Davids, K. & Stephenson, J. (1999). *The effects of practicing with a small, heavy soccer ball on the development of soccer related skills.* In proceedings of British Association of Sport and Exercise Sciences Annual Conference, Leeds Metropolitan University.

Chapman, G.J. (2003). *The effect of manipulating equipment constraints on the acquisition of lower limb interceptive actions.* England: Department of Sport Sciences, Manchester Metropolitan University [master thesis].

Chapman, S. (1968). Catching a baseball. *American Journal of Physics, 36,* 868-870.

Crowdy, K.A., Hollands, M.A., Ferguson, I.T. & Marple-Horvat, D.E. (2000). Evidence for interactive locomotor and oculomotor deficits in cerebellar patients during visually guided stepping. *Experimental Brain Research, 135,* 437-454.

Crowdy, K.A., Kaur-Mann, D., Cooper, H.L., Mansfield, A.G., Offord, J.L. & Marple-Horvat, D.E. (2002). Rehearsal by eye movement improves visuomotor performance in cerebellar patients. *Experimental Brain Research, 146,* 244-247.

Davids, K., Bennett, S.J., Kingsbury, D., Jolley, L. & Brain, T. (2000). Effects of postural constraints on children's catching behavior. *Research Quarterly for Exercise and Sport, 71,* 69-73.

Davids, K., Lees, A. & Burwitz, L. (2000). Understanding and measuring co-ordination and control in kicking skills in soccer: Implications for talent identification and skill acquisition. *Journal of Sport Sciences, 18,* 703-714.

Dudink, A.C.M. (1994). Birth date and sporting success. *Nature, 368,* 592.

Durand, M., Geoffroi, V., Varray, A. & Préfaut, C. (1994). Study of the energy correlates in the learning of a complex self-paced cyclical skill. *Human Movement Science, 13,* 785-799.

Fischman, M.G., Moore, J. & Steele, K. (1992). Children's one-handed catching as a function of age, gender, and ball location. *Research Quarterly for Exercise and Sport, 63,* 349-355.

Gallahue D.L., & Ozmun, J.C. (1995). *Understanding motor development: Infants, children, adolescents, adults.* Madison, WI: Brown & Benchmark.

Gibson, J.J. (1966). *The senses considered as perceptual systems.* Boston: Houghton Mifflin.

Gibson, J.J. (1979). *The ecological approach to visual perception.* Boston: Houghton Mifflin.

Heise, G.D., Caillouet, L., Cornwell, A. & Sidaway, B. (1996). *The exploitation of task characteristics during skill acquisition as reflected by temporal EMG changes.* Presented at the 20th annual meeting of the American Society of Biomechanics: Atlanta, Georgia.

Kugler, P.N., Kelso, J.A.S. & Turvey, M.T. (1982). On the control and coordination of naturally developing systems. In J.A.S. Kelso & J.E. Clark (Eds.), *The development of movement control and coordination* (pp. 5-78). New York: Wiley.

Land, M.F. & Hayhoe, M. (2001). In what ways do eye movements contribute to everyday activities? *Vision Research, 41,* 3559-3565.

Marple-Horvat, D.E. & Crowdy, K.A. (2005). Direct visualisation of gaze and hypometric saccades in cerebellar patients during visually guided stepping. *Gait and Posture, 21,* 39-47.

McBeath, M.K., Shaffer, D.M. & Kaiser, M.K. (1995). How baseball outfielders determine where to run to catch fly balls. *Science, 268,* 569-573.

McLeod, P. & Dienes, Z. (1993). Running to catch the ball. *Nature, 362,* 23.

Michaels, C.F. & Oudejans, R.R.D. (1992). The optics and actions of catching fly balls: Zeroing out optical acceleration. *Ecological Psychology, 4,* 199-222.

Newell, K.M. (1986). Constraints on the development of coordination. In M. Wade & H.T.A. Whiting (Eds.), *Motor development in children: Aspects of coordination and control* (pp. 341-360). Dordrecht, the Netherlands: Martinus Nijhoff.

Oudejans, R., Michaels, C.F., Bakker, F.C. & Davids, K. (1999). Shedding some light on catching in the dark: Perceptual mechanisms for catching fly balls. *Journal of Experimental Psychology: Human Perception and Performance, 25,* 531-542.

Oudejans, R.R.D., Van de Langenberg, R.W. & Hutter, R.I. (2002). Aiming at a far target under different viewing conditions: Visual control in basketball jump shooting. *Human Movement Science, 21,* 457-480.

Savelsbergh, G.J.P., Bennett, S.J., Angelakopoulos, G.T. & Davids, K. (2005). Perceptual-motor organization of children's catching behaviour under different postural constraints. *Neuroscience Letters, 373,* 153-158.

Savelsbergh, G.J.P. & van der Kamp, J. (1994). Effects of body orientation to gravity on infant reaching. *Journal of Experimental Child Psychology, 58,* 510-528.

Savelsbergh, G.J.P. & van der Kamp, J. (2000). Information in learning to co-ordinate and control movements: Is there a need for specificity of practice? *International Journal of Sport Psychology, 31,* 467-484.

Savelsbergh, G.J.P. & van der Kamp, J. (2001). Training must be as specific as possible, but not always! *Insight, 4,* 48-49.

Savelsbergh, G.J.P., van der Kamp, J., Williams, A.M. & Ward, P. (2005). Anticipation and visual search behaviour in expert soccer goalkeepers. *Ergonomics, 373,* 153-158.

Savelsbergh G.J.P. & Whiting, H.T.A. (1992). The acquisition of catching under monocular and binocular conditions. *Journal of Motor Behavior, 24,* 320-328.

Savelsbergh, G.J.P., Williams, A.M., van der Kamp, J. & Ward, P. (2002). Visual search, anticipation and expertise in soccer goalkeepers. *Journal of Sports Sciences, 20,* 279-287.

Strohmeyer, H.S., Williams, K. & Schaub-George, D. (1991). Developmental sequences for catching a small ball: A prelongitudinal screening. *Research Quarterly for Exercise and Sport, 62,* 257-266.

Thelen, E. & Fisher, D.M. (1983). The organization of spontaneous leg movements in newborn infants. *Journal of Motor Behavior, 15,* 353-377.

Thelen, E., Fischer, D.M. & Ridley-Johnson, R. (1984). The relationship between physical growth and newborn reflex. *Infant Behavior & Development, 7,* 479-493.

Thelen, E., Fisher, D.M., Ridley-Johnson, R. & Griffin, N. (1982). The effects of body build and arousal on newborn infant stepping. *Developmental Psychobiology, 15,* 447-453.

Van der Kamp, J., Savelsbergh, G.J.P. & Davis, W.E. (1998). Body-scaled ratio as control parameter for prehension of 5-9 year old children. *Developmental Psychobiology, 33,* 351-361.

Van der Kamp, J., Vereijken, B. & Savelsbergh, G.J.P. (1996). Physical and informational constraints in the coordination and control of human movement. *Corpus, Psyche et Societas, 3,* 102-118.

Vereijken, B., Van Emmerik, R.E.A., Whiting, H.T.A. & Newell, K.M. (1992). Free(z)ing degrees of freedom in motor learning. *Journal of Motor Behavior, 24,* 133-142.

Vereijken, B., Whiting, H.T.A. & Beek, W.J. (1992). A dynamical systems approach to skill acquisition. *Quarterly Journal of Experimental Psychology, 45A,* 323-344.

Vickers, J.N., Rodrigues, S.T. & Edworthy, G. (2000). Quiet eye and accuracy in the dart throw. *International Journal of Sports Vision, 6,* 30-36.

Wellman, B.L. (1937). Motor achievements of preschool children. *Childhood Education, 13,* 311-316.

Wickstrom, R.L. (1983). *Fundamental motor patterns.* Philadelphia: Lea & Febiger.

Wilson, G. (1999). The birthdate effect in school sports teams. *European Journal of Physical Education, 4*(2), 139-145.

Zelazo, P.R., Zelazo, N.A. & Kolb, S. (1972). "Walking" in the newborn. *Science, 177,* 1058-1059.

chapter fourteen

Core-Based Motor Teaching

Veikko Eloranta
Timo Jaakkola
University of Jyväskylä, Finland

After reading this chapter, you will be able to do the following:

- Define core-based motor teaching
- Describe the strategy of core-based motor teaching
- Understand why core-based motor teaching has been developed
- Understand the teaching method of positive cheating

The teaching of motor skills has traditionally been based on a behaviourist concept of learning. According to this concept, the teacher plans the contents and implementation of instruction based on target analysis. Teaching aims at concretely measurable target performances. The skills are divided into parts and developmental stages corresponding to the intermediate goals, which are then practised one at a time. The teacher attempts to teach one part at a time before moving to the next part. Teaching is based on the idea that the parts can be used to logically build a whole, which is the target skill. Teaching the skill of hurdling, for example, might progress as follows: (1) practising the hurdler position, (2) bringing the free leg over the hurdle from the side, (3) bringing the takeoff leg over the hurdle and (4) taking various steps over the hurdles. Only if there is time at the end of the lesson do students move on to the fifth stage, actually running over 'real' hurdles. Practice time during the lesson is cut short because the teacher spends a lot of time giving instructions for various skill parts, as well as demonstrating and arranging the setup to practise these skills. The time to practise and learn the actual skill (the whole) is very limited.

In this teacher-centred concept, the teacher's task is to transfer knowledge and skills to students and afterward monitor how much of the transferred knowledge has remained in their memory. The students' task is to receive knowledge, save it in their memory and repeat the taught skill. In this teacher-centred approach, the students' activity is perceived as computer-like information processing (e.g., Schmidt, 1988, 1991), which consists of three levels: receiving sensory information, processing information and producing a motor activity. To carry out information processing, students are believed to have more or less permanent motor programmes stored in their central nervous systems. Measuring learning according to the behaviourist approach is easy because the teacher only needs to evaluate whether the performance is successful, or correct. Teaching generally aims at creating one correct, flawless performance. Because other kinds of performances are considered incorrect, the teacher focuses on finding and correcting mistakes.

During the last few decades, education experts have become concerned about the ineffectiveness of the behaviourist teaching–learning process. In behaviourist education, only about 10 percent of the general learning is transferred to students' independent activities after school (Baldwin & Ford, 1988). As a result, both researchers and hands-on educators have become increasingly interested in individual learning. During the last decade, a teaching–learning process based on a modern, constructivist concept of learning has taken an increasingly prominent role (e.g., Bereiter, 1994; Biggs, 1996; Cobb, 1994; Driver, Asoko, Leach, Mortimer & Scott, 1994). In this concept, students are perceived as independently acting and thinking individuals who, with their own experiences and skills, build their individual learning entities. Researchers agree that students learn only what they process in their minds. The responsibility for learning has, therefore, switched from the teacher to the students, and the teaching–learning process has become, or is becoming, student centred.

For the modern teaching process to be effectively realised, students need to be perceived as humanly behaving, dynamic 'wholes', instead of as computer-like information processors. According to this ecological approach, because students function in constant interaction with their environment, they cannot arrive at solutions and performances expected by teachers using the information-processing method (Handford, Davids, Bennett & Button, 1997). Instead, different performance variations arise constantly, even if the dynamic system functions quite regularly as a whole. The principles of dynamism and reciprocity of the ecological approach consider perception to be more important than information processing. Practice means continually studying the perceptual-motor problem and looking for a solution within the framework of the task at hand. Depending on the individual, there are several strategies or routes in this approach for finding the 'right solution'. The traditional teaching approach, on the other hand, aims for the one and only right solution.

Contentwise, the ecological approach means practising the whole performance in an actual learning environment, which, in a constructive sense, gives students an opportunity for meaningful, independent practice (Davids, Handford & Williams, 1994; Handford et al., 1997; Vereijken & Bongaardt, 1999; see also chapter 13 in this volume). A **core-based motor teaching** model includes the ecological and constructivist concepts of learning. Its goal is to motivate students makes learning more effective and enlivens instruction—thereby providing each student with an independent strategy of learning to learn. Teaching is informed by the students' knowledge of, skill in and experiences of the task to be learned. Students progress by creating inner **images** corresponding to the learned skills. Unlike traditional technique instruction, the main emphasis is on helping students create and edit these inner images. For example, the image of water buoyancy in swimming is much more important for learning than is the technical performance of an arm stroke.

The core-based concept of teaching attempts to give students versatile preconditions for learning. This offers dynamic, flexibly processing individuals an opportunity to engage in meaningful reflection in an ecological environment. Students are offered numerous practice and problem-solving situations in which they can experience learning journeys that suit them personally. Core-based thinking emphasises a modern viewpoint in the teaching–learning process: Practice and the process are more important than the result of learning the skill itself.

Principles of Core-Based Motor Teaching

In the traditional, behaviourist learning concept, all students practise the same skills and progress along the same stereotypical development lines. The technical core parts of a particular skill determine every developmental stage or step of skill practice. According to the core-based concept, each student gets to practise according to his or her own skill level and motor activity habits. During the same lesson, students might practise very different performances at the same time. For example, a lesson in long jumping might include jumps from different heights to practise elementary jumping skills, jumps from a trampoline to soft mats to practise takeoff and flight skills and practise jumping steps and flight positions with various platforms and ropes. In addition, the lesson would include actual full-speed long jumping performances.

The core-based concept of teaching, as well as the core-based concept of motor learning that guides it (Eloranta, 2003b), are based on

biomechanical research results that describe motor behaviour (Eloranta, 1994, 1997, 2003a). According to the results, skill learning is guided along a path of previous experiences and learned skills. Therefore, a new skill includes features that are characteristic of an individual student's motor behaviour. A skill is not a traditionally perceived, separate and specific act that is added to the supply of previously learned skills during the learning process. As a result, it is natural that the **core-based motor learning** concept differs from the traditional concept of learning in terms of both goals and content. The following section will introduce the central concepts of core-based motor learning, an understanding of which is essential for an understanding of the core-based concept of teaching.

Concepts of Core-Based Motor Learning

According to the core-based motor teaching concept, the student's behaviour is guided and directed by three central systems: the 'inner boss', skill reflexes and perception cycles. The student's behaviour and learning are controlled by an **'inner boss'**, which is an unconscious proclivity to revert to previously learned behaviours. The inner boss uses and controls **skill reflexes,** which are automated motor performance techniques. The inner boss and the skill reflexes together form the motor skill structure that resists changes in the student's motor behaviour.

The actual learning process is guided by a **perception cycle.** The perception cycle is started when the student forms the first inner image of the task to be learned by means of the inner boss and the skill reflexes. This image directs the student's perceptions during the teaching situation (i.e., the practice). The changes that the student perceives in his performance formulate his image, which in turn changes his skill **schema,** and the new image that is formed starts the next round of the perception cycle. The slowness and difficulty in learning are due to the fact that the image is affected by the inner boss and the skill reflexes. Even when students try to learn new skills, the unconscious structures (inner boss and skill reflexes) prevent or slow down the learning process.

Unconscious Decision Maker: The Inner Boss

Through years of experiences and learning, each student has an in-built individual network of skills, a schematic structure also known as the inner boss. This holistically functioning structure—containing knowledge, skills, feelings and attitudes—determines, unbeknownst to the student, her unique way of behaving. The inner boss decides whether to start practising and how the practice will progress.

In ball games, for example, scoring is considered meaningful; it motivates players of all skill levels. During a traditional football lesson, students practise individual part performances or developmental stages, such as kicks or passes. Because they don't practise actually playing football and scoring, they often find the lesson meaningless. The teacher can lure the inner boss into playing football by starting the practice session with goal kicks because goal kicks are fun for students. In the future, making goals will continue to have a central role in developing the game and game understanding.

Motor Ability: The Skill Reflex

A skill reflex is a motor skill that has been learned to the point of becoming automatic. Hierarchically structured skill reflexes characterise all motor behaviour. A learned skill affects the coordination of another skill, and in this way, skill reflexes form the students' motor handwriting.

Figure 14.1 (showing antagonist muscle activity for a swimmer and a jumper) provides an example of the interference of muscle coordination. The antagonist muscle coordination of elite jumpers follows the normal jumping movement model. The antagonist muscles at the back of the thigh (semimembranosus/SM) and at the front of the leg (tibialis anterior/TA) are activated before the jump to cause stiffness in the agonist side and to protect the joints against injuries at the end of the jump (reciprocal reflex). The swimmers' intensive training produces muscle coordination that does not contain activity peaks of preparation and ending that are typical in jumping. Instead, the antagonist muscles act in the same way as the agonist muscles; that is, the highest activity is in the middle of the contact, which produces cocontraction. Because all the muscles are activated at the same time, the jump is ineffective.

A skill reflex always affects the learning of a new skill. It can make learning easier or harder. A good example of this is the effect the tennis stroke has on learning the squash stroke. Traditionally, the learning process starts off easily because both events are racket sports, in which estimating the ball's path, hand–eye coordination and the game idea are similar (positive transfer). As the skill level improves, technical differences between the two events become obvious. Because the movement paths and performance images of the tennis and squash stroke are opposite, the earlier learned skill might make the learning of the new skill

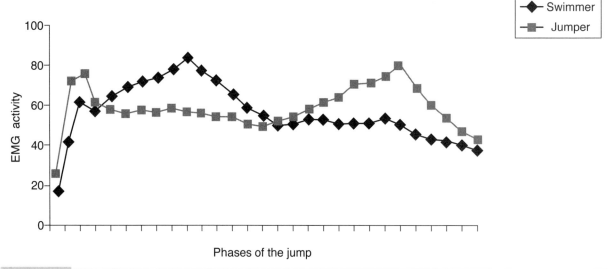

Figure 14.1 Electric activity of antagonist muscles for a swimmer and a jumper.

Adapted from V. Eloranta, 2003, "Influence of sports background on leg muscle coordination in vertical jumps," *Electromyography and Clinical Neurophysiology* 43: 141-156.

more difficult (negative transfer). In the end, the student has to relearn and repractise the squash technique from the beginning to form an image characteristic of the squash stroke. In core-based teaching, the important skill-specific technical content is included in practising from the very beginning of the learning process.

The skill reflex can be seen during a physical education class when, for example, swimmers or gymnasts, who tend to have extended joints (particularly in the ankles), play ball games (they execute skills, such as the tennis stroke, with extended joints). Similarly, ball players and track and field athletes have their joints flexed during swimming and gymnastics. During a jump, a football player might be heading the ball, a swimmer might be going through the motions of a starting dive and a wrestler might be throwing an opponent. A gymnast's straddle jump can be seen during hurdles running, and the muscle coordination of a high jumper stiffens his downhill skiing position. The skill reflexes of different athletes are made obvious in their physical education performances.

Learning Tool: The Perception Cycle

One of the central tasks of teaching is to guide students' attention and perception because perception is the basis and prerequisite of learning (see also chapter 13 in this volume). Students' schematic structures, with the help of images, maintain and guide their perception activities, allowing them to observe only stimuli that match their own skill levels.

In a learning situation, the student forms an image of the task based on her skill schema (see figure 14.2). The schema, which is based on her long-term experiences, is a concrete and three-dimensional conceptualisation that encompasses her knowledge, skills, feelings and attitudes (see the preceding discussion of the inner boss and the skill reflex). This is why the student is only able to produce images that match her skill level. Consequently, she is able to perceive only what matches her schema. By comparing the perceptions formed during the practice with her existing images, the student may produce a slightly different image and

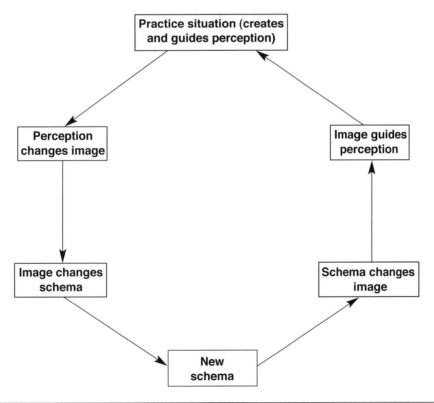

Figure 14.2 Perception cycle.

Adapted from V. Eloranta, 2003, "Who decides my motor learning?" Paper presented in the *Exercise and Psychological Well-Being* 4:12. (Viveca Symposium, Jyvaskyla).

schema, thus starting a new round of the perception cycle.

For example, beginning downhill skiers cannot feel the weight shift from ski to ski because they do not have a prior experience/schema/image of it. Similar problems might come about in dribbling a basketball or in choosing the takeoff foot in high jumping.

Core-based motor teaching attempts to guide learning according to the specific preconditions of learning (i.e., the inner boss, skill reflex and perception cycle). The preconditions create divergent demands and challenges for teaching, when compared to the traditional method. The student's inner boss dictates the terms for the progress of the teaching process. The skill reflexes regulate the development of the level and quality of the task to be learned. To facilitate students' development of their perceptual skills, the teacher must come up with concrete practice situations that take into account the students' individuality. Core-based motor teaching responds to these challenges with two central principles that guide and support learning. The following section gives a short conceptual description of these principles.

Concepts of Core-Based Motor Teaching

The aim of teaching is to get students to learn skills. Teaching should therefore be focused on the individual knowledge and skills of the student. In the core-based motor teaching concept, the student's **skill core** determines both the learning and the teaching strategy. Because the skill core is controlled by an unconscious system, the traditional rational teaching method does not work. Because the receiver in the teaching situation is a sensitive, unconsciously acting inner boss and not a rational student, teachers must use the core-based motor teaching concept to encourage the change-resisting unconscious system to practise and learn new performance models.

Content of Teaching: The Image

Students interpret the task to be learned individually and formulate an image in their learning and memory processes (Eloranta, 2003b). They start to investigate and construe their personal images, which are always whole and real performances.

This kind of performance is familiar and safe and thus meaningful to practise. Initially, the image is a very small and frail presentation of the actual performance to be learned. The goal of core-based teaching is to first awaken the image and then create a learning situation that helps the student expand his skill core within the limits of his own perception of reality.

For example, the starting point in teaching ball games to a student whose background is in swimming is the image that his swimming-oriented inner boss has formed of ball games. The teacher has to accept, and even compliment, the swimmer's image, even if his joint extensions and spatial orientation (characteristic of a swimmer) limit his specific ball skills. A swimmer may have difficulty catching, dribbling or passing a basketball or throwing it into the basket. Most of all, as a swimmer and an individual event athlete, he might have a hard time understanding and visualising the open action environment of basketball and the idea of team play.

Guidance of Learning: Positive Cheating

To be motivated, the unconscious inner boss that controls a student's motor behaviour requires positive experiences, meaningful learning and significant practice that is in line with the student's unique reality. Hence, guiding students onto individual learning paths requires a specific teaching method—**positive cheating** (see figure 14.3). The method attempts to steer students toward learning something new with exercises that motivate them and are familiar and sufficiently easy to bring about feelings of success. Cheating gradually directs practice toward the learning path of a new skill that is suitable for a particular student. Traditional didactic methods that target the conscious self do not necessarily reach the inner boss, which is flavoured with attitudes and reacts automatically.

For example, long jump practice can be started with any kind of jumping that motivates students. Jumping down from a platform to soft mats may provide pleasurable flight experiences and feelings of success that inspire their training motivation. Once the teacher has awakened the students' motivation, it will be much easier in the future to motivate them to practise skills that are closer to the actual long jumping performance.

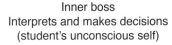

Inner boss
Interprets and makes decisions
(student's unconscious self)

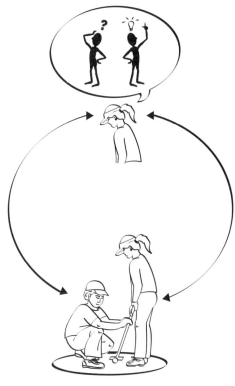

Teacher teaches   Student practices
(positive cheating)   (conscious self)

Figure 14.3   Core-based motor teaching–learning process.

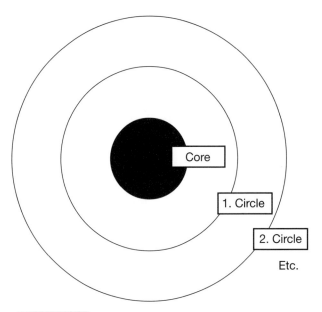

Figure 14.4   Core-based motor learning. The core is the pupil's schema of the skill to be learned. The surrounding circles are the learning circles.

Adapted from V. Eloranta, 2003, "Who decides my motor learning?" Paper presented in *Exercise and Psychological Well-Being* 4:12. (Viveca Symposium, Jyvaskyla).

Core-based motor teaching requires individual guidance for each student; motor skill practice is initiated and guided along a development path that is marked by each student's unique experience background (cf. Ausubel, 1968). This means that teaching emphasises students' unique learning processes by creating inspiring learning conditions. At the beginning of the process, a core-based teacher strives to find each student's skill core (see figure 14.4). During the process, the teacher attempts to expand and direct the core toward the skill to be learned (learning circles). Because learning is governed by each student's unconscious inner boss, all the solutions and implementations of the teaching–learning process need to use the methods of positive cheating in guiding the learning process (see figure 14.3). In reality, the core-based method puts the consciously acting student and teacher in a similar role. They work together to solve the problems that come up while the unconscious inner boss is practising and learning. Rather than having the role of an authority, boss or traditional teacher, the core-based teacher is more like an expert, helper and consultant.

Because student activity consists of experimenting and learning by doing, core-based teaching emphasises the significance of the learning environment. Appropriate environments are helpful in activating students and teaching them to learn (cf. Handford et al., 1997). The goal is to maximise the amount of meaningful activity in physical education settings. Similar teaching ideas have been presented, for example, under the guise of game-centred teaching (teaching games for understanding [TGFU]; Bunker & Thorpe, 1982; Launder, 2001) and gestalt theory (Singer, 1982). A core-based learning situation that activates all students gives the teacher time to act as an observer, allowing her to see the students as individuals with their own physical backgrounds and skills. This gives the teacher crucial information to use in guiding and assisting the students' unique learning processes. Perception skills allow the core-based teacher to reflect on the contents and progress of instruction and shape it to be appropriate to each student's skills and development.

In the core-based concept of teaching, the planning of activities is governed and guided by the students' preconditions to learn a new skill and the opportunities for personal interaction offered by the learning environment. Thereafter, planning considers the principles and possibilities of human movement. In the final stages of planning, teachers address technical principles such as the type of sport and the main technical points of the event. The order is almost opposite to that of traditional lesson planning, which principally begins by focusing on the main technical points of the event. Core-based teaching focuses on the motor learning of students, whereas traditional teaching emphasises specific skills and techniques (see the example of teaching the skill of hurdling during a traditional lesson in the introduction to this chapter).

Core-based motor teaching makes practice more effective than traditional teaching does, and it helps students in all stages of motor learning. Throughout the teaching–learning process, students are given space to practise different performances, test their limits and learn spontaneously. Unlike traditional teaching, core-based teaching has an especially strong effect at the cognitive stage. Traditional teachers introduce a new skill to students and try to get them to understand it. In core-based motor teaching, students start off by practising the core of the skill (in a reduced performance model) within the framework of their own schemata and resources—in a familiar environment, in a familiar activity and under facilitated and attractive conditions.

A physical education class conducted using the core-based method may seem chaotic to an outside observer because students are participating in activities of different levels and types throughout the teaching space. There are numerous performance stations, and all students are practising at the same time in their own learning environments with their own **assistant teachers** (see the section 'Using Assistant Teachers to Create an Effective Learning Environment' later in this chapter). Core-based teachers must be able to control chaos-like activity, while also reflecting on their observations. They must be able to observe simultaneous and different activities, have a comprehensive knowledge of human motor activity and have good interaction and human relations skills. A command of biomechanics and of different sport skills and events helps the teacher in thinking up

and building learning environments that fit the situation. In addition, core-based lessons include various assistive equipment that guide learning ('assistant teachers'), which not only encourage the students to practise, but also guide them to learn independently.

A professional core-based teacher, with a positively analytical eye, accepts many kinds of performances and allows the learning path of an individual student to be wide enough for practice and experimentation—in other words, for learning.

Learning Goals of Core-Based Motor Teaching

Learning is effective when the students themselves are active and prepared to practise. Because the inner boss of a student has to be enticed to practise a single task, or to learn in general, teaching has to be meaningful and motivating. The skill core offers a familiar and safe learning base for all kinds of practice. In this way the student understands what learning is about. A familiar performance idea allows the student to act spontaneously, experience how her logical skills develop and have strong and positive learning insights. By focusing on the student's spontaneous activity, the core-based motor teaching concept aims toward a wider objective in learning: learning to learn. Core-based teaching includes three learning goals: logical learning, discovery learning and deep learning.

Logical Learning

Instruction attempts to maximise learning by teaching students to act logically. Logical activity and long-range self-evaluation skills develop through all practice, with the skill core expanding from a basic level to a level of more detailed coordination. The preconditions for spontaneous learning to learn are created when students practise a performance in a meaningful way, understanding its basic idea and experiencing feelings of success, development and skill. The students develop and learn to come up with appropriately difficult challenges for themselves (cf. mind-map, portfolio; see Valencia, 1990).

Discovery Learning

Learning that is structured around a skill core grows like a snowball. On the other hand, growth is slow in routine-like learning because learning is based on repetition. It could be compared to the familiar biological concept of adaptation, which states that the lower brain centres are stimulated by the repetitions. Initiating discovery learning calls for waking up the emotional brain and offering motivation and appropriate learning challenges. A mechanism to speed up discovery learning (or spontaneous learning) is found in the nervous networks of the higher brain centres: The emotional brain stimulates the centres of thinking, reasoning and creating into reciprocal relationships (Brooks, 1986). Students continuously define their tasks as problems at higher and higher skill levels (Bereiter & Scardamalia, 1993). While helping students to open up new image windows, core-based motor teaching also develops their creative capabilities.

Deep Learning

The aim of teaching is to have students remember the skills they have learned when they are active later on. Meaningful learning based on experiences of success includes strong positive emotional reactions and experiences. In addition, learning is always task and situation bound, which strengthens the image in the brain. A learned or successful performance remains in students' memories because they have produced it themselves and because the event is important to them. They save the experience in their long-term memory in an episode-like manner—empirically—and in this way the saved performance image is comprehensive. It includes their successes and failures, their knowledge of circumstances and their own reactions. Practice is shaped into a 'story' of learning to learn, made up of different situations in which each skill image is related to the total picture. Therefore, teaching should focus on giving all students plenty of experiences of success (see Brooks, 1986).

Characteristics of Core-Based Motor Teaching

According to core-based thinking, physical education should activate students and promote learn-

ing. The teacher has to pay special attention to each student's activity level and preconditions to learn on the one hand, and to the content of practice and the learning environments that affect learning opportunities on the other hand. This requires constant observation as well as evaluation, acceptance and creation of different performance options. It also requires constant interaction with students as the teacher guides individual learning. Detailed management of the lesson takes less of the teacher's time in core-based teaching than it does in traditional teaching. Core-based teaching lets the teacher use the many-sided professional skills acquired during training in a comprehensive and challenging manner. In the following sections we present the principles by which core-based motor teaching can be recognised.

Generating Student Motivation

Motivation regulates people's behaviour and learning (Deci & Ryan, 2000). Without motivation, students will not learn motor skills, let alone acquire a lifestyle of physical activity. Core-based motor teaching focuses on individual student skills, previous positive experiences and optimal learning experiences. These three areas are the crucial starting point of the learning process: motivating and inspiring experimentation and practice.

The core-based teacher aims to make the activity so motivating and meaningful for the students that their intrinsic motivation starts to grow. At its best, as the activity progresses, the intrinsic

Core-based teaching requires constant interaction with students as the teacher guides individual learning.
© Bob Vincke.

motivation starts to feed itself. When this happens, the activity itself offers students of all skill levels the opportunity to participate, succeed and develop their skills. According to motivation literature, factors that affect our intrinsic motivation are perceived autonomy, competence and social relatedness (Deci & Ryan, 1985). Therefore, the starting point of the core-based method is activities and exercises that interest students. During the early phases of learning, it is not important whether practice progresses according to the technical phases of the skill to be learned. The main goal is to motivate students to practise. Once the motivation is born, the teacher has a much better chance of directing activities toward the core points of the skill and other lesson goals.

Student motivation is most likely to be born when the teacher creates a positive, learning-oriented atmosphere that supports individual learning. A crucial motivation-building aspect is that all participants have the opportunity to try out and practise the task. A motivation climate study has shown that a task-involving motivational climate is positively related to the intrinsic motivation of participants (Duda, 2001; Duda & Whitehead, 1998; see also chapter 1 in this edition). Core-based teaching includes the features of a task-involving motivational climate (Epstein, 1988). Tasks that are differentiated according to each student's skill level, a democratic teacher and support of each participant's own decision making are emphasised in all activities. Giving feedback and evaluating the activity are based on individualism and the effort that each student puts forth. The use of time in core-based activities is flexible, allowing students to practise a certain task as long as they find necessary. Teaching does not recognise faulty performances. When exercises promote learning, unnecessary or faulty performances or techniques, being unsubstantiated, can be forgotten.

In core-based teaching, feelings of success and challenges that are individually scaled (problem-based learning) strengthen student motivation, and the resulting positive learning climate increases the amount of practice—and as a result, the amount of learning.

Maximising the Amount of Activity and Practice

In the behaviouristic teacher-centred approach, the teacher describes ('gives a lecture on') the

technical core points of the skill to be learned at the beginning of the lesson. In javelin throwing, for example, a teacher may lecture on five or six core skills. After this, the teacher demonstrates the model performance himself or lets a skilful student do it. The demonstration might be given from several angles. During the lecture and demonstration, the students stand in a line and watch. After this, the teacher divides the students around the available space to practise the skill that was just taught. In most cases, students take turns practising with the few available pieces of equipment. Practice continues until the teacher calls everyone in to make performance corrections or start teaching a new skill by 'lecturing and demonstrating'. This cycle is repeated over and over again. The lesson includes a lot of waiting and passive time, and teaching is done on the teacher's terms. The teacher is very busy throughout the lesson, managing and organising student activities.

Because physical activity is learned by doing, core-based motor teaching attempts to maximise the amount of activity (e.g. Kolb, 1984; Launder, 2001). This means that the teacher does not use much time instructing, showing or organising. The time that is usually spent in these activities is shortened in two ways. First, because students are practising the same familiar core content (smaller or larger core entities), instruction does not take much time after the initial start-up. As soon as the learning process is initiated, students start practising the new skill based on their individual starting points; therefore, traditional technical

Core-based teaching is a departure from the traditional method of lecturing and demonstrating.
© Bob Vincke.

instruction is not needed. The teacher's instructions in core-based motor teaching are primarily directed at the environment and less at the technical details of the performance (cf. Handford et al., 1997). As a matter of fact, once the learning process has started, students themselves come up with their next exercises. Second, because a core-based lesson does not break the skill down into parts, students can spend more time participating in the actual activity.

In core-based motor teaching, the entire learning environment is being effectively used because it is full of performance stations. Abundant equipment allows students to practise tasks that are appropriate for them and to develop and change the tasks as needed. An effective learning environment offers plenty of practice opportunities for students at different skill levels. Core-based motor teaching attempts to create a differentiated learning environment that activates everyone. Students need to be free to explore opportunities to be active rather than be inhibited by artificial limits, such as technical step-by-step instructions (cf. Handford et al., 1997). An attractive environment that encourages exploration guides students toward spontaneous perceptual-motor learning.

A proper warm-up is important in maximising the amount of student activity. In a core-based physical education lesson, students begin practising the actual skill during the warm-up, which should offer plenty of performance repetitions. A good warm-up in a javelin-throwing lesson includes a number of throws with different kinds of equipment. The throwing theme during the warm-up should be enjoyable to the students; for example, it can be in the form of play and games.

Using Assistant Teachers to Create an Effective Learning Environment

In the model of core-based motor teaching, the teacher complements the practice-oriented learning environment with 'assistant teachers', which are usually concrete apparatus and equipment that arouse and guide the students' images. The positive effect of assistant teachers on learning is very strong; it might even be stronger than the teacher's instructional effect because assistant teachers aim at awakening and motivating spontaneous activity by the learners.

Concrete assistant teachers can be built with platforms, obstacles, rings, tape, lines or chalk. They facilitate, vary and guide the performance, making learning more efficient. With assistant teachers, the teacher can vary the possibilities and boundaries offered by the environment and the task, thereby allowing for the cultivation of the students' images in a perceptual-motor exploration environment (cf. Handford et al., 1997). Assistant teachers assist the teacher, as the name suggests, and guide students along their individual learning paths. For example, pieces of tape and plastic give feedback about the rhythm of running the hurdles, hurdling technique and the fluency of running. Students get to evaluate their images (performances) by using both internal and external senses, and at the same time build their own learning toward a goal. Via self-evaluation, assistant teachers give students information about the success of their performance—and simultaneously change their images and improve their skills. Practice becomes a personal and many-sided individual process. The use of concrete assistant teachers increases the imagination and inventiveness of students, which enables the development of imaginary assistant teachers. For example, to learn the rhythm of cross-country skiing, one could create an image of the rhythm of a waltz or of a boat rocking on the waves.

Assistant teachers convert practice and learning into exciting experimentation, spontaneous adventure and positive experiences. Only the imaginations of the teacher and students limit the possibilities of using assistant teachers.

For example, many kinds of equipment that make swimming easier and develop the imagination have been invented to practise swimming. Concrete assistant teachers in swimming include equipment such as buoys, flippers and boards, which allow even the less skilled students to be successful in learning the core skill of swimming—that is, gliding. Furthermore, these kinds of equipment help make sure that the students are performing the technique correctly. As a result, the teacher does not need to give feedback on each individual performance; she can instead focus on her actual task, which is guiding learning.

Expanding the Skill Core of Students

Teaching has traditionally been built on breaking skills down into parts to support the core technique of a specific event. In core-based motor teaching, students carry out actual—or real—performances throughout the learning process, but always at their own level of readiness.

The technical starting point of the core-based approach is practising the most essential part of the skill—the substantive core. Examples of cores are the flow of motion in throwing, gliding in swimming and game understanding in ball games.

The core of practice does not change, even if the skill level of the group changes—for example, from primary school students to elite athletes. The students' skill levels or skill cores determine how many challenges or core circles can be built around the substantive core (see figure 14.4). As many exercises as necessary can be built inside the core circle. Because small qualitative challenges make practice versatile and interesting, student-created exercises serve quite well in core-based teaching. Students can move between core circles during practice, and in case of regression, they can also move back toward the core. If reviewing a lower-level core circle seems meaningful to a student, the lesson is still successful because the student is practising and repeating the skill core that is necessary for learning.

A core-based physical education lesson includes a lot of practice and development of the essential content for the target task. The motivation levels is high because students get to do what they can, which is practise according to their own levels of readiness. In this way, by following the constructivist concept of learning, students find it easy to construct their own learning. New learning tasks are necessarily built on top of old, familiar, already existing, and learned knowledge structures. This is the construction of inner models or schemata, which then further direct the learning process (Piaget, 1962).

A common view of motor behaviour is based on the permanence and specialisation of motor skills. According to many studies, there is hardly any correlation or transfer between two skills (e.g., Schmidt, 1988). The model of core-based motor teaching is based on modern knowledge about motor behaviour, according to which skills are not, after all, independent and unchanging. Instead, certain kinds of long-term practice will change a person's physical activity behaviour (Eloranta, 2003a). Proponents of the model believe that intensive, event-specific training (e.g., swimming or football) that has lasted for years will change the coordination of muscle activity for other events. A skill reflex or automatic motor skill has been built (Eloranta, 1997, 2003a). In practice, this kind of a change means that a swimmer will use the muscle coordination of swimming during jumping practice (see figure 14.1). When compared to the 'normal' muscle coordination of jumping, the swimmer has an activity model whose central features are simultaneous activity of agonist and antagonist muscles, as well as lack of sequential activity flow and reciprocal innervation. Her individual motor handwriting is characterised by the innervation of swimming (Eloranta, 2003a). Because the motor handwriting, under the authority of the student's inner boss, affects the learning of new skills, it is necessary to emphasise the differentiation of students and the individual guidance of learning at all skill levels—that is, core-based motor teaching (cf. core-based motor learning, Eloranta, 2003b).

Practising the Whole Performance

In traditional teaching, the whole is developed by practising parts that represent the main technical points (see Magill, 2004; Schmidt & Lee, 2005; also, the hurdling example in the introduction to this chapter). In core-based teaching, students practise the whole performance from the start because individual students always perceive the schema corresponding to their own skill level as a whole performance (Brooks, 1986; Vereijken & Bongaardt, 1999). A schema that is saved in memory is based on each student's own experiences, perceptions, interpretations and personally meaningful memories. It is part of a hierarchical entity of nervous networks, intertwined in individually unique ways. A student's schema is marked by his own creation, and, as a result, all of his actions are bound up together. Therefore, the image based on the schema, created by the individual student, is a unique whole that is concrete and three-dimensional and contains information, skills and feelings.

During the early stages of instruction, students perform the whole skill using a reduced performance model that is at the level of their individual image. The standard of the performance or technique is purposefully set so low that even the least skilled students have a chance to succeed.

For example, tennis practice could be started with simple rallying in the service area. Students use a reduced forehand stroke (short lever; light, short racket) to hit the ball over the net to their partners. The goal is to perform as many repetitions as possible, allowing one or more bounces.

Students are immediately provided an image of the whole performance that is easy to accept. At the same time, they find the task meaningful and important because it is an event-specific task, yet easy enough to carry out successfully considering each student's schematic limits.

According to the cognitive concept of learning, meaningful practice is a precondition for learning (Ausubel, 1968). Learning develops with the help of a perception cycle (see figure 14.2). A student first performs a new task based on an image born out of her skill schema. During the performance she perceives and compares her perceptions to this image. A changed image initiates the correction of the schema, which then produces a new image, and so forth (Neisser, 1976; Piaget, 1962). After each turn of the perception cycle, the student can open a new learning window only slightly. She can only perceive with image windows that are already available to her. The target of teaching is, with the help of a versatile learning environment, to develop the student's readiness to open the new windows that are necessary for continued learning.

At the beginning of learning ball games, students are motivated to be actually playing. Therefore, the lesson should focus on teaching the whole: guiding the skill of playing and developing game understanding (practising the whole). From the start of the learning process, the teacher should attempt to provide students with the core aspect of ball games, which is game understanding, or the game idea. Later, if they wish to become better players, students will find the desire to develop their technical skills to a higher skill level (practising skill parts). With better technical skills, they can further develop their actual playing to be more effective (practising the whole). In general, once practice of the whole performance has developed the scheme of playing sufficiently, both part and whole practice can be included in the learning process, as needed.

Positive Cheating of the Student's Unconscious Self

Positive cheating motivates students to practise and develop toward a target performance on their own terms. Cheating combines the technical core content of the skill to be learned and each student's skill core. The technical core is the event's 'idea' that is a necessary and central part of the performance, thereby representing the teacher's target image (e.g., flow of motion in throwing, gliding in swimming and game understanding in ball games). The content of teaching comprises the tasks and exercises by which the teacher offers the contents of the technical core to the students within the limits of their skill capacity on the one hand, and in a way that is meaningful and motivating for them on the other hand (e.g., throwing a ball into a goal, diving for objects from the bottom of a pool). By engaging in positive cheating, the teacher attempts to change behaviours that are managed by the students' inner boss and that resist change (see figure 14.3). Learning is more likely to be initiated if the students themselves think up appropriate exercises. The teacher tries to guide and activate the students—with the help of an attractive learning environment and 'assistant teachers'—toward independent work. The students' main focus is on pleasant and motivating activity, and not on practising teacher-directed technical skills. Once the students realise the point of the task, they might get enthusiastic about cultivating the learning environment to be appropriately challenging for them as individuals (e.g., throwing into a smaller goal or basket or into a moving target).

Traditional teacher-centred teaching attempts to change the student's image of the skill externally, with factual, information-based teaching material about the event. In positive cheating, images corresponding to the student's skill level determine the teaching material.

The true core of core-based teaching to be developed and guided is the student's image of the subject to be taught. In simple terms, the teaching material is in the student's head and not in a sports manual. Teaching attempts to expand and develop the image inside the student's head toward the learning objective.

In traditional teaching, the teacher usually does not accept alternative performance models created by the students because they are different from his own image. The teacher's image is of a correct, faultless performance; other kinds of performances are, therefore, wrong. Traditional teaching aims at finding and correcting mistakes. A teacher is considered an expert if he has a good eye for mistakes. In the background is the general view that people learn from their mistakes. A core-based teacher, on the other hand, accepts different student performances at different skill levels. The teacher encourages and persuades the students to experiment with different performances, have positive experiences, enjoy the practice and activate spontaneous physical activity patterns.

Summary

Core-based motor teaching is a teaching model that motivates students, makes learning more effective and enlivens instruction—thereby providing each student with an independent strategy of learning to learn. The core of teaching is formed by the students' knowledge of, skills in, and experiences of the task to be learned. Learning progresses through images corresponding to the learned skills. Unlike in traditional instruction, the main emphasis of core-based motor teaching is on creating and editing images and guiding the unconscious inner boss, which requires positive experiences, meaningful learning and significant practice that are in line with each student's own reality. Guiding students onto individual learning paths requires a specific teaching method—positive cheating. The method attempts to steer students toward learning something new with exercises that motivate them and are familiar and sufficiently easy to bring about feelings of success. Cheating gradually directs practice toward the learning path of a new skill that is suitable for a particular student. Students are offered numerous practice and problem-solving situations in which they can experience learning journeys that suit them personally. Core-based thinking emphasises a modern viewpoint in the teaching–learning process: Practice and the process are more important than the result of learning—the skill itself.

Review Questions

1. What is the difference between traditional and core-based teaching methods?
2. Why is the perception cycle so important in core-based motor teaching?
3. How can a physical education teacher maximise practice time?
4. What can you do to increase the kind of practice that results in learning?
5. Why should teachers use positive cheating?
6. Why does a teacher not need to react to faulty performances in core-based teaching?

Critical Thinking Questions

1. How can a teacher plan a lesson according to the principle of whole performance?
2. How can the student's learning process be guided by positive cheating?

Key Terms

assistant teachers—Equipment that guides learning.

core-based motor learning—A style of learning that develops along a path of previous experiences and learned skills.

core-based motor teaching—A style of teaching that guides skill learning along a path of previous experiences and learned skills.

image—A picture in one's mind of a task to be performed.

inner boss—An unconscious proclivity to revert to previously learned behaviours.

perception cycle—A tool through which learning develops.

positive cheating—A teaching method that steers the unconscious inner boss toward learning.

schema—A three-dimensional inner conceptualisation that encompasses one's knowledge, skills, experiences and attitudes.

skill core—A student's interpretion of the task to be learned.

skill reflex—A motor skill that has been learned to the point of becoming automatic.

References

Ausubel, D. (1968). *Educational psychology: A cognitive view.* New York: Holt, Rinehart & Winston.

Baldwin, T.T. & Ford, J.K. (1988). Transfer of training: A review and directions for future research. *Personnel Psychology, 41*(1), 63-105.

Bereiter, C. (1994). Constructivism, socioculturalism, and Popper's world 3. *Educational Researcher, 23,* 21-23.

Bereiter, C. & Scardamalia, M. (1993). *Surpassing ourselves: An inquiry into the nature of expertise.* Chicago: Open Court.

Biggs, J. (1996). Enhancing teaching through constructive alignment. *Higher Education, 32,* 347-364.

Brooks, V.B. (1986). *The neural basis of motor control.* Oxford: Oxford University Press.

Bunker, D. & Thorpe, R. (1982). A model for the teaching of games in the secondary school. *Bulletin of Physical Education, 10,* 9-16.

Cobb, P. (1994). Where is the mind? Constructivist and sociocultural perspectives on mathematical development. *Educational Researcher, 23,* 13-20.

Davids, K., Handford, G. & Williams, M. (1994). The natural physical alternative to cognitive theories of motor behaviour: An invitation for interdisciplinary research in sport science? *Journal of Sports Sciences, 12,* 495-528.

Deci, E.L. & Ryan, R.M. (1985). *Intrinsic motivation and self-determination in human behaviour.* New York: Plenum Press.

Deci, E.L. & Ryan, R.M. (2000). The "what" and "why" of goal pursuits: Human needs and the self-determination of behaviour. *Psychological Inquiry, 11,* 227-268.

Driver, R., Asoko, H., Leach, J., Mortimer, E. & Scott, P. (1994). Constructing scientific knowledge in the classroom. *Educational Researcher, 23,* 5-12.

Duda, J.L. (2001). Goal perspective research in sport: Pushing the boundaries and clarifying some misunderstandings. In G.C. Roberts (Ed.), *Advances in motivation in sport and exercise* (pp. 129-182). Champaign, IL: Human Kinetics.

Duda, J.L. & Whitehead, J. (1998). Measurement of goal perspectives in the physical domain. In J.L. Duda (Ed.), *Advances in sport and exercise psychology measurement* (pp. 21-48). Morgantown, WV: Fitness Information Technology.

Eloranta, V. (1994). Comparison of static muscle coordination in two different movement models. *Electromyography and Clinical Neurophysiology, 34,* 165-169.

Eloranta, V. (1997). Programming leg muscle activity in vertical jumps. *Coaching and Sport Science Journal, 2*(3), 17-28.

Eloranta, V. (2003a). Influence of sports background on leg muscle coordination in vertical jumps. *Electromyography and Clinical Neurophysiology, 43,* 141-156.

Eloranta, V. (2003b, December 4). *Who decides my motor learning?* Paper presented at the Exercise and Psychological Well-Being—Viveca Symposium, Jyväskylä, Finland.

Epstein, J.L. (1988). Family structures and student motivation: A developmental perspective. In C. Ames & R. Ames (Eds.), *Research on motivation in education* (pp. 13, 259-295). San Diego, CA: Academic Press.

Fitts, P.M. & Posner, M.I. (1967). *Human performance.* Belmont, CA: Brooks-Cole.

Handford, G., Davids, K., Bennett, S. & Button, C. (1997). Skill acquisition in sport: Some applications of an evolving practice ecology. *Journal of Sports Science, 15,* 621-640.

Kolb, D.A. (1984). *Experimental learning: Experience as a source of learning and development.* Englewood Cliffs, NJ: Prentice Hall.

Launder, A.G. (2001). *Play practice.* Champaign, IL: Human Kinetics.

Magill, R.A. (2004). *Motor learning concepts and applications.* Dubuque, IA: McGraw-Hill.

Neisser, U. (1976). *Cognition and reality.* San Francisco: Freeman.

Piaget, J. (1962). *Play, dreams and imitation in childhood.* London: Routledge & Kegan Paul.

Prawatt, R.S. (1996). Constructivisms, modern and postmodern. *Educational Psychologist, 31,* 215-225.

Schmidt, R.A. (1988). *Motor learning and performance: A behavioural emphasis.* Champaign, IL: Human Kinetics.

Schmidt, R.A. (1991). *Motor learning and performance: From principles to practice.* Champaign, IL: Human Kinetics.

Schmidt, R.A. & Lee, T.D. (2005). *Motor control and learning: A behavioral emphasis.* Champaign, IL: Human Kinetics.

Singer, R.N. (1982). *Motor learning and human performance.* New York: Macmillan.

Valencia, S. (1990). A portfolio approach to classroom reading assessment: The whys, whats, and hows. *The Reading Teacher, 43*(4), 338-340.

Vereijken, B. & Bongaardt, R. (1999). Complex motor skill acquisition. In Y.V. Auweele, F. Bakker, S. Biddle, M. Durant & R. Seiler (Eds.), *Psychology for physical educators* (pp. 233-256). Champaign, IL: Human Kinetics.

epilogue

A review of current general discussions about physical education reveals differences of opinion regarding what constitutes best practice. This book is a compilation of ideas from a number of authors representing various disciplines and several European countries. However, despite differences, all authors reflect the same opinion about the main directions for physical education in the 21st century:

1. Physical education curricula should be designed to increase the likelihood of enhancing pupils' physical and psychosocial well-being throughout their lives.

2. Physical education curricula on each level (national, local, classroom) should be balanced to function in the following educational domains: physical activity, motor development, health and fitness, the development of positive self-perceptions and social skills. Professional training programmes should prepare future teachers to be effective in all these domains.

We believe that the application of these themes would constitute a new approach to physical education in many countries, and we are aware that such a shift is no simple task. It was essential to all of us involved in the writing of this textbook, as well as in the first edition of it, that the ideas and concepts discussed here be available in a concrete and practical way so that physical educators could use them in their educational practice. It was also our intention to promote a more systematic examination of psychology as it relates to physical education.

With the preceding issues in mind, we end this book with our sights set firmly on the future. What will physical educators be able to do with what they have learned from this book, and which topics will be important to include in future research into the psychology of physical education? To get some answers to these questions, the authors of the chapters in this book were invited to give their comments after they had submitted their texts. We wanted to know where they thought research priorities should be in the near future regarding the field of the psychology of physical education. Additionally, they gave ideas about what would help or hinder physical educators in implementing the practical recommendations presented in this book. The comments and feedback we received from the authors of this edition of the text, in addition to the comments from the authors of the first edition, constituted the raw material for this epilogue. The discussion here is not meant to be exhaustive, and it is not a summary or review of the rich ideas found in the chapters. We wish only to touch on some of the major issues related to their implementation.

Research on the Psychology of Physical Education in the Near Future

In addition to the research needs in specific fields that are mentioned in the chapters, authors pointed out two new research elements: the construction of valid measurement devices and the incorporation of psychological skills training in the physical education curriculum. We note that concepts specifically applicable to physical education have been adapted from sport psychology, and we suggest that controlled research (e.g., in the form of experimental designs and interventions) on most of the guidelines and recommendations in this book would be invaluable to the field.

The development of ecologically valid measurements and evaluations of the outcomes of physical education should be targeted as research tasks. Future research problems include psychological outcomes, developmental effects, and difficulties facing teachers who try to carry out educational programmes based on student-focused, psychologically based approaches. The use of observational and qualitative methods would be especially suitable for such research.

There is a definite need for more and better assessments of what physical education teachers achieve. The lack of such data undermines physical educators' ability to explain to local, regional and national authorities the values of physical education to European societies.

Although at first blush it might appear to be beyond the scope of this book, it seems quite likely that physical education teachers and students could well benefit from learning the psychological skills largely applied in elite sports, such as goal setting, imagery, concentration and relaxation. Traditionally, these skills have been used to assist athletes in competitions, to enhance their functional abilities and to help them cope with stress. More and more, companies are using these mental skills to enhance the creativity, productivity and mental well-being of managers, production engineers and others in positions of responsibility. These skills are certainly also relevant for physical educators and their students. Future research into empirical evidence to support the value of teaching psychological skills, as well as the practical information physical education teachers need to apply such skills, would be useful.

Knowledge in exercise and sport psychology relies on research carried out mostly in competitive sport or exercise settings. Consequently, few of the many apparently appropriate and useful suggestions given in this book have been tested in physical education settings. Controlled research into the implementation of the guidelines, as well as outcome research into the benefits and consequences of the application of the recommended classroom practices, would make a major contribution to the advancement of the field.

Hindrances and Facilitators of Implementation

The majority of the responses from authors referred to barriers or impediments to the implementation of the proposed guidelines, although some mentioned facilitating or advantageous circumstances. The contexts they addressed ranged from the broad, such as the sociopolitical context, physical education teacher training and the organisation of schools and their regulations, to the specific, including the beliefs, attitudes and expectations of teachers. The authors confirmed

that a textbook, however good, is just the start of the process of executing the recommended guidelines in day-to-day physical education settings.

Sociopolitical Context

For physical activity and physical education to benefit society, society must value them. We must create the objectives of our physical education lessons in light of our political, social and economic circumstances as well as the health status of our populations. These objectives should be discussed not only at the national level but also at the European and even broader international levels. Hopefully we will be able to stop the worldwide evolution from 'homo movens' to 'homo sedens' ('the person in motion' to 'the sedentary person'). Although countries and regions generally share the major physical education goals, different geographical, language and cultural areas will likely adapt and implement the guidelines provided in this book differently.

The low status of physical educators may be the major impediment to implementation in some European countries. The lack of incentives and the marginalisation of the profession discourage physical educators in these countries from striving for continuous professional improvement and education. This discouraging note is in marked contrast to the opinion of authors from other countries (such as the United Kingdom and France) who observe an increasing willingness not only to involve PE in the context of health promotion but also to resolve social issues (for example, integration of immigrants). The versatility of opinions related to PE and the status of the PE teacher reflects different values and educational systems in European countries.

An important question related to the role of physical education in our societies is: 'What can it contribute to the training of future citizens?' This contribution can include ethical, ecological and social aspects and themes such as health, security, responsibility and solidarity in relation to sports and leisure. The fact that many people today are aware of the importance of physical activity in youth and adulthood is reflected in part in the public health programmes that stress the relationship between physical activity and health.

Although the link between physical education and social behaviour and social responsibilities may still be a new concept for some, it has seen strong support during the last decade. Given the increased tension in many cities, schools have an increased responsibility to teach students interpersonal and communication skills. At school, physical education may be one of the best settings for the teaching and learning of social values.

Teacher Education

The basic factor in implementation is teacher education. Knowledge without a bridge to practice remains ineffective. If there is no specific instruction on how to teach something, as interesting as that content might be, it will remain a dead letter.

One of the most important tasks in teacher education programmes is to elucidate the discrepancy between the educational goals teachers want to strive toward and the goals they actually pursue in their courses. Because this is a difficult task, teachers need help from social sciences, observing educational practice and trying to select what could be helpful to close this discrepancy. The effort made by the authors to put this book together should be seen in this perspective. This awareness should lead to the incorporation of psychological knowledge and may eventually lead to pedagogical innovation.

Next to a scarce input from social sciences, the lack of methodology for applying theory to actual teaching practice is a fundamental shortcoming. Even textbook writers seem to assume that teachers will 'intuitively' understand how to apply the theories they carefully and extensively have worked out. But this is not usually the case. The development of a methodology for the application of new ideas and theories deserves to be the object of extensive study in itself. Such a methodology should be scientifically based and presented at a level as comprehensive as the ideas and theories themselves.

Teachers' Attitudes, Beliefs and Expectations

Unfortunately, the statement 'Teachers teach the way they were taught' is still applicable in many cases, at least in Europe and probably worldwide. Without continuing teacher education, teachers will continue implementing their own modifications of how they have learned to teach. Even teachers who have a great desire to develop

themselves professionally and to do well for their students tend to have traditional views that focus on performance rather than on the process of teaching. Teachers who expect to receive concrete answers to their everyday teaching problems are difficult to respond to, unless they are flexible and accommodating in the application of guidelines. The authors of this book implied that teachers are typically rather traditional or conservative in their teaching methods.

As a result of modern PE teacher education curricula in many European universities, a good number of teachers seem to continuously adapt their knowledge and practice by drawing on their own experiences and perceptions of practical situations. Another aspect to be considered, then, is the shortcomings of the theoreticians themselves. Asking for more flexibility on the part of teachers may sometimes conceal theoreticians' own lack of interest or ability to translate general principles into useful guidelines. Physical educators with their day-to-day concerns and educational psychologists with theoretical models and theories must be able to listen to and learn from each other.

The Challenge of Change

Society's desire to improve areas strongly associated with physical activity (i.e., public health and the personal and social well-being of individuals) is a reason for optimism about the move toward deeper professionalism in physical education. Consider the following:

- The low level of physical activity is increasingly found to be related to health problems and to social problems, which interfere with healthy psychological development.

- Physical activity in schools can help to ameliorate both health and social problems.

- If experts can demonstrate and convincingly present the benefits of physical education in terms of health and personal and social well-being, societies will insist on finding a way to develop and implement effective physical education programmes.

We are not entirely convinced of the logic apparently underlying the preceding argument.

In the fields of public health and exercise psychology, information alone has not been shown to be sufficient in stimulating change. And from educational psychology we learn that even when society and school authorities have endorsed small social changes, bringing about the change can still be a slow and difficult process.

Perhaps physical education is so different from subjects such as math or science that change in educational practice can occur more quickly. Physical education curricula are more flexible than traditional academic curricula and relatively unregulated. That academic freedom should give physical education teachers the latitude to design their course content themselves to a certain degree. 'So, although we may strive to turn a profession that has the inertia of a supertanker, as individuals each of us is a speed boat that can turn on a dime'.*

We certainly cannot discount the barriers that have been discussed here. But, as we know, too much emphasis on the numerous difficulties involved can lead to powerlessness and inertia. Therefore, we are quite willing to follow Pate and Hohn's suggestion and invite you, the physical educator, to incorporate the most striking and outstanding ideas in this textbook . . . today.

Jarmo Liukkonen and Yves Vanden Auweele

*Pate, R.R. & Hohn, R.C. (Eds.). (1994). *Health and fitness through physical education.* Champaign, IL: Human Kinetics.

Addresses of Editors and Contributing Authors

Alfermann, Dorothee
University of Leipzig
Faculty of Sports Science
Jahnallee 59
D-04109 Leipzig
Germany
E-mail: alferman@uni-leipzig.de

Barkoukis, Vassilis
Aristotle University of Thessaloniki
School of Physical Education and Sport Science
54124 Thessaloniki
Greece
E-mail: bark@phed.auth.gr

Bjerke, Øyvind
Norwegian University of Science and Technology
Human Movement Science Programme
7491 Trondheim
Norway
E-mail: oyvind.bjerke@hist.no

Chroni, Stiliani
University of Thessaly
Department of Physical Education and Sport
  Science
42100 Trikala
Greece
E-mail: schroni@pe.uth.gr

Digelidis, Nikolaos
University of Thessaly
Department of Physical Education and Sport
  Science
42100 Trikala
Greece
E-mail: nikdig@pe.uth.gr

Eloranta, Veikko
University of Jyväskylä
Department of Sport Sciences
P.O. Box 35
40014 Jyväskylä
Finland
E-mail: veikko.eloranta@sport.jyu.fi

Fjørtoft, Ingunn
Telemark University College
Faculty of Teacher Education
Lærerskolevegen 40
3679 Notodden
Norway
E-mail: Ingunn.Fjortoft@hit.no

Goudas, Marios
University of Thessaly
Department of Physical Education and Sport
  Science
42100 Trikala
Greece
E-mail: mgoudas@pe.uth.gr

Gundersen, Kari Aasen
Agder University College
Faculty of Health and Sports
P.O. Box 604
4809 Arendal
Norway
E-mail: Kari.A.Gundersen@hia.no

Hatzigeorgiadis, Antonis
University of Thessaly
Department of Physical Education and Sport
  Science
42100 Karies Trikala
Greece
E-mail: ahatzi@pe.uth.gr

Hovelynck, Johan
Katholieke Universiteit Leuven
(K.U. Leuven)
Centre for Organizational and Personnel Psychology
Tiensestraat, 102
B-3000 Leuven
Belgium
E-mail: johan.hovelynck@psy.kuleuven.ac.be

Jaakkola, Timo
University of Jyväskylä
Department of Sport Sciences
P.O. Box 35
40014 Jyväskylä
Finland
E-mail:

Kosmidou, Evdoxia
University of Thessaly
Department of Physical Education and Sport Science
42100 Trikala
Greece
E-mail: ekosmid@pe.uth.gr

Kuusela, Marjo
University of Jyväskylä
Department of Sport Sciences
P.O. Box 35
40014 Jyväskylä
Finland
E-mail: marjo.kuusela@surfeu.fi

Lemyre, Pierre-Nicolas
The Norwegian School of Sport Sciences
Department of Coaching and Psychology
P.O. Box 4014, Ullevaal Stadion
0806 Oslo
Norway
E-mail: nicolas.lemyre@nih.no

Lintunen, Taru
University of Jyväskylä
Department of Sport Sciences
P.O. Box 35
40014 Jyväskylä
Finland
E-mail: taru.lintunen@sport.jyu.fi

Liukkonen, Jarmo
University of Jyväskylä
Department of Sport Sciences
P.O. Box 35 (L)
40014 Jyväskylä
Finland
E-mail: jarmo.liukkonen@sport.jyu.fi

Marple-Horvat, Dilwyn
Manchester Metropolitan University
Institute for Biophysical and Clinical Research into Human Movement
Hassall Road
ST7 2HL Alsager
United Kingdom
E-mail: d.e.marple-horvat@mmu.ac.uk

Milosis, Dimitris
Democritus University of Thrace, Greece
Department of Physical Education and Sport Science
Erythraias 5
55132 Thessaloniki
Greece
E-mail: dmilosis@yahoo.com

Mouratidis, Thanasis
Katholieke Universiteit Leuven, Belgium
(K.U. Leuven)
Faculty of Kinesiology and Rehabilitation Sciences
46, Damaskinou Str.
71305 Heraklion, Crete
Greece
E-mail: thanmour@yahoo.com

Ommundsen, Yngvar
The Norwegian School of Sport Sciences
Department of Coaching and Psychology
P.O. Box 4014, Ullevaal Stadion
0806 Oslo
Norway
E-mail: yngvar.ommundsen@nih.no

Papaioannou, Athanasios G.
University of Thessaly
Department of Physical Education and Sport Science
42100 Trikala
Greece
E-mail: sakispap@otenet.gr

Polvi, Singa
University of Jyväskylä, Finland
Department of Sport Sciences
Etu-Hätiläntie 7b
13270 Hämeenlinna
Finland
E-mail: singa.polvi@pp.inet.fi

Savelsbergh, Geert J.P.
Free University of Amsterdam
Institute for Fundamental and Clinical Human
   Movement Sciences
Van der Boechorststraat 9
1081 BT Amsterdam
The Netherlands
E-mail: g_j_p_savelsbergh@fbw.vu.nl

Stiller, Jeannine
University of Leipzig
Faculty of Sports Science
Jahnallee 59
D-04109 Leipzig
Germany
E-mail: stiller@rz.uni-leipzig.de

Telama, Risto
University of Jyväskylä
Department of Sport Sciences
Keltavuokko 4C
40520 Jyväskylä
Finland
E-mail: risto.telama@sport.jyu.fi

Theodorakis, Yannis
University of Thessaly
Department of Physical Education and Sport
   Science
42100 Trikala
Greece
E-mail: theodorakis@pe.uth.gr

Tsigilis, Nikolaos
University of Thessaly
Department of Physical Education and Sport
   Science
42100 Trikala
Greece
E-mail: tsigilis@uom.gr

van der Kamp, John
Free University of Amsterdam
Institute for Fundamental and Clinical Human
   Movement Sciences
Van der Boechorststraat 9
1081 BT Amsterdam
The Netherlands
E-mail: j_van_der_kamp@fbw.vu.nl

Vanden Auweele, Yves
Katholieke Universiteit Leuven
(K.U. Leuven)
Faculty of Kinesiology and Rehabilitation
   Sciences
101, Tervuursevest
B-3001 Leuven
Belgium
E-mail: Yves.Vandenauweele@faber.kuleuven.be

Vereijken, Beatrix
Norwegian University of Science and Technol-
   ogy
Human Movement Science Programme
7491 Trondheim
Norway
E-mail: beatrix.vereijken@svt.ntnu.no

Verheul, Martine
University of Edinburgh
Perception-Movement-Action Research Centre
EH8 8AQ Edinburgh
United Kingdom
E-mail: martine.verheul@ed.ac.uk

index

Jarmo Liukkonen, PhD, is a professor of sport pedagogy at the University of Jyvaskyla, Finland, and deputy head of the Department of Sport Sciences, in charge of research and education of doctoral students. He was a member of the managing council for the European Federation of Sport Psychology (FEPSAC) from 1991 to 2003. He is currently president of the Finnish Association of Sport Psychology and works as a psychological consultant to several Finnish national sport teams. His main research interests include motivational climate in school physical education and sports, psychosocial determinants of physical activity, and physical activity and psychological well-being.

Yves Vanden Auweele, PhD, is a professor emeritus of psychology at Katholieke Universiteit Leuven in Belgium. Since 1980, he has taught psychology to physical education and psychology students and has been the Belgian co-coordinator of the European Masters Programme for Exercise and Sport Psychology. He was president of the Belgian Society of Sport Psychology and also a member of the managing council for the European Federation of Sport Psychology (FEPSAC) from 1991 to 1999. He has published on many sport and exercise psychology topics, including promoting physical activity in sedentary adults, personality of the elite performer, dysfunction versus optimal functioning of elite athletes and judging bias in aesthetic sports relying on the subjective evaluation of a panel of judges.

Beatrix Vereijken, PhD, is a professor and head of the Human Movement Science Programme at the Norwegian University of Science and Technology. With a formal background in experimental psychology, developmental psychology and human movement science, she covers a range of research topics including complex motor skill acquisition, movement coordination dynamics, balance and gait in infants and the elderly, and changes in force control with age. She is currently chairman of the Nordic Council for Higher Education in Sport Sciences, and serves on the editorial boards of Infant Behavior and Development and Infant and Child Development.

Dorothee Alfermann, **PhD,** is a professor of sport and exercise psychology at the University of Leipzig, Germany. She is a former vice president of the International Society of Sport Psychology and, since 2004, co-editor in chief of *Psychology of Sport and Exercise,* an official journal of the European Federation of Sport Psychology (FEPSAC). Her research topics include career transitions and career termination, physical self-concept, coach–athlete interaction and gender roles and gender identity.

Yannis Theodorakis, **PhD,** is a professor of sport psychology in the Department of Physical Education and Sport Science at the University of Thessaly, Greece. He was elected a member of the managing council for the European Federation of Sport Psychology (FEPSAC) from 1999 to 2003, head of his department and president of the Greek Society of Sport Psychology. He is currently on the editorial board of *Psychology of Sport and Exercise* journal and editor of *Inquiries in Sports and Physical Education.* He has published six books and more than 150 articles in Greek and international journals covering topics such as goal setting, self-talk, attitude and behavior relationships, injury rehabilitation and health psychology.

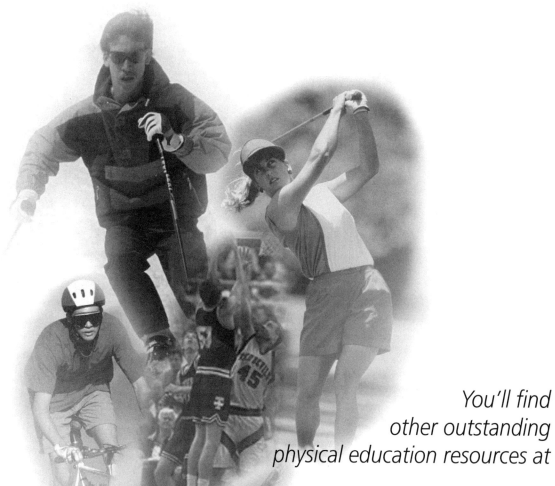